CINEMA AND NATION

In *Cinema and Nation* leading film scholars, philosophers and sociologists consider the ways in which film production and reception are shaped by ideas of national identity and belonging. The contributors discuss a wide range of cinemas, in Europe, Asia and the Americas, exploring the relationship between film policy and film cultures, and examining the implications of globalisation and the reconfiguration of nation states for both the concept and the reality of national cinema.

In the book's first three sections, contributors explore sociological approaches to national identity, challenge established ideas about 'national cinema', and consider the ways in which nation states – from the former Soviet Union to contemporary Scotland – use cinema in their efforts to create a national culture. The final two sections focus on the diverse strategies involved in the production of national cinema, and consider how images of the nation are understood by audiences both at home and abroad.

Contributors: Asu Aksoy, Sally Banes, Tim Bergfelder, Noël Carroll, Sumita S. Chakravarty, Paul Coates, Jane M. Gaines, John A. Hall, Susan Hayward, Ulf Hedetoft, Andrew Higson, Mette Hjort, Ian Jarvie, Charles Lindholm, Scott MacKenzie, Duncan Petrie, Eric Rentschler, Martin Roberts, Kevin Robins, Philip Schlesinger, Anthony Smith.

Mette Hjort is Associate Professor in the Department of Languages and Intercultural Studies, Aalborg University. **Scott MacKenzie** is Lecturer in Film and Television Studies at the School of English and American Studies, University of East Anglia, Norwich.

CINEMA AND NATION

*Edited by Mette Hjort and
Scott MacKenzie*

London and New York

First published 2000
by Routledge
2 Park Square, Milton Park, Abingdon, Oxon, OX14 4RN

Simultaneously published in the USA and Canada
by Routledge
270 Madison Ave, New York NY 10016

Routledge is an imprint of the Taylor & Francis Group

Transferred to Digital Printing 2010

Typeset in Galliard by Taylor & Francis Books Ltd

British Library Cataloguing in Publication Data
A catalogue record for this book is available from the British Library

Library of Congress Cataloging in Publication Data
Cinema and nation / [edited by] Mette Hjort and Scott MacKenzie.
p. cm
Includes bibliographical references and index.
1. National characteristics in motion pictures. 2. Motion picture
ndustry–Government policy. 3. Motion pictures–Political aspects. I. Hjort, Mette.
II. MacKenzie, Scott, 1967–
PN1995.9.N33 C56 2000
791.43'658–dc21   00-036636

ISBN 0–415–20862–9 (hbk)
ISBN 0–415–20863–7 (pbk)

Publisher's Note
The publisher has gone to great lengths to ensure the
quality of this reprint but points out that some
imperfections in the original may be apparent.

FOR SIRI, ERIK AND DARLENE

CONTENTS

CONTENTS

CONTENTS

LIST OF FIGURES

CONTRIBUTORS

Asu Aksoy is a researcher at Goldsmiths College, University of London. She is currently working on the implications of Turkish satellite television for the Turkish immigrant communities in Europe.

Sally Banes is Marian Hannah Winter Professor of Theatre History and Dance at the University of Wisconsin-Madison. Her books include *Terpsichore in Sneakers: Post-Modern Dance* (Wesleyan University Press, 1986), *Democracy's Body: Judson Dance Theater 1962–64* (Duke University Press, 1995), *Writing Dance in the Age of Postmodernism* (Wesleyan University Press, 1994), *Dancing Women: Female Bodies on Stage* (Routledge, 1998) and *Subversive Expectations: Performance Art and Paratheater in New York 1976–85* (University of Michigan Press, 1998), and she is the director of the documentary video *The Last Conversation: Eisenstein's Carmen Ballet*. She is past president of the Society of Dance History Scholars.

Tim Bergfelder is Lecturer in Film Studies and German at the University of Southampton, UK. He has previously taught film at the Merz Akademie in Stuttgart, Germany and the University of East Anglia, Norwich, UK.

Noël Carroll is the Monroe C. Beardsley Professor of the Philosophy of Art at the University of Wisconsin-Madison and he is the president of the American Society for Aesthetics. His books include *The Philosophy of Horror* (Routledge, 1990), *A Philosophy of Mass Art* (Clarendon Press, 1997), *Interpreting the Moving Image* (Cambridge University Press, 1998) and *Philosophy of Art: A Contemporary Introduction* (Routledge, 1999). He is the screenwriter for the documentary video *The Last Conversation: Eisenstein's Carmen Ballet*.

Sumita S. Chakravarty teaches in the Media Studies program and in the Graduate Faculty at New School University, New York. She is the author of *National Identity in Indian Popular Cinema, 1947–1987* (University of Texas Press; OUP-Delhi, 1996) and editor of *The Enemy Within: The Films of Mrinal Sen* (Flicks Books, 2000). She is part of the editorial collective of *Immediacy*, a new online journal devoted to a discussion of art, media and culture in the new millennium. Her current research includes a study of eroticism and visual culture, and an investigation of the social implications of technological change.

Paul Coates is Reader in Film Studies in the English Department of the University of Aberdeen, Scotland. His books include *The Story of the Lost Reflection: The Alienation of the Image in Western and Polish Cinema* (Verso, 1985), *The Gorgon's Gaze: German Cinema, Expressionism and the Image of Horror* (Cambridge University Press, 1991) and *Film at the Intersection of High and Mass Culture* (Cambridge University Press, 1994). He is editor of *Lucid Dreams: The Films of Krzysztof Kieslowski* (Flick Books, 1999).

Jane M. Gaines is a Professor in the Literature Program at Duke University and Director of the Program in Film and Video. She is the author of *Contested Culture: The Image, The Voice and the Law* (BFI, 1991) and co-editor (with Charlotte Herzog) of *Fabrications: Costume and the Female Body* (Routledge, 1990) and (with Michael Renov) of *Collecting Visible Evidence* (University of Minnesota Press, 1999). She recently completed *Fire and Desire: Mixed Race Movies in the Silent Era* (University of Chicago Press, 2001).

John A. Hall is Professor of Sociology at McGill University in Montreal and Research Professor in Sociology at Queen's University in Belfast. His own books include *Diagnoses of Our Time* (Heinemann, 1981), *Powers and Liberties* (Penguin, 1986), *Liberalism* (Paladin/University of North Carolina, 1987), *Coercion and Consent: Studies on the Modern State* (Polity, 1994), *International Orders* (1996) and most recently (with Charles Lindholm) *Is America Breaking Apart?* (Princeton University Press, 1999). He has edited collections on the rise of the West, the nature of civil society, the state, Ernest Gellner and his theory of nationalism and the contemporary world polity. He is at present writing (with Brendan O'Leary) a biography of Ernest Gellner and an analytic history of sociological thought.

Susan Hayward is the endowed Chair of French at Exeter University. She is the author of numerous articles on French cinema. Her books include *French National Cinema* (Routledge, 1993), *Key Concepts in Cinema Studies* (Routledge, 1996) and *Luc Besson* (Manchester University Press, 1997). She is currently working on a book on Simone Signoret. She is the General Editor of the National Cinema Series for Routledge.

Ulf Hedetoft is Professor of International Studies, Aalborg University and Director of SPIRIT (School for Postgraduate Interdisciplinary Research on Interculturalism and Transnationality). He is the author of *British Colonialism and Modern Identity* (Aalborg University Press, 1985) and of *Signs of Nations: Studies in the Political Semiotics of Self and Other in Contemporary European Nationalism* (Dartmouth, 1995). He is editor of *Political Symbols, Symbolic Politics: European Identities in Transformation* (Ashgate, 1998) and co-editor (with Mette Hjort) of *Reimagining Belonging: Self and Community in an Era* *of Nationalism and Postnationality*. He is currently working on a book on the culture of states in Europe.

Andrew Higson is Professor of Film Studies and Deputy Dean of the School of English and American Studies at the University of East Anglia. He has written widely on British cinema, including *Waving the Flag: Constructing a National Cinema in Britain* (Oxford University Press, 1995) and *English Heritage, English Cinema* (forthcoming, Oxford University Press). He is editor of *Dissolving Views: Key Writings on British Cinema* (Cassell, 1996) and co-editor (with Richard Maltby) of '*Film Europe*' *and* '*Film America*': *Cinema, Commerce and Cultural Exchange, 1920–1939* (University of Exeter Press, 1999) and (with Justine Ashby) of *British Cinema: Past and Present* (Routledge, 2000).

Mette Hjort was for several years Associate Professor of English at McGill University, where she was director of Cultural Studies. She is now Associate Professor of Intercultural Studies at Aalborg University. She is the author of *The Strategy of Letters* (Harvard University Press, 1993), editor of *Rules and Conventions* (Johns Hopkins University Press, 1992) and co-editor (with Sue Laver) of *Emotion and the Arts* (Oxford University Press, 1997). She is co-editor (with Ib Bondebjerg) of a volume of interviews with Danish film-makers entitled *The Danish Directors: Dialogues on a National Cinema* (Intellect Press, 2001) and (with Ulf Hedetoft) of *Reimagining Belonging: Self and Community in an Era of Nationalism and Postnationality* (forthcoming).

Ian Jarvie is Professor of Philosophy, York University, Toronto, Ontario, Canada. He is the author of *Movies and Society* (Basic Books, 1970), *Towards a Sociology of the Cinema* (Routledge, 1970), *Thinking about Society: Theory and Practice* (Reidel, 1986), *Philosophy of the Film: Epistemology, Ontology, Aesthetics* (Routledge, 1987), *Hollywood's Overseas Campaign: The North Atlantic Movie Trade, 1920–1950* (Cambridge University Press, 1992) and (with Garth Jowett and Kathryn Fuller) *Children and the Movies* (Cambridge University Press, 1996). He is currently working on a sociological study of mass-media pornography.

Charles Lindholm is University Professor of Anthropology at Boston University. He is the author of several books, including *The Islamic Middle East: An Historical Anthropology* (Blackwell, 1996) and (with John A. Hall) *Is America Breaking Apart?* (Princeton University Press, 1999). His current research deals with psychological issues, especially idealisation.

Scott MacKenzie is Lecturer in Film and Television Studies in the School of English and American Studies at the University of East Anglia, Norwich, UK. His articles have appeared in many journals, including *Cinéaction*, *Canadian Journal of Film Studies*, *Public* and *Screen*. He has taught previously at McGill University and the University of Glasgow. He is presently completing a book-length study on Québécois cinema, national identity and the public sphere.

Duncan Petrie is Director of the Bill Douglas Centre and Senior Lecturer in the School of English, University of Exeter, UK. He was previously Research Officer at the BFI in London. His publications include *Creativity and Constraint in the British Film Industry* (Macmillan, 1991), *Bill Douglas: A Laternist's Account* (BFI/Scottish Film Council, 1993) and *The British Cinematographer* (BFI, 1996). He is also the editor of *Screening Europe: Image and Identity in Contemporary European Cinema* (BFI, 1992) and of *New Questions of British Cinema* (BFI, 1992).

Eric Rentschler is Professor and Chair of the Department of Germanic Languages and Literatures at Harvard University. He is the author of *West German Film in the Course of Time* (Redgrave, 1984) and *Ministry of Illusion: Nazi Cinema and Its Afterlife* (Harvard University Press, 1996). He is the editor of *German Film and Literature: Adaptations and Transformations* (Methuen, 1986) and *West German Filmmakers on Film: Visions and Voices* (Holmes and Meier, 1988). He is currently writing a history of film in the Federal Republic of Germany.

Martin Roberts is a faculty member in the Media Studies Program at New School University, New York, and has taught at Harvard University and MIT. After completing a Ph.D. in French Studies at Cambridge University, his research interests have focused on ethnography, postcolonialism and transnational media studies, with a special interest in cinema and music. His previous publications include articles on ethnographic film, 'world music' and 'world cinema', and Indonesian *gamelan* music. He is currently working on a book on cinema and globalisation.

Kevin Robins is Professor of Communications at Goldsmiths College, University of London. He is the author of *Into the Image: Culture and Politics in the Field of Vision* (Routledge, 1996) and (with Frank Webster) of *Times of the Technoculture* (Routledge, 1999).

Philip Schlesinger is Professor of Film and Media Studies at the University of Stirling, Scotland where he is also Director of the Stirling Media Research Institute. He is Visiting Professor of Media and Communication at the University of Oslo, a member of the board of the Scottish Screen agency and co-editor of the *Media, Culture and Society* journal. His publications include *Putting 'Reality' Together* (Methuen, 1987, 2nd edn), *Televising 'Terrorism'* (Comedia, 1983), *Media, State and Nation* (Sage, 1991), *Women Viewing Violence* (BFI Publishing, 1992), *Reporting Crime* (Clarendon, 1994) and *Men Viewing Violence* (Broadcasting Standards Commission, 1998). He is currently completing research on political communication and national identity in the European Union, UK and Scotland.

Anthony Smith is Professor of Ethnicity and Nationalism at the European Institute, London School of Economics. His main interest is in ethnicity and nationalism and his publications include *The Ethnic Origins of Nations* (Blackwell, 1986), *National Identity* (Penguin 1991), *Nations and Nationalism in a Global Era* (Polity, 1995) and *Nationalism and Modernism* (Routledge, 1998).

ACKNOWLEDGEMENTS

Susan Hayward deserves thanks for her generous advice at key moments. At Routledge, Rebecca Barden and Alistair Daniel provided expert guidance, as did the anonymous readers who assessed the initial project. Thanks to The Danish Film Institute (Copenhagen), The Museum of Modern Art (New York), The Kobal Collection (London), Heritage Films (Warsaw) and the National Film, Video and Sound Archives (Pretoria, South Africa) for permission to print stills from their collections. Mette Hjort would like to thank the Social Sciences and Humanities Research Council of Canada for a generous grant in support of her research on national cinema.

INTRODUCTION

Mette Hjort and Scott MacKenzie

Poststructuralism and psychoanalytic semiology have taught several generations to view literary and cinematic texts, not as works with distinctive traits expressing in some instances the intentions of creative agents, but as mere epiphenomena of language, desire, ideology and a unified, 'logophallocentric' Western metaphysics (Hjort 1993). However, over the past ten years or so, we have seen a dramatic shift from this sort of theory to what is beginning to look like a promising emphasis on the specificity of relevant cultural, social, and historical contexts in accounts of literature, film, and the other arts. More specifically, the influential critical vocabulary associated with deconstruction and psychoanalytic semiology must compete with a new set of terms: 'hybridity', 'multiculturalism', 'transnationalism', 'nationalism', 'internationalism', 'globalisation', 'cosmopolitanism', 'exile', 'postcolonialism', to mention but some of the most salient terms. While the specific meaning of some of these terms – 'hybridity' is a good example – is linked to poststructuralist premises, many of the terms bring into play concepts and approaches that are able to mediate successfully between macrosociological and agential levels of description. Any successful attempt, for example, to deal cogently with the nationalist dimensions of a given work is likely to involve some account of the historical specificity of a given nationalist context, as well as an exploration of the ways in which the artist's focal beliefs about national identity, and self-deceptions linked to the psychologies of nationalism, find expression.

The nascent critical vocabulary is anything but a matter of settled doctrines or a stable consensus. In the disciplines from which this vocabulary is, to a certain extent, borrowed, there is disagreement, not only about the precise meaning of many of the key terms, but also about their relevance for certain cultural realities. Whereas for some scholars globalisation and postnationality are salient features of the modern landscapes of artistic production, others (Hall and Lindholm 1999) contest the idea that nation-states are being rapidly undermined. For some scholars (Smith 1991), nations are enduring, primordial entities that can be expressed in art, while others (Gellner 1983) assume that nations are constructed in a process of myth-making linked to the needs of the modern, industrial state. In short, following in the wake of academic trends marked by strong internal cohesion and settled doctrines – poststructuralism and psychoanalytic semiology – the new tendency provides a stimulating opportunity to redefine certain critical agendas, as well as to revisit with fresh insight some of the debates that were believed, perhaps wrongly, to have been finally settled.

One such debate has to do with the nature of national cinema, for the various permutations of 'nation' – 'transnationalism', 'multinationalism', 'national identity', 'internationalism' and 'nationalism' – that figure centrally in the new critical vocabulary have the effect of foregrounding for critical scrutiny this basic cornerstone of film studies. And although there is much talk these days about the erosion of nation-states and the need to rethink the link that has been assumed for some time to exist between nations and cinematic cultures, Benjamin Barber's (1995) claim that globalisation and nationalism in many cases are two sides of the same coin suggests that film scholars should be intent, not so much on avoiding concepts of nationhood and nationality, but on refining them and clearly identifying their continued, although changing pertinence for film studies. The recent surge in the study of national cinemas (Chakravarty 1993; Higson 1995; Sorlin 1996; Street 1997), coupled with the framing of various image cultures in terms of new nationalisms (Parker *et al.* 1991) – such as that of a queer nation – clearly suggests that concepts of national cinema and identity belong both to the future of film studies and to its beginnings. At the same time, it is important to note that many current attempts to articulate the national or nationalist dimensions of cinematic cultures draw on only the most limited corpus of relevant theoretical texts. Indeed, in many cases it is a matter of mobilising Benedict Anderson's (1991) modernist conception of the nation as an imagined community. That Anderson's work is seminal and can be usefully extended from print to cinematic cultures is undeniable. At the same time, the quality of film scholars' discussions of central issues can only profit from an increased awareness, not only of the place of Anderson's concepts and frameworks within the context of larger debates, but of competing accounts. This observation is in many ways the premise underwriting *Cinema and Nation* and explains both the choice of organising categories and contributors, about which more below.

Since *Cinema and Nation* is a collective attempt to focus a sharp light on national cinemas and closely related phenomena, a brief overview of the relevant concept's history is in order. In the early days of the institutionalisation of film as an academic discipline, the study of national cinemas – in conjunction with *auteur* theory – was widely and unproblematically accepted, and these two critical approaches provided the categorial framework for the first film courses in North American universities in the late 1960s. National cinema at that point was understood both as a descriptive category and as a means of systematising an emerging university curriculum. There was not much in the way of critical writing on national cinemas at the time – the key exception to the rule was the quickly canonised study by Siegfried Kracauer, *From Caligari to Hitler: A*

Psychological History of the German Film (1947). Kracauer's text, however influential, did not inspire extensive writing about national cinemas, for the model of psychological determinism found in this key work was thought to pertain to the particulars of the German psyche, rather than to national cinemas more generally. Instead, national cinemas were by and large organised in terms of a literary conception of 'great works': Ingmar Bergman was largely synonymous with Sweden, Jean-Luc Godard and François Truffaut with France and Alfred Hitchcock, Howard Hawks and John Ford with America.

The influx of semiotics, Lacanian psychoanalysis, structuralism and feminism into film theory and criticism in the 1970s and 1980s changed much of this. What David Bordwell and Noël Carroll (1996) refer to as 'grand theory' arose as a result of the influence of these theoretical paradigms and was closely associated with journals such as *Screen, Ciné-tracts, Cahiers du cinéma, Cinéthique, Frauen und Film* and *Camera Obscura*, where it was a matter of problematising notions of the national, while sustaining national cinema as a descriptive category. Thomas Elsaesser's (1980) influential work on German cinema, for instance, examined the tensions within German cinematic texts (most importantly, the works of Rainer Werner Fassbinder) as so many attempts to come to terms with the nation's past (*Vergangenheitsbewältigung*). The idea that there was something essentially 'German' about these films was not questioned. Mention should nonetheless be made of some major exceptions to these critical tendencies. A significant exploration of how films manifest national characters was Martha Wolfenstein and Nathan Leites' *Movies: A Psychological Study* (1971). An early, formalist analysis of aspects of a national cinema was Pierre Sorlin's influential *Sociologie du cinéma: ouverture pour l'histoire de demain* (1977). And Francis Courtade's *Les malédictions du cinéma français: une histoire du cinéma français parlant, 1928–1978* (1978) provided a detailed and penetrating account of ways in which the specificity of French political and economic conditions constrained film production and reception in the period in question.

The late 1980s saw the emergence of a range of critical studies on national cinemas and careful analytic work on the concept of national cinema itself. What kinds of extradiegetic materials and practices are pertinent in a thorough account of the role played by nation-states in the production and reception of cinematic works? To what extent, and how exactly, do cinematic works contribute to the kinds of imaginings that sustain nation-states? And what are the implications for national cinema of claims to the effect that nations and states increasingly are going their separate ways? Andrew Higson (1989, 1995), Stephen Crofts (1998) and John Hill (1999), among others, have attempted to answer these questions. The approach here is analytic, for it is a matter of generating a carefully differentiated categorial framework capable of identifying a wide range of factors underwriting diverse manifestations and conceptualisations of national cinema. Crofts, for example, contends that national cinemas are best analysed in terms of the following kinds of categories: 'production', 'audiences', 'discourses' , 'textuality', 'national-cultural specificity', 'the cultural specificity of genres and nation-state cinema movements', 'the role of the state' and 'the global range of nation-state cinemas' (1998: 387–9). These categories, claims Crofts, help to draw attention, among other things, to the styles and conventions of national cinemas and the ways in which specific national contexts encourage the development of certain genres of cinematic production.

Some of these scholars have reconsidered the very nature of national cinemas. Andrew Higson, for example, writes that '[h]istories of national cinema can only ... be understood as histories of crisis and conflict, of resistance and negotiation' (1989: 37). On this view it is important to acknowledge the limitations of a conception of national cinema as a seamless totality that somehow accurately expresses, describes, and itemises the salient concerns and features of a given national culture. That this line of argument involves certain political commitments is underscored by Christopher Faulkner, who claims that any attempt 'to construct the history of a nation or national cinema as coherent, unified, homogeneous, is to lend support to its erasure of difference and to the maintenance of a centrist and neo-conservative cultural politics' (1994: 7). Following this approach national cinema is more fruitfully understood in terms of notions of conflict. Films, it is claimed, do not simply represent or express the stable features of a national culture, but are themselves one of the loci of debates about a nation's governing principles, goals, heritage and history. It follows that critics should be attuned not only to the expressive dimensions of a nation's films, but to what these films and their categorisation as elements of a national cinema may elide or strategically repress. In this vein Vincendeau and Dyer (1992) have argued for the need to resist the tendency systematically to overlook nations' popular cinematic cultures in the most common constructions of national cinemas, which focus largely on the kind of 'art' products that tend to reach international audiences.

The question of national cinema is thus currently very much on film scholars' critical agenda, where it figures alongside such terms as 'nationalism', 'postnationalism', 'transnationalism' and 'supranationalism', which are held to identify related or competing phenomena, depending on the specificity of the theoretical account in question. *Cinema and Nation* is designed to contribute to the project of conceptual clarification that orients discussions of national cinema during the late 1980s and 1990s. To this end, we have attempted to create a dialogic space that brings into play voices that do not typically speak to each other, although they may well talk about similar issues. Included are pieces by sociologists such as John A. Hall and Anthony Smith, figures who are associated, not with film studies, but with the influential modernist and perennialist accounts of nationalism and national identity that they respectively espouse. *Cinema and Nation* includes a co-authored contribution by Sally Banes and Noël Carroll, the latter being one of the philosophers who have instigated an influential cognitive turn in film studies. Essays by Susan Hayward and Sumita Chakravarty, on the other hand, involve approaches that reflect some of the central tendencies and premises of cultural studies. Figuring here are also pieces by leading scholars of specific national cinemas: Paul Coates, Jane M. Gaines, Andrew Higson, Duncan Petrie and Eric Rentschler. Together the pieces by Ulf Hedetoft, Kevin Robins and Asu Aksoy and Martin Roberts identify some of the salient relations among national, postnational and globalising tendencies. The result of these and other pieces is a volume that is an invitation to the kind of dialogue across disciplinary boundaries and methodological divides which can unsettle received views and promote greater clarity about the issues at hand.

In Part I, 'The Sociology of Nationalism', the aim is to explore a range of sociological approaches to nationalism and their relevance for film studies. In 'The Sociological Scope of "National Cinema"', Philip Schlesinger identifies the tradition of sociological inquiry into the nature of nations and nationalism that converges with, or directly underwrites, influential conceptions of national cinema. He argues that key elements in the social communication approach associated with Karl W. Deutsch (1996) resurface in Michael Billig's (1995) account of nation-maintenance by means of 'banal nationalism', as well as in the modernist views of Ernest Gellner and Benedict Anderson. These sociological theories are all predicated on an assumption that nations are constituted and sustained by certain communicative specificities. As a result, the focus is on processes occurring within what is construed as a national communicative space. Yet, the view that the sovereign nation-state provides the 'politically salient container for communicative space' is less and less persuasive, claims Schlesinger, as various decouplings of nation and state are effected by transnational and supranational arrangements. It is Schlesinger's contention that the weaknesses marring the social communication tradition of sociological inquiry resurface in the work of key film theorists such as Susan Hayward (1993), Sarah Street (1997) and Andrew Higson (1989, 1995), who, drawing on Benedict Anderson's notion of imagined communities, variously assume that a given national cinema expresses communicative specificities developed by a relevant and clearly delimited nation-state. Schlesinger claims that inasmuch as globalising processes are increasingly undermining the unity of state and nation and thereby making implausible the idea of a single, national communicative space, national cinema is best construed, not as a corpus of films that defines a nation's specificity, but rather, as Pierre Sorlin puts it, as 'the chain of relations and exchanges which develop in connection with films, in a territory delineated by its economic and juridical policy' (1996: 10). Schlesinger's piece amounts ultimately to an invitation to both sociologists and film theorists to rethink the nature of nation and culture in ways that accurately reflect the impact of globalising tendencies as well as the wide range of media.

Charles Lindholm and John A. Hall are concerned with the following question: why are explicitly political films unpopular in the United States when the country's citizens can be legitimately described as 'strongly patriotic and nationalistic'? The answer, they claim, has to do with the centrality in American national identity of key anti-political attitudes. Lindholm and Hall explore the relevant distrust of institutionalised politics by means of a careful analysis of Frank Capra's political films, *Mr Deeds Goes to Town* (1936), *Mr Smith Goes to Washington* (1939) and *Meet John Doe* (1941). Their argument hinges on key differences between the first two films, where a virtuous individual with roots in a given community successfully challenges official authority, and the third, which is concerned with how an amoral, rootless individual can be induced to participate in civil life. *Meet John Doe* fails, claim Lindholm and Hall, because here Capra steps outside the individualist paradigm that is operative in the first two films in order to explore the possibility of amoral individuals being transformed into moral citizens by means of inclusion in political communities. The deeply problematic mob scene in *Meet John Doe* is symptomatic, they argue, of the questionable nature of Capra's starting assumption, which is that 'people alone are amoral, together they achieve morality, but as soon as that togetherness is organised politically they become immoral'. Much like de Toqueville and many other theorists of American politics, Capra wrongly assumes that individuals are amoral and prone to irrational, conformist, group behaviour. Lindholm and Hall conclude that Capra, like de Toqueville, accurately captures the hostility to political action that is central to American national identity. In their view, however, both the film-maker and the political theorist are wrong to link American individualism with conformity and ultimately fascism.

Anthony Smith provides an account of the relationship between cinema, painting and national identity. Smith's aim is to outline an ethno-symbolic approach to the visual representation of national identity, one that is able accurately to account for painters' and film-makers' tendency to converge on certain moral and symbolic themes and increasingly to favour naturalistic aesthetic styles. His discussion focuses on key features of nineteenth-century history painting and their recurrence and further development in film, especially in the later work of Sergei Eisenstein. Smith situates his discussion within the larger context of debates over the nature of nationalism and national identity. He takes issue, more specifically, with the modernist conceptions of Gellner (1983), Hobsbawm (1990) and Anderson (1991), who define the nation as a quintessentially modern phenomenon created by nationalism, by the fabrication and dissemination of myths of nationhood by a secular intelligentsia. Smith's influential perennialist account, on the other hand, construes nationalism as an affirmation of enduring ethnic identities that find expression through shared memories, collective myths and so on. On the perennialist view, then, national identity is a matter, not of the imposition of 'invented traditions' (Hobsbawm and Ranger 1983) with largely fictive connections to the past, but rather of the rediscovery and authentification of already existing myths and symbols with collective value. Modernists, claims Smith, fail to take seriously the 'content and the tone of the nationalist message' and his proposed ethno-symbolic approach is clearly designed to take issue with the McLuhanesque notions of medium as message that variously underwrite what he refers to as the 'presentist' position. By focusing on these neglected elements, Smith aims to show that while representations of national identity may not be authentic in a 'strictly factual' sense, they do in many cases have an 'emotional and moral' authenticity.

Part II, 'The Concept of National Cinema', brings together pieces designed to probe the validity of some of the most influential definitions of one of film studies' organising categories. In 'The Limiting Imagination of National Cinema' Andrew Higson subjects his earlier, seminal piece entitled 'The Concept of National Cinema' (1989) to critical scrutiny. In this article Higson identified various accounts of national cinema and suggested that a 'text-based' approach focusing, among other things, on themes and concepts of nationhood and national identity, was to be preferred over 'economic-oriented', 'criticism-led' and 'consumption-based' conceptions. In his contribution here Higson takes issue with the sociological framework underwriting his earlier claims. More specifically, it is a matter of questioning the extent to which Benedict Anderson's concept of the nation as a community imagined as limited, finite and sovereign provides an appropriate framework for conceptualising the specificities of national cinema. Higson argues that although mass communication does indeed provide a salient means of constituting and sustaining a national community, as film scholars indebted to Anderson have suggested, it is important to note that contemporary media practices involve various forms of transnationalism. The challenge, then, claims Higson, is to provide an account of national cinema that acknowledges not only the nationalising effect of certain discourses and state policies, but also the increasingly transnational dimensions of cinematic production, distribution and reception. Higson concludes that the boundaries defining cinematic cultures cannot legitimately be seen as coinciding neatly with the 'limits of the nation-state'. Indeed, the claim is that the communities imagined by cinematic means tend at this point to be local or transnational, rather than national.

Ian Jarvie's 'National Cinema: A Theoretical Assessment' examines arguments in favour of national cinema in the light of Gellner's (1983) influential, modernist account of nationalism. In essence, Gellner's view is that nations are the product of nationalism, which itself arises during the industrial period and ultimately serves the particular needs of the modern state. Jarvie identifies three recurring arguments in the literature on national cinema: a 'protectionist' argument; a 'cultural defence' argument; and a 'nation-building' argument. Protectionism, claims Jarvie, is indeed a means, although a culturally neutral one, of promoting a national cinema. That is, there is no necessary connection between a thriving domestic film industry and national film, for the industry in question might prosper by producing films with little or no national specificity. Following Jarvie, the protectionist argument, unlike the other two arguments, can be readily reconciled with the Gellnerian picture of modernising states. That is, if movies in fact foster the kinds of basic skills that citizens of modern states require, then the promotion of a domestic industry through protective measures is warranted. Jarvie considers the other two arguments dubious. The cultural defence argument is held to rest on two questionable assumptions: that viewers exposed to cultural difference will imitate foreign patterns of behaviour and that movies provide the principal means of cultural transmission. Jarvie argues that any mobilisation of the cultural defence argument is likely to be symptomatic, not only of weaknesses inherent in the relevant national culture, but of a lack of self-confidence in those who seek to defend it. Jarvie's approach to the nation-building argument is to ask what national cinema contributed in the context of those 'settled' and 'satisfied' nations that first began to articulate a concept of national cinema around 1915. He argues that the internal dimensions of national cinema are at least as important as its external aspects. For national cinema was first and foremost a strategy designed to facilitate the absorption of newly emancipated groups into an already existing hierarchical social framework. And the resistance to Hollywood products that accompanied the emphasis on national cinemas in various European countries was ultimately a matter of countering a spirit of multicultural egalitarianism held to be at odds with an internal nation-building project. Jarvie's point here is that the nation-building argument requires careful scrutiny inasmuch as it insists on internal cohesion through processes of strong centralisation at the expense of regional and other forms of differentiation. It is this internal connection between nation-building and centralisation that is overlooked, claims Jarvie, in leftist critics' recent and unconvincing attempts to salvage the project of national cinema by pointing to the possibility of films reflecting differences or tensions within nation-states.

The concept of, and discourses about, national cinema are also subjected to critical scrutiny in Susan Hayward's 'Framing National Cinemas'. As a way of pinpointing characteristic weaknesses, Hayward draws on the insights of key anthropologists and sociologists of nationalism and national identity. She largely adopts the modernist perspective associated with Gellner, who has argued that nationalism creates the very nations from which it is wrongly held to emanate. She affirms the idea that the construction of nations involves a selective appropriation of history and tradition, as well as significant degrees of amnesia, which obscure the true origins of nations, lending them the appearance of enduring essences. Hayward insists that while 'nation' is used to refer to unified collectivities, it is important to remember that the relevant convergences and solidarities are forged and sustained by certain networks of power. Hayward claims that thinking about national cinema has relied on the following wrongheaded assumptions: national cinema simply articulates the cultural specificities of a given pre-existing nation; nations are enduring, primordial entities; and Hollywood provides the only relevant point of contrast in the context of cinematically mediated national identities. Hayward's proposed corrective involves acknowledging the way in which cinema contributes to the construction of nations. As an ideal she posits a discourse about national cinema that resists the assimilationist and integrationist imperatives of nationalism and reflects, among other things, the multicultural tendencies of cinematic production within nation-states and, increasingly, various supranational or even postnational arrangements.

In 'Themes of Nation' Mette Hjort examines the implications of regarding national cinema as a phenomenon that to an important extent is constituted by national themes. Having canvassed some of the salient meanings of 'theme' and 'nation', she goes on to distinguish between perennial and topical themes, arguing that themes of nation belong to the latter category and typically play only a secondary role in contemporary Danish cinema, which provides the empirical context for her analysis. She contends that the call, within various Danish contexts, for films about Danes and Denmark does not in fact amount to an invitation to make films that embody themes of nation. Instead, claims Hjort, proponents of Danish film as a form of identity politics seem to be interested in cinematic works involving what Michael Billig (1995) has called banal nationalism. She concludes that themes of nation play a much less important role in the creation of a national cinema than has previously been suggested. In the course of her discussion, Hjort considers examples of ethnic, polemical and ironic thematisations of nation in films by contemporary Danish film-makers, such as Lotte Svendsen, Gabriel Axel, Erik Clausen and Lars von Trier.

Part III, 'Film Policy, Nationalism and the State', addresses the ways in which a variety of state-formations, ranging from the totalitarianism of a Stalinist Soviet Union to the federalism of the UK, aim at producing national culture through the cinema. In 'Cinematic Nation-Building: Eisenstein's *The Old and the New*', Noël Carroll and Sally Banes discuss an example of cinema being yoked to a project of civic nationalism, where it is a matter, not of harking back to some bygone cultural moment that allegedly captures the essence of a given people, but rather of imagining the specificity of a nation that has yet to be realised. Eisenstein's *The Old and the New* (1929), they claim, is an attempt to translate Soviet agricultural policies of the 1920s into a galvanising regulative ideal involving a perfect synergy between agriculture and industry. Following Carroll and Banes, Eisenstein used intellectual montage in *The Old and the New* to evoke instances of fantastic causation linking present-day agricultural activities to desirable forms of industrialisation in the future. The Soviet project of nation-building, claim Carroll and Banes, is also reflected in the film's unfolding narrative which thematises the virtues and benefits of co-operation. The central figure, Marfa Lapkina, is held to be important in this regard and to pre-figure in interesting ways future Eisensteinian characters, such as Alexander Nevsky and Ivan the Terrible. Carroll and Banes identify a number of narrative similarities between Russian fairy tales and *The Old and the New* and argue that they were established by Eisenstein for purely communicative purposes. That is, the relevant elements cannot be used to counter the authors' main contention, which is that *The Old and the New* aims to assimilate, not the past to the present, but the present to the future in a form of prospective nation-building.

Tim Bergfelder takes issue with the idea that the transnationalism effected by increased globalisation can be contrasted with some bygone period when the boundaries of cinemas and nations coincided perfectly. Rather, claims Bergfelder, cinema was from the outset a matter of transnational co-operation. Bergfelder also squares off against the idea that European cinemas and transnational initiatives were unable, as a result of the linguistic and cultural diversity of Europe, to compete successfully against the global reach and inherent internationalism of Hollywood. A careful analysis of aspects of cinematic production in the 1950s and 1960s reveals that while European co-productions may have been prompted by the threat of Hollywood, they were also effective instances of pan-European co-operation, both culturally and economically. Bergfelder disputes the recurrent claim that the European co-productions of the 1950s and 1960s involved more or less successful attempts to imitate Hollywood genre films. Bergfelder's contention is that the formulae adopted were at least to some extent a matter of reviving a long-established pan-European tradition of popular culture. European co-productions from the period in question are typically examples, not of pure genres, but of a mixing of genres, and this feature, claims Bergfelder, is precisely a reflection of a tendency to draw, not on Hollywood, but on early European cinema, nineteenth-century pulp fiction and various popular European narratives.

Duncan Petrie's 'The New Scottish Cinema' identifies the key institutional developments that made possible the emergence in the 1990s of a Scottish cinema within British national cinema more generally. Channel 4, established in 1982, is considered important for economic and especially cultural reasons, for its emphasis on diversity had the effect of opening up an institutional space for Scottish cinematic expression. Petrie emphasises the role played by the Scottish Film Production Fund (1982), which later becomes Scottish Screen (1997), in fostering much-needed continuity within Scottish feature-film production. Petrie also points to the Glasgow Film Fund (1993) and the Scottish Lottery Panel (1995), other successful initiatives designed to promote ongoing activity within the industry. He emphasises a number of schemes aimed at boosting short-film production – Tartan Shorts, Prime Cuts and First Reels – all of which have helped to create and sustain a viable infrastructure for Scottish film production. Petrie concludes by assessing two rival approaches to Scottish film, the one favouring primarily economic considerations, the other issues of cultural specificity. He rejects the suggestion that the Scottish Film Council and Scottish Film Production Fund have been overly concerned with a purely economic conception of film and should be promoting what Colin McArthur (1993) calls a 'Poor Scottish Cinema'.

In Part IV, the focus shifts to some of the diverse reasons and strategies involved in the production of national images. In 'Indonesia: The Movie' Martin Roberts analyses the role played by official state nationalism, globalisation and postcolonialism in the production and reception of three IMAX films entitled *Beautiful Indonesia* (1984), *Indonesian Children* (1988) and *Indonesia: A String of Emeralds on the Equator* (1991), all of which were produced by MacGillivray Freeman Films, at the behest of Madame Tien Suharto, for screening in the IMAX theatre situated in the heritage park, Taman Mini, in the environs of Jakarta. Roberts argues that these IMAX films are continuous with the project of national self-imagining initiated by the Suhartos in the 1970s in an effort to create the so-called 'New Order regime'. Whereas influential theorists of nationalism, such as Benedict Anderson, have emphasised the role played by print culture in the creation and affirmation of national cultures, Roberts shows that in this case nationalising intentions are supported by a culture of images designed to display national unity in and through regional and ethnic diversity. The relevant films, claims Roberts, also involve various transnational dimensions, for they are at once an instance of the 'globalisation of North American popular culture' and of the 'Javanisation of global cultural forms'. For example, in these American-produced films about Indonesia the conventions of the 'destination' film genre are made to accommodate a range of references to practices associated with the tradition of shadow-puppet theatre. This indigenising tendency within a more general process of globalisation has the effect of providing Western audiences with touristic images of Indonesia and Indonesian audiences with the elements constitutive of a national identity. Roberts points out that the 'Indonesia Indah' films provide the means, not only of construing local traditions as national traditions, but of staging the Indonesian nation as a modernising nation. Roberts concludes his discussion by construing the 'Indonesia Indah' films as a form of colonial film-making that is likely to be challenged in the future by Indonesian film-making in a postnational vein that foregrounds regional differentiation and thwarts the centralising tendencies of an official nationalism.

In 'Notes on Polish Cinema, Nationalism and Wajda's *Holy Week*', Paul Coates identifies romanticism as a salient feature of Polish cultural production over the past two centuries. The romantics in question, he claims, all saw themselves as exiles within a state imposed by foreign rule while communing with the nation in an imagined nation-state where cultural and political borders coincide perfectly. He discusses some of the communicative strategies adopted by these artists in an effort to circumvent the existing state apparatuses and sustain a dialogue among members of the Polish nation. Coates is interested in determining whether the relevant modes of expression can be characterised as a form of nationalist discourse and, if so, what the relation is between this discourse and a dominant public sphere governed by socialism. Coates argues that nationalist discourse in post-war Poland is best thought of as comprising a number of components which can be variously stressed or repressed depending on the specific nature of Soviet policies at a given moment. Coates surveys a wide range of Polish films, with special reference to *Holy Week*, in support of his central contention, which is that a conception of the heroic constitutes the main element in a cinematically sustained nationalist discourse in post-war Poland.

Kevin Robins and Asu Aksoy explore the implications for national cinema of national communities' tendency to repress and deny diversity in a piece entitled 'The Deep Nation: The National Question and Turkish Cinema Culture'. The modern Turkish state, created in the wake of the First World War, was at once a matter of effacing an earlier cosmopolitanism and of valorising as real an ideal image of the Turkish nation by means of a selective appropriation of Anatolian folk culture. Kemalist legislators, claim Robins and Aksoy, understood the task of Turkish cinema to be one of projecting an ideal and essentially unified Turkish nation, rather than accurately reflecting the diversity of Turkish identities. Turkish cinema, then, was to be an ideological instrument instead of the film-makers' preferred means of mediating and acquiring knowledge about actual Turkish realities. Turkish film-makers, however, rejected the role assigned to them, insisting instead on exploring the complexities of the 'empirical nation'. The result, Robins and Aksoy argue, was a system of censorship that rendered impossible the creation of the very national cinema that legislators believed themselves to desire. Robins and Aksoy trace the history of cinematic censorship in Turkey from early concerns about the representation of the Anatolian people to later worries about depictions of class difference. They go on to identify some of the ways in which critics and film-makers have attempted to construe Turkish cinema from the mid 1960s onwards. In this context they consider the critics' emphasis on a 'universal' cinema and film-makers' preferences for a cinema oriented by either local traditions and identities or religious practices. Robins and Aksoy contend that in the case of Turkish cinema attention should be paid, not to how 'cinema has struggled to reflect the unity of the Turkish nation', but 'how it has struggled to disorder the ideals of the Kemalist nation'. They conclude by briefly discussing Yesim Ustaoğlu's *Journey to the Sun* (1999), which they construe as precisely the kind of postnational or counternational film that is needed to challenge Kemalist priorities.

In 'Fragmenting the Nation: Images of Terrorism in Indian Popular Cinema', Sumita Chakravarty analyses popular Indian film-makers' growing interest over the past two decades in producing cinematic representations of terrorism. Chakravarty's larger claim is that the influential concepts of national cinema that are in some way shaped by Anderson's notion of imagined communities cannot account for this recent tendency, which instead requires an understanding of how nations deal with the threat of fragmentation through cultural imagining. The call for an account of fragmentation is not, however, based only on the historical realities of ethnic nationalism with which many Indian film-makers concerned with the issue of terrorism grapple, but also on assumptions about fundamental differences between literary and cinematic modes of narration. The iconic nature of cinematic representation, claims Chakravarty, foregrounds the particular and does not as a result foster the kinds of metonymic processes required readily to imagine collective, national identities. Chakravarty briefly outlines key stages in the history of Indian cinema before focusing in detail on Mani Ratnam's so-called 'terrorism trilogy'. On Chakravarty's view, the nationalism promoted by these films is not a matter of fuelling a prior patriotism, nor is it prompted by a cinematic mobilisation of the official symbols of the relevant nation-state. Instead, claims Chakravarty, Ratnam's films thematise the nation's relation to its constituent parts – its fragments – in a way that makes strong, cohesive ties seem desirable.

In the final part, 'The Reception of National Images', the emphasis is on the function of national images within the public sphere. Here the contributors are concerned primarily with questions such as: How are national images used and understood? Can national images be contestatory? How do they change over time and as a result of their remobilisation in other cultures? One of the contributors in this section, Scott MacKenzie, goes beyond the perimeters of film to address the roles played by television and video in the dissemination of the national, for the advent of television and video challenged the specificity of the cinema as a means of producing national images, in much the same way that globalisation now throws into question the idea of clearly bounded national cultures.

MacKenzie's 'Mimetic Nationhood: Ethnography and the National' examines the relevance of concepts of nationhood and national identity for minor, third, alternative or aboriginal cinemas. MacKenzie draws on key instances of ethnographic film and video production in Ghana, Brazil and Québec and his central concern throughout has to do with a strategic construction of national identity involving various highly ritualised or staged appropriations of the signs of nationhood privileged by some dominant other. MacKenzie situates his analysis within the larger context of anthropological debates about the role of ritualised mimicry, taking issue, for example, with Victor Turner's suggestion that inversions of the relevant kinds necessarily contribute to, rather than destabilise, the dominant order. The mimetic manipulation of the signs of national identity, claims MacKenzie, can serve many different functions, depending on larger contextual determinants. MacKenzie substantiates this point by way of analyses of Jean Rouch's treatment of the Hauka possession ritual in *Les Maîtres fous* (1957), Pierre Falardeau's references to this same ritual in a video dealing with Québécois national identities, *Le Temps des bouffons* (1993) and Vincent Carelli's ethnographic videos (1989–93) of the Waiãpi Indians in Brazil. MacKenzie's analysis provides further evidence in support of the modernist idea that national identities involve myth-making, rather than an articulation of enduring essences. What is also underscored, however, is the extent to which the myth-making in question can hinder, rather than promote the autonomy and equality of nations.

In 'From New German Cinema to the Post-wall Cinema of Consensus', Eric Rentschler identifies the factors that undermined the New German Cinema and allowed for the emergence of a quite different conception of German national cinema in the 1990s. Rentschler focuses on the recent popular comedies (by film-makers such as Rainer Kaufmann, Dominik Graf, Doris Dörrie, Sönke Wortmann, Katja von Garnier, Joseph Vilsmaier, Helmut Dietl, and Detlev Buck) that have met with acclaim domestically and with disinterest or even disdain internationally. These films, claims Rentschler, are symptomatic of a decisive break with the *auteurs* of New German Cinema, for they seek to entertain, rather than instruct, and explore trivial rather than deep conflicts, typically by means of conventions associated with popular genres and tastes. Whereas

13

New German Cinema, following Rentschler, is best thought of as an oppositional 'cinema of disenchantment' committed to thematising questions of
national identity, post-wall German cinema is oriented by the idea of an
unproblematic consensus, one made possible precisely by neglecting deeper
questions of history and identity. If the specificity of national cinema is
contrastively defined, then today's Cinema of Consensus squares off, not
against Hollywood, but rather against the New German Cinema and its
provocative *auteurs*. In the emerging conception of German cinema, the cinema
of disenchantment appears merely as a stage, rather than as a defining moment
within a larger process of historical development. The Cinema of Consensus,
claims Rentschler, finds its conditions of possibility in a series of events and
developments, including the death of Fassbinder and simultaneous demise of
New German Cinema, subsidy policies favouring commercial films and
enhanced co-operation between film and television, a radical transformation of
the public sphere by new media, changing self-conceptions and significant
investments in German film by five major American distributors.

Ulf Hedetoft examines selected reviewers' reactions to a particular
Hollywood blockbuster – Steven Spielberg's *Saving Private Ryan* (1998) – in
France, Denmark and the US. Hedetoft's intention is to show that while talk of
cultural globalisation may account accurately for the increasingly transnational
nature of contemporary cinematic production, it tends to obscure the persistence of national optics at the level of reception. Responses to *Saving Private
Ryan* clearly suggest that Hollywood's globalising cinematic culture tends to be
nationalised by reviewers and other gatekeepers whose task it is to frame films
for what are essentially national publics. Not only do the French and Danish
reviewers identified by Hedetoft respond to what they construe as the
Americanness of *Saving Private Ryan*, they do so in ways that reflect current
national attitudes toward the US. The global reach of this particular Hollywood
blockbuster, claims Hedetoft, is a matter of a typical 'transboundary process'
that has the effect of generating 'third cultures'. These cultures, he argues,
should not be thought of as detached from nation-states and somehow global
in a nation-transcending sense, but rather as a fusion of indigenous and foreign
national elements. Hedetoft's main point is that nationalising modes of reception are a corollary of globalising national cinemas, just as nationalism may be
provoked by economic and other forms of globalisation.

In 'Birthing Nations', Jane M. Gaines examines two films that are often
considered to involve racism and nation-building: D.W. Griffith's *The Birth of a
Nation* (US, 1915) and Harold Shaw's *De Voortrekkers* (South Africa, 1916).
Gaines argues that any attempt to theorise the racism of films must take into
account key features of relevant contexts of production and reception. This
point is substantiated in an analysis of the extent to which historical reconstruction in *The Birth of a Nation* and *De Voortrekkers* rests, not only on the past, but
on the very myth-making processes that modernists consider central to the
forging of national identities. Gaines examines, for example, the way in which

14

Harold Shaw has the Zulus replace the British as the villains of his film. This substitution, she argues, helps to articulate a historical myth centred around the twin concepts of whiteness and white supremacy. And this myth, she points out, departs radically from the historical record, for the Boer War was not in fact a conflict between black and white, but between colonisers. Gaines is interested in the effective history of the myths articulated in *De Voortrekkers*, particularly their emerging function as South African, national myths during the centenary celebrations of the Great Trek in 1938. She concludes by exploring the relationship between gender, genre and nationalism in the construction of nation-building texts.

Despite apocalyptic claims on various fronts, cinemas and nations are unlikely to disappear any time soon. While they may continue to change and assume new forms, their ubiquity at this point in time seems inescapable. It is to be hoped, then, that *Cinema and Nation* will expand existing debates about image-making and the nation and engender new ones.

Bibliography

Anderson, B. (1991) *Imagined Communities: Reflections on the Origins and Spread of Nationalism*, 2nd edn, London: Verso.

Barber, B. (1995) *Jihad vs. McWorld*, New York: Ballantine Books.

Billig, M. (1995) *Banal Nationalism*, London: Sage.

Bordwell, D. and Carroll, N. (eds) (1996) *Post-Theory: Reconstructing Film Studies*, Madison, WI: University of Wisconsin Press.

Chakravarty, S. (1993) *National Identity in Indian Popular Cinema 1947–1987*, Austin, TX: University of Texas Press.

Courtade, F. (1978) *Les malédictions du cinéma français: une histoire du cinéma français parlant, 1928–1978*, Paris: A. Moreau.

Crofts, S. (1998) 'Concepts of National Cinema', in Hill and Church-Gibson (eds).

Deutsch, K.W. (1996) *Nationalism and Social Communication: An Inquiry into the Foundations of Nationalism*, 2nd edn, Cambridge, MA: MIT Press.

Elsaesser, T. (1980) 'Primary Identification and the Historical Subject: Fassbinder and Germany', *Cinétracts* 11: 43–52.

Faulkner, C. (1994) 'Affective Identities: French National Cinema and the 1930s', *Canadian Journal of Film Studies* 3, 2: 3–24.

Gellner, E. (1983) *Nations and Nationalism*, Oxford: Blackwell.

Hall, J.A. and Lindholm, C. (1999) *Is America Breaking Apart?*, Princeton, NJ: Princeton University Press.

Hayward, S. (1993) *French National Cinema*, London: Routledge.

Higson, A. (1989) 'The Concept of National Cinema', *Screen* 30, 4: 39–47.

—— (1995) *Waving the Flag: Constructing a National Cinema in Britain*, Oxford: Clarendon Press.

Hill, J. (1999) *British Cinema in the 1980s*, Oxford: Clarendon Press.

Hill, J. and Church-Gibson, P. (eds) (1998) *The Oxford Guide to Film Studies*, Oxford: Oxford University Press.

Hjort, M. (1993) *The Strategy of Letters*, Cambridge, MA: Harvard University Press.

Hobsbawm, E. (1990) *Nations and Nationalism Since 1780*, Cambridge: Cambridge University Press.

Hobsbawm, E. and Ranger, T. (eds) (1983) *The Invention of Tradition*, Cambridge: Cambridge University Press.

Kracauer, S. (1947) *From Caligari to Hitler: A Psychological History of the German Film*, Princeton, NJ: Princeton University Press.

McArthur, C. (1993) 'In Praise of a Poor Cinema', *Sight and Sound* 3, 8: 30–2.

Parker, A., Russo, M., Sommer, D. and Yaeger, P. (eds) (1991) *Nationalisms and Sexualities*, London: Routledge.

Smith, A.D. (1991) *National Identity*, London: Penguin.

Sorlin, P. (1977) *Sociologie du cinéma: ouverture pour l'histoire de demain*, Paris: Aubier Montaigne.

—— (1996) *Italian National Cinema, 1896–1996*, London: Routledge.

Street, S. (1997) *British National Cinema*, London: Routledge.

Vincendeau, G. and Dyer, R. (1992) 'Introduction', in Vincendeau and Dyer (eds), *Popular European Cinemas*, London: Routledge.

Wolfenstein, M. and Leites, N. (1971) *Movies: A Psychological Study*, New York: Hafner.

I

THE SOCIOLOGY OF
NATIONALISM

THE SOCIOLOGICAL SCOPE OF 'NATIONAL CINEMA'

Philip Schlesinger

Introduction

Questions about 'national cinema' may usefully be resituated as part of a line of sociological inquiry that centres on the prior matter of how the *nation* may be conceived as a communicative space. I want to restate some of this anterior thinking here because it forms the intellectual hinterland to contemporary debate in film studies.

In what follows, I shall first sketch out the highly influential line of inquiry embodied in social communication theory that contains recurrent, underlying assumptions about the relationship between the nation and communication. Second, I shall briefly examine some recent writing on national cinema and show how the main arguments deployed are largely worked out within a social communication framework, although this is never explicitly recognised.

The selfsame framework of ideas also appears to infuse, and underpin, much everyday thought and governmental policy assumptions about nationhood and nationality in ways entirely congruent with the concern for the nation in film studies, the transfixing obsession of which is the world-wide influence of Hollywood and its impact on particular national film cultures.

The nation and social communication

Karl W. Deutsch (1953; 2nd edn 1966) articulated one of the most explicit and wide-ranging theorisations of the role of communication in nationalism. In his introduction to the second edition of *Nationalism and Social Communication*, Deutsch (1966: 4) highlighted a cardinal theme that remains pertinent for current debate: he observed that the nation-state was 'still the chief political instrument for getting things done', and underlined his view that supranational integration had inherent limits given the resilience of nationality. The key proposition of Deutsch's theory is this: 'The essential aspect of the unity of a people ... is the complementarity or relative efficiency of communication among individuals – something that is in some ways similar to *mutual rapport, but on a larger scale*' (1966: 188, emphasis added). Deutsch sees a 'people' as providing the basis for the forging of a nationality. This, in turn, is distinct from 'nation-statehood', where political sovereignty is harnessed to the pursuit of a group's cohesion and the continuity of its identity. Without expressly naming it, the theory therefore entertains an idea – that of 'the nation without a state' – which has become increasingly significant of late both as an analytical category and as a political project aimed at redefining the autonomy of national groups within the existing international system of states (cf. McCrone 1998; Nairn 1997). For Deutsch (1966: 75), the eventual exercise of national power relies upon 'the relatively coherent and stable structure of memories, habits and values' which in turn 'depends on existing facilities for social communication, both from the past to the present and between contemporaries'.

'*Social* communication' is, therefore, very broadly understood: it is akin to an all-embracing anthropological notion of culture as a way of life, an interactively sustained mode of being that integrates a given people and provides it with singularity (Deutsch 1966: 96–7). This idea is otherwise represented as a principle of coherence for a community, and has a basis in the 'facilities for storing, recalling, and recombining information, channels for its dissemination and interaction, and facilities for deriving further information' (Deutsch 1966: 75).

Social communication theory embraces the ways in which socio-cultural groups cluster and how forms of cohesion affect institutions and socio-cultural interaction. Communicative integration has a key significance because it produces social closure. Central to the argument is the view that nations and nation-states are strongly bounded by their socially communicative structures of interaction: 'Peoples are held together "from within" by this communicative efficiency, the complementarity of the communicative facilities acquired by their members' (Deutsch 1966: 98). Nationality therefore becomes an objective function of communicative competence and belonging.

One key implication is that the communicative practices of nations lead to the exclusion of foreigners. 'Ethnic complementarity' (which for Deutsch broadly equates to nationality) sets up 'communicative barriers' and engenders '"marked gaps" in the efficiency of communication' relative to other groups (1966: 100). Although some nations, those based on immigration and openness to assimilation, are well adapted to the integration of new members, others may throw the process into reverse by expulsion or even extermination.

A further consequence is that the creation of wider collectivities via, for instance, supranational political arrangements such as federation or confederation, is inherently difficult to achieve, especially where communicative complementarity is weak or does not exist. In a negative anticipation of the techno-utopia of the global village, Deutsch argues that the construction of a universal communication system is impossible in a non-uniform world (1966: 176). Deutsch is, therefore, more struck by the likely persistence of the nation-state than by its disappearance. As he neatly puts it, 'the present distribution of sovereign states' is 'necessary in its essential features, though not in its accidents' (1966: 187).

This functionalist conception of cultural integration has a decisive weakness when the level of analysis shifts *outside* the nation-state. There is no general principle for analysing the interaction between communicative communities, for assessing cultural and communicative flows in a global system – matters of central concern to contemporary film studies – because that is not where the theoretical interest lies. Social communication theory is therefore about how shared cultural and communicative practices strengthen the identity of a group by creating boundaries.

High cultures, imagined communities, banal nationalisms

Deutsch's underlying conception of social communication – if not his theoretical idiom – lives on strongly, mostly half-recognised at best, in more contemporary work, such as, Ernest Gellner's noted *Nations and Nationalism* (1983), the lodestar exposition of the 'modernist' conception of nationalism.

Gellner argues that the formation of nation-states is the inevitable outcome of industrialisation, with its concomitant complex division of labour. The social relations created by industrial society mean that to function effectively one needs to be able to do anything, in principle, and that requires 'generic training'. This transmission of know-how necessitates a universal, standardised system of education, using a standardised linguistic medium. It is this process that brings about an inevitable 'deep adjustment in the relationship between polity and culture', namely nationalism, which is 'the organisation of human groups into large, centrally educated, culturally homogeneous groups' (Gellner 1983: 35). Gellner's theory, then, connects the explanatory motor of industrialisation to a quintessentially Deutschian conception of social communication.

Gellner takes culture to refer to 'the distinctive style of conduct and communication of a given community', which in the modern world takes the modal form of a nation-state. For the members of such political formations 'culture is now the necessary shared medium' (1983: 37–8). Cultural boundaries become defined by national cultures, which diffuse a literate 'high culture', in which the key agency is a national education system. In this account, the culture of a nation is broadly identified with official culture. The theory is less focused on sources of internal differentiation and conflict than it is concerned with what makes the nation cohere. Consequently, like Deutsch's theory, Gellner's is mainly concerned with how a national culture comes to be created, rather than with how it is maintained and renewed. It likewise stresses the self-containedness of cultures protected by the nation-state. So, although Deutsch is mentioned only *en passant*, as the springboard for Gellner (1983: 126) to think briefly about the role of media in the national culture, his influence actually runs far deeper than it seems.

Whereas contemporary media and cultural theories are especially concerned with cultural flows and relations of dominance within the global communication order (cf. e.g., Sreberny-Mohammadi *et al.* (eds) 1997; Thussu (ed.) 1998) this is not a key interest for Gellner, any more than it was for Deutsch. In a way still quite characteristic of most sociological theorising, mass-mediated communication is dealt with as a relative triviality. Gellner argues, in a cryptic passage, that it is not the content of such communication that matters, but rather:

> the media themselves, the pervasiveness and importance of abstract, centralised, standardised, one to many communication, which itself automatically engendered the core idea of nationalism, quite irrespective of what in particular is being put into the specific messages transmitted. The most important and persistent message is generated by the medium itself, by the role which such media have acquired in modern life. The core message is that the language and style of the transmissions is important, that only he who can understand them, or can acquire such comprehension, is included in a moral and economic community, and that he who does not and cannot, is excluded.
>
> (1983: 127)

Echoing Marshall McLuhan, Gellner therefore argues in part that the media are the message. But the formula is modified to take account of 'language and style', of how common codes invite the audience to consider and understand themselves to be members of a given community. The media therefore function as a categorical system: widespread public identification with the national space is held to be an effect of this form of cultural organisation. Media are boundary markers, intimately related to the 'political roof' that caps a culture and makes it into a nation-state.

This argument overstates the point. 'Language and style' are about more than the medium that transmits them: they are closely related to the question of 'content'. This is of cardinal interest for the cultural industries that produce it and a central issue for film and television policies. The attitude of the state to its own 'national' content is frequently a matter of high importance in international cultural trade and often embedded in national communication policies. Hence, Gellner's rendition of social communication theory reproduces the original Deutschian fixation on what is internal to the communicative community rather than considering the import of what lies outside and how it may affect the interior. It ignores the 'otherness' that may well substantially condition any given national identity.

This internalist line of argument also runs through another pivotal text of recent years, Benedict Anderson's *Imagined Communities* (1983), which has evidently provided the theoretical starting point for most recent writing on national cinema. In his account of the emergence of European nations, Anderson, like Deutsch and even more so than Gellner, takes mediated communication to be of central importance in the formation of a nationalist consciousness (or, as we now say, national identity): 'What, in a positive sense, made the new communities imaginable was a half-fortuitous, but explosive, interaction between a system of production and productive relations (capitalism), a technology of communications (print), and the fatality of human linguistic diversity' (Anderson 1983: 46). Whereas for Gellner national systems of education that produce cultural affines (a community of 'clerks') take centre-stage, Anderson's key contention is that '[p]rint-language is what invents nationalism, not *a* particular language per se' (1983: 122). Thus, what is highlighted is the importance of the media of communication in the construction of an imagined community, given the appropriate material conditions.

According to Anderson, 'print language' was the means whereby given vernaculars became standardised, being disseminated through the market for books and newspapers. His account is resolutely Gutenbergian: the impact of the moving image is not addressed. Mechanically reproduced print-languages unified fields of linguistic exchange, fixed 'national' languages, and created new idioms of power. The 'nationalist novel' (its plot enacted in a socially recognised common space) together with the newspaper, with 'calendrical consciousness' as its principle of organisation, were, Anderson argues, the two key vehicles in shaping national consciousness. By co-ordinating time and space these could address an imagined national community even before it had been formed into a nation-state.

Hence, the collective consumption of mediated communication serves to create a sense of national community. Like Gellner, from whom he would differentiate his approach, Anderson actually understands the confines of the nation to be inescapably implicit in the way that the media categorise reality and address their audiences. Strikingly, like Deutsch, who writes of a large-scale 'mutual rapport', Anderson speaks of the nation's 'deep, horizontal comradeship' (1983: 16).

Subsequently, Anderson has considered how the national story has been told in postcolonial states by way of the cultural institutions of the census (enumerator and sorter of populations), the map (definer of the political boundaries) and the museum (vehicle for the establishment of legitimate ancestry) (1991: 184). Although the moving image is not part of Anderson's story, its formative role in postcolonial nation-formation has been justly underlined by others (Martín-Barbero 1993). And while (unlike Gellner) Anderson makes no reference to Deutsch's work, his approach is still unmistakably located in a social communication framework: the imagined community is situated within the socio-cultural and communicative space of the nation-state and it is the internal processes of nation-formation that are of predominant interest.

Anderson's argument about the 'imagined community' has been taken up, with a distinctive twist, by Michael Billig (1995: 70) who stresses nationalism's 'banality': namely, the demonstrable proposition that a great deal of nationalist practice is embedded in the rituals and practices of everyday life.

Billig argues that in the contemporary world, entire peoples are simply embedded in their national deixes. Their flags flutter diurnally, largely unnoticed as adornments to public buildings; the news categorises some events as home affairs and distinguishes these from foreign reports; the weather forecast reinforces the awareness of political geography; sporting heroes embody national virtues and mobilise collective loyalties; moments of crisis – especially war – produce patriotic addresses from political leaders; national languages and histories, through their transmission constitute a sense of communality. And so forth. Thus are the internal props of national identity routinely and unremark-ably reproduced. In line with Gellner and Anderson, Billig's analysis fills in the space of 'communicative complementarity' and underscores its tenacious grip on how we categorise the world. But, notably, unlike his precursors, Billig is less interested in the question of nation-formation than that of nation-maintenance.

The boundary of the national

Thus far, it has been argued that social communication theories have two key features: a tendency to think in terms of a close functional fit between commu-nication and the nation; and an overwhelming concern with the interior of the national communicative space, whether this be in respect of its formation or its maintenance. This internalism may, at times, acknowledge how nations are defined by their positions in the relations of an interstate world, but that is of secondary interest. Taken together, therefore, these positions carry a major implication: that the politically salient container for communicative space is the sovereign nation-state. It is striking just how much this way of constructing the problem has been reproduced in recent film theory. Indeed, viewed from the standpoint of sociology, present concerns with national cinema in film studies are a sectoral application of social communication theory.

The scope of 'national cinema'

Film studies' concern with the role of cinema in the nation is inherently inter-nalist. Its central concern is with how – if at all – the production, circulation and consumption of the moving image is constitutive of the national collectivity. However, this internalism is necessarily tempered by an awareness of exteriority as a shaping force. Indeed, it is precisely the extra-territorial cultural pressure of Hollywood's production, imported into the national space, that sets up the contemporary issue of national cinema. This outside challenge to ideas of the national is at once interpreted as cultural, economic and political as well as ideo-logical. I shall discuss a number of recent contributions to this line of argument. In general, these are motivated by the desire to characterise the cinematic output that occurs – or ought to occur – within the boundaries of a given state, while at the same time recognising that this may be both an elusive and rather contested goal. It is striking how much of this thinking plays itself out within the characteristic problematic of the social communication theory of nation-hood and national identity outlined above. I shall take, by way of illustration, some well-known contemporary accounts of British, French and Italian cinema.

For Susan Hayward, writing about France, the problem of how to delineate a national cinema is deeply influenced by a statist paradigm. For Hayward (1993: ix), the issue is firmly rooted in the development of a political culture, the process 'whereby myths are erected about a nation's various and particular institutions':

> film functions as a cultural articulation of a nation … [it] textualises the nation and subsequently constructs a series of relations around the concepts, first, of state and citizen, then of state, citizen and other … a 'national' cinema … is ineluctably 'reduced' to a series of enunciations that reverberate around two fundamental concepts: identity and difference.
>
> (Hayward 1993: x)

In this kind of formulation, the nation is treated as *singular*, and national cinema is to be investigated by a study of a given country's cinematographic production. The latter, it is held, can be studied by analysis of the films themselves, the written discourses that they evoke, and the patrimony embodied in archiving and exhibiting practices. Hayward's view is greatly influenced by the French state's self-conscious predilection for fashioning the history of the nation and for its long-standing and highly explicit confrontation with Hollywood along the way.

It is the concept of 'identity' that underlines the inward focus, whereas it is the concept of 'difference' that, by its invocation of contrast and comparison, points outside the confines of the national cinematic territory. For Hayward, the practical solution to analysing French national cinema lies in stressing questions of production, and the distinctive film stylistics that are embodied in this output. For Sarah Street (1997), writing on Britain, a similarly pragmatic definition of national cinema is also most easily arrived at by stressing domestic production, understood as 'films registered as British', whatever the ambiguities this creates, given the diverse national mixes of finance, producer partnerships and creative personnel typical of movie-making. However, this simplification is tempered by an acceptance of Britishness as 'one element in the increasingly international, intertextual diversity of modern genre cinema' (1997: 113).

Based on similar terrain, Andrew Higson (1995) has argued that both national identity and national cinema should be seen from a processual point of view. He suggests that we might define a national cinema by looking at a range of features: its industrial and business aspect, exhibition and consumption and their impact on national culture, the definitions used in cultural policy-making and critical circles, and finally, questions of representation, in particular the favouring of particular genres. Higson goes on to describe the process thus:

> Individual films will often serve to represent the national to itself, as a nation. Inserted into the general framework of the cinematic

experience, such films will construct imaginary bonds which work to hold the peoples of a nation together as a community by dramatising their current fears, anxieties, pleasures and aspirations. A diverse and often antagonistic group of peoples are thus invited to recognise themselves as a singular body with a common culture, and to oppose themselves to other cultures and communities. Of course, this work is never completely achieved.

(1995: 7)

This framing of the problem, highly derivative of Anderson on the calling into existence of a national community, fits perfectly into a social communication perspective. As with Hayward's formulation, it is complemented by a sense of how a national cinema may be taken to affirm a singular national self-identity and at the same time be situated in an international system of differences. British cinema, Higson's focus, must perforce define itself in relation to Hollywood, on the basis of a familiar mix of economic competition considerations and cultural anxieties about 'Americanisation'. Hollywood presents a major problem, precisely because of its protean capacity to enter the national space and not be seen as 'other' due to the popularity of many of its offerings.

While Higson proposes one version of how a British national cinema may be characterised, and argues that film cultures offer a means of drawing boundaries around a collectivity, he also evidently holds the arguments for cultural defence espoused by government policy-makers and national cultural intellectuals to be unachievable. Higson – by contrast to Hayward – moves the argument away from questions of production and underlines the key importance of how *audiences* consume. The issue thus becomes one of 'how actual audiences construct their cultural identity in relation to the various products of the national and international film and television industries' (1995: 279).

This argument has its detractors. For instance, John Hill (1992, 1997) distinguishes between economic arguments in defence of a national film industry and cultural arguments in favour of a diverse representation of the nation. It is the latter he believes need most careful attention, since the global political economy of communication sets the terms of trade for production outside Hollywood. He argues that to emphasise consumption, as does Higson, and to raise the importance of the ways in which audiences make sense of what they see, is to make use of an indefensible notion of national cinema. Addressing himself specifically to the case of the UK, Hill argues that Higson's approach would allow Hollywood films to be classified as part of British national cinema merely because they are consumed by British audiences. It is important, he counters, to distinguish between 'cinema in Britain' and 'British national cinema'. To defend the latter category is to head into normative territory, to argue that a national cinema *ought* to represent cultural diversity and that it has no necessary nationalistic mission.

Hill argues that a homogeneous idea of the 'nation' falls apart in the face of the UK's increasingly evident diversity. Black cinema and Scottish and Welsh film-making are challenges to narrow conceptions of Englishness. We are left wondering whether it makes sense to talk of a 'national' cinema in the British case, or whether we must now talk about national cinemas (cf. Petrie 1992: 3). Such arguments begin to throw the question of the *state* into relief – how much of the argument about national cinema is actually about state cinema? – as well as to put on to the agenda the growing complexities of the cultural relations between states and nations in a world increasingly dominated by regional trade groupings such as NAFTA, Mercosur and the European Union.

On the one hand, Hollywood patently is part of how cinema circulates in given national spaces. And on the other, what actually constitutes a 'national' space may begin to be seriously challenged by processes of socio-political change and modes of popular identification. So arguably, in some situations at least, we have to address the question of what is 'national' at a time of cultural fragmentation. In the discourse of political philosophy and much recent media studies, there has been, first, an identification of the national communicative space with 'the' public sphere. Latterly, there have been increasing efforts to rethink this space, in line with growing social diversity and political change, as a 'sphere of publics' in which national identities are seen as subject to much more explicit negotiation (Calhoun 1992; Habermas 1997; Schlesinger 1999). It seems evident that parallel moves are taking place in film studies, although without, for the most part, explicit connections being made with current socio-logical thought. Underlying all of these developments is a desire to see the interior of the national space as more complex and diverse, while at the same time wishing to sustain the idea that there is still some retaining boundary wall, if not of nationhood, then at least of statehood.

Hill's argument may be read as a plea for retaining the role of critical cultural discourse in thinking about cinema in the national public space. It is true that to reduce cultural production to a question of economics is indeed severely to restrict possible frameworks of debate, although it plainly accords with the will of the *Zeitgeist*. Yet it should be noted that to recognise how consumption may constitute collective identities does not necessarily entail abandoning arguments about the cultural value of national production. Rather, it provides another, parallel, mode of understanding how cinema works in the national space along-side normative and economic arguments. This line of argument has been developed by Pierre Sorlin, for whom it is the consumption of films across successive generations that is the key to understanding Italian national cinema:

> Four generations of cinema-goers built up an enormous palimpsest of different sounds and images, domestic as well as alien, and used it to organise their lives in the particular place where they were residing, Italy. The films they enjoyed were American as often as domestic, but the manner in which they assimilated and re-used this material was

theirs and it is their appropriation of various cinematic sources which has made up Italian national cinema.

(Sorlin 1996: 172)

Underlying this argument is a view of culture as inherently syncretic. It is closely aligned with a number of contemporary Latin American attempts in cultural and communication theory to rethink the nature of cultural dependency. At root, it is an argument about the popular appropriation and refashioning of global culture that re-theorises questions of cultural domination (cf. Schlesinger and Morris 1998).

Sorlin has encapsulated the essential ambiguity behind the project of defending a national cinema when he observes that on the one hand 'before it was twenty years old, the cinema extended beyond national frontiers' but that on the other, '[f]ilms have long been taken to be part of a nation's culture, more complex than the institutions and companies that make and circulate them, but still fundamentally governed by national traditions' (1996: 1).

In an analysis much influenced by the peculiarities of the historically weak Italian state formation, Sorlin argues that nations are 'fractured, self-contradictory structures'. In an approach that itself, therefore, presumes an irreducible diversity of cultures within the nation, he suggests that the best way to envision a national cinema is not 'as a set of films which help to distinguish a nation from other nations' but rather to see it as 'the chain of relations and exchanges which develop in connection with films, in a territory delineated by its economic and juridical policy' (Sorlin 1996: 10). And furthermore, he remarks that:

> The evolution of community feelings is linked to the unstable, permanently moving relationship between the social organisation, the institutions, and the set of symbols (linguistic, visual and aural) which human beings use to make sense of the world that surrounds them. This process is itself determined by the existence or absence of a standardised, shared system of reference. The cinema was part of a cluster of tools which enabled the Italians to build a picture of themselves, both individually and as members of a group.
>
> (Sorlin 1996: 170)

This formulation is entirely consistent with Deutsch's own idea of 'communicative complementarity' and with Gellner's related emphasis on a shared, integrative culture – although here it is 'ciné-literacy' rather than Gellnerian clerkly high literacy that is being emphasised. Indeed, when Sorlin turns to language – Anderson's key vehicle for establishing a common discourse – the congruence of thinking with the social communication tradition is even more evident. Cinema – like the Andersonian novel and newspaper – has been the vehicle for producing a common spatio-temporal horizon for Italians: 'Far from taking their identity from the language they use, film-makers have actively co-operated in giving official Italian its present status of most common idiom in the peninsula', a process in which this role for cinema subsequently has been reinforced by that of nationwide radio and television broadcasting (Sorlin 1996: 10, 170).

Sorlin's conception of the national audience is a historical one. He identifies successive cinema-going 'generations' in terms of their different configurations of experience. The precise adequacy or otherwise of this conceptualisation is perhaps less important than the recognition that the national audience is not frozen in time. This allows us to broaden questions of national cinema to those of the national audio-visual space. It permits us to acknowledge, for instance, how film has increasingly become diffused by television and video and how these media have substantially displaced the theatrical cinema circuit as a site of consumption. A historical conception of the audience also allows us to note the shifts in audience demographics among cinema-goers and how the viewing nation may be diversely constituted and reconstituted over time (cf. Hill 1997).

Concluding observations

Contemporary analyses of 'national cinema' are entirely congruent with a well-established line of sociological thinking about the nation. That is because they depart from the same deeply embedded assumptions. Consciously or unconsciously, social communication thought is an expression of the cultural geography of the nation-state in a world of sovereign states. This is the bedrock on which film studies has been based when it invokes a largely derivative sociological argument about nationalism and national identity as a necessary starting point for studies of national cinema. The guiding interest lies in what a national cinema *is* or *might* be and is broadly connected to the political project of constituting the national collectivity. The main task has been to define and depict the relations between nations (usually meaning 'states') and film cultures. The inevitable cross-border flow of moving images has been firmly at the forefront of concern because – the United States excepted – the film studies discourse is always wrestling with the consequences of cultural dependency.

Film studies' use of sociological thinking has been heavily applied to an argument about how the moving image plays variously into the constitution of cultural boundaries. However, the work of film scholars has yet to be explicitly integrated into mainstream sociological analyses of how national identities are formed. At best, like all treatments of the media in mainstream studies of nationalism and national identity, the moving image is more invoked in passing than analysed in depth. It is striking, therefore, that we have two lines of inquiry that ought not only to converge but also to be thoroughly integrated as part of a broad programme of work on nation and culture in the age of so-called globalisation.

Social communication theory's functionalism produces an image of a strongly bounded communicative community. Under present conditions clearly this needs to be revised given the increased attention afforded the 'globalisation' of communication – especially the border-circumventing flows resulting from the rapid transformation of electronic media and of information and communication technologies. That said, the new wave of concern with global interconnectedness should not make us now envisage the world as definitively 'postnational'. The continuing strong links between modes of social communication and national political spaces remain fundamental for conceptions of collective identity. And it is precisely that connectedness that informs, constructs and reproduces the problematic of a national cinema. But as this issue begins to be rethought in conditions of greater complexity, the underlying social communication theory will need substantial revision. It now must offer an explanatory grasp of the increasingly evident contradictions between the various levels of culture and identity that are tending to decouple state and nation.

Acknowledgements

The first half of the present essay draws extensively on 'The Nation and Communicative Space', in Howard Tumber (ed.), *Media Power, Professionals and Policy*, London: Routledge, 2000. The present work is based on research carried out as part of the 'Political Communication and Democracy' project in the ESRC's 'Media Economics and Media Culture Programme' (Reference No.: L126251022). The author is grateful to the Council for its support.

Bibliography

Anderson, B. (1983) *Imagined Communities: Reflections on the Origin and Spread of Nationalism*, London: Verso, 2nd edn 1991.

Billig, M. (1995) *Banal Nationalism*, London: Sage Publications.

Calhoun, C. (ed.) (1992) *Habermas and the Public Sphere*, Cambridge, MA: MIT Press.

Deutsch, K.W. (1953) *Nationalism and Social Communication: An Inquiry into the Foundations of Nationalism*, Cambridge, MA: MIT Press, 2nd edn 1966.

Gellner, E. (1983) *Nations and Nationalism*, Oxford: Blackwell.

Habermas, J. (1997) *Between Facts and Norms*, Cambridge: Polity Press.

Hayward, S. (1993) *French National Cinema*, London: Routledge.

Higson, A. (1995) *Waving the Flag: Constructing a National Cinema in Britain*, Oxford: Clarendon.

Hill, J. (1992) 'The Issue of National Cinema and British Film Production', in D. Petrie (ed.), *New Questions of British Cinema*, London: BFI, pp. 10–21.

——(1997) 'British Cinema as National Cinema: Production, Audience and Representation', in R. Murphy (ed.), *The British Cinema Book*, London: BFI, pp. 244–54.

Martín-Barbero, J. (1993) *Communication, Culture and Hegemony: From the Media to Mediations*, London: Sage Publications.

McCrone, D. (1998) *The Sociology of Nationalism: Tomorrow's Ancestors*, London: Routledge.

Nairn, T. (1997) *Faces of Nationalism: Janus Revisited*, London: Verso.

Petrie, D. (ed.) (1992) *New Questions of British Cinema*, London: BFI.

Schlesinger, P. (1999) 'Changing Spaces of Political Communication: The Case of the European Union', *Political Communication* 16, 3: 263–79.

Schlesinger, P. and Morris, N. (1998) 'Communication, Cultural Identity and the State in Latin America: A Perspective from Europe', pp. 267–303, in Hedetoft (ed.) (1998) *Political Symbols, Symbolic Politics: European Identities in Transformation*, Aldershot: Ashgate.

Sorlin, P. (1996) *Italian National Cinema, 1986–1996*, London: Routledge.

Sreberny-Mohammadi, A., Winseck, D., McKenna, J. and Boyd-Barrett, O. (eds) (1997) *Media in Global Context: A Reader*, London: Arnold.

Street, S. (1997) *British National Cinema*, London: Routledge.

Thussu, D.K. (ed.) (1998) *Electronic Empires: Global Media and Local Resistance*, London: Arnold.

2

FRANK CAPRA MEETS JOHN DOE

Anti-politics in American national identity

Charles Lindholm and John A. Hall

Nationalism is often seen as a force – characteristically, as a disease – that affects others. Gellner's very sophisticated theory, for example, defines nationalism as the struggle of a cultural group to establish its own political roof (Gellner 1983; Hall 1998). This will not do. The nationalisms which most affected the historical record were those of France and of Germany – that is, the nationalisms of large and established states rather than those of peoples struggling to secede from larger polities. In our own time the nationalism which matters most for world affairs is that of the United States. If this is one justification for the focus of this chapter, another background consideration must be that the United States is the leading producer of film. But the story to be told here is complex, certainly far less simple than views of an all-encompassing and confident American cultural imperialism would allow. Bluntly, while American citizens are strongly patriotic and nationalistic,[1] overtly political films have never been popular. As Phillip Gianos has recently remarked: 'The United States has developed over the years a richer film vocabulary for gangsters, cowboys, and mummies raised from the dead than it has for citizens and presidents ... '. In the world of Hollywood, 'politics is not consequential; politics is not interesting; happiness is purely an individual matter; things will be all right. This is what virtually all American films tell their audiences' (Gianos 1998: 4, 7).[2] So our subject must be that of the curious case of an anti-political national identity.

The best way to tease out these issues is by considering Frank Capra. He is the sole major American director to have devoted a major part of his career to the exploration of American political culture. Further, no other major American film-maker has dealt seriously with central themes of citizenship, responsibility and participation in civic life; certainly no one has confronted the internal contradictions of America in a more powerful and revealing way. This paper contextualises the rise and eventual collapse of Capra's attempt to develop a positive American cinematic vocabulary for political action, connecting the failure of his project with fundamental contradictions inherent in American national identity.

Frank Capra and American political cinema

From the mid 1930s until the early 1940s Capra, the son of illiterate Sicilian immigrants, exemplified the American dream by becoming one of the most popular and successful men in America. Capra was not only the best paid director in Hollywood, he was the only director whose name was featured above the title, and the only one given free rein in production (Capra 1971).[3] Capra presided over the golden age of film, before the advent of television, when over ninety million people went to the movies at least once a week. The unparalleled cultural dominance of Hollywood film during this period has led Neal Gabler to discern the presence of a 'new civic religion' (Gabler 1988: 102) binding a fragmented American society together during the Depression and the Second World War. If this is so, then Capra was Hollywood's high priest.

Capra's early movies were witty romantic comedies where class divisions were overcome by the force of love. The most popular was *It Happened One Night* (1934), in which a manly proletarian hero brings a snobbish rich girl down to earth and gains her devotion, her father's approval and her fortune, without compromising his independence or integrity. The democratising messages were that what really matters is character, that love conquers all, and that the only real sin is snobbery. However, immediately after the huge financial and critical success of *It Happened One Night* Capra suffered a major physical and psychological breakdown, torn by doubts about his own creative ability and personal worth – an identity crisis that resonates with characteristic American cultural anxieties about authenticity and status (McBride 1992). As Capra reports in his lively but often unreliable autobiography, he was rescued from his depression by a visit from an anonymous 'little man' who chided him for not making use of his talents to better the lot of humanity. In response, Capra self-consciously resolved to inspire his fellow citizens by reaffirming and updating national myths in his films (Glatzer 1989).

The first of his 'depression trilogy', *Mr Deeds Goes to Town* (1936), established the basic formula. In it, Mr Deeds, a naive country boy (Gary Cooper), inherits a fortune and goes off to experience life in New York, where his basic American values of fairness and honesty are challenged by the cruelty and hypocrisy of the city. He also meets a street-wise media woman (Jean Arthur) who first manipulates him for her own ends, but who ends by falling in love with him. Moved by the plight of his fellow citizens, Deeds decides to give away most of his fortune (prudently keeping two million dollars for his own use – he may be charitable, but he is no saint). He is then accused of being crazy and taken to court by venal lawyers, but wins everyone over in a stirring speech (later quoted extensively by Ronald Reagan during his presidential campaign). In it, Deeds says: 'From what I can see, no matter what system of government we have, there'll always be leaders and always be followers. ... And I say the fellows who can make the hill on high should stop once in a while to help those who can't' (McBride 1992: 341–2). Capra's (and later Reagan's) appeal to charity and individual goodness – combined with a distaste for the complexities of political life – struck a chord with most Americans.[4]

In *Mr Smith Goes to Washington* (1939) Capra expanded on his pet themes, making them more obviously political. Jefferson Smith (James Stewart), the son of a crusading newspaperman, is a sweet and childlike Western everyman who imitates birdcalls and spends his spare time as a boy scout leader. He is elected to the senate as a stooge for crooked special interests led by a greedy boss (Edward Arnold). His fellow senator, Paine (Claude Rains), was his late father's best friend, but has now been corrupted. He counsels Smith to learn to compromise his ideals, but Smith responds that lost causes are the only ones worth fighting for. Meanwhile, Smith has been taken up by a savvy newspaper woman (again played by Jean Arthur) who aims to exploit his innocence for publicity purposes; but she falls in love with him instead, and encourages him to stand up against the lobbyists and special interests. Smith duly tries to expose the plots of the political bosses, but is made to face trumped up charges on the floor of the Senate, where he fights back through a filibuster. In contrast to Deeds, who convinced the court of his integrity with his arguments, the Senate is unmoved. Smith collapses with exhaustion, and is only victorious because Paine, overcome by guilt, first tries to commit suicide and then tells the truth.

After the completion of *Mr Smith*, some politicians, furious at Capra's portrayal of the Senate as a nest of corruption, denounced the film as un-American; there were demands that it not be released. But Capra's depiction of the depraving influences of governmental power appealed to an American public traditionally leery of politicians and official authority; similarly, the story of a lone hero struggling against all odds for what he knows to be right evoked the American myth of the rugged individual, reliant solely on his own moral compass for direction. The film also tapped an equally American faith in the sacred rule of law, which allows Smith his right to be heard before the full Senate (just as Deeds had his say in court). And of course, the movie featured the necessary (though completely unbelievable) happy ending, along with the message that love can conquer all. *Mr Smith Goes to Washington* was a great success both at home and abroad. The *London Sunday Graphic* called it the best American patriotic film ever made, which could only be equalled by 'Mr Capra Goes to America' (McBride 1992).

In these two films, Capra and his collaborators built a myth of the American everyman hero as 'the honest and forthright fellow – confused, inconsistent, but always sincere – who believes in the basic goodness of people and has the courage to fight hard for principles' (Crowther 1989: 221). Each film utilised the same sets of populist oppositions: small-town innocence against the wise-guy corruption of the city; the integrity and decency of the individual everyman versus the power and venality of 'special interest groups' run by rapacious 'bosses'; the necessity of charity as a counter to greed; faith in the legal system and suspicion of the compromises of politics; love as the solvent of cynicism and the conqueror of class divisions. Each movie was centred on the lonely and courageous stand of an honest innocent hero against corporate evil. The United States, Capra's political films seemed to suggest, was a place where virtuous political action, love, naivety, bravery, integrity and charity went hand in hand with a faith in the individual and a deep distrust of official authority. But neither of these hugely popular films really touched on the fundamental problem that was to preoccupy Capra in his next, and crucial, work; the problem of reconciling heroic individualism with the practice of collective action.

Meet John Doe

Meet John Doe (1941) was the third and most ambitious of Capra's political films. The film was to deal with the masses rather than with heroes. They are described in the film as follows:

> If anybody should ask you what the average John Doe is like, you couldn't tell him, because he's a million and one things. He's Mr. Big and Mr. Small. He's simple and he's wise. ... He's the man the ads are written for. He's the fellow everybody sells things to. He's ... the world's greatest stooge and the world's greatest strength.
>
> (Wolfe 1989a: 97–8)

Prior to release, the film had a huge publicity build up that conflated the lead character with the American public and even with America itself. One ad proclaimed that John Doe is '3,000 miles wide and 1,000 miles tall' and superimposed a sketch of the character over a map of the United States. Another showed John Doe's silhouette fleshed in with line drawings of hundreds of tiny figures. The text announced 'One Man in a Million! ... A Million Men in One!'. Yet another portrayed a giant John Doe bending to greet a field of miniatures, with the headline reading 'John Doe ... Meet America'. At some theatres life-sized cardboard cutouts of John Doe extended a hand to greet the incoming public. As Charles Wolfe remarks, 'To enter the front door of a movie theater and meet John Doe was perhaps to discover yourself, or your neighbor, or yourself as part of the national neighborhood that Capra's "camera eye" envisioned' (Wolfe 1989c: 22).

In many respects, the storyline of *John Doe* followed the well-tested plots from *Deeds* and *Smith*. A rural innocent, John Willoughby (Gary Cooper) is thrust into a corrupt political arena where he is first manipulated and then helped by a cynical newspaper woman (Ann Mitchell, played by Barbara Stanwyck) who has fallen in love with him. He is suborned by a political boss and newspaper owner, D.B. Norton (again played by Edward Arnold) who makes him a media star for his own nefarious purposes. The naive hero finally realises he is being duped and stands up for himself against the forces of evil.

But a closer look shows significant divergences from the earlier plots. A major difference is that in *John Doe* the hero does not have a solid base in family and community. Instead, he is a hobo, an ex-baseball pitcher with a bad arm; in Capra's words, he is 'a drifting piece of human flotsam as devoid of ideals as he was of change in his pocket' (Capra 1971: 303). By beginning with an amoral and rootless individual, Capra touches on a central American ambivalence about social life. In the United States a strong ideal of individualism correlates with real fluidity in social status and spatial mobility, a frontier mentality, a Protestant cosmology, and capitalist entrepreneurism. Like the standard assumptions of classic social contract theory and Western liberalism, this ideal posits that individuals exist prior to the social world. As one commentator has noted, for Americans 'individualism is natural, community problematical. *Society has to be built*' (Varenne 1977: 70). The premise of individual responsibility for the manufacture of a fragile society is in marked contrast to the European assumption that people live within a pre-existent social and political hierarchy.

The American belief in the primacy of the individual coincides with anxiety that the demands of the community might destroy one's personal freedom. This anxiety nurtures fantasies of escape from all social entanglements and mundane responsibilities; fantasies expressed in characteristic American tropes of the lone cowboy riding into the wilderness, get-rich-quick schemes, desert island idylls, and so on. In his romantic comedies Capra had been content to play along with these typical fantasies. As one critic writes, his films showed 'only a sense of dissatisfaction, an urge to escape – on to the open road with the daughter of a millionaire, back to small-town simplicity on a safe income' (McBride 1992: 383).

In his first political movies, Capra had not considered how an independent individual could reconcile his freedom with a social conscience. Instead, he had assumed that his heroes were upright simply because they had been born into traditional communities and families. The conflict was between rural values and urban corruption. But in *John Doe* Capra asked how a free man could be induced to give up his liberty and accept the necessary but burdensome obligations and responsibilities of participation in civil life. To highlight the issue, he paired his hero with a true anarchist, the Colonel (played with brio by Walter Brennan), who believes that 'the world's been shaved by a drunken barber' and that the best strategy is to opt out of social life altogether. According to the Colonel's Rousseauean philosophy, relationships, responsibilities and social participation inevitably lead to status competition and envy, turning the free individual into 'a Heelot' driven by desire for possessions and status, and borne down by regulations and duties.[5] In the movie, the Colonel responds to all talk of love or community with cynicism, and continually seeks to lure John back toward the masculine, unsocialised life of hobo freedom. Unfortunately for the coherence of the plot, the Colonel's beliefs are presented with such conviction that they erode the movie's main message of co-operation and community – just as antisocial impulses remain a central aspect of American thought, undermining awareness of interdependence.[6]

Given this context, it is not surprising to find that the asocial Willoughby is initially drawn into the social world for purely materialistic reasons. Penniless and starving, he accepts Ann's offer to play the part of a non-existent 'John Doe' who has vowed to commit suicide on Christmas to protest the miserable state of the world. Ann has made up 'John Doe' as a publicity stunt in order to keep her job on Norton's paper, which is being 'streamlined' by Norton's employee, the hard-bitten newspaperman Connell (James Gleason). Willoughby's job is to read the speeches that Ann writes, meet the public, and to keep his mouth shut. The Colonel warns Willoughby that he is on the way towards selling his freedom and becoming a 'Heelot', but despite the advice, Willoughby accepts the job.

However, the stunt soon proves to have more serious consequences than had been anticipated. By reading speeches prepared by Ann (making use of her saintly dead father's diaries), the fake John Doe begins to inspire a mush-rooming growth of grass-roots 'John Doe clubs' based on simple values of neighbourliness and voluntarism. Capra thus takes on another issue he had previously skirted: the role of popular political action in the American context. As noted, Capra's earlier movies had already shown his deep suspicion of polit-ical professionals and official government (along with his faith in the law). The John Doe movement too is determinedly anti-institutional; politicians are not allowed to join; there is no official organisation or hierarchy; the John Doe clubs 'ask for nothing' from government agencies and rely solely on the personal kindness of members toward one another to transform society (Wolfe 1989a: 119). This too is an attitude deeply rooted in American culture, one that has its roots in a shared premise of egalitarianism.

It was Tocqueville who argued that the highest value held by the citizens of the United States is equality. Every individual in America, Tocqueville said, is believed to be the moral equivalent of all others, with an equal potential and right to life, liberty and the pursuit of happiness – an ideology, it should be stressed, that continues to be eagerly embraced even by those at the very bottom of the socio-economic order as well as by the rest of the society.[7] This pervasive faith helps explain why the United States has never been friendly to the emergence of distinct social groups with self-consciously different ways of life, and why socialism has always had a hard time in the United States. It accounts as well for the massive popularity of Capra's earlier comedies in which class differences were dissolved by love and good fellowship.

Because Americans consider themselves to be morally equivalent, consider-able resentment is reserved for those who make claims to be superior. This applies in particular to the minions of the state, and to those who wield political authority in 'the name of the people'. Partly this antipathy stems from the fact that the United States was founded by means of a revolution directed against state power; it remains the least centralised modern nation, with the least amount of governmental intervention in the lives of citizens. As egalitarian indi-vidualists Americans continue to view central state organisation with great trepidation, fearing curtailment of individual liberty.[8] Americans therefore tend to believe that political organisation in its ideal form ought to be a personal matter spontaneously achieved between neighbours meeting over the back fence, inspired solely by love and friendship; otherwise it risks the dangers of bureau- cratic rationalisation and entanglement with corrupting official state power. The John Doe clubs exemplify the ideal small-scale form of communal participation, arising outside of official channels and reliant on the good fellowship of its members to draw isolated individuals out of themselves and into social life.

This is illustrated clearly in the effect of the clubs on 'John Doe' himself. During the course of the movie, the hero – who was moved at first purely by self-aggrandisement – slowly becomes more socially committed, first as a result of his growing love for Ann. She also begins to love him, in large part because she hears the voice of her father in the inspirational speeches she has written for John to deliver (confusions between paternal and sexual love abound in the movie). But the turning point in his transformation is when Doe/Willoughby realises the common humanity he shares with the humble members of the clubs who come to listen to him speak:

> I could feel that they were hungry for something. Do you know what I mean? Maybe that's why they came. Maybe they're just lonely and wanted somebody to say hello to. I know how they feel. I've been lonely and hungry for something practically all my life.
>
> (Wolfe 1989a: 129)

Realising his own need for others, John is now committed to the ideals Ann had put in his mouth in his first speech. The struggle of the John Does throughout history, the speech said, has always been to gain freedom. But this can only be accomplished through co-operation; average Americans therefore need to seek out their neighbours and help each other as teammates; they must tear down the fences that separate them (the Colonel's response is: 'Why if you tore one picket off of your neighbor's fence, he'd sue you!'). The pivotal speech ends as follows:

> The meek can only inherit the earth when the John Does start loving their neighbors. You'd better start right now. Don't wait till the game is called on account of darkness. Wake up, John Doe, you're the hope of the world.
>
> (Wolfe 1989a: 102, 100)

The rule of the mob

The movie reaches its dramatic turning point as Ann's boss, the power-hungry newspaper magnate Norton, plots to make use of the Doe movement's popu- larity to launch his own bid for the presidency. Norton is portrayed as an American fascist who commands a uniformed private army of motorcyclists. He believes the American people have too much freedom, and has enlisted a cadre of corrupt politicians, labour leaders and financiers to back him in his takeover bid. Willoughby/Doe discovers Norton's plan and threatens to expose him at the huge public rally where he is supposed to announce his support for Norton's candidacy. In return, Norton derides him:

> 'You're the fake! We believe in what we're doing!' John responds that the John Doe idea is 'bigger than whether I'm a fake'. ... 'It may be the one thing capable of saving this cockeyed world!' and he vows to speak out, 'in my *own* words this time'.
>
> (Wolfe 1989a: 143, 144, 146)

However, where Deeds and Smith had their chance to represent themselves to the public, Doe does not. The unscrupulous Norton exposes Doe as a fraud to the crowd of club members. In a remarkable and frightening scene, the cheering crowd is transformed into a violent mob. Egged on by Norton's planted henchmen, they turn on Doe, who is unable to defend himself, since his microphone has been disconnected by Norton.[9] Even when he does manage to speak personally to some of his most loyal supporters, they brutally repudiate him. The humiliated Doe is battered and bruised by the mob, Ann stands helplessly weeping, and Connell offers a cynical toast: 'You can chalk up another one to the Pontius Pilates' (Wolfe 1989a: 159).

This was hardly the sort of uplifting tale Capra had told in his earlier movies, where Deeds and Smith had each stood up alone for their beliefs and had won out against all odds. Instead, the message was that the American public are nothing more than 'decent, credulous sheep', 'a fickle, easily manipulated and easily stampeded herd' (Gianos 1998: 102; McBride 1992: 221) who blindly destroy their own capacity for brotherly unity. Capra had previously said that 'the people are right ... people's instincts are good, never bad' (Glatzer 1989: 245). But in this movie, he concluded that 'people can become mobs, and one of the occasions they can become mobs is when they become disillusioned, when somebody has tricked them' (Schickel 1975: 81).

Having reached this juncture, Capra was at an impasse. As he wrote later: 'But now, what happens to John Doe? To the thousands that believed? To the forces of evil? We didn't know' (Capra 1971: 303). His inability to end the film became infamous in Hollywood. Five different endings were scripted. In all of them, Willoughby decides to redeem himself by actually committing suicide, as the false note had promised, and mounts to the top of City Hall on Christmas eve. But in none of the alternative scripts does the redemptive suicide actually occur. As Capra wrote, 'my argument against that is that his blood would be on the souls of the John Does' (Capra 1989: 206).

He first released a print in which Norton, moved by Willoughby/Doe's willingness to sacrifice himself, repents and offers to confess his wrongdoing to the public, but this sentimental ending was rejected by the audience. Capra finally settled on a script suggested, he said, in a letter by an anonymous 'John Doe' who was incensed with the way the ordinary man was shown in the film. In this final version, Ann entreats John not to die, reminding him that Jesus had already sacrificed himself for the ideal of brotherly love. But the last straw in persuading John to live is the arrival of John Doe club members, who ask his forgiveness and beg him to continue to lead them. When John relents, Connell has the last word: 'There you are Norton! The people! Try and lick that!' (Wolfe 1989a: 171). The film ends with 'Ode to Joy' and the pealing of church bells.

But despite Capra's blatant use of a 'hieratic register' meant to hush all doubts (Andrew 1989: 267), it was obvious that the ending was not successful. Belying Connell's defiant words, the people had hardly triumphed: Norton remained powerful and the so-called people's representative was a fraud who had no message to give other than his willingness to die. The failure was obvious to Capra himself. The movie he had hoped would lead him into the future had instead 'fizzled into the Great American Letdown. ... What our film said to bewildered people hungry for solutions was this, "No answers this time, ladies and gentlemen. It's back to the drawing board." And the people said, "Oh, nuts!"' (Capra 1971: 304, 305).

The inadequacy of *Meet John Doe* had a profound effect on Capra's career. His next (and last) successful film, *It's a Wonderful Life* (1946) retreated completely from politics towards a saccharine apotheosis of private life and small-town nostalgia.[10] His attempt to return to political discourse in *State of the Union* (1948) produced a movie not only of poor technical quality but also of unrelieved cynicism, confusion and weariness. The hero (Spencer Tracy) is a successful businessman who decides to run for political office, only to discover that he has nothing to offer and is merely a selfish phoney. 'I have no cause', he admits (McBride 1992: 540). Capra was speaking for himself. He had nothing more to offer, and never again produced any work of merit.

Politics and the individual

In his old age, Capra warned American film-makers to 'Forget all politics. Because if you politicize yourself, what you do is cut yourself in half' (McBride 1992: 635). How did America's foremost political film-maker come to such a conclusion, and what does his trajectory tell us about the problems of political cinema in America?

There are many reasons, personal and social, for Capra's withdrawal from political film-making. One could argue that the grandiosity that led him to try to reformulate the American myth hid a fragile sense of identity; in *John Doe* he was confronted with the limits of his narcissism, and found he really had no message; that he, like his hero, was empty of content. His long decline and depression was the inevitable result. Equally, one could note the repressive and censorious American political climate of the era and Capra's fear of being perse-cuted – not an unrealistic anxiety. His screenwriter on *Mr Smith*, Sidney Buchman, was indeed blacklisted and driven into exile.

But also responsible for Capra's impasse are the logically incoherent implications of the premises that he operated from – premises that prevail very widely in American political theory. They can be summarised as follows: 'People alone are amoral, together they achieve morality, but as soon as that togetherness is organized politically they become immoral' (Andrew 1989: 256).

This view of politics resonates with Tocqueville's widely accepted notions about the nature of the American experiment. To recapitulate briefly, Tocqueville believed that in the American world of proudly egalitarian individualists 'no man is obliged to put his powers at the disposal of another, and no one has any claim of right to substantial support from his fellow man' (Tocqueville 1969: 672). As noted earlier, the egalitarian value of personal independence lies behind the suspicion of central authority and the appeal to anarchy that is so notable in Capra's films and in American culture in general.

Capra and Tocqueville both assumed that the egalitarian individualist is inevitably disconnected from the world of society and politics. In fact, the major theme of American social thought, and of Capra's movie, is how to relate the isolated individual to the larger social whole. Here is where the fundamental problem lies, since it is presumed that the asocial individual does not have any moral core. As Tocqueville argued, without a larger social and moral framework within which to locate their identities, Americans 'increasingly let themselves glide with the stream of the crowd and find it hard to maintain alone an opinion abandoned by the rest' (Tocqueville 1969: 520). In other words, despite their affirmations of independence, Americans are actually unable to stand up for themselves. And because America is a place where 'men are weak, isolated, and changeable', without firm social positions, rules and precedents, it follows that 'when ambitious men have once seized power, they think they can dare to do anything' (Tocqueville 1969: 631).

Tocqueville believed that the tendencies toward conformity, withdrawal and tyranny he found beneath the surface in the United States could be offset by training in civic virtue, which occurred in institutions like the jury system and in the numerous voluntary associations of neighbours and co-workers that he saw proliferating in the United States. But all this would come to naught without some kind of religious faith:

> Despotism may be able to do without faith, but freedom cannot. ... How could society escape destruction if, when political ties are relaxed, moral ties are not tightened? And what can be done with a people master of itself if it is not subject to God?
>
> (Tocqueville 1969: 294)

Tocqueville's analysis of American culture thus rests on the premise that the ordinary individual in American democratic society has no moral compass, and will follow wherever led. The citizen can really only be rescued from tyranny by faith. This is the same fear and the same unrealistic solution found in *John Doe*.

Capra's earlier political movies about heroic individuals worked because he was able to set them *against* society and *against* politics, and thereby stay within the boundaries of the individualist paradigm. But when he sought to express the development of a moral sense through participation in a political community, the ideological framework within which he worked, and which he shares with Tocqueville and other social theorists of American culture, inevitably led him to portray the American public as a dangerous and mindless mob who end by crucifying their own representative, who is portrayed as just as empty of content as are the people he embodies. The only ones with inner conviction, it seems, are the power-hungry Nortons of the world.

Conclusion

Durkheim once noted that every social representation tells us something about society. This is true, but it should be seen as the beginning rather than the end of inquiry *for the key challenge is to locate the precise part of society which is being represented*. In artistic matters it is often crucial to go beyond any generalised notion of art 'reflecting' society towards a more precise notion of the particular social referent of an individual work (Hall 1977, Chapter 2). An example that brilliantly makes this point is Chesterton's essay on the 'slum novelists' of Edwardian England. Chesterton demonstrated that these novels were written from the outside, but did not as a result accuse them of falsity: to the contrary, he recognised that they were a marvellous record of middle-class attitudes to the poor (Chesterton 1970: 27).

This principle can usefully be applied to the argument that has been made. The sharpest way of so doing is to insist that Tocqueville, for all his cult-like status, may well not be a perfect guide to American life. It is important to make a distinction which will help us understand both Tocqueville and Capra. On the one hand, Tocqueville and Capra did capture a general feature of American national identity, namely its hostility to political action. On the other hand, Tocqueville and Capra may mislead when describing an insatiable urge to conformity, capable of resulting in fascism.[11] Fascism did not triumph in America and its sociology is such as to suggest that this eventuality was always unlikely. But this is not to say that *Democracy in America* and *Meet John Doe* are simply false, and so unable to tell us anything. To the contrary, we are here presented with characteristic evidence of elite fear of popular culture in America.

It is worth concluding that the problems that defeated Capra have also undercut later attempts by American film-makers to portray the complex relationship between individualism and citizenship in the United States. Instead, Hollywood has embraced the paranoid vision of politics that Capra had tried and failed to surmount. As a consequence, American political movies focus purely on the flawed character of leaders (examples include *Citizen Kane* (1940) and the underrated *Nixon* (1995)) or else show all too graphically how power corrupts (*The Candidate* (1972) and *Primary Colors* (1998)). Many American political films, such as *A Face in the Crowd* (1957) and *All the King's Men* (1949), follow *John Doe* in warning against populist movements, gullible publics and fascist demagogues, while others, like *JFK* (1991) or *The Manchurian Candidate* (1962), assume from the outset that democracy is an illusion, and that Americans are dupes of various conspiracies. Rare films such as *The President's Plane is Missing* (1971), turn the president into an action hero; but far more commonly it is simply assumed that political actors are evil, stupid, treacherous and rapacious, and that political action is only viable if it occurs outside of, and against, the government. With this imagery in mind, it is easy to understand why the most popular American president in recent years was a film actor who was overtly suspicious of the very institutions that he was supposed to represent.

Notes

1 See Lipset 1996 for a comparison of American and European patriotic sentiments.
2 Gianos also quotes Samuel Goldwyn's famous dictum that 'Messages are for Western Union'.
3 McBride 1992 points out the degree to which Capra characteristically exaggerated his own independence, and underplayed his reliance on his co-workers, especially his cameraman Joseph Walker and his screenwriters Robert Riskin, Jo Swerling and Sidney Buchman. The problem of reconciling independence with community and co-responsibility is central in Capra's political films, as we shall see.
4 See Lipset 1996 for a recent cross-national comparison of values of individualism, charity and anti-authoritarianism.
5 The 'Heelots' are 'a lot of heels'. For the Colonel's full statement, see Wolfe 1989a: 67–8.
6 Capra always portrayed himself as completely independent, conspicuously denying the role of his family in helping him gain success, and ignoring the contributions of others in making his projects. See note 3.
7 For evidence, see Hochschild 1995.
8 The ambivalent relation of Americans to the state is discussed in more detail in Hall and Lindholm 1999.
9 The treatment of the media is another complex and self-contradictory aspect of the film. The message is that control over information by the powerful suborns democracy. Yet, at the same time the movie industry in which Capra worked is itself a huge corporate enterprise. For more on this problematic, see Browne 1989.
10 Significantly, this film, with its dark subtext of hopelessness and its use of a literal *deus ex machina* to save the suicidal protagonist became the iconic American movie during the Reagan years, shown over and over again during the Christmas season. It remains Capra's most famous and beloved work.
11 For an argument in favour of an alternative view, see Hall and Lindholm 1999.

Bibliography

Andrew, D. (1989) 'Productive Discord in the System: Hollywood Meets John Doe', in C. Wolfe (ed.) (1989b).

Browne, N. (1989) 'System of Production/System of Representation: Industry Context and Ideological Form in Capra's *Meet John Doe*', in C. Wolfe (ed.) (1989b).

Capra, F. (1971) *My Name Above the Title*, New York: Macmillan.

—— (1989) 'Letter from Frank Capra to Viewer', in C. Wolfe (ed.) (1989b).

Chesterton, G.K. (1970) 'Slum Novelists', in G.K. Chesterton, *Chesterton: A Selection of His Non-fictional Prose*, selected by W.H. Auden, London: Faber.

Crowther, B. (1989) 'Review of *Meet John Doe*', in C. Wolfe (ed.) (1989b). Originally published in *The New York Times* 13 March 1941.

Gabler, N. (1988) *An Empire of their Own: How the Jews Invented Hollywood*, New York: Anchor Books.

Gellner, E.A. (1983) *Nations and Nationalism*, Oxford: Blackwell.

Gianos, P. (1998) *Politics and Politicians in American Film*, Westport, CT: Praeger.

Glatzer, R. (1989) 'Meet John Doe: An End to Social Mythmaking', in C. Wolfe (ed.) (1989b).

Hall, J.A. (1977) *The Sociology of Literature*, Harlow: Longman.

—— (ed.) (1998) *The State of the Nation: Ernest Gellner and the Theory of Nationalism*, Cambridge: Cambridge University Press.

Hall, J.A. and Lindholm, C. (1999) *Is America Breaking Apart?*, Princeton, NJ: Princeton University Press.

Hochschild, J. (1995) *Facing Up to the American Dream: Race, Class, and the Soul of the Nation*, Princeton, NJ: Princeton University Press.

Lipset, S.M. (1996) *American Exceptionalism: A Double-Edged Sword*, New York: Norton.

McBride, J. (1992) *Frank Capra: The Catastrophe of Success*, New York: Simon and Schuster.

Schickel, R. (1975) *Men Who Made the Movies*, New York: Atheneum.

Tocqueville, A. (1969) *Democracy in America*, Garden City, NJ: Doubleday.

Varenne, H. (1977) *Americans Together: Structured Diversity in a Midwestern Town*, New York: Teachers College Press.

Wolfe, C. (1989a) 'Continuity Script for Meet John Doe', in C. Wolfe (ed.) (1989b).

—— (ed.) (1989b) *Meet John Doe*, New Brunswick, NJ: Rutgers University Press.

—— (1989c) 'Meet John Doe: Authors, Audiences and Endings', in C. Wolfe (ed.) (1989b).

3

IMAGES OF THE NATION

Cinema, art and national identity

Anthony Smith

My theme is the visual representation of national identity. My argument is that, in painting as in film, we can see how the historicist vision of the nation, and its ethnic fund of myths, memories, symbols and traditions, is unfolded through an increasingly naturalistic mode of expression, and is made to carry an ever wider range of meanings and emotions as the visual arts are opened up to a greatly enlarged national membership. This occurred pre-eminently with the invention of the moving image and the cinematic revolution at the turn of this century; but many of the latter's themes and modes of representation were foreshadowed in the visual art of the preceding century. In this exploratory essay, I can only attempt to show the ways in which certain national themes and historicist modes of expression in history painting have found parallels in the cinema as some directors in turn sought to evoke and portray aspects of national identity.

Historicism and nationalism

In his classic treatment of neo-classical art, *Transformations in Late Eighteenth Century Art*, Robert Rosenblum claims that the relatively novel viewpoint of historicism:

> became more and more vulgarised until, in our own century, it reached its inevitable conclusion, the presentation of different historical milieux through animated, photographic verisimilitude. The roster of popular historical films today offers the most restricted narrative themes within the most unrestricted range of environments – the Ice Age, Ancient Troy, Imperial Rome, Renaissance France, Colonial America, the Third Reich – all carefully reconstructed in Technicolor by a learned staff of experts whose historical specialties may range from archeology and decorative arts to coiffures and ballistics. Such movies, in which the audience may find comfort in a familiar dramatic situation and adventure in an unfamiliar but almost palpably real visual confrontation, are the ultimate descendants of the late eighteenth century's combination

45

of an easily communicable emotion and a search for the appurtenances of historical truth.

(Rosenblum 1967: 49)

Leaving aside his normative standpoint, the art historian here seeks to relate his field to the later developments of film art, suggesting a lineage in terms of specific similarities of purpose and method, and of the new cultural outlook which he labels 'historicism'. In a note, Rosenblum explains that:

This broad concept, suggesting the new retrospective and archeological attitudes towards the historical past that appeared in the mid eighteenth century and that continue to be elaborated and refined in our own time, is found most often in modern German historical studies.

(ibid.: 34, n. 106)

This new approach permitted 'a growing chronological and geographical mobility' in both painting and architecture from the late eighteenth century onwards. At the same time, the older Christian and classical traditions 'began to lose their living actuality and became part of a dead past that could only be regarded retrospectively, from the dawn of another historical epoch' (ibid.: 48).

That epoch was the age of nationalism and capitalism, the epoch *par excellence* of the citizen-nation. In the currently dominant modernist interpretation of this age, nations and nationalism are seen as exclusively modern phenomena. Indeed, for Ernest Gellner, the most forthright exponent of this view, nations and nationalism, though logically contingent, are sociologically necessary components of modernity. The nation is a product of nationalism, which in turn is an expression of modernity's need for 'high cultures' – linguistic cultures based on literacy and schooling, and supported by an infrastructure of mass, public, standardised education. Only in a mobile, literate, modernising society where much work is semantic and linguistic culture is needed to bind together uprooted and anonymised populations in large cities, do nations and nationalism become necessary, in order to create mass loyalties and cohesion (Gellner 1964: chap. 7; and 1983: chaps 1–6).

Post-war historians too have generally shared this modernist perspective. Eric Hobsbawm, for example, sees the nation as a creation of the nineteenth century, following in the wake of the French Revolution and the Napoleonic Wars. At first, nationalism was an inclusive, mass-democratic and political movement; but after 1870, a more divisive, small-scale, right-wing nationalism appealed to language and ethnicity. This period saw a spate of 'invented traditions' – national mythologies, symbols, rituals and histories – through which ruling elites aimed to control and channel the energies of the recently enfranchised masses (Hobsbawm and Ranger 1983: Introduction and chap. 7; Hobsbawm 1990).

Hobsbawm's concept of 'invented tradition' is particularly pertinent here. The many new themes of artists, writers and composers, who expanded and enriched the language of poetry, drama, music, painting and sculpture, can be read as so many 'invented traditions', forged to meet new needs through iterative symbolic practices which claim a putative link with the communal past. Such a link is largely fictive. For Hobsbawm, attempts to supply historical continuity for modern English, French and German nations with ancient pasts through such semi-fictions as Boadicea, Vercingetorix and Arminius the Cheruscan are no more than imaginative nationalist fabrications 'beyond effective historical continuity' (Hobsbawm and Ranger 1983: 7).

For Benedict Anderson, too, nationalism creates nations in a world of human mortality and linguistic diversity. But this can occur only when 'print-capitalism' has, through the dissemination of books and newspapers in vernacular languages, created large reading publics based on print-languages. Only when sacred monarchies and religious civilisations have declined, and when time is measured in linear fashion by clock and calendar, does it become possible for these reading publics to 'imagine' themselves as nations, that is, as sovereign, finite, cross-class political communities (Anderson 1991: chaps 1–4).

In sum, for modernists, not only is the nation recent and novel, it is the *product* of modernisation and modernity, and of the secular, modern intelligentsia which creates and disseminates the historical myths of nationhood. This was the focus of Elie Kedourie's diatribes against nationalist historiography and anthropology. Nationalism, he claimed, was a doctrine invented in Europe at the beginning of the nineteenth century, under the influence of the Enlightenment, by excluded and alienated German intellectuals. But these doctrines spread rapidly like a virus across the globe, through the agency of historicist intellectuals who imitated and adapted the original European ideas to their peculiar ethnic circumstances, bringing in their wake a trail of terror and destruction. The historical mobility of these intellectuals, and their historicist world-view, enabled them to create for their nation the myth of a glorious ethnic past and an equally promising national destiny. The problem, of course, was to convince the mass of the designated 'national' population that this was indeed *their* nation, and that they should identify with it and defend it (Kedourie 1960 and 1971: Introduction).

In fact, this is a problem for all modernist explanations of nationalism, not just for nationalist intellectuals. What these elitist and presentist perspectives so often omit is an analysis of the *content* and the *tone* of the nationalist message. That message is certainly addressed to the imagination of the elite, but even more to the moral will, the emotions and the shared memories of the masses. Rosenblum himself draws attention to these moral and affective aspects, when he discusses the stoic moralities offered by history painters from the late eighteenth century onwards, to edify and exhort their audiences; in the eyes of nationalists, the nation is a historic community of political will and moral purpose, a sacred communion of all the citizens (Rosenblum 1967: chap. 2).

This is why nationalist intellectuals seek to rediscover and authenticate pre-existing collective myths, symbols, values, memories and traditions of 'the people', and to locate the 'old-new' nation they seek to recreate within its evolutionary ethnic framework. The artist and the writer alike have been at the heart of this project of popular national representation and renewal, clothing the ideal of the nation and its historical myths, memories and symbols in palpable, dynamic forms which are easily accessible to the mass of the 'national' membership. And the greater the pre-existing sense of ethnic community and the more intense the ethnic ties binding 'the people', the easier and more credible has been their task (Smith 1986: chap. 8 and 1998: chap. 8).

Public moralities of national heroism

But it is not only these moral and symbolic themes that are common to the artistic representations of the nation. The analogies are also expressive and aesthetic: a growing interest in archaeological verisimilitude, in dramatic reconstruction and in atmospheric evocation of myths, symbols, traditions and memories. I shall first consider the public moralities and didactic messages conveyed by the visual arts and the cinema, and then explore some of the more expressive and aesthetic aspects of dramatic reconstruction and 'ethnic atmosphere'.

Exempla virtutis, classical and biblical, but also increasingly medieval and modern, were the most obvious vehicles for moral didacticism in painting from, at least, the Renaissance; one thinks of Michelangelo's *David* or Lorenzo Lotto's *Death of Lucretia*, preaching the virtues of courage and chastity. The late eighteenth century developed a widespread taste for these moralities. Along with Judith and David, Moses and Elijah, came a veritable torrent of Greco-Roman moralities, exhibited at the regular Paris Salon and London Royal Academy exhibitions: the remorse of Oedipus and the self-sacrifice of Antigone, the choice of Hercules, the departure of Hector for battle, the calm resolve of Socrates drinking the hemlock, the oath of Brutus against the Tarquin tyrants, the heroism of Regulus returning as a hostage to Carthage, the continence of Scipio, the courage of the dying Cleopatra, the virtue of Cornelia, mother of the Gracchi, the sacrifice of the Roman matrons, and many more (Smith 1979).

In each of these *exempla virtutis*, the artist has chosen a crucial moment of psychological tension in which a very public moral choice is realised through a life-like portrayal of the protagonists' drama. Such is the message of an early picture like Benjamin West's *Choice of Hercules* (1764), where the handsome hero wavers between female representations of virtue and pleasure; or of Gavin Hamilton's rendering of *The Oath of Brutus* (1764), in which the life-size protagonists, their figures pushed towards the picture plane, swear to rid Rome of the Tarquins. Now, at last, the moment of swearing has become the pivot of the drama, displacing the suicide of Lucretia herself, a moment in an unfolding political drama, set on a 'stage', with the 'actors' grouped round the upturned sword, declaiming to an invisible audience their oath to rid Rome of tyranny (Rosenblum 1961).

Oath-taking was a favourite theme in the late eighteenth century. It combined ideas of the compact (contract) of citizens and of self-sacrifice. A striking example is Henry Füseli's *Oath of the Rütli* (1778–81), commissioned by the Zürich Rathaus. Here three towering Michelangelesque figures are placed in a barren landscape filling the picture space, their muscular bodies and raised arms joined to the sword held aloft in defiance of the Habsburg tyrant and in defence of cantonal liberties. Similar ideas pervade Jacques Louis David's celebrated *Oath of the Horatii* (1784). This invents an episode in the battle of Rome against Alba Longa, when the three Horatii brothers were pitted in combat against their three Curatii counterparts. The extraordinary power and concentration of David's 'spartan' portrayal of the oath derives both from the electric impulse that unites the taut, outstretched arms of the three Horatii brothers as they swear to die for their country on the sword held aloft by their father, and from their drastic separation from their female relatives grieving and swooning on the right, unable to prevent the doom that awaits the combatants of both cities (Antal 1956: 71–4; Brookner 1980: chap. 5).

Moral resolve was another favourite lesson of the history painters. In *Joan of Arc at the Coronation of Charles VII* (1854), Jean Auguste Dominique Ingres presents a memorable image of the warrior saint standing at the altar in Rheims Cathedral in her shining armour holding aloft the oriflamme, her eyes turned heavenward in fixed gaze. Ingres portrays her as an exemplar of piety, simplicity and fortitude, but also as the soldier of the Church militant and of a resurgent France; and through the depiction of ecclesiastical and patriotic accessories, he recreates the *tone* or *atmosphere* of the fifteenth century, at a time when a wave of medievalist religious nationalism was sweeping France (see Rosenblum 1985: 160–3).

Heroic self-sacrifice constituted a third, and supreme, public morality for the history painters. West's *Death of General Wolfe* (1770) on the plains of Quebec in 1759 was one of the first images of contemporary war reportage; yet it is equally an icon of self-sacrificing patriotism, echoing in its tripartite composition and gestures a Christian *pietà*. Probably the best-known of these contemporary fallen patriots was Marat, slain in his bathtub by Charlotte Corday, as recorded immediately afterwards by David (*Marat Assassiné*, 1793). Here the painter sets an authentically naturalistic depiction of the immediate event within an almost sacred, and timeless, ambiance of awe and veneration for the republican patriot-hero blessed, as it were, by martyrdom. It is the large void above Marat's slumped corpse that bids us to noble sorrow, respectful silence and elevated meditation, the same emotions that had been inculcated by the Church down the ages in respect of Christian saints and martyrs (Wind 1938–9; Rosenblum 1967: chap. 2; Brookner 1980: chap. 8, esp. 112–16; Abrams 1985: chap. 8).

These emotions were also tapped over a century later in a variety of cinematic images. Some, of course, were translations of dramatic texts and theatrical portrayals, as with the various British Shakespearian films, in which moral resolve in battle (*Henry V*, and *Richard III*), or courage in the face of conspiracy (Antony in *Julius Caesar*, and *Hamlet*), were memorably conveyed. In the first case, too, there was also a much more overt national-historical message, purveying explicit national propaganda during the Second World War (1944). Similarly, Marlon Brando's defiant rendering of the role of Emiliano Zapata (in *Viva Zapata!*), at the time of the Mexican Revolution, projects the doomed hero as the true embodiment of national purpose and popular Mexican virtues, and his death as a national tragedy of betrayal. In the same way, the heroisation of the Russian prince in *Alexander Nevsky* marked the official return to a Russian nationalism at a time (1938) of rising fascist threat and failing Soviet foreign policy. In accepting the pleas of the people of Novgorod, Alexander embodied the open traditions of Russian nobility, generosity and courage, in contrast to the dark menace and destructive brutality of the (Western) Teutonic Knights. The moral is clear: not only is the communist system superior, but so also is the 'old-new' Russian man and woman. The implication is that the perfect political system finds fertile soil in the superior morality of the Russian soul, unsullied by the class conflicts and moral degradation of the West. In this respect, Sergei Eisenstein harks back to a familiar Slavophile tradition (see Thaden 1964; Taylor 1998: chap. 8; cf. Perrie 1998).

These are just a few examples of the historical genre of films which offer simplified public moralities of heroism, courage and self-sacrifice, tied to a community of will and purpose on whose behalf the hero or heroine strives and dies. Whether it be Moses in Cecil B. De Mille's *The Ten Commandments* or Ruy de Bivar in Anthony Mann's *El Cid* or *St Joan* or Richard Attenborough's *Gandhi*, the drama is as much that of a national community of will and purpose whom the hero(ine) embodies and leads as of the leader. These cinematic portrayals stand firmly in the tradition pioneered by the history painters of the late eighteenth and nineteenth centuries, both in the portrayal of national virtues being inculcated and in their use of *exempla virtutis*.

Cultivating 'ethnic atmosphere'

But there is more to nationalism and national identity than public moralities and virtuous patriots. In the eyes of its devotees, the nation possesses a unique power, pathos and epic grandeur, qualities which film, perhaps even more than painting or sculpture, can vividly convey. In this respect, the moving image is more akin to music, which also unfolds its character and identity over a finite sequence of time; and in which the meaning of the composition becomes apparent only at the conclusion. That is why we find an increasing concern for archaeological verisimilitude and distinctive 'ethnic atmosphere' in the portrayal of national drama. In part, this is the result of technical advances in the field of visual representation, such as photography; but it also springs from a desire to engage a wider range and greater depth of emotions by evoking and re-presenting the panorama of nationhood in all its historical and geographical variety in as naturalistic a manner as possible.

These developments in the visual representation of the evocative and emotive qualities of 'ethnic atmosphere' and national identity, can be broken down into a number of dimensions. They include: character development, historical recon-struction, pictorial tableaux, accessories, ethnoscape and the 'people'. Let me take these in turn, highlighting parallels between the visual arts and cinematic imagery, and concentrating in the main on Eisenstein's later historical films, where these parallels are most in evidence.

Character development

In *Ivan the Terrible*, Eisenstein portrays several stages of the first Tsar's develop-ment: precarious childhood surrounded by quarrelsome boyars; vigorous young manhood bent on Russian unity, war and victory; cruel, suspicious and tormented old age with his army of *Oprichniks*. There is a particularly memo-rable flashback to his childhood at the beginning of Part II: eight-year-old Ivan sees his mother poisoned and then sits on his throne between two enormous, overpowering and quarrelling boyars. He looks down at his feet; they dangle in the air, unable to reach the ground (Eisenstein 1989: 142, shot 174). This is a striking image of fear, loneliness and helplessness, soon to be transformed, as young Ivan has Shuisky arrested and killed in his first act of self-assertion. Part I has shown the new Tsar, in Moscow and at the battle of Kazan, and then betrayed by his friend, Kurbsky. At the end of Part I, Ivan leaves Moscow for Alexandrov and in Part II forms his 'iron guard', the *Oprichnina*, who terrorise the boyars, till in old age Ivan becomes *grozny* ('formidable') and (in the famous colour sequence) crushes the plots of Staritsky and others. There is another celebrated tableau at the end of Part I, where we see a bearded Ivan bending forward, staff in hand, through an archway of the Alexandrov palace, as he looks down and out on to a procession of the people 'advancing like a long serpent across a snow-covered plain' (ibid.: 119, shot 780 and 120–1, shots 791–806). Here, it is tempting to think that Eisenstein has in mind the famous picture by Victor Vasnetsov of *Ivan the Terrible* (1897), clad in a heavy, buttoned caftan, descending a Kremlin staircase, staff in hand, and casting a suspicious, black, sideways look, betraying violent passions on his furrowed brow (Shanina 1979: 110–13, and plates 87–9). And perhaps, still further back, we may recall Ingres' icon of *Napoleon on his Throne* (1805), a frightening monument of cold, impassive haughtiness and imperial power (Rosenblum 1985: 68–9, Pl. 7).

The same traits of arrogance, cruelty and suspicion are almost caricatured in Olivier's portrait of *Richard III*, notably in the scene where a newly enthroned Richard, having confined Anne, his wife, refuses Buckingham the gift of lands he had promised ('I am not in the giving vein today'), as he stares ahead with fearful menace. But in this case, we see far less of that development of character which Eisenstein, despite all the political obstacles, attempted to realise, and which he attempted to explain in his letter to the editors of *Kultura i Zhizn* in 1946:

> We all know that Ivan the Terrible was a man of great willpower and strong character. But does this exclude the presence of certain doubts in particular cases? ... Is it in these hesitations and doubts, or rather in the fact that he surmounted them without compromise, in the implacable continuity of his actions, that we find the essence of this powerful figure of the 16th century?
>
> (Eisenstein 1989: 12; cf. Perrie 1998)

Historical reconstruction

In both *Ivan the Terrible* and *Alexander Nevsky*, as in his earlier contemporary films, Eisenstein attempted to reconstruct the historical narrative of events, even while taking the necessary liberties, as in the Alexandrov sequence. Of course, in all historical films, as well as in the texts from which they stem, the sequence of events provides the essential framework, not for a detached and 'truthful' account of *wie es eigentlich war*, but to convince the spectator of the epic grandeur of the nation, that is to say, in the first place, his or her nation. This was, after all, Shakespeare's own purpose in his historical plays based on the chronicles of Holinshed and others. In other words, even if they are not a species of overt national propaganda, such works aim to provide a 'historical map' of the national past in order to bind the spectator more firmly to the present national identity. This is obvious in the case of films like *Alexander Nevsky* and *Henry V*; but it also comes across in those Hollywood epics, which aim to recreate episodes from the pasts of a variety of countries and civilisations from Fred Niblo's *Ben Hur* to Basil Dearden's *Khartoum*. In each case, the search for epic grandeur is built up around a reconstruction of key events which follow an accepted sequence of episodes, so as to create a convincing picture of the nation moving forward, as Anderson puts it, through 'empty, homogeneous time'. Here, Cecil B. de Mille and others could look back to the dramatic historical panoramas of artists like John Martin and Gustav Doré, as well as to the battle scenes of the Napoleonic and later wars by artists from John Singleton Copley, Baron Gros and Horace Vernet to Paul Nash and Stanley Spencer. Of course, considerable liberties were often taken with historical facts. At the same time, the best directors aimed for convincing historical reconstructions and strove to ascertain as much of the truth about the period in question as they could, in the manner of the history painters before them (see Rhode 1978: 224–6; Fraser 1996: chap. 2, esp. 24–5, 41–2).

Pictorial tableaux

For obvious reasons, the example and influence of painting can be realised only through the *tableau*, in which a scene that is part of a longer sequence of events is abstracted and made to epitomise the whole sequence. Two examples must suffice. One is Eugène Delacroix's celebrated *Massacre of Chios* (1824), in which the miseries and heroism of the Greek War of Independence are encapsulated in one great image of national oppression and ethnic slaughter. For the massacre of the Greeks by the Turks on the island of Chios, like the death of Byron, came to symbolise the drama of nationalism and the 'awakening' of nations; but also the ethnic contrast between the noble, suffering Greeks, revealed through their beautiful 'classical' bodies, and the savage, merciless, scimitar-bearing Turkish horsemen. The second example is Diego Rivera's series of tableaux of the Mexican Revolution and the Mexican past which he, along with the other Muralists, frescoed on the walls of public buildings in Mexico City, with the active support of the revolutionary government. Rivera's *The History of Mexico: From the Conquest to the Future* (1929–30, Palácio Nacional) and the later frescoes of the pre-Columbian civilisations (1942–51) present a virtual panorama of that past through a series of symbolic images of events and cultures, thereby creating an illusion of forward movement, even without the cinema's ability to conjure a sense of actual movement in time (see Eisenmann 1994: 71–3; Ades 1989: 151–79, esp. 172–4).

That sense is most memorably conveyed to evoke equally distant events in two great historical films, both of which are immeasurably enriched by music that heightens the tension and unfolds the action to build to its climax in the clash of armies. In Olivier's *Henry V*, Walton's evocative score, notably in the Agincourt sequence, increases the sense of expectancy and of forward movement of each tableau, as the English and French armies march inexorably towards each other and join battle, under a hail of arrows from the archers. Similarly, the power of certain scenes in *Alexander Nevsky* is greatly enhanced by the menace and beauty of Prokofiev's score. The scenes of the invasion of Pskov by the Teutonic Knights and the brutalities of their rule there provide a medieval (but also modern) equivalent of Delacroix's massacre. True to his theory of '*typage*' (type-casting), Eisenstein contrasts the human openness and generosity of the Russian characters with the meanness and evil of the invaders: 'The Germans are faceless, often hooded and frequently shot in profile, with cruel, animal-like features' (Taylor 1998: 90). Though only a rough parallel to Cortes' slaughter of the Aztecs, the famous *Battle on the Ice of Lake Peipius* depicts a similar bloody denouement to a clash of civilisations, and of good and evil. Perhaps here painting follows the moving image: the slightly later stylised painting by Nikolai Roerich of *Prince Igor leading out his Host* (1941) against the Polovtsii in 1185, which was prompted by the Nazi invasion of Russia, takes us back to a similar period, if a much more southerly zone, of Kievan Rus, and harks back to the Russian musical

53

nationalism of *Prince Igor* (1890), Borodin's great opera, to give us a hieratic tableau of the Russian army marching out with their flags and religious banners – much as the Russian and Teutonic armies carried their banners to Lake Peipius in 1242 (see Korotkina 1976: 10; Leyda 1974: 124–33).

Period accessories

Ever since the neo-classical and medieval revivals in the late eighteenth century, artists had sought increasing verisimilitude through the accurate period rendering of furnishings, costume, coiffure and armour, in their portrayal of heroic events and national dramas in distant ages and climes. Already in the work of David, for example, his *Hector and Andromache* (1783) and *The Death of Socrates* (1787), we see a much greater concern for the authentic period depiction of furniture, armour, dress and household objects. This is carried even further by Ingres, who, in his portrayal of Joan of Arc, as well as in his early medievalist hallucinatory fantasy, *The Dream of Ossian* (1813), and his minutely observed spectator view of *Pope Pius VII in the Sistine Chapel* (1814), took great pains to render accurately details of armour, robes, vessels and furniture (see Rosenblum 1985: 96–7, 100–3). This concern with fidelity to nature was carried to extremes by the Pre-Raphaelites, so that, while evoking the dream-like worlds of early British legend, they could give them realistic and 'authentic' expression through the detailed study and rendering of early medieval dress, armour and furnishings, in paintings like Morris' tapestry-like *La belle Iseult* (1858) and Burne-Jones' richly ornamented *King Cophetua and the Beggar-Maid* (1884), or his pure, almost Gothic, *The Dream of Sir Lancelot at the Chapel of the Holy Grail* (1896) (Wilton and Upstone 1997: 147–9, 250–1; Poulson 1999: 162–3).

A similar passion for archaeological fidelity in rendering period accessories became a staple of Hollywood epics. Biblical, Greek, Roman, medieval, Tudor, Stuart, Georgian and Victorian costume and furnishings became the distinguishing features and hallmark of the 'real' historical epic, sometimes requiring considerable research, as for the chariot race in *Ben Hur*. Eisenstein's enthusiasm for authentic recreation of period furnishings, costume and armour was perhaps even greater, even if the effects were less lavish; witness the armour and helmets of the Teutonic Knights, the furnishings of Ivan's Kremlin palace, and the royal robes of the Tsar. In *Alexander Nevsky*, in the scenes where the Russian troops play the pipes and tabors, and the Germans sound the horn, Eisenstein even filmed his property instruments for Prokofiev to provide a musical equivalent for the montage – an example of Eisenstein's passion for research into historical documents, artefacts and period atmosphere (Taylor 1998: 93–4).

Homeland and ethnoscape

As one might expect, 'ethnic atmosphere' is closely linked to the poetic landscapes of distinctive ethnic communities (*ethnies*), or 'ethnoscapes'. Here the territory mirrors the ethnic community and is historicised by the communal events and processes whose relics and monuments dot its landscape, so that the land comes to belong to a people in the same way as the people belong to a particular land – creating an ancestral 'homeland' (see Smith 1997).

Cinema and historical film, of course, specialised in the reconstruction of ethnoscapes – from the great temples of ancient Egypt and the basilicas and monuments of the Roman empire to the windswept Russian steppes and the idyllic hamlets of southern England. But in these matters they were only following in the footsteps of the history and landscape painters. John Martin's colossal swirling biblical dramas, Jean Léon Gérôme's, Thomas Couture's and Lawrence Alma-Tadema's grandiose evocations of Roman festivals and rituals, Edward Poynter's and Edwin Long's richly detailed portrayals of ancient Egypt and Babylon, Akseli Gallen-Kallela's vivid depictions of ancient Finnish land-scape and mythology in the *Kalevala*, Ferdinand Hodler's majestic Swiss mountain ranges, the setting of great battles and heroic feats, and Victor Vasnetsov's and Vasily Surikov's images of the Russian steppe and the medieval Kremlin, pointed the way for Griffith, de Mille and Bronston – and Eisenstein – and not always in the direction of vulgarity. Indeed for artistry, and evocation of ethnic atmosphere, the scenes in Pskov and Novgorod (in *Alexander Nevsky*) and at Kazan and Alexandrov (in *Ivan the Terrible*) were worthy successors of the best Russian landscapes and townscapes by Vasnetsov, Surikov and Repin (Gray 1971: chaps 1–2; Harding 1979: chap. 2).

Eisenstein, indeed, was such a perfectionist in matters of archaeological verisimilitude that he had the sets for the Pskov and Novgorod scenes in *Alexander Nevsky* rebuilt in the studio according to their original proportions, because the old palaces and churches had sunk several feet into the ground, altering their proportions and perspective. And the great Battle on the Ice had to be artificially simulated in order to shoot the film swiftly – in the middle of a Moscow heatwave! – by ploughing up a vast field, covering it with asphalt and putting a mixture of chalk and naphthalene on it (Taylor 1998: 89, 92–3, citing V. Shklovskii, *Eizenshtein*, Moscow 1973: 247). The aim, and the result, was a Russian ethnoscape matching, and amplifying, Eisenstein's national theme, namely, the defence of the motherland: 'The theme of patriotism and national defence against the aggressor is the subject that suffuses our film' (Taylor 1998: 86, citing Eisenstein, *Selected Works*, vol. 3, p. 118).

This example, like that of the Odessa steps sequence in *Battleship Potemkin*, appears to confirm the artifice and 'invention' which, for Hobsbawm and Anderson, characterise the cult of the nation. Yet, these are only technical means to an 'authenticity' of ethnoscape and homeland that is poetic and popular rather than strictly factual. Historically documented fact (of which there is little in thirteenth century Russia) furnishes the basis of the reconstruction, but the authenticity sought is emotional and moral; as Eisenstein put it, speaking of the relationship of man and nature in Japanese painting:

'Everywhere the emotional landscape turns out to be an image of the mutual absorption of man and nature one into the other' (Taylor 1998: 89 and 226, n. 15, citing S.M. Eisenstein, *Nonindifferent Nature*, trans. H. Marshall, Cambridge 1987: 359).

'The people'

Ethnoscapes formed one element in a 'national dialogue', the other being constituted by the 'the people', the folk (*Volk*), or 'ethnic populace', suffering, celebrating or revolutionary, but always 'chosen', who so often provided the pivot, and real subject, of the drama. Not till the end of the eighteenth century, the era of revolution, did 'the people' begin to occupy centre stage, starting with David's excited rendering of the Third Estate in *The Oath of the Tennis Court* (1791) and continuing through Delacroix's insurrectionary *Liberty leading the People* (1830), Surikov's desolate *The Morning of the Execution of the Strelstii Guard* (1881) and, in a more relaxed, rural mode, Anders Zorn's *Midsummer Dance* (1897), to Diego Rivera's vivid panorama of Mexico's pre-Columbian peoples, and the visionary English recreations of Stanley Spencer's Cookham and war-time Macedonia, in the 1920s and 1930s.

One could equally argue that, from the first, cinema has not only been popular, it has taken 'the people' as its prime subject-matter. In comedy and documentary film, 'the people' has often signified the 'common folk', rather than the 'ethnic folk'; but in history, mythology and war films, this motif is combined with the distinctive ethnic culture of 'the people' – be they Jews, Greeks, Romans, Scots, French or Russians. Perhaps Eisenstein recalled for his own patriotic-religious crowd scenes Repin's depiction of a *Religious Procession in Kursk Province* (1880–83), traversing the Russian countryside with their banners and relics – not to mention the religious processions and anthems of the suffering Russian people, the true 'hero' of Mussorgsky's *Boris Godunov* (1868–74). But there are other sides to 'the people': the rebellious rioting people in Part I of *Ivan the Terrible* (Eisenstein 1989: 47–53, shots 171–238), egged on by the Simpleton – a familiar Russian literary figure, also found in *Boris Godunov* – demanding to see their Tsar and make him put down the Glinskys, his wife Anastasia's boyar family; or the resolute, patriotic people, like the common people of Novgorod in *Alexander Nevsky* opposing the merchants and the Church and calling on Alexander to lead them against the invading Teutonic Knights – answering the martyred beggar Avvakum's call, which became their battle hymn:

> Arise, people of Rus,
> To glorious battle, mortal battle!
> Arise, men of freedom,
> For our fair land!

> (Taylor 1998: 90; Leyda 1974: 103, 105)

In both cases, Eisenstein had plenty of precedents on which to draw, from David and Delacroix to Griffith and his own portrayals of revolution and popular resolve in *Battleship Potemkin* and *Oktober*. And in showing 'the people' as an active, conscious political force, he diverged considerably from the rather passive, supportive role granted them in many Hollywood historical films (see Rhode 1978: chap. 4).

Conclusion

Here I have been able to do little more than scratch the surface of a vast topic area – an area which, more than most, admits of multiple approaches (see, for example, Hayward 1997: Introduction and chap. 2, especially 95–8, on French First World War films like Gance's *J'accuse* and Poirier's *Verdun, visions d'histoire*, as well as Marc de Gastyne's *La merveilleuse vie de Jeanne d'Arc*; and further on Gance's *J'accuse*, in Winter 1995). The relationship between history (and landscape and genre) painting and historical film, on which I have focused, requires much more detailed scholarly research, by those well versed in both fields of study. From the standpoint of the study of ethnicity and nationalism, I can only highlight a few of the issues, theoretical and empirical, that present themselves in reflecting on the relationship between the imagery of cinema and art and the interpretations of national identity. My aim has been only to initiate discussion of some parallels and analogies, thematic and formal, of the visual representation of national identity, and to suggest a framework for making further cultural comparisons, on the basis of an 'ethno-symbolic' approach which highlights the role of various ethnic elements – myths, symbols, traditions and memories – in the formation of nations and in the shaping of national identities (see Smith 1995).

If I have concentrated on the role of one film director in particular, it is because in the later work of Sergei Eisenstein we find one of the clearest expressions of artistic and cinematic analogies and one of the most compelling representations of key themes of national identity. For not only are we dealing with the products of a kaleidoscopic 'historical mobility', but more importantly with the materials and methods by which artists help to create and reproduce the very fabric of national communities to which they belong, and thereby disseminate and perpetuate the idea of the nation itself, its history, development and destiny. Even where artists cast doubt on the morality of the actions committed in the name of the nation, as did Nash in his Great War paintings, even where they show us a different or more universal code of myths, memories and values, as with Renoir in *La grande illusion*, the nation and its collective identity has remained central to the imagination and activity of the modern era. Few have done more to confirm, express and disseminate the ideals and problems of the nation than the artist in painted or in moving images.

Bibliography

Abrams, A.U. (1985) *The Valiant Hero: Benjamin West and Grand-Style History Painting*, Washington, DC: Smithsonian Institution Press.

Ades, D. (ed.) (1989) *Art in Latin America: The Modern Era, 1820–1980*, London: South Bank Centre, Hayward Gallery.

Anderson, B. (1991) *Imagined Communities: Reflections on the Origin and Spread of Nationalism*, London: Verso.

Antal, F. (1956) *Füseli Studies*, London: Routledge and Kegan Paul.

Brookner, A. (1980) *Jacques Louis David*, London: Chatto and Windus.

Eisenmann, S. (1994) *Nineteenth Century Art, A Critical History*, London: Thames and Hudson.

Eisenstein, S.M. (1989) *Ivan the Terrible*, London: Faber.

Fraser, G.M. (1996) *The Hollywood History of the World, Film Stills from the Kobal Collection*, London: The Harvill Press.

Gellner, E. (1964) *Thought and Change*, London: Weidenfeld and Nicolson.

—— (1983) *Nations and Nationalism*, Oxford: Blackwell.

Gray, C. (1971) *The Russian Experiment in Art, 1863–1922*, London: Thames and Hudson.

Harding, J. (1979) *Artistes Pompiers: French Academic Art in the Nineteenth Century*, London: Academy Editions.

Hayward, S. (1997) *French National Cinema*, London: Routledge.

Hobsbawm, E. (1990) *Nations and Nationalism since 1780*, Cambridge: Cambridge University Press.

Hobsbawm, E. and Ranger, T. (eds) (1983) *The Invention of Tradition*, Cambridge: Cambridge University Press.

Hosking, G. and Service, R. (eds) (1998) *Russian Nationalism, Past and Present*, Basingstoke: Macmillan.

Kedourie, E. (1960) *Nationalism*, London: Hutchinson.

—— (ed.) (1971) *Nationalism in Asia and Africa*, London: Weidenfeld and Nicolson.

Korotkina, L. (1976) *Nikolay Roerich*, Leningrad: Aurora Art Publishers.

Leyda, Jan (ed.) (1974) *Battleship Potemkin, October and Alexander Nevsky by Sergei Eisenstein*, London: Lorrimer Publishing Limited.

Perrie, M. (1998) 'The Cult of Ivan the Terrible in Stalin's Russia', in Hosking and Service (eds).

Poulson, C. (1999) *The Quest for the Grail: Arthurian Legend in British Art, 1840–1920*, Manchester: Manchester University Press.

Rhode, E. (1978) *A History of the Cinema, From Its Origins to 1970*, Harmondsworth: Penguin.

Rosenblum, R. (1961) 'Gavin Hamilton's *Brutus* and its Aftermath', *Burlington Magazine* 103: 8–16.

—— (1967) *Transformations in Late Eighteenth Century Art*, Princeton, NJ: Princeton University Press.

—— (1985) *Jean Auguste Dominique Ingres*, London: Thames and Hudson.

Shanina, N. (1979) *Victor Vasnetsov*, Leningrad: Aurora Art Publishers.

Smith, A.D. (1979) 'The "Historical Revival" in Late Eighteenth Century England and France', *Art History* 2: 156–78.

—— (1986) *The Ethnic Origins of Nations*, Oxford: Blackwell.

—— (1995) 'Gastronomy or Geology? The Role of Nationalism in the Reconstruction of Nations', *Nations and Nationalism* 1, 1: 3–23.

—— (1997) 'Nation and Ethnoscape', *The Oxford International Review* 8, 2: 11–18.

—— (1998) *Nationalism and Modernism*, London: Routledge.

Taylor, R. (1998) *Film Propaganda: Soviet Russia and Nazi Germany*, 2nd rev. edn, London: I.B. Tauris.

Thaden, E. (1964) *Conservative Nationalism in Nineteenth Century Russia*, Seattle, WA: University of Washington Press.

Wilton, A. and Upstone, R. (eds) (1997) *The Age of Rossetti, Burne-Jones and Watts: Symbolism in Britain, 1860–1910*, London: Tate Gallery Publishing.

Wind, E. (1938–9) 'The Revolution of History Painting', *Journal of the Warburg Institute* II, 116–27.

Winter, J. (1995) *Sites of Memory, Sites of Mourning: The Great War in European Cultural History*, Cambridge: Cambridge University Press.

II

THE CONCEPT OF
NATIONAL CINEMA

4

THE LIMITING IMAGINATION
OF NATIONAL CINEMA

Andrew Higson

In 1989, I published an essay about national cinema in *Screen* (Higson 1989).[1] Ten years on, much of what I wrote still seems valid, but there are also some issues I would want to reconsider. One of the problems with that essay is that I was very much extrapolating from my knowledge of just one national cinema (British cinema). As Stephen Crofts has suggested, scholarly work on national cinema often operates from a very limited knowledge of the immense diversity of world cinemas (Crofts 1993: 60–1). In my case, there is undeniably a danger that my essay transformed a historically specific Eurocentric, even Anglocentric version of what a national cinema might be into an ideal category, a theory of national cinema in the abstract that is assumed to be applicable in all contexts.

'When is a cinema "national"?', asks Susan Hayward (1993: 1). As if in answer, Crofts delineates several different types of 'national' cinema that have emerged in different historical circumstances (1993, 1998). They have performed quite distinct functions in relation to the state. They have had very different relationships to Hollywood. Divergent claims have been made for them. They adopt a range of formal and generic characteristics. They are 'national' cinemas in a variety of ways. Faced with such variety, a single, all-encompassing grand theory may be less useful than more piecemeal historical investigations of specific cinematic formations. How have specific national cinemas been defined as such, for instance? How have they come to be understood as national cinemas, in what historical circumstances? How have politicians, trade organisations, distributors, critics, historians, journalists and audiences demarcated one national cinema from another? How has a particular body of films or a particular economic infrastructure come to be seen as embodying a distinct national cinema? Which strands or traditions of cinema circulating within a particular nation-state are recognised as legitimate aspects of the national cinema? How have particular policies and practices been mobilised in the name of particular national cinemas?

While these are undoubtedly important questions, and while I have attempted to explore some of them elsewhere, I do in fact want to deal with some of the more abstract and theoretical issues here.[2] First, I want to revisit the idea that the modern nation, in Benedict Anderson's terms, is an imagined community (Anderson 1983). Second, I want to reconsider the traditional idea of the 'national' as a self-contained and carefully demarcated experience. In particular, I want to suggest that the concept of the 'transnational' may be a subtler means of describing cultural and economic formations that are rarely contained by national boundaries. Third, I want to examine John Hill's argument that the concept of national cinema is of vital importance at the level of state policy, particularly as a means of promoting cultural diversity and attending to national specificity (Hill 1992, 1996). For better or worse, I will again be drawing examples from the British context.

My intention overall is to question the usefulness of the concept of national cinema. It is clearly a helpful taxonomic labelling device, a conventional means of reference in the complex debates about cinema, but the process of labelling is always to some degree tautologous, fetishising the national rather than merely describing it. It thus erects boundaries between films produced in different nation-states although they may still have much in common. It may therefore obscure the degree of cultural diversity, exchange and interpenetration that marks so much cinematic activity.

The nation as imagined community

Following Anderson (1983), it is now conventional to define the nation as the mapping of an imagined community with a secure and shared identity and sense of belonging, on to a carefully demarcated geo-political space. The nation, from this perspective, is first forged and then maintained as a bounded public sphere. That is to say, it is public debate that gives the nation meaning, and media systems with a particular geographical reach that give it shape. Those who inhabit nations with a strong sense of self-identity are encouraged to imagine themselves as members of a coherent, organic community, rooted in the geographical space, with well-established indigenous traditions. As David Morley and Kevin Robins put it, 'the idea of the "nation" ... involve[s] people in a common sense of identity and ... work[s] as an inclusive symbol which provides "integration" and "meaning"' (1990: 6).

National identity is, in this sense, about the experience of belonging to such a community, being steeped in its traditions, its rituals and its characteristic modes of discourse. This sense of national identity is not of course dependent on actually living within the geo-political space of the nation, as the émigré experience confirms. Thus some diasporic communities, uprooted from the specific geo-political space of the nation or the homeland, still share a common sense of belonging, despite – or even because of – their transnational dispersal. On the one hand community, on the other, diaspora. On the one hand, modern nations exist primarily as imagined communities. On the other, those communities actually consist of highly fragmented and widely dispersed groups of people with as many differences as similarities and with little in the sense of real physical contact with each other. If this is the case, it follows that all nations are in some sense diasporic. They are thus forged in the tension between unity and disunity, between home and homelessness. Nationhood thus answers to 'a felt need for a rooted, bounded, whole and authentic identity' (Morley and Robins 1990: 19).

The public sphere of the nation and the discourses of patriotism are thus bound up in a constant struggle to transform the facts of dispersal, variegation and homelessness into the experience of rooted community. At times, the experience of an organic, coherent national community, a meaningful national collectivity, will be overwhelming. At other times, the experience of diaspora, dislocation and de-centredness will prevail. It is in times such as these that other allegiances, other senses of belonging besides the national will be more strongly felt.

It is widely assumed that the rituals of mass communication play a central role in re-imagining the dispersed and incoherent populace as a tight-knit, value-sharing collectivity, sustaining the experience of nationhood. But is that collectivity necessarily national? Consider three prominent media experiences that might be seen at one level as enabling the British to imagine themselves as a distinctive national community. First, consider the funeral of Diana, Princess of Wales, which of course became a major media event in which millions participated. Second, consider the consistent ratings success of long-running, home-grown, British-based soap operas depicting everyday inner-city life. Programmes such as *Coronation Street* and *EastEnders* are of course routinely transmitted on a nationwide basis by British broadcasters with at least some sense of a public service remit. Third, consider the immense success at the box-office and subsequently on video and the small screen of a handful of 'typically British' films of the 1990s, among them *Four Weddings and a Funeral* (1994), *The Full Monty* (1997) and *Shakespeare in Love* (1998), all of them British-produced and British-set. Each of these media events has had repercussions far greater than mere viewing figures suggest, given their wide discussion in print, on television, on the Internet and through word-of-mouth.

But are these media events best understood as national phenomena? For a start, there are always dissenters. Some Britons did not mourn Diana's death or participate in the media event of her funeral. Some Britons don't watch soaps, go to the cinema, or take any interest in popular culture. Nor do they recognise themselves in films like *Four Weddings* or *The Full Monty*, or feel interpellated by the invitation through such texts or viewing experiences to share in a collective sense of national identity. Second, the audiences for all three cited events were by no means simply national. To talk about these events as global phenomena would surely be an overstatement, but they undoubtedly were, and in some cases continue to be, considerable transnational experiences. Third, there is of course no guarantee that all audiences will make sense of these experiences in the same way, since audiences will translate each experience into their own cultural frames of reference, using them in different contexts and for different ends.

Fourth, the 'national' audience for a film like *The Full Monty* also 'gathers' to watch non-indigenous films, especially Hollywood films. On the one hand, their coming together for a Hollywood film surely underlines the transnational experience of the 'imagined community', rather than a solely national experience. On the other hand, it is clear that American films play a strong role in the construction of cultural identity in the UK. Fifth, the community that we might imagine 'gathered' around, say, the exhibition and dissemination of *The Full Monty* is always a fortuitous, contingent, abstract amalgam of dispersed and specific audiences or cultural subjects that have come together for a very specific event. At the end of this particular experience or event, the imagined community disperses again, while other communities reassemble quite differently for other relatively fleeting experiences. Such communities are rarely self-sufficient, stable or unified. They are much more likely to be contingent, complex, in part fragmented, in part overlapping with other senses of identity and belonging that have more to do with generation, gender, sexuality, class, ethnicity, politics or style than with nationality. The sense of community, of shared experiences and common identities that was mobilised around the death of Diana, for instance, was clearly mobilised beyond the boundaries of the nation. National identity did not always or necessarily come into it. Thus in some quarters, the popular groundswell of empathy registered as feminism or sisterliness; in other quarters, or even at the same time, it took the shape of anti-authoritarian and especially republican principles.

The 'imagined community' argument, in my own work as much as anywhere else, is not always sympathetic to what we might call the contingency or instability of the national. This is precisely because the nationalist project, in Anderson's terms, imagines the nation as limited, with finite and meaningful boundaries. The problem is that, when describing a national cinema, there is a tendency to focus only on those films that narrate the nation as just this finite, limited space, inhabited by a tightly coherent and unified community, closed off to other identities besides national identity. Or rather, the focus is on films that seem amenable to such an interpretation. The 'imagined community' argument thus sometimes seems unable to acknowledge the cultural difference and diversity that invariably marks both the inhabitants of a particular nation-state and the members of more geographically dispersed 'national' communities. In this sense, as with more conservative versions of the nationalist project, the experience and acceptance of diversity is closed off. This seems particularly unfortunate as modern communication networks operate on an increasingly transnational basis and cultural commodities are widely exchanged across national borders.

The media are vital to the argument that modern nations are imagined communities. But contemporary media activity is also clearly one of the main ways in which transnational cultural connections are established. Hollywood of course is one of the longest standing and best organised media institutions with a transnational reach capable of penetrating even the most heavily policed national spaces. Should this fact be celebrated or bemoaned? As Hollywood films travel effortlessly across national borders, they may displace the sort of 'indigenous' films that might promote and maintain specific national identities. On the other hand, the entry of 'foreign' films into a restricted national market may be a powerful means of celebrating cultural diversity, transnational experiences and multinational identities. Certain British films may have been identified as projecting a core sense of national identity – the consensus films made at Ealing Studios and elsewhere in the latter half of the Second World War, for instance – but it is equally possible to identify 'British' films that seem to embrace the transnational or even quite self-consciously to dissolve rather than to sustain the concept of the nation.[3]

Nationalism and transnationalism

In 'The Concept of National Cinema' (Higson 1989), I suggested that national cinemas were the product of a tension between 'home' and 'away', between the identification of the homely and the assumption that it is quite distinct from what happens elsewhere. In this sense, there are two central conceptual means of identifying the imaginary coherence or specificity of a national cinema. On the one hand, a national cinema seems to look inward, reflecting on the nation itself, on its past, present and future, its cultural heritage, its indigenous traditions, its sense of common identity and continuity. On the other hand, a national cinema seems to look out across its borders, asserting its difference from other national cinemas, proclaiming its sense of otherness.

The problem with this formulation is that it tends to assume that national identity and tradition are already fully formed and fixed in place. It also tends to take borders for granted and to assume that those borders are effective in containing political and economic developments, cultural practice and identity. In fact of course, borders are always leaky and there is a considerable degree of movement across them (even in the most authoritarian states). It is in this migration, this border crossing, that the transnational emerges. Seen in this light, it is difficult to see the indigenous as either pure or stable. On the contrary, the degree of cultural cross-breeding and interpenetration, not only across borders but also within them, suggests that modern cultural formations are invariably hybrid and impure. They constantly mix together different 'indigeneities' and are thus always re-fashioning themselves, as opposed to exhibiting an already fully formed identity.

The cinemas established in specific nation-states are rarely autonomous cultural industries and the film business has long operated on a regional, national and transnational basis. The experience of border crossing takes place at two broad levels. First there is the level of production and the activities of film-makers. Since at least the 1920s, films have been made as co-productions, bringing together resources and experience from different nation-states. For even longer, film-makers have been itinerant, moving from one production base to another, whether temporarily or on a more permanent basis. When a German director like E.A. Dupont is based in England, and makes an Anglo-German co-production simultaneously in English and German (*Atlantic*, 1929), can it usefully be called a British film?[4] When a British director like Alan Parker makes a Hollywood film about an Argentinean legend (*Evita*, 1996), to which nation should the film be attributed? When a British director teams up with an American producer, a multinational cast and crew, and American capital, to adapt a novel about the contingency of identity by a Sri Lankan-born Canadian resident (*The English Patient*, 1996), can its identity be called anything other than transnational?

The second way in which cinema operates on a transnational basis is in terms of the distribution and reception of films. On the one hand, many films are distributed far more widely than simply within their country of production. Occasionally, even the small, 'home-grown', indigenous film can become an international box-office phenomenon given the right backing and promotional push. On the other hand, when films do travel, there is no certainty that audiences will receive them in the same way in different cultural contexts. Some films of course are physically altered for different export markets, whether in terms of subtitling, dubbing, re-editing or censorship. But even where they are not altered, audiences can still take them up in novel ways.

The debates about national cinema need to take greater account of the diversity of reception, the recognition that the meanings an audience reads into a

Figure 4.1 Shifting sands, shifting identities: *The English Patient*
Source: Tiger Moth/Miramax, courtesy of the Kobal Collection

film are heavily dependent on the cultural context in which they watch it. The movement of films across borders may introduce exotic elements to the 'indigenous' culture. One response to this is an anxious concern about the effects of cultural imperialism, a concern that the local culture will be infected, even destroyed by the foreign invader. A contrary response is that the introduction of exotic elements may well have a liberating or democratising effect on the local culture, expanding the cultural repertoire. A third possibility is that the foreign commodity will not be treated as exotic by the local audience, but will be interpreted according to an 'indigenous' frame of reference; that is, it will be metaphorically translated into a local idiom.[5]

Cultural diversity and national specificity: a matter of policy

One of the ways in which the nation talks to itself, and indeed seeks to differentiate itself from others, is in terms of state policy. The fear of cultural and economic imperialism has of course had a major impact on state policy in a great many different nations. Consequently, if the concept of national cinema is considered troublesome at the level of theoretical debate, it is still a considerable force at the level of state policy. One of the problems with legislating for a strong and healthy national cinema untroubled by foreign interlopers is that national legislation can rarely have more than a cosmetic effect on what is really a problem of the international capitalist economy. One of the solutions is that even governments occasionally operate on a transnational basis, notably in terms of the pan-European media funding infrastructure established under the auspices of the European Union and the Council of Europe.

Even so, there is no denying that at the level of policy, the concept of national cinema still has some meaning, as governments continue to develop defensive strategies designed to protect and promote both the local cultural formation and the local economy. Such developments have traditionally assumed that a strong national cinema can offer coherent images of the nation, sustaining the nation at an ideological level, exploring and celebrating what is understood to be the indigenous culture. Of equal importance today is the role that cinema is felt able to play in terms of promoting the nation as a tourist destination, to the benefit of the tourism and service industries. Also at the economic level, governments may legislate to protect and promote the development of the local media industries. They may encourage long-term investment (often from overseas). They may create the conditions that might generate significant export revenue. And they may seek to maintain an appropriately skilled domestic workforce in full employment.

To promote films in terms of their national identity is also to secure a prominent collective profile for them in both the domestic and the international marketplace, a means of selling those films by giving them a distinctive brand name. In this respect, it is worth noting how national labels become crucial at prestigious prize-giving ceremonies, such as the Oscars, for the kudos that can spill over from successful films on to their assumed national base. Note for instance the way in which the British press celebrated the success of films like *Chariots of Fire* (1981), *The English Patient* and *Shakespeare in Love* as British films, even though they all depended on significant amounts of foreign investment.

Given that the nation-state remains a vital and powerful legal mechanism, and given the ongoing development of national media policies, it remains important to conduct debate at that level and in those terms. It would be foolish in this context to attempt to do away altogether with the concept of national cinema. Yet it is important to ask to what precisely the concept refers, what sorts of cultural developments it can embrace and what it makes difficult. The implication of what I have argued so far is that the concept of national cinema is hardly able to do justice either to the internal diversity of contemporary cultural formations or to the overlaps and interpenetrations between different formations. This is surely true if we define a national cinema as one that imagines, or enables its audiences to imagine, a closed and coherent community with an already fully formed and fixed indigenous tradition. Ironically, it is very often the case that a government that legislates for a national cinema, or a pressure group that lobbies for such legislation, is in fact advancing an argument for cultural diversity. Those western European nations, for instance, that have erected defensive mechanisms in their own marketplace and economy against an apparently imperialist Hollywood have almost invariably done so as a means of promoting a film culture and a body of representations other than those that Hollywood can offer.

Given the extent to which state media policy is still overwhelmingly defined in nationalist terms, it may then make sense to continue to argue for a national cinema precisely as a means of promoting cultural difference. A government-supported national cinema may be one of the few means by which a film culture not dominated entirely by Hollywood can still exist. This is an argument that John Hill has developed, with specific reference to British cinema. He suggests that the case for a national cinema is best made in terms of 'the value of home-grown cinema to the cultural life of a nation and, hence, the importance of supporting indigenous film-making in an international market dominated by Hollywood' (Hill 1992: 11). Such a statement of course begs the question of what exactly the value of that home-grown cinema is. This is particularly pressing in the light of the argument that the presence and popularity of Hollywood films in Britain is in itself a means of ensuring a populist diversity within British culture, a valuable means of broadening the British cultural repertoire.

Hill however is dismissive of the claim that the presence of Hollywood films within British culture should be seen as a potential democratisation of that culture. He argues that national cinemas have a much greater potential to act as forces for diversity and for the re-fashioning of the national cultural formation. 'It is quite possible to conceive of a national cinema', he writes, 'which is none the less critical of inherited notions of national identity, which does not assume the existence of a unique, unchanging "national culture", and which is capable

70

of dealing with social divisions and differences' (Hill 1992: 16). In other words, to question tradition and to embrace cultural difference is not necessarily to reject altogether the idea of a national cinema that can speak eloquently to a multicultural audience. On the contrary, Hill argues, it is important that a national cinema is maintained in Britain, one that is 'capable of registering the lived complexities of British "national" life' (Hill 1996: 111). Hill suggests that this was precisely the national cinema that Britain enjoyed in the 1980s, when 'the "Britishness" of British cinema ... was neither unitary nor agreed but depended upon a growing sense of the multiple national, regional and ethnic identifications which characterised life in Britain in this period' (Hill 1999: 244).

Is this a sufficient reason for persevering with the concept of national cinema? In fact, it seems to me that Hill is arguing less for a national cinema than for what might be called a critical (and implicitly left-wing) cinema, a radical cinema, or as he puts it, a cinema 'characterised by questioning and inquiry' (Hill 1992: 17). His concern is to ensure that the range of cultural representations available to audiences is not restricted by the operations of the marketplace. In this respect, as he puts it, 'The case for a national cinema ... may be seen as part of a broader case for a more varied and representative range of film and media output than the current political economy of the communications industries allows' (Hill 1992: 18).

There are two problems with formulating a defence of national cinema in these terms. First, in order to promote a cinema characterised by questioning and inquiry is it necessary to do so on national grounds? A critical cinema surely need not be nationally based in its funding, its textual concerns or its reception. Likewise, cultural diversity within a national film-culture may just as easily be achieved through encouraging a range of imports as by ensuring that home-grown films are produced. Second, the British films of the 1980s that Hill favours are by no means the full range of British-made films produced in that decade, but those whose radical subject-matter and critical approach appeal to his own ideological preferences. Most histories of national cinema have of course been written in this way. Canons of critically favoured home-grown films are created to the neglect of other films circulating within the film culture, whether home-grown or imported. The formation of such canons also tends to overlook the relative popularity of the canonical films with 'national' audiences. As far as Hill is concerned, 'the most interesting type of British cinema, and the one which is most worthy of support' does not 'exemplify ... the virtues and values of Britain'. Instead, what he calls for is 'the provision of diverse and challenging representations adequate to the complexities of contemporary Britain' (Hill 1992: 18–19).

What sort of cinema does this imply? It seems to me that it is really a call for a very specific type of film: social dramas set in contemporary Britain, attending to the specificities of multiculturalism and employing a more or less realist mode of representation. It is thus hardly surprising that Hill's book on British cinema in the 1980s presents the British costume dramas and heritage films of the period as of less *relevance* than the films of Ken Loach, Stephen Frears and Isaac Julien. It is not necessarily the case, however, that audiences will find more relevance in contemporary dramas than in period films. Nor is it the case that only British-made or British-set films can address matters of importance or value to audiences in Britain. After all, questions of gender, sexuality and ethnicity, for instance, can be addressed in very poignant ways in displaced or exotic settings, whether the displacement is in terms of period or geography. In this sense, films by a Spike Lee, a Jane Campion or an Emir Kusturica can make what Hill describes as 'a valuable contribution to British cultural life' (Hill 1992: 17). The case for supporting a home-grown cinema, it seems to me, is thus weakened rather than strengthened by Hill's call for a critical cinema that promotes cultural diversity.

Given his emphasis on national specificity, there is even a sense in which Hill's argument depends on a rather enclosed sense of the national, in which borders between nations are fully capable of restricting transnational flow. He does of course argue that films made in a particular nation-state need not necessarily invoke homogenising national myths and may precisely be sensitive to social and cultural differences and to the plurality of identities *within* that state. He seems less sensitive to the hybrid or the transnational, however. Central to his argument is the distinction between a cinema that indulges in homogenising national myths and one that 'works with or addresses nationally specific materials' (Hill 1992: 16). It is a distinction he draws from the work of Paul Willemen, who argues that a nationally specific cultural formation need not necessarily be characterised by a preoccupation with national identity (Willemen 1994). As Willemen points out, the discourses of nationalism will always try to repress the complexities of and internal differences within a nationally specific cultural formation. But he also argues that a cinema that attempts to engage with the nationally specific need not be a nationalist cinema.

The terms in which Hill and Willemen make this distinction seem to me confusing and therefore problematic because they persist in using the concept of the national. Willemen is of course right to insist that 'national boundaries have a significant structuring impact on ... socio-cultural formations' (Willemen 1994: 210). We cannot therefore simply dismiss the category of the nation altogether, but nor should we assume that cultural specificity is best understood and addressed in national terms. To persist, as Hill does, in referring to a 'nationally specific' cinema that deals with 'national preoccupations' (Hill 1992: 11) within 'an identifiably and specifically British context' (Hill 1992: 16) seems once more to take national identity, and specifically Britishness, for granted. It seems to gloss over too many other questions of community, culture, belonging and identity that are often either defiantly local or loosely transnational. Concepts like 'national life' and 'national culture' thus seem destined to imply a homogenising and enclosing tendency.

Conclusion

I stated at the outset of this chapter that I wanted to question the usefulness of the concept of national cinema. It would be impossible – and certainly unwise – to ignore the concept altogether: it is far too deeply ingrained in critical and historical debate about the cinema, for a start. Even so, as Crofts has argued, it is important to question 'the ongoing critical tendency to hypostatize the "national" of national cinema' (1993: 61). The questions I have posed above suggest that it is inappropriate to assume that cinema and film culture are bound by the limits of the nation-state. The complexities of the international film industry and the transnational movements of finance capital, film-makers and films should put paid to that assumption. Should policy then be developed to ensure that cinema can operate at a national level? On the basis of the British experience, I have suggested that to make assumptions about national specificity is to beg too many questions. In other political circumstances, however, it may be that lobbying or legislating for a national cinema will usefully advance the struggle of a community for cultural, political and economic self-definition. As Crofts points out, in some contexts it may be necessary to challenge the homogenising myths of national cinema discourse; in others, it may be necessary to support them (1993: 62).

Are the limits of the national the most productive way of framing arguments about cultural diversity and cultural specificity? It is certainly valid to argue for a film culture that accommodates diverse identities, images and traditions, and it is undoubtedly important to promote films that deal with the culturally specific. But it doesn't seem useful to me to think through cultural diversity and cultural specificity in solely national terms: to argue for a national cinema is not necessarily the best way to achieve either cultural diversity or cultural specificity. In any case, the contingent communities that cinema imagines are much more likely to be either local or transnational than national.

Notes

1 This was an early version of material subsequently revised in Higson 1995, in which I explore some of the ways in which British cinema has been constructed as a specifically national cinema. See also three other papers in which I discuss the concept of national cinema: Higson 1997, 2000a and 2000b.

2 I look at some of the ways in which British cinema has been constructed as a national cinema in Higson 1995 and 2001; Higson and Maltby 1999 look at the development of a pan-European, transnational cinema in the 1920s and 1930s.

3 For a more detailed version of this argument, see Higson 2000b.

4 For a discussion of Dupont's career in Britain in the late 1920s, see Higson 1999.

5 For enlightening discussions of this process of cultural translation, see Bergfelder 1999a and 1999b; also chapters by Bergfelder and Hedetoft elsewhere in this book.

Bibliography

Anderson, B. (1983) *Imagined Communities: Reflections on the Origins and Spread of Nationalism*, London: Verso.

Ashby, J. and Higson, A. (eds) (2000) *British Cinema, Past and Present*, London: Routledge.

Bergfelder, T. (1999a) 'The Internationalisation of the German Film Industry in the 1950s and 1960s', unpublished Ph.D. thesis, Norwich: University of East Anglia.

—— (1999b) 'Negotiating Exoticism: Hollywood, Film Europe and the Cultural Reception of Anna May Wong', in A. Higson and R. Maltby (eds).

Bondebjerg, I. (ed.) (2000) *Moving Images, Culture and the Mind*, Luton: University of Luton Press/John Libby Media.

Briggs, A. and Cobley, P. (eds) (1997) *The Media: An Introduction*, London: Addison Wesley Longman.

Crofts, S. (1993) 'Reconceptualising National Cinema/s', *Quarterly Review of Film and Video* 14, 3: 49–67.

—— (1998) 'Concepts of National Cinema', in J. Hill and P. Church Gibson (eds).

Hayward, S. (1993) *French National Cinema*, London: Routledge.

Higson, A. (1989) 'The Concept of National Cinema', *Screen* 30, 4: 36–46.

—— (1995) *Waving The Flag: Constructing a National Cinema in Britain*, Oxford: Clarendon Press.

—— (1997) 'Nationality and the Media', in A. Briggs and P. Cobley (eds).

—— (1999) 'Polyglot Films for an International Market: E. A. Dupont, the British Film Industry, and the Idea of a European Cinema', in A. Higson and R. Maltby (eds).

—— (2000a) 'National Cinemas, International Markets, Cross-Cultural Identities', in I. Bondebjerg (ed.).

—— (2000b) 'The Instability of the National', in J. Ashby and A. Higson (eds).

—— (2001) *English Heritage, English Cinema*, Oxford: Oxford University Press.

Higson, A. and Maltby, R. (eds) (1999) *'Film Europe' and 'Film America': Cinema, Commerce and Cultural Exchange, 1920–1939*, Exeter: Exeter University Press.

Hill, J. (1992) 'The Issue of National Cinema and British Film Production', in D. Petrie (ed.).

—— (1996) 'British Film Policy', in A. Moran (ed.).

—— (1997) 'British Cinema as National Cinema: Production, Audience and Representation', in R. Murphy (ed.).

—— (1999) *British Cinema in the 1980s*, Oxford: Oxford University Press.

Hill, J. and Church Gibson, P. (eds) (1998) *The Oxford Guide to Film Studies*, Oxford: Oxford University Press.

Moran, A. (ed.) (1996) *Film Policy: International, National and Regional Perspectives*, London: Routledge.

Morley, D. and Robins, K. (1990) 'No Place like *Heimat*: Images of Home(land) in European Culture', *New Formations* 12: 1–23.

Murphy, R. (ed.) (1997) *The British Cinema Book*, London: BFI.

Petrie, D. (ed.) (1992) *New Questions of British Cinema*, London: BFI.

Willemen, P. (1994) 'The National', in P. Willemen, *Looks and Frictions: Essays in Cultural Studies and Film Theory*, London/Bloomington: BFI/Indiana University Press.

5

NATIONAL CINEMA

A theoretical assessment

Ian Jarvie

Culture and social organisation are universal and perennial. States
and nationalisms are not.

(Ernest Gellner 1997: 4)

Preliminaries

As an assiduous young movie-goer trying to grasp the intellectual approach to
movies, I would often read about the importance of British national cinema. In
a recent formulation national cinema is 'the realist project that ... would reflect
the times, the lives and the culture of a country's population' (Anon., *Sight and
Sound* 1999: 3). National cinema talk always struck me as vaguely threatening.
Lauding the positive qualities of the national product was one thing (although a
steady diet of realism seemed unlikely to be satisfying); effectively slighting the
pleasures of the films one paid for, was another. British films, one learned,
enjoyed a quota of screen time – though its workings scarcely affected my
1950s cinema-going. In the provincial British town where I grew up there were
four cinemas, three showing weekly double-bills, the fourth showing bi-weekly
double-bills: ten first-run movies a week. On Sundays all four cinemas would
show double bills of older films, adding another eight to the week's total.
Almost all of these movies were American. One escaped from the drabness and
boredom of provincial Britain to the magic kingdom of Hollywood movies.
Occasionally an entertaining British movie, war subject or Ealing comedy
perhaps, would come along. More likely a British film was an Edgar Lustgarten
semi-documentary, or a low budget comedy starring the likes of Norman
Wisdom.

This personal opening exposes at once my bias. I guess I was an internal
cultural exile from Britain long before emigration. My sympathies were not
aroused by the nationalism and protectionism so taken for granted in writings
about movies. Later, more reflectively, I came to think that as long as I could
get what I was willing to pay for, and as long as I was not heavily taxed to
support the local film industry, then national cinema was OK. There were, after
all, obvious cultural arguments. If you speak a different language from English

there is the same call for films in that language as there is for the publication of books in that language and the performance of plays. If all films are imported then local people who would like to make films will have to go abroad, where it may not be easy to make films about their homeland (assuming they want to).

From now on the paper will be impersonal and systematic. My aim is to test the robustness of the idea of national cinema by pitting it against current thinking about nationalism. After setting out the main arguments for national cinema, I shall subject them to scrutiny in the light of current theorising. Throughout, my main focus is Europe, with only glancing reference to other continents.

Discussions of national cinema presuppose certain ideas about culture, social organisation, nation, state and land. Most history of film uses the nation-state as its primary organising category. If it was ever reasonable to take that category for granted, it is no longer. We are in a period of rich theorising about nationalism. So far from its categories being taken for granted, there is wide agreement that they are social constructions. Hence the popularity of Benedict Anderson's *Imagined Communities* (1983), much cited in recent national cinema literature. Marxists and functionalists would object that it is not consciousness of mankind that determines their existence – rather, it is their social existence that determines their consciousness. People have many ideas, but those that get a purchase in the world are favoured by circumstances in the world. Against Anderson's idealism (and Kedourie's 1960), I find Gellner's approach appealing because he tried to steer a middle course between such idealism and a materialist reduction of nationalism. Declaring nationalist ideas worthless, poor imaginings, as it were, Gellner took up instead the problem of the power of nationalism as a social force, the nature of its widespread appeal and the social conditions that permitted it to flourish (Gellner 1983: 123–5; see also Anderson 1983: 5). This makes Gellner's theory, to my mind as well as Ferdinand Mount's, 'the least unconvincing' among the many on offer (Mount 1999: 28). What Gellner held is that to be a competent person in the modern world required a certain cultural access; provision of the culture and access to it required a state tied to a cultural complex that embraced the citizens, most often in the form of a nation.

Gellner further argued that culture, social organisation, nation, state and land, should be sharply separated. Culture (and its spine, language) and social organisation surround everyone from birth. Whatever nations are, they are not identical, or even co-extensive with, culture or social organisation. States are a particular governmental form, not found with some nations, not found necessary by many tribes. Finally land: Gellner was vehement that culture was portable equipment only contingently linked to land. Indeed, the linking of culture to land he labelled 'fetishizing' (Gellner 1997: 102–8). This latter point, on which I shall not dwell, aims to disconcert those who attach nationalism to landscape.

Arguments for national cinema

Kristin Thompson suggests that claims about national cinema begin to emerge in Europe in the decade after 1915 (Thompson 1996: 259). The basic category of the nation, or rather the nation-state, is rapidly taken for granted, naturalised, with the unfortunate consequence that more often than not its value and appropriateness are not argued. After 1915, the main alternative before each European nation-state was American cinema, so such arguments as are found for national cinema direct themselves to the deficiencies, from the point of view of the receiving nation, of American movies (de Grazia 1989; Higson 1995).[1] The quality of these arguments is disappointing. That American *mores* are different from those of each and every European nation is scarcely news. That commentators prefer their own *mores* scarcely surprising. That it would be nice for people to see their own *mores* on film does not follow from the first two points, but no one is likely to want to deny it.

Sifting through the various writings on these matters I have come across three arguments with some life in them. (I ignore obviously invalid or nakedly prejudiced arguments.)[2] Let me label them: (a) the protectionist argument; (b) the cultural defence argument; (c) the nation-building argument. All three presuppose the idea that movies are different. They are different from traditional high culture, for example, since few nation-states regard the national origin of music, painting, sculpture, or theatrical works as matters on which to develop public policy. Mass culture seems to raise public policy questions in ways that (subsidised) traditional high cultural products do not. This view in turn presupposes that mass cultural works are cultural and not merely trade goods. One can find interesting equivocations here. Supporters of traditional high culture were slow to grant that movies were part of that culture at all. Yet apprehensions about possible influence could lead the same group to fret about the 'cultural damage', of a regime of free trade in movies.

The protectionist argument

Classical economics allows the following protectionist arguments: the infant industry argument, the anti-dumping argument, the excess capacity argument and the defence argument. The defence argument would require first showing that movies were vital to defence. By and large this argument has not been used to advocate protection of national cinemas. The other three arguments have separately, or in combination, been used in advocating national cinema. Since each is a valid argument in economics the proof is in all cases in the pudding. Did the protected *infant industry* eventually prove strong enough to compete internationally? Did the protection measures successfully neutralise *dumping*? Did the utilisation of *excess capacity* increase aggregate income? None of these proofs, however, bears on national cinema in the cultural sense. From the economic point of view, a successfully protected infant industry could be one that is a wholly owned branch plant, producing international or cosmopolitan films suitable for overseas as well as domestic consumption. Governments usually tried to devise additional protectionist measures to prevent any such outcome. This shows that the cultural defence and nation-building arguments are more fundamental than the protectionist argument. Protectionism is one instrument with which to nurture national cinema. By itself it is culturally indifferent – a charge often levelled at capitalism. We shall however rehabilitate the argument below.

The cultural defence argument

This argument, as its name implies, is largely negative in form. Non-national movies are seen as cultural or national threats, invaders, or occupiers. The language of colonialism or war seems unavoidable. Typically, the foreign film is seen to be presenting as normal different *mores*, a different outlook on life, different values and a different vision of the individual and society. Under various conditions, this normalisation of the foreign is claimed to be an influence for social change. Social change towards the foreign may be for good or for ill; if for ill, then it should be resisted. In American films, for example, wrongs are righted and justice served more often than not by a lone hero taking matters into his own hands; the authorities cannot be relied upon and, indeed, may be part of the problem. In European films the authorities can be relied on and impetuous heroes need to be curbed, especially from taking the law into their own hands. More generally, Wolfenstein and Leites (1950) argued that in European films authority figures, including parents and teachers, are respected, while in American films they are judged wanting. The amount and severity of violence in American as opposed to European films was often adversely remarked upon by proponents of national cinema. Britain of course was a special case, sharing a version of the spoken language with the United States. This led, in the talkie era, to persistent expressions of fear that 'slovenly' American speech habits would infect British children and adolescents (Russell 1951).

Undergirding the cultural defence argument are two very interesting but controversial presuppositions, one about influence, the other about the nature of *mores* and outlooks. The presupposition about influence is that the portrayal of difference in the context of entertainment may have an imitative effect. Associationist folk psychology and common sense take this to be obvious, yet it has not been easy to demonstrate experimentally. Children playing at cowboys and Indians need to be balanced against *mores* and outlooks absorbed from parents, peers, teachers and the like. It goes without saying that, *if* influence is clear and direct, and *if* the content of the influence is clearly objectionable, then protection is warranted. These are big ifs. It is easy to see why countries might fear the possible influence of violent content and prudently seek to protect against it. It is less easy to see quite what the objection might be to British people learning, i.e. choosing, to talk more like Americans. This brings us to the presupposition about the nature of *mores* and outlooks, the nature of culture.

Cultures differ: that is one of the main things about them. However, they also resemble one another. This is not surprising, since any given culture emerged historically from an earlier or neighbouring culture, just as languages have emerged and differentiated themselves from older languages, and borrowed from neighbouring ones. That Americans speak the way they do compared to Britons is often related to the particular way people in the British West Country spoke at the time of the Pilgrim Fathers. British pronunciation, idiom, spelling, vocabulary, are all deeply marked by the influence of French. This normal process of language change is not sensibly treated as a threat, invasion, or occupation. A language is enriched by its borrowings and additions. Language is at the core of what we mean by culture, so why are not open cultural borders enriching? Why, that is, are *mores*, outlooks and the rest of culture treated as having a purity that warrants preservation and a fragility that warrants protection? If languages are enriched by borrowing, perhaps cultures are enriched by exposure to other national cinemas. In France, which is very culturally proud, an argument for national cinema is precisely that it will display French culture to the world when screened abroad. If you see your culture as a civilising influence you can consistently resist reciprocity only by judging other cultures inferior. Thus we expose a further presupposition: many voices in the European national cinema debates despised America as a culture (Morpurgo 1951 is a mild expression).

What is at issue here, then, seems to be one of balance. American and other outland cinema might be acceptable in smaller doses, because informative and possibly culturally enriching. In large doses it is dangerous, capable of overwhelming the influence of local enculturation processes. In this form the argument is not valid. If people learned their culture from the movies the argument might work. But people learned their culture very well before movies, and they still learn it largely independently of movies (and of television). Since the media are only one bunch of the many paths by which culture is transmitted, and not the most influential bunch, there is reason to think that a non-stop diet of American movies (and television programmes) would not greatly alter the culture of receiver countries. Any alteration at all, however, can be taken as a corruption of identity. To avoid discussing the whole issue of identity and culture one can refer back to language. If people take their identity from language then they have somehow to accommodate themselves to the fact that languages are normally subject to influence and to change. Can cultural defence be any more successful than language-defence?

The argument from nation-building

This argument has then to be formulated carefully. Movies (and television) are not sufficient for nation-building. Indeed, they are not necessary, for the obvious reason that nation-building was accomplished long before the mass media were around. This allows that at most a national cinema can be a contribution to nation-building, neither necessary nor sufficient. If Kristin Thompson is correct, it is interesting that arguments for national cinema first arose not in emergent nations in the 1920s (Yugoslavia, Czechoslovakia, Poland) but somewhat earlier in the relatively stable western European nation-states: Scandinavia, the Low Countries, Britain, France, Germany and Italy. None of these countries was lacking in clear national identity or in a strong language and culture. What then was the building that nation-building was to achieve, and how did a national cinema contribute to that project?

One clue is that western European political elites were indeed faced with new problems, even in these stable countries. All were in the process of absorbing massive extensions of the franchise, eventually to every adult citizen of both sexes. The wishes and whims of this new mass electorate were unknown. The masses were thought to be particularly susceptible to the mass media, especially the press and the movies. This was taken to be a political fact. Traditional political groupings, which emerged from somewhat more restricted political participation, were faced with a new problem: how to bring the inchoate masses to accept the sense of nation and culture possessed by the elites? In my view this is the project of nation-building of the time, and it is less a case of building than of absorption. We might compare it to the absorption of immigrants: well-established nation-states with political systems adapted to nineteenth-century conditions found themselves with the task of socialising those with lesser stakes in the nation into a national consciousness. Recall how delighted the political elites were with the patriotism of the masses in the First World War (progressive intellectuals with internationalist aspirations were dismayed). Undoubtedly the unstated hope was that accepting traditional elite views of nation and culture would assist acceptance of the continuing leadership and dominance of the elite.

In the project of creating a universal sense of citizenship and culture the mass media were thought to be vital. Whatever one may think of this assimilationist project, it was a real one. All the countries keen on the project of national cinema were engaged in what one might characterise as the transition politics of government by the votes of all adult citizens. This was the era of mass society and mass politics. Both of these were served by the mass media. The political elites knew little of the masses or of the mass media (Hollins 1981). The masses read the tabloids, or equivalent, and watched movies. The elites read *The Times*, or local equivalent, and did not go to the movies. But these masses were internal immigrants; from second class to full citizenship, not foreigners to be absorbed – however strange their *mores* and outlook might be. This was also the era of radical parties hoping to recruit the masses (before or after their enfranchisement) to the side of a total transformation of the system. Thus it was not that imported movies, especially American movies, were going to damage robust *mores* and outlooks. Rather it was that they would at the very least not contribute to the socialisation of the emancipated masses, but at worst they would confuse those who were going through an important transformation. Thus I believe it was that advocates of national cinema with a simple commercial interest, and also those with a confused cultural defence message, could find a sympathetic audience in western European countries with a secure cultural or national identity. That identity was articulated by political, social and cultural elites who themselves felt threatened by the task of socialising the unknown and unreliable masses of their fellow citizens. These were citizens with little or no financial or property stake in the nation-state, in some cases no political sympathy with the elite consensus, and in not a few cases members of religious, linguistic, or ethnic minorities with an unhappy history in the land. They also included women, traditionally excluded from decision-making generally, and the subject of many male myths and superstitions about temperament and capacity.

National cinema as nation-builder, then, was a project to socialise newly emancipated populations away from radicalism and towards acceptance of the *mores*, outlook, and continuing hegemony of the governing and cultural elites. Movies were to be part of this undertaking, along with the mass-circulation press. Only thus can we explain the concern of a social, political and cultural mandarin such as Britain's Sir Philip Cunliffe-Lister in the strange project of building up a British film industry (Jarvie 1992).

Assessment of the arguments for national cinema

Armed with this analysis of the arguments for national cinema, we can take a hard look at its nationalist elements. Before proceeding to examine the arguments for national cinema in light of Gellner's theory of nationalism, a couple of cases provide food for thought. The immigrant nations of North America are striking for the weakness, indeed virtual absence, of calls for national cinema. The United States had almost no such calls. Historians have argued that the movies did in fact function to assimilate immigrants, but not as the outcome of policy. Canada has had weak calls, and the National Film Board was partly an outcome. But the mandate of nation-building and cultural defence has stressed more press, radio and, later, television. By contrast, western European nations, long after their nineteenth-century struggles for unification, are singularly prone to such arguments for national cinema, as in Great Britain, which emerged in its modern form in 1707. In these countries legislation and taxpayers' money were and are directed to support indigenous movies as something of a cultural 'good thing'.

Whether or not it is a good thing for each and every nation-state, and each and every nation not yet having a state (McArthur 1982), to have a national cinema, is not the sort of issue I want to discuss here. As I have suggested, in more cases than not, national cinema is touted as an alternative to, even a replacement for, American movies. Partial though I am to American movies, it is easy to agree that the world would be a culturally poorer place if there were no other kinds of movies. Judging by the investment American companies have made in theatres, studios and movies abroad there would seem to be a commercial benefit to diversity also. My aim is only to cast a sceptical eye on the way national cinema is construed.

The protectionist argument revisited

We concluded above that the protectionist argument does not support cultural versions of national cinema. Gellner's view of nationalism helps us revive this argument. Buried within the infant industry argument is a corollary about the acquisition and mastery of new technology. In Gellner's view modernisation entails, among other things, acquisition and mastery of technology. He uses the motor car as an example of a relatively opaque technology for most of its users, which, because of a friendly interface, can be almost universally mastered (Gellner 1983: 24–9). To be mastered a technology has to be acquired. On the way to acquiring television and computer technology, the movies are a way-station. (I include here not just the physical and electronic aspects of movies and television, but also content: ways to construct exposition, whether of fact or fiction; the interplay of sound and visuals; means of generating anticipation and excitement; and the like.)

Movies are part of the nuts and bolts kit of modern communication technologies, especially those for dramatising fictions, and for presenting news and information. In the overall project Gellner envisages nationalist regimes undertaking, namely being vehicles of modernisation, communication technology is vital. Modernity empowers partly by mastering a technology: that is, acquiring it, training the necessary support personnel, but also creating an interface so that its mastery can be widely diffused. Since many nationalisms centre on the identification of a culture, in turn centred on a language, centring the project at least to some extent in each (linguistic) nation makes good sense. The technology will need translation, adaptation and modification for each language and hence, obviously, for each culture. Not just manuals and instruction plates need to be translated, but local skills and prejudices, local traditions of communication, narrative and drama have to be accommodated if the technology is to be incorporated with ease.

Movies may be an early communications technology, and I can imagine that some would argue that it is a prime candidate for skipping – that phenomenon where technology-acquiring societies leap over the phylogenetic stages and acquire the latest ontogeny. That is not my view. It is my guess that cadres and audiences which have mastered the movies are better grounded for the later technologies. This dispute is particular, and scarcely affects the general argument. If movies are an indispensable, or at least very instructive, basic communications technology, then building a node of the industry in or near each distinct modernising cultural entity is warranted. In order to build that node, it is very possible that responsible authorities will need to protect the industry by fostering it. That may well be done under the rubric of building national cinema.

The cultural defence argument revisited

Applying Gellner's theory is more complicated here. Nationalism is a solution for societies struggling with the travails of modernisation. Thus colonial and postcolonial societies can envisage part of their task as fostering whatever is culturally indigenous against whatever they view as colonial imposition. Yet early and vociferous calls for national cinema came from countries that were not emerging from a colonial past: Britain, Germany, France, the Netherlands, the Scandinavian countries. Gellner's theory also postulates an inward flow of modernisation. Yet these countries have fair claim to be creators and exporters of the modern world.

A further wrinkle is that in some parts of the world nationalism preaches an ambivalent message about modernity. To the extent that modernity is associated with the West, that may be a reason for rejecting it. As a recent book on Egyptian cinema reminds us, elements in the Islamic world have in the past called for the prohibition of movies altogether (Shafik 1999). In a paper written thirty years ago, Joseph Agassi and I argued that the dream of many emerging nations was to acquire Western technology (modernity of one kind) while rejecting Westernisation (modernity of another kind) (Jarvie and Agassi 1969).

As far as movies go, the technology is western European and North American in origin and, mostly, in manufacture. The programme content and presentation is a joint product of Western traditions, mostly perfected in the United States (Tunstall 1977). Movies thus have an indelible Western stamp. In business terms the American industry colossus is universally seen as an invader whose activities invite cultural defence. If there is invasion it is a metaphorical one. International trade is not normally thought of as invasion, but as exchange. One of the problems for those who see invasion, is that there are large audiences which welcome the invaders with cash at the box office. Given that the United States has become the international symbol of modernity, we might see the readiness to consume American films, even among those with strong nationalist feelings, as part of the romance with modernity.

In the earlier discussion the question arose as to whether cultures are robust or fragile; their need for defence turns upon the answer. We will search in vain in Gellner's work for a clear statement of how he viewed the robustness of cultures. He argues that as the nature of work becomes ever more semantic, there is the need for cross-cultural, cross-language communication. This process he calls phonetic diversity without semantic diversity. Engineers may speak different languages, but they all drink Coca-Cola, wear jeans and operate Visual Basic. Gellner also says that nationalism achieved less than one might expect in Europe, except in one field, ideology (i.e. literature).

Gellner seems, then, to take the strength of cultures for granted. Perhaps, as a social anthropologist, he was loath to reify culture beyond necessity. Jewish opponents of assimilation, French-Canadian sovereigntists, Asian Confucianists, British writers deploring American modes of speech and generally sloppy habits, all of these take the view that a culture is fragile and needs maintenance. They are also Platonists in the sense that they see foreign cultural influence both as possibly damaging and as possibly corrupting. The same divide affects views of language. The strenuous attempts of French elites to protect the purity of the French language through legislation and the Académie are well known. By contrast, the English language is left to drift, grow and absorb, most of its dictionary-makers now accepting the view that it is their task to record, describe and analyse, but not to prescribe or defend.

Treating a language or a culture as needing defence or propping up smacks of insecurity. Insecurity suggests that the invader is attractive as well as damaging. There is then a grudging acknowledgement of the potency of American movies lying behind the fear of them as culturally damaging. American movies are remarkably good at what they do: delivering popular entertainment at an affordable price. Also, one might note, doing it without condescension, without excessive seriousness, and with much allusion, open and disguised, to story-telling traditions from all over the world.

Where does all this leave the cultural defence argument? It seems to me that one should ask, if a national culture really needs defence what are its problems? Second, a film culture is a very expensive matter, and many traditional cultures do not have a film culture. Those that have striven to have one should be encouraged to make a cost-benefit analysis. If the culture has problems, is introducing or sustaining a movie culture the best expenditure of tax money? Finally, of course, clear goals should be set. It is not so long ago that ambitious European governments dreamed of taking away from the United States a significant share of the international film market (Jarvie 1992). But that is a different ambition from cultural defence. Cultural defence would be achieved by sustaining a national film culture that makes popular films of local interest, such films as the international industry would not make because of their poor international prospects. But here again there is ambivalence. British films with George Formby, French films with Louis de Funes, French-Canadian films about the *famille Plouffe* on the whole do well at home, displease the critical elite, and do not travel well. Because they make money, most of these films would have been made without the presence of defence policies. Sometimes, as in the quintessentially British 'Carry On' series, they make quite a lot of money. Much money has been wasted on over-ambitious goals (Wood 1952).

The nation-building argument revisited

Gellner, as we have seen, sharply differentiates nation and culture. People are born into cultures; nations are created, indeed, invented. The rigid demand for monogamy of one nation/one culture is also in his view a modern invention. It faces the reality of multicultural empires and nations; and cultures or ethnicities without national status. By Gellner's lights, then, nations always have to be built.

In his more nuanced close-up view of Europe, Gellner distinguishes four time zones, moving west to east (Gellner 1994a: 112–18; Gellner 1994b: 29–31). On the Atlantic coast he notes the fact that culture and nation by and large do correspond in settled polities. He thus simplifies the divisions in the Low Countries and plays down Basque nationalism. Nevertheless, on the western littoral of Europe, as compared to the situation further east, the monogamous marriage of one nation to one culture makes sense. The next zone is, roughly, coincident with the erstwhile Holy Roman Empire. It is characterised by many cultures that only latterly gained states. Since nationalism made no sense of multicultural states, declaring them unnatural and unworkable, its devotees had to resort to elaborate boundary-drawing and ethnic cleansing. The story in zones three and four, still further east, need not concern us. Suffice it to say that many new nations had the project of nation-building. This does not explain why settled and satisfied nations (in the language of power politics) still clamoured for a film industry for purposes of nation-building.

Using ideas outlined earlier I can offer two arguments to the purpose. One is that nation-building had an internal as well as an external aspect. The internal aspect was the presence in most nations of social mobility, residual regional and ethnic identities, and other phenomena which did not easily fit the nationalist model of the unified nation and its monolithic culture (Weber 1979). In the same way that the BBC was thought likely to teach British regionals how to speak 'properly', many nation-states thought of the movies as one component in the building of a more harmonious nation-culture marriage. Movies were mass entertainment and might therefore have the wide reach such efforts required.

The external aspect was less the model of better unified states, but rather the invasive and disruptive threat of movies from a nation that did not have a single culture – the United States. The vitriolic descriptions of the United States by European intellectuals, especially German and French, are some indication of how it was feared. Ignoring the snobbery of such arguments, there was a danger: American movies did depict a society that was emphatically egalitarian in outlook, even if not in outcomes, democratic to a populist T, and manifestly multicultural. Through all the distortions of American films, no audience could imagine that the Wild West, the southern plantations, the urban jungles and the idyllic small towns, all depicted so deftly, amounted to a single culture. One reason, perhaps, why the United States was so often denounced as a 'mongrel' society. In other words, the actual nation-building project under way in many recipient countries was not consonant with the national and cultural model of the United States. The American model de-naturalises purificatory nationalisms and tends therefore to undermine them.

A harsher analysis might show that nation-building is also about nation-crushing. In light of *Peasants into Frenchmen* (Weber 1979) it is hard to deny that even the stable states of the western European littoral had to cope with internal divisions. Some of these were of class and sex, others were of region, culture, language, even nation. National, and, of course, metropolitan control of the mass media brought new hope that the centre could dominate the periphery, the elites the masses. To the extent that this underlies the nation-building argument for national cinema its appeal to progressives is puzzling (Hill 1992). Only the extra premise that the centre was modernising made it palatable – perhaps with the addition of the super-major premise that modernisation is not just good, but inevitable. Hence nation-building arguments need careful scrutiny.

Conclusion

Somewhat to my surprise, the arguments for national cinema have emerged from the challenge of Gellner's theory of nationalism rather better than expected. Of the three arguments we have surveyed, we can see that the protection argument survives Gellnerian scrutiny. The cultural defence argument reveals lack of cultural self-confidence in those who use it; this is self-defeating. The nation-building argument is by far the most disreputable, both in its inward-looking form, and in its outward-looking form. In both, proponents are looking to movies to create a particular kind of nation–culture marriage, one which homogenises internal differences, and which rejects American models that offer diversity controlled by citizenship and law.

Much of our discussion has inevitably been backward-looking because policy interest has shifted from movies to TV. Calls for national cinema should naturally come, under all three arguments, from conservatives of various stripes. What is surprising is how they sometimes come from the progressive left. The official internationalism of the left is translated into multiculturalism and the claim is made that there is no reason why a national cinema should not acknowledge internal differences and tensions. Perhaps this is true. But the three arguments we have reviewed, and they are the main ones, scarcely envisage very much difference or tension, otherwise the infant industry will fragment its audience, the culture will not defend itself, and the project of nation-building will be subverted.

Notes

1 There are of course exceptions: ambivalence toward French cinema was expressed in both Québec and Belgium.
2 I have in mind arguments that are simply anti-American; or that deplore the Jewish presence in the movie industry.

Bibliography

Anderson, B. (1983) *Imagined Communities: Reflections on the Origins and Spread of Nationalism*, London: Verso.

Anon. (1999) 'Editorial: How British Is It?', *Sight and Sound* 9, 3: 3.

Gellner, E. (1983) *Nations and Nationalism*, Oxford: Blackwell.

—— (1994a) *Conditions of Liberty*, London: Hamish Hamilton.

—— (1994b) *Encounters with Nationalism*, Oxford: Blackwell.

—— (1997) *Nationalism*, London: Weidenfeld.

Grazia, V. de (1989) 'Mass Culture and Sovereignty: The American Challenge to European Cinemas, 1920–1960', *Journal of Modern History* 61: 53–87.

Higson, A. (1995) *Waving the Flag: Constructing National Cinema in Britain*, Oxford: Clarendon Press.

Hill, J. (1992) 'The Issue of National Cinema and British Film Production', in D. Petrie (ed.).

Hollins, T.J. (1981) 'The Conservative Party and Film Policy Between the Wars', *English Historical Review* 95: 359–69.

Irwin, R. (1999) 'In the Heart of Cairo-Babylon', *Times Literary Supplement* 5, 15, 14 May: 10.

Jarvie, I. (1992) *Hollywood's Overseas Campaign: The North Atlantic Movie Trade, 1920–1950*, New York: Cambridge University Press.

Jarvie, I. and Agassi, J. (1969) 'A Study in Westernization', in I.C. Jarvie and J. Agassi (eds), *Hong Kong: A Society in Transition*, London: Routledge.

Kedourie, E. (1960) *Nationalism*, Oxford: Blackwell.

McArthur, C. (ed.) (1982) *Scotch Reels: Scotland in Film and Television*, London: BFI.

Morpurgo, J.E. (1951) 'Hollywood: America's Voice', in B. Russell *et al.* (eds).

Mount, F. (1999) 'Reinventing the Union: Must Scottish Devolution Lead to Separatism?', *Times Literary Supplement* 5, 14, 7 May: 28.

Petrie, D. (ed.) (1992) *New Questions of British Cinema*, London: BFI.

Russell, B. (1951) 'The Political and Cultural Influence', in B. Russell *et al.* (eds).

Russell, B., Lehmann, J., O'Fadain, S., Morpurgo, M., Cooper, M. and Miller, P. (eds) (1951) *The Impact of America on European Culture*, Boston, MA: Beacon.

Shafik, V. (1999) *Arab Cinema*, Cairo: American University in Cairo.

Thompson, K. (1996) 'Nation, National Identity and the International Cinema', *Film History* 8: 259–60.

Tunstall, J. (1977) *The Media Are American*, London: Constable.

Weber, E. (1979) *Peasants into Frenchmen: The Modernization of Rural France, 1870–1914*, London: Chatto.

Wolfenstein, M. and Leites, N. (1950) *Movies: A Psychological Study*, Glencoe, IL: Free Press.

Wood, A. (1952) *Mr. Rank*, London: Hodder and Stoughton.

6

FRAMING NATIONAL CINEMAS

Susan Hayward

In this chapter I want to address a series of questions which the concept 'national cinema' raises and to argue the case that debates around what is national cinema are still extremely important ones to be having, as indeed is the production itself of a national cinema (whatever that might happen to mean). I should make the point too that, as general editor of the National Cinema Series for Routledge (since 1989), I am acutely aware that *the* national of cinemas has been quite uppermost in my mind for over ten years now; and I am also acutely aware that there are no easy definitions – nor do I seek to establish any. What I do bear in mind, however, is Terry Eagleton's statement that 'To wish class or nation away ... is to play straight into the hands of the oppressor' (1990: 23).

In the light of the above comments, the questions I am raising are: What is the value of a 'national' cinema? What needs does it fulfil? How can we think in terms of framing or conceptualising it? What function does it serve? And, why is it still extremely important to be talking about it?

Introduction: nation and culture

Clearly, a starting point is to turn to the debates around the key concepts of nation, national identity(ies), nationalism and culture as ways to help clarify some issues in relation to national cinema and to enable us to pose other questions or to question differently what is meant by national cinema. And my introductory comments, which will be reasonably brief, are going to pull on the work of Ernest Gellner, Benedict Anderson, Anthony Smith, Patrick Hall and Thomas Erikson – because between them we can come up with a first set of useful rubrics (or key words) for leading our discussion of framing national cinemas. These key words which I have established in relation to the concept of nation constitute a neat triumvirate: that of *history-masquerade-symbolism*. Let me lay these before you and try to explain what I mean.

Gellner (1983: 55–6) argues that nationalism invents nations where they do not exist and not the other way round. In other words, to quote Smith, 'nationalism is an ideological movement for the attainment and maintenance of (the) unity and identity of a human population sharing an historic territory' (1996:

359). Both Gellner and Anderson (1991) stress that nations are ideological constructions seeking to forge a link between a self-defined cultural group and the state, creating *abstract* or *imagined* communities that we loosely refer to as 'the nation' or indeed 'the nation-state' and which get passed off as 'natural', although of course they are in fact not natural. It holds then that national identities are *also* constructions and equally get passed off as 'natural'. As such, then, they too are not 'natural', and to identify culture with a particular identity is to *reify* a one-to-one relationship. As Erikson (1993: 103) says, nationalism reifies culture in the sense that it enables people to talk about their culture as though it were a constant and also distinctive, but it isn't. Nationalism leads us to think in terms of bounded cultural objects. That is, cultural artefacts are *made* (in the French sense of *fabriqué* [fabricated] and *obligé* [obliged]) to represent a nation, to function as evidence of the nation's distinctiveness. And the question that immediately pops into my mind is: 'is the cuckoo clock as intrinsically Swiss as Orson Welles would have us believe?'.

The question is of course why there is this need to reify culture in such a way? Why is there the need to create a nation, a social cultural community? And lastly why is nation hyphenated to state? A first answer is the importance of wholeness, of belongingness. As Erikson says: 'an important aim of nationalist ideology is to ... *recreate* a sentiment of wholeness and continuity with the past to transcend that alienation or rupture between individual and society that *modernity* brought about' (1993: 105). Here modernity refers broadly to the Industrial Revolution and subsequent urbanisation of citizenry/subjects and the loss of kinship and family. In other words, nation comes to stand for/in for lost issues/concepts/realities of kinship and family obligations. This is why, argues Erikson (ibid.: 108), threats to the nation get read as issues of kinship and family. The nation becomes a collective individual that one dies for (the father- or more particularly and pertinently, the motherland). Or again, the nation is a collective (female) individual that suffers rape at the hands of the enemy. Thus a closed, self-referential, even vicious circle gets established whereby one concept feeds the other: threat to nation leads to (manifestations of) kinship, and kinship leads to nationalist discourses (in the name of the mother nation etc.) – i.e., a nationalism which in turn engenders the notion of nation. Each concept *masquerades* as a grounded reality, disguising the fact that, as such, these are imagined abstractions.

This closed discursive circle nonetheless does the trick: it bounds the notion of nation to the individual and has an embodied ideal (the maternal body). There are other boundings at play however, between nation and state. The state is a legal and political concept, and is not a community. The nation for its part is defined as a social cultural community and yet it is one that must comply with the state. Nationalist discourses around culture work to forge the link – the hyphen – between nation and state. Nationalist discourses act then to make the practice of the state as 'natural' as the concept of nation: 'In the name of the nation, the state may govern'. By binding the concept of nation to state (literally by hyphenating it), the state has legitimate agency *over* and *of* the nation. Another closed, self-referential circle is born, therefore: the state is founded in the nation and the nation is constituted as the state. As Erikson says: 'the distinguishing mark of nationalism is by definition its *relationship* to the state. A nationalist holds that political *boundaries* should be coterminous with *cultural* boundaries' (ibid.: 6, emphasis added). And of course the standardisation of culture is one very important way of forming the nation-state, of founding cultural boundaries that then become political boundaries. The obvious example of this is education, but one cannot underestimate the importance of visual and print media and their role in disseminating this relationship between nation and state – a role which cinema necessarily shares.

A third very important point is how is this abstract and therefore potentially unstable concept of nation secured? Rather than secured, we would say that it becomes consecrated as a concept by its invocation as a historical subject. As Smith (1996: 375) says, nationalisms have an investment in the past (why for example were national costumes invented? what do they mean?). Nationalisms are forged in part in an apprehension (a seizing and remodelling) of the past. Nationalisms make use of the past, go back to 'ancestral' traditions or indeed *invent* them. In this regard, says Smith, nations are a product of a territorialisation of memory. Memory here stands for collective memory, a shared culture, shared memories of a collective past. All well and bad/so far so clear. But memory also means amnesia and, as Smith goes on to say, 'the importance of national amnesia and getting one's own history *wrong* (is essential) for the maintenance of national solidarity' (ibid.: 382). We need only think all too briefly of the post-occupation period in France to realise the self-serving purpose and necessity of national amnesia.

Nationalism's investment in history to create its nation and its identity means that the modern nation is built on shared memories of some past or pasts that can mobilise and unite its members. Memory is then very much bound to the notion of place, to a homeland and therefore to identity. Memory is, as Smith says, 'crucial to identity. In fact one might almost say: no memory, no identity; no identity, no nation' (ibid.: 383). What happens then to a nation newly emerging from colonialism, postcolonialism or post-apartheid? To a nation – in other words – that has suffered erasure of its own collective memory? This is a point I shall be raising in the last section of this chapter.

History then is a crucial player in this construction of a nation. But, and this is the point, viewed in this context the nation is constructed as a historical subject from nationalist discursive practices. Now, according to Hegel's definition of history, history becomes knowledge of itself – both subject and object – and *not* the subject of knowledge. In Hegelian terms, history is then very self-regarding/self-reflexive. Another closed-circle. As a historical subject, the nation becomes itself a self-regarding concept/object, displaying a narcissism that conceals what really is at stake, namely *practices* of power and knowledge (the real function of the (nation-) state). But says Patrick Hall, in his clever and persuasive essay on nationalism and historicity, the nation is not a 'historical subject, but instead a social relation of power and knowledge'. What has happened, he argues, is that this relation has 'become *represented* as a discursive régime where the nation *appears* to be the historical subject' (1997: 3, emphasis added). In other words, the concept of nation is disguised, masquerades as an abstract 'out-there-ness' while (also already) being a set of 'concrete practices of *power and knowledge*' (and I am reminded here of parallels we could establish with mainstream cinema and the construction of the feminine as masquerade). Hall (ibid.: 5) goes on to say that by disguising the nation as a historical subject (to disguise what it really does) nationalist discourses mobilise the nation into 'a surrogate religion of modern society'. To this effect 'nation' both masquerades and has symbolic value – it is represented as and acts as the precise opposite of what it truly is: (which is) a 'fictional', one might say pathological, construction to ease the fear of alienation. But as Terry Eagleton (1990: 30–1) suggests, nationalism involves an impossible irony: the fact that it is itself a form of alienation, that of individual life into collective anonymity.

Debates around national cinemas

It will be fairly self-evident that in the light of the above comments there will always be problems in defining 'national' cinema. Yet it is a fruitful, albeit as Tom O'Regan (1996: 2) puts it, *messy affair*. In defining/framing a national cinema, or is it *the* national of a cinema, what is instructive are the discourses mobilised to do so – what they include and exclude; *how* they choose to frame matters; the assumptions and presuppositions they make. These framings – be they a matter of mappings/typologies, be they structuralist, political or cultural – all tend to *set* the very territory of the nation *and* artefact, and the nation *as* artefact. In other words, they assume a one-to-one relationship between 'cultural artefact' – 'cultural identity' – 'nation/national identity': in other words, the artefact 'film' speaks of/for/as the nation. While of course this is in part true, there are significant problems with this set of assumptions, which I'll come to in a minute. A second set of problems is that these discourses/framings tend to assume/infer that a nation is in place as it moves through history in its own peculiar development. Europe warns us that this is an unstable practice (and I am reminded here of the sigh of relief from the author, who originally was to write the Soviet national cinema book, when the Soviet Union dissolved – 'now', he declared, 'I need only write the *Russian* National Cinema book'). Finally these discourses, at least in the West, ineluctably frame the 'national' against the dominance of Hollywood – which is useful and not useful – because it reduces the idea of a national cinema to economies of scale and therefore to one concept of *value*: namely, economic wellbeing. It also reduces the ideology of national cinema to a set of binaries.

To come back to these issues, the territorialisation of the cultural artefact, the cinema, as 'national bounded cultural artefact' produces a first set of problems.

This territorialisation makes cinema into a historical subject. It stands for the nation – it is a means by which the nation can represent itself to itself (*qua* subject) and to its subjects (as object). This produces a narcissistic, self-reflexive and self-fulfilling view of national cinema, one in which the historical subject/object becomes knowledge of itself and not the subject of knowledge. Writing a national cinema as a territorialised historical subject runs the risk then of colluding with the idea of (re)producing the meaning (a history) of the nation, of setting false boundaries that limit one's understanding of what really might be occurring in terms of practices of power and knowledge (these are points I will develop in a moment). And this ties in with the other issue which concerns the concept of value and the ideology of national cinema as a set of binaries which start from the primary one of Hollywood/other. The problem I am hinting at here is the risk we run of providing an essentialist view of national cinemas. Thus when Dudley Andrew states that 'from the standpoint of economies, there is but one viable national cinema – Hollywood – and the world is its nation' (1995: 54) and when *Le Monde* reiterates this idea by declaring that 'there is no European cinema only American cinema' (6 November 1996), we must be very chary of what they are saying because – intentionally or not – such statements feed into the essentialist approach to national cinema.

Tom O'Regan's (1996) discussion of Australian national cinema helps us see where we might better go in our attempts at framing national cinema – it is a first set of steps in an alternative direction. There are no claims that these are the only ones, but they do help move the debate along as indeed will others which I will come to in my fourth and final section.

Having established a triangular formation: film/nation/production-company as the praxis for a national cinema, O'Regan (ibid.: 45) argues that national cinemas are a series of sets of relations between national film texts, national and international film industries, and the films' and industries' socio-political and cultural contexts. This allows us to distinguish between cinemas in domestic and international circulation. It also allows us to see a national cinema as being 'in conversation' with Hollywood and other national cinemas (i.e., Hollywood is not the only referent) (O'Regan 1996: 115). Finally, it affords us the means to see how these national cinemas carve out a space (economic/market/audience spaces) locally and internationally for themselves in the face of the dominant international cinema, Hollywood. That is the first point. Second, we are also talking here of the need for an interdisciplinary approach when dealing with national cinemas, which is something that is now reasonably commonly practised in film studies. Thus what gets taken into account, in this context, is cinema in relation to its economic industrial base, but also in relation to film and criticism, film history, cultural studies and film, cultural policies and film, political culture and film. But, as O'Regan points out we are really in fact practising national cinema analysis rather than answering the question 'what is national cinema?' (ibid.: 334).

However, a major step forward is forged when we bring these two conceptual approaches together: the relational and the interdisciplinary. In this double parametric context, as O'Regan explains, national cinema becomes an object of knowledge (ibid.: 27) and a problem of knowledge (ibid.: 261–362) :

- First as an *object of knowledge*: that is, cinema becomes a domain in which different knowledges about national cinema are produced (from production to reception) and are brought into relation.
- Second, national cinema becomes/manifests itself as a *problem of knowledge*: that is, by viewing cinema in a relational and interdisciplinary context it does not allow for a 'naturalising' of the concept of national cinema but rather it causes a calling of things into question and in so doing generates problems in three areas, the critical, the political and policy-wise.

Thus questions arise that generate problems of knowledge.

- Critically, these questions bring us to ask is there such a thing as national cinema and what purpose does it fulfil?
- Politically, what gets raised are questions of exclusion/inclusion (race, gender, age and so on).
- Policy-wise, here we ask questions about what might be the effects of public and private sector strategies (i.e., government/state, but also supranational strategies (as in the European Union) versus/alongside the private sector strategies of film and independent TV industries).

In other words, O'Regan suggests that rather than talk about nationalism and national cinema as exclusive terms we should seek to investigate the way in which society as a national whole is problematised and the kind of nation that has been projected *through* such problematisation. In this regard we can begin to see cinema as an effect of and as affecting that problematisation.

So far then what this seems to help us do is to get away from 'historicising the *subject*' and to see emerging (ideas of) the practices of power and knowledge (the very thing that nationalisms in their discursivity attempt to conceal). This approach, the one suggested by O'Regan, goes against the narcissistic notion of self-reflexivity of which historicity is a central practice. And it does more than expose the 'masquerading' practices of the nation as a categorical concept. Yes, it shows how the nation is imagined (as subject and object in and of itself) and how it shapes objects and subjects in contemporary social practice of which cinema is one – all of this exposing of practices is already a good thing. But this approach also carves out spaces that allow us to *revalue* the concept of national cinema. It makes it possible to reterritorialise the nation (to rewrite Paul Virilio, echoing Deleuze perhaps) not as bounded, demarcated and distinctive but as one within which boundaries constantly criss-cross both haphazardly and *unhaphazardly*. Let us now pursue this idea.

SUSAN HAYWARD

Re-evaluating/revaluing the concept and the value of national cinema

*Or: why Marianne Jean-Baptiste did not go to Cannes (May 1997) and
David Thewlis did as part of Britain's special envoy of the new, young
and aspiring faces of Britain's actors (as Thewlis himself pointed out in
an interview he is neither young nor new ... !)*

Paul Virilio speaks of boundaries no longer surrounding and demarcating a
territory, but of boundaries criss-crossing inside every territory (1991: 9–27).
Homi Bhabha talks of 'national' cultures increasingly being produced from the
perspective of disenfranchised minorities (1990: 303–19). Undeniably in non-
Western nations and cultures Bhabha's comments are strongly borne out by
practice. But there is now evidence of this in Western cultures and nations as
well, in that there has been a foregrounding of the margins of the nation-space
of which so-called marginal-cinema is but one manifestation. To quote Kristeva,
there has been a 'demassification of the problematic of difference' (1986: 209),
a questioning of the legitimacy of the state-representing-the-nation, challenges
to nationalist discourses which represent the nation as one. How is this so, how
did it come about? Well there are two partial answers which I'd like to put
forward. First, the paradox of globalisation and the concomitant valuation of
the local – this has meant that the parochial and ultimately/eventually the
periphery find a new relevance and importance within discourses of nationalism.
We look to signal our difference from other nations and in so doing look to our
own sets of differences. However, and here is the problem, it is in that set of
differences that we seek to forge our national identity as one: calling it multicultural (i.e. different but as one) whereas in fact it is patently pluricultural (i.e.
segregated cultures) as those on the margins, occupying what Bhabha terms (re-
writing Fanon) the place of 'cultural undecidability' (1990: 304), never cease to
make evident. In fact what is presently going on in Europe (particularly within
the European Union in terms of nationalist discourses) is very revelatory.
European nations have become, more evidently than ever before, territories of
struggles between competing subject positions, narratives and voices, which
nationalist discourses attempt to win either by appropriating the diverse cultures
and placing them under some sort of illusionist rainbow coalition and integrated whole, or by some vain attempt to wipe out the traces of these struggles
(although not of Europe, the cultural and national history of South Africa is
extremely relevant in this context).

A second point that needs to be made about the 'enfranchisement' of
voices/cultures (that Virilio, Bhabha and Kristeva speak of) is that it is not just
the effect of globalisation, though that has played a significant role. It is also an
effect of an earlier set of events – the effect of the post 1960s in the West, the
1960s revolt against the lack of tolerance of difference that prevailed before. If
we look at the pre-1960s discourses it is clear what a profound effect the

1960s had nations-wide and internationally. The social revolution of the 1960s created gaps and legitimate spaces for diversification and the possibility of *multi*culturalism – gaps which are constantly being renegotiated (despite the attempts in the UK under Thatcherism to wipe out the effect of the 1960s). And the importance of the role of cultural studies within this revolution must not be underestimated in its making visible the 'popular' and in turn the multiplicity of points of differentiation. The multiplication of points of differentiation has come to mean an expansion of points of contact in the context of palpable diversity: i.e. race, class, age, sexuality and/or gender. In other words, the political and the sexed body have become palpably visibilised. So too has the body of other excluded persons. The ailing body.

What we can make of this enfranchisement and visibilisation is that, within a limited sphere of cultural expression at least, identity co-existing with difference(s) has become a reality – the very thing that nationalisms seek to deny. The paradox of a national cinema becomes clear in that henceforth it will always – in its forming – go against the underlying principles of nationalism and be at cross-purposes with the originating idea of the *nation* as a unified identity.

But, as is clear from my earlier remarks on nationalisms, this is not yet a widely enough practised reality. Not yet. Nations are still power-related concrete practices even though they disguise themselves as abstract historicised subject-objects (nineteen years of Thatcherism prove how alive this political discursive masquerading still is). In fact, the picture is complex because nations are both things at once – at the same time – thus it is hard to make a distinction between what nations really are and what they are masquerading as. And so one must beware of invoking an 'alternative' form of essentialism as a solution since, in the final analysis, it merely mirrors the practice of dominant ideology. It is not enough to say that this invocation is part of a strategy of 'demystifying' concepts and practices that rule our life, valuable though that is. And in a moment I shall attempt to outline some ways in which we can think anew the concept of nation, nationalism, and the framing of national cinema. But before we get there I need to put in one more piece of the puzzle.

It is important to recall, as Tom O'Regan (1996: 305) does, that many nations are settler nations which have practised various tactics of annihilation of the indigenous societies. Many of these nation-states are ones that have reproduced in the settler nation Europe and European nationalism with its ultimately profoundly anti-humanist principles (starting with racist, colonialist atrocities). And it is important to recall also that most nations (whether self-evidently settler-nations or not) practice some form of apartheid or another, legitimated or not (hence the title of this section and its reference to Marianne Jean-Baptiste). And this practising of apartheid includes nations that have themselves been victims of colonialisation or apartheid. So we are always in the presence of the complex issue of *exclusion/inclusion* – there is always an investment in repressing history/memory, of evacuating the 'colonised's' culture as aberrant, as abject. As Edward Saïd says, imperialism/colonialism is an act of geographical violence disguised as humanism; it is a form of making the colonised country into images of what has been left behind (1990: 77). What we are saying then is that these practices occur not just between nation and colonised country but they also happen within a nation-state. And the role of culture (within the nation-state as well as the colonised/settler nations), the role of national culture is (still) to suppress political conflict and disguise it as imagination – *image/nation* – a function that is so clearly manifest in the very problematic issue and conceptualisation of national cinema. For, to rewrite Judith Butler (1993), there is still a cinema that matters and one that doesn't. However, it is when the latter penetrates into the material boundaries of the former (material in all the senses of the word: physical, economic, etc.) that we jubilate because it does cause fissures that allow for changes. We witness the effect of the 'occult instability' of the peripherals (to quote Fanon 1990: 83).

Towards a framing of national cinemas

Let us now look at this question of fissuring and see what it tells us in the context of national cinemas. I'm very much tempted to subtitle these remarks: *cinema's pathology and visual culture – or what's Fanon got to do with it?*

If we start from the premise that Hollywood's hegemony can be viewed as a nationalism (not necessarily a new idea), then we can start to look at some of the issues of power and knowledge (which nationalism seeks to hide) in a very interesting and destabilising way. In other words, we can make our own 'techniques of trouble' (to re-write Butler 1990: 34) – that is, pose questions provocatively (and in turn ensure that these questions filter on through to question other national cinema practices).

What I am proposing to do here is to come back to the earlier essentialist and binaried reading of national cinemas (as Hollywood/other which sets in motion a chain of other binaries – e.g. Europe/other) and to rethink it both in the light of the above framings and focusings and through a Fanonian optic. And I want to speak first in terms of what conceptualising Hollywood's hegemony as a form of *para-nationalism* might produce, *para* in the triple Greek sense of *near-beyond-defective/abnormal*. Near and beyond are I think quite self-evident, the latter 'defective-abnormal' is less so and that is the one that will be my main focus. And it is here that I invoke Fanon and his reading of colonialism and indeed alienation and madness (1990: 201–50). Hollywood has of course effected forms of colonialism, the first of which is economic. Apart from France, where Hollywood 'only' takes around 60 per cent of the market, American film-products garner 80 per cent (plus) of the western European film market. The second form of colonialism is cultural (dress-codes, eating practices, American look-alike movies and TV programmes, etc. – known hostilely as 'Cocacolonisation'). According to Fanon, colonialism (which is a practice of nationalism) is a narcissistic practice – an imposing on the colonised 'other' of colonialist discourses and images: the nation 'colonises' itself on to (in-to?) the colonised body. Economically speaking at least, as we have just stated, the United States is not exempt from this colonising practice of imposing its own images and discourses. And its para-nationalist cinema (Hollywood) makes this abundantly clear even to the point that the 'colonised' seek to imitate the Hollywood product (the clones clone!).

However (but/also) this self-reflexivity within colonialism produces all sorts of blindnesses (race, gender blindness, etc.) which is of course a blindness (a visual defectiveness) that initiates from within nationalism. A prime example of this blindness – as Fanon (1996:10) makes clear through his post-Freudian statement 'what does the black man want?' – is blindness to the fact that sex and gender and race are inextricably linked to and involved in nationalism and therefore colonialism (something which the Senegalese film-maker Diop Mambéty addresses right up front in his film *Hyènes*, 1992). Furthermore, this self-reflexivity/narcissism produces pathologies (the abnormal). But this does not just take the form of pathologising the culture of the 'other' as 'less-than' (to the point of erasure, as could be argued is the case for South Africa and its cinema – 'no memory, no identity, no identity, no nation'). It also takes the form of an internal set of pathologies which in Hollywood occur around its own industrial practices, for example, its current 'the budget is all' approach whereby the production costs signify as *more* than the actual product (e.g., 'go and see this film because it cost x billion $'). Cost, not the actual film product is what matters. In this pathology, capitalistic pathology, money is the sign and referent all rolled into one. These internal pathologies also revolve around Hollywood's own particular sets of representations. For example, Hollywood's focus on white masculinity springs to mind and the consequent hystericisation of 'otherness' within its own film culture. Thus we think of the modernisation of white masculinity in the 1930s and early 1940s (heroic and complex characterisation), the threat to it in the 1940s and 1950s (*film noir*), the reconstruction of it in the light of the 1960s and 1970s into new masculinities, and of course now the post-modernisation and virtualisation of white masculinity/ies over the past two decades – as in Forrest Gump (a.k.a. Tom Hanks), Sylvester Stallone, Arnold Schwarzenegger. Representations which in *this* context lead (unintentionally as far as nationalist discursivity is concerned) to a performance, a display of an erotics of nationalism through the male body that reflects the very pathologies these sets of representations-as-a-discourse-of-nationalism seek to deny.

The way in which the body is a site of performance in film displays yet further contradictions within the concept/conceptualisation of 'nation' as one and indivisible. The nation pretends to be gender-neutral (in that it purports to dissolve difference) and yet the woman's body is closely aligned/identified with nationalist discourses. We fight and die for our mother-nation; when we leave we return to our mother-nation; the colonised referred to the colonising country as mother-country. When 'she' is invaded by the enemy, she is 'raped'. However, as Mary Layoun says (in a wonderful collection of essays entitled *Scattered Hegemonies*) 'the metaphoric equation of inviolable woman and inviolable motherland is as unsurprising as it is fearfully problematic' (1994: 65). The symbolic equation mobilised by nationalist discourses goes as follows:

> violated motherland = violated woman
> invasion by the enemy = rape of the mother-land/woman
> rape = occupation of the mother-body by the enemy
> occupation = reproduction of the enemy within the mother-body

It is inconceivable (para-logic is the term Mary Layoun uses) within nationalist discourses that the woman might choose to sleep with the enemy. So it is not diffi-cult to see that and why nationalist discourses do militate for a gendered proscription of agency and power (so that, implicitly, agency becomes naturalised as male), and that they use the very real concept of rape in an abstract (but also extremely concrete) way to keep that proscription in place. Rape, then, becomes one way of eroticising the nation's plight in male-driven narratives that have appropriated the female body. But that isn't all. In these male-driven narratives, the female body by extension becomes the site of life and death of a nation, the rise and fall of a nation. And, by way of an example, I am thinking here of Jean Stelli's film *Le voile bleu* (1942) – a sado-masochistic fantasy based in natalist discourses. In Stelli's film the female body is appropriated by nationalist discourses that begin with the representation of the female/mother-body as the site of life and death. To give the context: the female protagonist's hero-husband has just been killed in the war, and this precipitates her prematurely giving birth to a son, who then dies. In turn, her body (and this is the core of the narrative) becomes the site for natalist discourses – cruel post-natalist discourses one might add – as in: 'there are lots more babies out there who need mothering' which is what the nurse declares to the heroine, upon which she embarks on a self-sacrificing life as nanny/-*maman*/proto-mother to the many (to the nation-state's need of motherhood).

Erotics is linked to image and display of the body and, therefore, to perfor-mance. And it is tempting here to agree with Bruce Brasell that 'all nationalism is performative' (which it is if we take nationalism as 'enunciation') (1995: 30). But while I agree that that is part of it, I think we can also say more. And this brings me to the question of national culture. National culture is a product of nationalist discourses and is based in the principle of representation and (of course) repression. Before getting there, however, let us start with the concept of nation first. The concept of nation as constructed by nationalist discourses is one that is in constant denial. It is:

- not concrete but abstract
- not based in amnesia but memory/history
- not gendered but gender-neutral
- not anti-humanist but enlightened
- not free and unbounded but delineated, fixed, unambiguous
- not divided, scattered, fragmented but united

The fact that these discursive concepts of the nation are based in a 'fictional' representation of the nation does not mean that they do not have real effects. Indeed we have seen how it is that the nation masquerades as these, the concepts create a reality which then acts upon actors' (those living the nation, therefore our) perceptions and behaviour. And it is here, as we shall see, paradoxically that there is the glimmer of hope, the fissuring moment. Because the fact that nations are invented and fictional means that they can be re-defined and re-appropriated by actors – in other words, a re-possessing of the nation by excluded groups is possible. And it is that very act of re-possession and re-definition that is liberating and empowering not only because it claims a geo-social, geo-political and geo-psychological space but also because it shows ineluctably *that* and *how* there is something wrong with the hegemonic discursive practice of defining the nation exclusively and essentially as 'in constant denial'.

Before developing that point, however, let us first return to the symbolic value of the female body within nationalist discourses as a way of discussing the *mise-en-scène* of national culture. We talked about the symbolic value of the female body as a means of playing out national insecurities (rape, natalist discourses, etc.). This symbolism disguises (albeit badly) real questions of gendered agency and power. Within the shifting discourses of nationalism, the image of woman shifts accordingly and serves the image of the nation-state (in different but analogous ways to the masculine body as evoked before; analogous because the body serves nationalist discourses; different, because agency and power are invested in the male not the female body). Thus the maternal body of the 1940s cinema in France might well give way to the liberated female body of the 1950s/1960s. However, the image of the liberated woman serves the nation-state just as much as the maternal one. In the first, the display of the woman's maternal body functions as a *mise-en-scène* for the nation's concern about demographic decline. In the latter, the liberated female body serves the nation's image as modern and not reactionary. The symbolic use of the female body is enough to tell us that nationalist discourses are invested in producing a national identity that is dialectically based in the principle of 'lack', and that national culture in this regard has as its starting (but disguised/absent) point: denial, deficiency/lacking and repression. In much the same way as nationalisms invent nations where they do not exist, national culture does not represent what is there but asserts what is imagined to be there: a homogenised fixed common culture. National culture then participates in the practice of repression which is in itself an act or form of alienation (starting with the fact that it alienates what it cannot tolerate) – it creates a common culture in which the individual is also alienated.

We can now begin to see how in relation to the idea of national cinemas, Hollywood's *para*-nationalism is pathologic – '*para*' in the sense of its internal nationalist discursive practices ('near'), '*para*' in the sense of its proto-colonialist practices ('beyond'). '*Para*' in the sense that, both near and beyond, its nationalism is abnormal and defective – in the final analysis, it reflects to itself its own strategies of repression and alienation at the same time as it attempts desperately not to do so. It is unwittingly counter-narcissistic – it exposes its own ideological practices. And this is an important point to make because, as Fanon so rightly points out, power and knowledge within colonialist practices (which as we recall function narcissistically) are not generally visible *except* when there is the visibility of difference (i.e. marked by colour/race) (1990: 29–30). To which I would add the audibility of difference. Language and language of the body. And Hollywood's ability only to reflect itself to itself, to repeat its discourses inter- and extra-nationally, is both its strength and its weakness (strength as in economically predatory, weakness as in endlessly self-reflexive). It denies and senses its own alienation – it repeats its own 'success formulas' and buys up, to remake (American-style), the successes of other national cinemas. This major film production industry is then the biggest recycling dream factory in the West.

'So what?' you might ask, 'does this tell us about framing national cinemas?'. Implicit in what I have been saying about the maternal body as occupied/colonised is the notion that the colonising culture will insert itself into the indigenous cultural body and be reproduced by 'her' – in short cultural rape. But also cultural erasure ('no memory, no identity, no nation'). Nothing however stays still. In every colonialism a post-colonialism is implicit. And this brings me back to considerations of Fanon and his discussion of the role of the native poet and the production of national culture (Fanon 1990: 166–99). Because it is here that the concept of national cinemas reveals its importance.

For my purposes, I shall read the term native poet as also native poet-film-maker. According to Fanon, in the evolution from colonialism to postcolonialism there are three moments: pre-liberation, liberation and post-liberation. During the colonised period, the native poet-film-maker experiences a double sense of alienation: alienation *from* his/her own society and *within* that of the settler nation. Alienation, we recall, is doubly experienced by the colonising nation. But the latter's alienation (that of the colonialist) is the result of denial and repression of 'otherness/difference'. The former's (the colonised) alienation results from exclusion as 'other/different'. The essentialised alienation of the one is not the same as the existential one of the other – and that also is why change can occur and nationalisms ultimately can function differently. As indeed Fanon goes on to make clear. The native poet-film-maker must progress, argues Fanon, from the pre-liberation moment of denouncing his (I add her) oppressor to the liberation moment of acting as mediator joining the people to their suppressed history. The native poet-film-maker, warns Fanon, must not however dwell nostalgically on that pre-history, that pre-their-past, and erect it as the cultural artefact that will stand for the nation. Instead, the poet-film-maker must negotiate that pre-history through the colonial past and call everything into question (problematise it to recall O'Regan's term) and do so by addressing his/her own people, by making a fundamental concession of the self to others – to make the people the *subject* not the *object* of his/her art. Only from that moment (the post-liberation moment), says Fanon, can 'we' speak of a national culture, which is a culture of combat in that it calls on the whole people to fight for their existence as a nation – to leave and to make traces. It is a culture of combat because it moulds the national consciousness both by giving it form and contours *and* by flinging open before it new and boundless horizons. Finally it is a culture of combat because it assumes responsibility and it is the will of liberty expressed in terms of time and space. Time and space, the very meaning of cinema.

But what is the territory that a 'national' cinema occupies? For cinema is not a pure product. It is inherently a hybrid of many cultures, be they economic, discursive, ethnic, sexed and more. It exists as a cultural miscegenation, a deeply uncertain product, therefore, as to its heritage – *patrimoine*, as the French put it, makes the point more clearly. Who and where is the father? While it may matter to hegemony, it does not to cinema in and of itself. For it is a production whose reproducers are wide and scattered and not one – not a single maternal body, nor a lone patriarchal one. Nor is it solely the offspring of maternal and patriarchal discourses. Its moreness, its hybridity challenges the deadliness of patriarchal (and modernist) binary thought. It is, in the end, as much about flux and difference as is the human body. In other words, it is as multicultural in its meaning as the nation is, finally, pluricultural. And this is a further way in which a national cinema can problematise a nation – by exposing its masquerade of unity (see above, p. 94).

So how now to speak of framing national cinemas? This writing of a national cinema is one that refuses to historicise the nation as subject/object in and of itself but makes it a subject and object of knowledge. This (ideal) writing of a national cinema is one that is invested in (defining) national cultural discourses as anti-assimilationist, anti-integrationist and pro-integralism. It is one which delves deep into the pathologies of nationalist discourses and exposes the symbolic practices of these forms of enunciation. Finally, this framing of national cinemas is one which perceives cinema as a practice that should not conceal structures of power and knowledge but which should function as a *mise-en-scène* of scattered and dissembling identities as well as fractured subjectivities and fragmented hegemonies.

Bibliography

Anderson, B. (1991) *Imagined Communities*, London: Verso.

Andrew, D. (1995) 'Appraising French Images', *Wide Angle* 16, 3: 53–66.

Bhabha, H. (ed.) (1990) *Nation and Narration*, London: Routledge.

Brasell, B.R. (1995) 'Queer Nationalism and the Musical Fag Bashing of John Greyson's *The Making of Monsters*', *Wide Angle* 16, 3: 27–38.

Butler, J. (1990) *Gender Trouble: Feminism and the Subversion of Identity*, London: Routledge.

—— (1993) *Bodies that Matter: On the Discursive Limits of 'Sex'*, London: Routledge.

Eagleton, T. (1990) 'Nationalism: Irony and Commitment', in Eagleton, Jameson and Saïd (eds).

Eagleton, T., Jameson, F. and Saïd, E. (eds) (1990) *Nationalism, Colonialism and Literature*, intro. S. Deane, Minnesota: University of Minnesota Press.

Erikson, T.H. (1993) *Ethnicity and Nationalism: Anthropological Perspectives*, London: Pluto Press.

Fanon, F. (1990) *The Wretched of the Earth*, preface J.-P. Sartre, trans. C. Harrington, Harmondsworth: Penguin.

—— (1996) *Black Skin, White Masks*, trans. C.L. Markmann, London: Pluto Press.

Gellner, E. (1983) *Nations and Nationalism*, Oxford: Blackwell.

Grewal, I. and Kaplan C. (eds) (1994) *Scattered Hegemonies*, Minnesota: University of Minnesota Press.

Hall, P. (1997) 'Nationalism and Historicity', *Nations and Nationalism* 3, 1: 3–24.

Kristeva, J. (1986) 'Women's Time', in T. Moi (ed.) *The Kristeva Reader*, Oxford: Blackwell.

Layoun, M. (1994) 'The Female Body and "Transnational" Reproduction; or, Rape by Any Other Name?', in Grewal and Kaplan (eds).

O'Regan, T. (1996) *Australian National Cinema*, London: Routledge.

Saïd, E. (1990) 'Yeats and Decolonization', in Eagleton, Jameson and Saïd (eds).

Smith, A.D. (1996) 'Memory and Modernity: Reflections on Ernest Gellner's Theory of Nationalism', *Nations and Nationalism* 2, 3: 371–88.

Smith, A.D. and Hutchinson, J. (eds) (1994) *Nationalism*, Oxford: Oxford University Press.

Virilio, P. (1991) *The Lost Dimension*, trans. D. Moshenberg, New York: Semiotext(e).

7

THEMES OF NATION

Mette Hjort

National cinemas, it has been argued (Higson 1989, 1995), are to an important extent thematically defined, yet little has been said about what exactly constitutes the relevant themes. My aim here, then, is to identify some of the key features of themes of nation. In the course of my discussion, I draw on examples from contemporary Danish cinema. I argue that themes of nation are topical, rather than perennial, and involve a process of marking and flagging that distinguishes them from instances of banal nationalism. I further contend that agents engaged in the construction of a national cinema emphasise a loose sense of aboutness which is constitutive, not of themes of nation, but of banal nationalism.

Theme as national policy? The case of contemporary Danish cinema

In 1998, the Danish Film Institute presented an ambitious 'Four-Year Plan' outlining a series of strategies designed further to develop the Danish film industry. Arguments having to do with economic viability figure centrally in the 'Four-Year Plan', but they are complemented throughout by a consistent attempt to articulate a set of artistic and cultural visions, one of which concerns the construction of a national culture through film. The document repeatedly emphasises the need to foster opportunities allowing film-makers to reflect, explore and imaginatively invent Danish realities:

> The point of the Danish Film Institute is to be the key site for ensuring that Danes are presented with artistically qualified offerings in an increasingly global media culture. The Institute's support policy is to guarantee the availability of films that express and sustain Danish culture, language, and identity.
>
> (Anon. 1998: 6)

Danish film-makers, it would appear, are to be encouraged to make films *about* Danes and their country. Does it follow that policy-makers concerned with the cultural viability of the Danish film industry have a preference for themes of nation? The short answer, which I shall defend in detail below, is 'no'.

Defining nation and theme

We may intuitively have some sense of what is meant by the phrase 'the theme of nation', but it is important to note that the meanings assigned to the two key terms – 'nation' and 'theme' – vary considerably and have given rise to numerous learned disputes. In her book, *Nationalism*, Liah Greenfeld (1993) surveys the changing meanings of nation in various historical contexts of use. The Latin term '*natio*' was originally derogatory, for 'in Rome the name *natio* was reserved for groups of foreigners coming from the same geographical region, whose status – because they were foreigners – was below that of the Roman citizens'. The meaning of the word 'nation' was subsequently transformed from 'community of origin' to 'community of opinion and purpose'. In the course of the medieval period, 'nation' was used to refer to 'representatives of cultural and political authority', to a social elite (Greenfeld 1993: 4). And by the sixteenth century, the term 'nation' became synonymous with a sovereign people, or a people aspiring to sovereignty on the basis of unique features. Not surprisingly, it is this modern meaning of the term with which we are most familiar today.

Although Greenfeld finds evidence of a modern conception of nation already in sixteenth-century England, most scholars associate the general concept of nation as sovereign people with the industrialisation of the Western world and emergence of nation-states during the nineteenth century. Attempts to pinpoint the exact, modern meanings of 'nation' abound in sociological and anthropological studies of nationalism, with authors admitting readily to the difficulty of the task. Ernest Gellner (1983) approaches the problem as follows:

> What then is this contingent, but in our age seemingly universal and normative, idea of the nation? Discussion of two very makeshift temporary definitions will help to pinpoint this elusive concept:
>
> 1. Two men are of the same nation if and only if they share the same culture, where culture in turn means a system of ideas and signs and associations and ways of behaving and communicating.
> 2. Two men are of the same nation if and only if they *recognise* each other as belonging to the same nation.
>
> (Gellner 1983: 7)

A certain number of individual agents do not become a nation on the basis only of shared traits that can be observed by agents belonging to other groups. A nation, rather, emerges when the agents in question recognise their mutual belonging as common knowledge. As philosophers such as David Lewis (1969) have pointed out, common knowledge involves a potentially expanding series of beliefs of the following kind: I know that you know that I know that you know that I know that x. In the context of nationhood, it is a matter of agents believing that their reasons for inscribing themselves within a given imagined community are mutually recognised and involve common knowledge or belief. It appears that a theme of nation, in contemporary cinematic contexts, presupposes notions of a sovereign people with its own political 'roof' and territory. Yet, the use of a national language and the development of stories set in national contexts do not alone suffice to establish a theme of nation. The forms of shared belonging, rather, must be explicitly thematised with the intention of bringing into *focal awareness* a given nation's mutual beliefs about belonging. That is, the subjective pole based on mutual recognition must be brought into play.

A rapid survey of recent work within the area of thematics quickly reveals theme to be a slippery, constantly transmuting phenomenon. Fortunately, at least some of the relevant work involves a number of convincing, overlapping claims. Here, then, are the traits that I take to be characteristic of themes. A theme, as Peter Lamarque and Stein Haugom Olsen point out, 'is not *found* in a literary work but *elicited*. It emerges as a result of the reader taking up the literary stance towards a text' (1994: 434). A theme is thus a semantic construct that emerges during the process of engaging with a given work. Lamarque and Olsen rightly claim that 'the expectation that a piece of writing is intended to have a theme is definitive of the literary stance' (1994: 415). An appropriate engagement with cinematic works of art involves, then, *mutatis mutandis*, a cinematic stance that motivates us to identify certain themes.

A film's theme is what the work in question is *about*. This aboutness is not, however, a matter of full-fledged referential meanings, for only in the case of specific genres do authors make literal claims about actual persons or events, which can and should be assessed in terms of notions of truth and falsity. Themes, claim Lamarque and Olsen, are not true or false, but more or less interesting, depending on the extent to which they shed light on certain perennial human concerns (1994: 437). A theme is intertextual, for, as Menachem Brinker remarks 'it is a semantic point of contact between the individual text and other texts'. What is more, the intertextuality in question involves a wide range of different kinds of texts. Themes, as Brinker puts it, 'are loci where artistic literary texts encounter other texts: texts of philosophy or the social and human sciences, texts of religion and social ideologies, journalistic texts, including gossip columns, and personal texts such as diaries and letters' (1995: 36). The point is that while themes may emerge as a result of a literary or cinematic stance, they are not themselves always specifically literary or cinematic.

Perennial and topical themes

Lamarque and Olsen (1994) discuss at length a distinction between what they call 'perennial' and 'topical' themes, which, as we shall see, helps to clarify the nature of the theme of nation. Put crudely, perennial themes bring into focus subject matter that resonates across historical and cultural boundaries. They are universal or quasi-universal in their thrust: 'Perennial themes and perennial thematic concepts are constant focuses for various types of culturally important discourses over the history of a culture' (1994: 417). In order to identify and grasp perennial themes, agents must have some understanding of the relevant perennial concepts, examples of which might be constancy and honour. Topical themes, on the other hand, involve only concepts that arise within, and remain relevant to, a highly specific historical or cultural formation. Lamarque and Olsen illustrate the distinction as follows:

> Concepts like 'sexual passion', 'pride', and 'human nature' are perennial thematic concepts. They can be used to formulate thematic statements of a much broader and more general human interest than the problems and themes which can be formulated by notions like 'the lack of intellectual standards among modern academics'.
>
> (1994: 424)

Lamarque and Olsen rightly assume that a work that encourages only thematic interpretations of a topical nature is likely to be less interesting than a work that calls for analysis in terms of perennial concepts. That is, the work is likely to be of interest to only a small number of people, and for only a limited period of time. The aspiration behind topical works is thus quite different from the aims guiding perennial works. Topical works are frequently politically motivated and serve as interventions in ongoing discussions within a given social context.

We are dealing here with terms that help us to pick out different kinds of emphases in works, rather than with criteria that allow us definitively to identify themes as belonging always to only one of two categories. Intuitively, the appeal of the line of argument proposed by Lamarque and Olsen is that it encourages us to ask the following kinds of questions: is the subject matter dealt with in a given film likely to be comprehensible and interesting primarily to regional, national, or international audiences? Is the structure of address in the film such that these audiences are appealed to in more or less the same way, or is the film's form of address at least dual? Does the film draw on and intervene in debates that are ongoing within a given community and linked to local or national politics?

Given that the very notion of nation points to the specificity of a people and its history and culture, the theme of nation is a likely candidate for topical theme *par excellence*. One could, of course, argue that since nationhood is based on imagined belongings, a work involving a thematisation of a given nation's concerns and values calls for interpretation in terms of the concept of imagined belonging, which can hardly be construed as a topical concept. The idea would be that it is possible to infer from a rich, culturally specific narrative an aboutness that is constituted by imagined belonging as such, rather than particular types of imagined belonging. The theme of a given work, in that case, would precisely be that of nation, rather than that of a particular nation. Although interesting, I think this line of reasoning is essentially misguided. The theme of nation almost always presents itself as a theme of *this* particular nation, and, as such, it provides a paradigmatic example of a topical theme and is inextricably linked to specific, explicitly acknowledged identities.

A quite different objection to classifying the theme of nation as topical draws on the theoretical literature on nations and nationalism, which emphasises the idea that nationalists typically regard nations as primordial.[1] Yet, modernist theorists of nationalism distance themselves from what they regard as the nationalists' false beliefs in order to present a picture of nations as social constructions produced by nationalism in response to specific historical developments. Why should a theoretical account of themes of nation be any more faithful to the (wrongheaded) beliefs of nationalists than theories of nationalism are? The theme of nation is defined here as topical because it finds its very conditions of possibility in the specificity of particular nations. Themes of nation may, however, be mobilised variously, which is why it is important to identify the overall thrust of a given topical thematisation. It is at the level of distinctions among *types* of thematisations of nation that it is relevant to speak of ethnic or primordialist attitudes.

The claim that the theme of nation is topical, rather than perennial, helps to explain why most film-makers would reject outright the idea that they are committed first and foremostly to the making of films that contribute to a thematics of nation. Interviews with Jytte Rex, Christian Braad Thomsen, Helle Ryslinge and many others, repeatedly bring to the fore an understanding of the film-maker's art as oriented by enduring, lasting concerns.[2] When, for example, Christian Braad Thomsen claims ultimately to be deeply interested only in love and death, he situates himself and his work within a thematic context that, precisely, is perennial rather than topical. Yet, many contemporary Danish film-makers do express views that are in harmony with the Danish Film Institute's insistence on some form of Danish content. The film-makers are not, however, committed to emphasising what they clearly regard as a set of narrow concerns that makes for insignificant art. Danish film-makers are just as uninterested in creating films based *only* on the narrowly topical theme of nation, as most audiences (including members of the Danish Film Institute) would be in viewing and funding them. Not surprisingly, then, topical themes of nation typically figure as secondary, rather than primary themes within contemporary Danish films.

Banal aboutness

Themes, I claimed above, are a matter of 'aboutness', and it is time now to look more closely at this notion. I have suggested that most Danish film-makers would be reluctant to work primarily with the highly topical theme of Denmark, yet Danish politicians, producers and the film-makers themselves repeatedly emphasise a commitment to producing films that in some sense are *about* Danish realities. There are, it would seem, different ways of interpreting the 'aboutness' of films. To state loosely that a film is *about* Denmark is not the same thing as claiming that a film is *about* Denmark in a properly *thematic* sense.

The casual use of 'about' assumes that all films that make use, for example, of recognisably Danish locations, the Danish language, Danish actors and props that mirror the material culture of Danes, qualify as being about Denmark. The question, then, is whether the presence of a significant number of such elements amounts to a theme of nation. My claim is that such elements can provide the basis for a given film's national quality, but that they cannot, in and of themselves, constitute a theme. Theme implies thematisation, that is, a self-conscious directing of focal awareness toward those meaningful elements that, when interpreted, reveal what a given film is strictly speaking about. A theme of nation will, of course, typically emerge as a result of a 'flagging' of precisely those elements listed above. But unless this flagging takes place, the elements do not amount to a theme.

Michael Billig's (1995) notion of banal nationalism can be usefully evoked here, for it helps us to clarify the distinction between background notions of Danishness and thematisations of Danishness. Billig's goal, in *Banal Nationalism*, is to show that theorists of nationalism have tended to construe nationalism as a less than desirable feature of the mentalities of others, and to overlook the banal forms of nationalism that are constitutive of everyday life within most nation-states. The image used repeatedly by Billig to illustrate the differences between banal nationalism and other kinds of nationalism involving focal beliefs is that of the national flag hanging limply in front of a government office: 'The metonymic image of banal nationalism is not a flag which is being consciously waved with fervent passion; it is the flag hanging unnoticed on the public building' (1995: 8). Banal nationalism is a matter of seemingly trivial evocations or indirect references to the nation in news, sports and weather reports, among other things. Banal nationalism involves the ongoing circulation and utilisation of the symbols of the nation, but in a manner that is so deeply ingrained and habitual as to involve no focal awareness. What we are dealing with here is what the French sociologist Pierre Bourdieu (1987), following Leibniz, would call a 'habitus'.

Banal aboutness is, I believe, what members of the Danish Film Institute and Danish film industry more generally have in mind when they call for films about Denmark. If we look at the context of contemporary Danish film-making it is not hard to find multiple examples of the kind of banal nationalism identified by Billig. The accomplished film-maker Søren Kragh-Jacobsen sees himself as a supporter of a liberal, civic nationalism, but does not believe that this self-conception plays a particularly important role in his film-making. In order to underscore this point, he foregrounds the banality of the national symbols in his films. He convincingly argues that the verisimilitude that is criterial for film-making in a realistic vein demands national symbols in certain contexts:

It is of course true that I've frequently included Danish flags in my films. But if I am making a film like *The Boys from St. Petri*, or *Rubber Tarzan*, which includes a cozy Danish lunch, then I obviously have to use some Danish flags. That at least is how I was raised.

(Hjort and Bondebjerg 2001)

Other examples of banal aboutness can be found in Bille August's early films. In *Tro, håb og kærlighed* (*Twist and Shout*, 1984), which is based loosely on *Når snerlen blomstrer* (*When the Bindweed Flowers*) by Bjarne Reuter, viewers are treated visually to an elaborate party celebrating a newly engaged couple, Bjørn (Adam Tønsberg) and Kirsten (Ulrikke Juul Bondo). At one point in the festivities, a rocket is lit, and, after a moment of suspense, it does finally take off, showering the guests with tightly rolled pieces of paper. As Danes know all too well, formal celebrations in Denmark, particularly in the milieu evoked by the film, typically involve the singing of songs that have been written for the occasion by the guests. Finding some original and interesting way of presenting the song lyrics to the other guests is an integral part of the custom in question. What we have here is a practice that, from the perspective of international audiences, is likely to seem striking as a result of its semantic opacity. From an indigenous perspective, however, the sequence of events is likely to seem unremarkable. What is noticed is not the cultural practice as such, but the suspense and relief generated by a rocket that initially fizzles and then performs as

Figure 7.1 Alex Svanbjerg as Ivan in Søren Kragh-Jacobsen's *Rubber Tarzan*

planned. Other examples of banal aboutness can be found in Christian Braad Thomsen's road movie about two female performers, *Koks i kulissen* (*Ladies on the Rocks*, 1983). Micha (Helle Ryslinge) and Laura (Anne Marie Helger) are treated after one of their performances in the provinces to 'natmad' (literally night food) in the home of a pretentious member of the culture industry. Once again, the national quality of the event in question is likely to go unnoticed by Danish audiences, for whom the concept of a formally arranged meal served late at night and involving a number of characteristic dishes is ordinary or banal. Typically Danish elements, then, provide a banal form of aboutness, unless there is something about their mode of presentation that suggests that the film-maker intends for us to pay special attention to them. Focal attention, then, provides the key to the difference between banal forms of aboutness and the kind of aboutness that is constitutive of full-blown themes of nation.

Thematisation and the directing of attention

Like all other themes, the theme of nation can only emerge in the course of a film's viewing if the relevant forms of aboutness are flagged or foregrounded. It is a matter, in other words, of directing the audience's attention toward those elements that signify the nation, and of doing so at key moments throughout the narrative. That is, I can think of no case in which a single instance of fore-grounding suffices to evoke a theme of nation.

Figure 7.2 Micha (Helle Ryslinge) and Laura (Anne Marie Helger) in Christian Braad Thomsen's *Ladies on the Rocks*

How, then, does this process of foregrounding or marking occur? In a useful article entitled 'Film, Attention, and Communication', Noël Carroll discusses what he calls 'scaling, bracketing and indexing' as key means of directing audience attention cinematically: 'Moving the camera forward not only indexes and brackets certain details rather than others. It also changes the scale of what the audience is looking at' (1996: 30). By zooming in on an object, for example, the film-maker alerts the audience to its importance in an indexical process that both enlarges the object's scale and brackets the larger context of its appearance. Carroll's concepts provide the basis for a useful, but not exhaustive account of how attention is directed in film. In the present context we need to take note of at least two other ways in which audience attention can be drawn to the constitutive elements of themes of nation. Acting styles, particularly if they are highly exaggerated or parodic, can focus attention and suggest a particular interpretive stance. And dialogue, it appears, is a favoured means of thematising or foregrounding the nation.

Foregrounding in film takes many forms, and I would like now to examine a number of different strategies utilised by Danish film-makers in their attempts to thematise the nation. I shall distinguish between two general types of approaches, which I shall label 'monocultural' and 'intercultural'. On my account, a given thematisation is monocultural if it is a matter uniquely of systematically foregrounding elements from the very national culture that is being thematised. The strategy here involves a *hyper-saturation* of the audio-visual field with national elements. The intercultural approach, on the other hand, is more efficient in many ways, for the contrastive mobilisation of *different* national cultures easily directs audience attention toward the very question of national identity and specificity. Hyper-saturation is an option in this case, but not a necessity. It is useful further to distinguish the relevant thematisations on the basis of their thrust and intended effect. I shall thus consider examples of nostalgic or ethnic, polemical and ironic thematisations.

Monocultural thematisations of nation

The strategy of hyper-saturation is characteristic of Denmark's most promising young female film-maker, Lotte Svendsen. Svendsen's film-making is characterised by political commitment, tightly constructed narratives, an intense attention to the details of scenographic design and an interest in reviving some of the popular indigenous genres that were trivialised by an earlier generation of film-makers. In *Royal Blues* (1997) Svendsen uses specifically cinematic techniques and dialogue to flag national elements. *Royal Blues* tells the story of a young, lower middle-class woman, Belinda, who becomes embroiled in a series of misadventures as she desperately seeks a royal pardon for her imprisoned lover, Henning. Through Belinda's pursuit of royalty, first the Queen, and subsequently her son, attention is *polemically* directed toward the place occupied by the royal family in the national imaginings of various social classes in

Figure 7.3 Belinda (Rikke Louise Andersson), her two sisters (Helle Dolleris and Sofie Stougaard) and her mother (Lone Helmer) in Lotte Svendsen's *Royal Blues*

Denmark. The opening sequence is already saturated with the kinds of elements capable of establishing a theme of nation. Belinda is shown at the gates of the royal palace, Amalienborg, where she interacts with a palace employee through a door-phone. As she is refused admission, the film's initials, R.B., appear on the screen in the manner of royal insignia, the viewer hears extra-diegetic marching music and witnesses a ceremonious march by a heavily uniformed royal guard. The next sequence takes place in the apartment of Belinda's mother, where the three daughters have gathered to celebrate their mother's birthday. This sequence is similarly characterised by a strategy of hyper-saturation. The viewer discerns a series of photographs on the wall behind the couch, and a close-up later reveals that the pictures are of the royal family. The royal family becomes the object of dispute as the drunken daughter (played by Sofie Stougaard) criticises her mother for having made a gift of her pension to the royals. This same daughter begins to roll cigarettes on her mother's latest issue of the tabloid publication entitled *Se & Hør,* and the mother's reprimand clearly indicates the extent to which she treasures this magazine for its endless pictures of, and narratives about, the royal family. Belinda has at this point shared her failure to gain access to the queen with the family, and the mother now suggests that she track the crown prince down by using the tabloids as maps to his regular haunts in Copenhagen's night life. The camera subsequently pulls back to reveal on the right a bust of a royal figure whom Stougaard later identifies as King Christian IX. In the birthday scene the bust is foregrounded through dialogue, for it becomes the occasion for further quarrelling when the imprisoned Henning's neurotic dog knocks over the stand and smashes the figure to smithereens. In these two opening sequences, the viewer is bombarded with a large number of monocultural aural and visual elements that work together to constitute a theme of nation. Subsequent scenes are similarly constructed, and the film's concluding image is of a crown-prince look-alike, in profile, with raised hand, bidding 34,000 Crowns for an Ask Hammerlund painting of the naked Belinda with dog.

Intercultural thematisations of nation

An intercultural approach to the thematisation of nation uses contrastive cultural elements to foreground and direct attention toward specifically national elements. An example is Gabriel Axel's *The Prince of Jutland* (1994) which usefully underscores the extent to which themes are merely elicited by cinematic texts and presuppose the viewer's ability to piece the relevant elements together in a process of thematic construction. Interestingly, in the case of *The Prince of Jutland* the theme of nation emerges only if the viewer grasps the relation between the narrative told by Axel and the story told by Shakespeare's *Hamlet*. Intertextual references, in this case, are an integral part of the thematisation process. A viewer focused uniquely on the information provided by the film's audio-visual elements will register only that an early title indicates that the story takes place in 'Jutland – an ancient Danish kingdom'. The use of English throughout the film, and prominent English-speaking actors, such as Gabriel Byrne and Helen Mirren, further militates against the construction of a theme that takes the specificity of the Danish nation as its content.

The situation changes radically, however, when the film is placed within a larger intertextual network, for Gabriel Axel's film is, by his own admission, very much about the Danish nation and the interesting task of reviving and affirming the original story of Amled as told by the medieval Danish monk, Saxo Grammaticus, one of Shakespeare's key sources. In interviews Axel repeatedly underscores differences between Shakespeare's conception of Hamlet, and Saxo's view of the young prince as a man of action. Axel's stated aim, in *The Prince of Jutland*, is to mobilise some of the conventions of the action genre in a narrative that is faithful to the original, properly Danish tale. Axel's statements regarding *The Prince of Jutland* clearly reveal that he is engaged in what I, following Charles Taylor, have called a politics of recognition, a foregrounding of the specificity of a certain identity accompanied by a demand that this identity be recognised as valuable (Hjort 1996). Unfortunately, it seems that the comparative process encouraged by *The Prince of Jutland* has served only, in various contexts of reception, to mark the film as a failure. Articles in the local and international press repeatedly suggested that *The Prince of Jutland*'s main failing is that it cannot compete with Shakespeare. The inability to compete here may have to do with the objective superiority of Shakespeare's version of the story. But it is also possible that the sheer historical weight bolstering the English story creates impediments to the appreciation of a significantly different approach. What is clear is that in *The Prince of Jutland* Axel adopts an intertextual, intercultural approach to the thematisation of nation. What is more, inasmuch as the thrust of the relevant thematisation involves an exploration and affirmation of a national past, *The Prince of Jutland* clearly exemplifies an *ethnic* or *nostalgic* form of thematic construction. *The Prince of Jutland* is in many ways an instance of what Andrew Higson (1995), following Charles Barr, calls a 'heritage film'.

The intercultural approach is also evident in Erik Clausen's *Tango* (1997) which was funded by New Fiction Film Denmark. In this case, however, the overall thrust of the process of thematisation is primarily *polemical*. The film focuses on a fictional character, Ole Jensen, who is played by Erik Clausen himself. Ole Jensen is described during the opening sequence in a documentary-style voice-over that is used regularly throughout the film. Ole Jensen, we are told, was once a passionate socialist, but has lost his passion for life. He was unemployed for many years and now receives early retirement allocations from the Danish state. Ole Jensen is the picture of passivity and loneliness, and his social worker is the only person who regularly talks to him. Bright yellow captions providing basic information about Denmark further underscore the quasi-documentary quality of the film and serve to contextualise the plight of Ole Jensen ('Denmark is a rich country. There are many lonely people there, especially men').

The comparative moment that provides the basis for a full-blown thematisation of nation is introduced when Jensen's social worker encourages him to take tango lessons. Jensen attends a tango class, is strongly attracted to a red-head, steals a ticket to Uruguay from the pocket of one of the other dancers, and decides to make use of it. The film becomes a comic travelogue at this point, with Jensen heading off to Uruguay to learn to dance the tango, so that he can return to Denmark and seduce his red-head. Jensen's explorations of Uruguay involve interviews with genuine musicians, dancers and former political prisoners, as well as staged, comic interactions with delinquent youths and gauchos. Captions, voice-over exhortations from the narrator and pronouncements by Ole Jensen and his interlocutors serve to establish Uruguay as a place of passion and engagement, a place where fear and uncertainty have been incapable of suppressing a basic hunger for life. Through a series of explicit and implicit contrasts, Denmark emerges as a land of plenty that has managed somehow to foster detachment and passivity, rather than passion and engagement. Ole Jensen eventually learns how to dance the tango, returns to Denmark, and with his new-found passion for life, easily engages with his desired red-head.

In an interview with Clausen on 14 February 1997, I asked the film-maker whether *Tango*, in his mind, was a so-called '*Danmarksfilm*'. Clausen agreed that *Tango* owes a great deal to the specific documentary genre that aims to provide an interpretation and picture of Denmark. The genre in question has a venerable tradition, and the first of these films was produced as early as 1917. The genre embraces promotional, critical and lyrical films, and the most famous is Poul Henningsen's highly controversial *Danmark* (1935), which was produced by the Ministry of External Affairs. Clausen's classification of *Tango* as a polemical '*Danmarksfilm*' serves usefully to underscore the theme of nation as a guiding element in the overall conception of the narrative and narration. The theme of nation is used here, not to affirm some inherent and enduring Danish identity, but to foreground the Marxist Clausen's commitment to the idea that human beings forge their own destinies and can become the vehicles of change. The polemical *Tango* is designed to awaken Danes from their lethargy and dogmatic slumber by focusing their attention critically on current Danish mentalities and identities.

The nation, as we have seen, can be thematised contrastively with the aim of reconnecting with national roots or re-imagining national identities. The contrastive approach can also, however, be utilised to call into question the very rationality and legitimacy of social differentiation along national lines. A striking example of this essentially *ironic* mode of thematisation is *Riget I/The Kingdom I* (1994) and *Riget II/The Kingdom II* (1997), directed by Lars von Trier and Morten Arnfred.

The Kingdom was originally made for television and subsequently released in 16 mm and 35 mm versions. *The Kingdom* marked Lars von Trier's transition from esoteric, art-film productions aimed at international audiences to popular film-making in Danish, with Danish actors. Prior to *The Kingdom*, von Trier was known in Denmark primarily as an eccentric, temperamental film-maker capable of garnering awards at Cannes for technically brilliant and mostly English-language films. *The Kingdom* was a conscious attempt on von Trier's part to appeal directly to indigenous audiences and to establish a national audience for his work. As a result of its postmodern fusion of internationally established genres and development of an aesthetics based on kitsch and camp, *The Kingdom* has further enhanced international interest in von Trier's work. At the same time, *The Kingdom* has provided von Trier with a new identity as popular Danish film-maker.

The very title of the film, *The Kingdom*, directs audience attention towards the notions of nationhood and national identity, which is a basic condition for thematisations of nation. As Gunhild Agger points out 'The title is ambiguous, meaning 1. Rigshospitalet, the national Danish hospital, in Copenhagen, 2. kingdom, empire, state' (1997: 127). The main site of the unfolding events is the Danish national hospital, and these events have implications for our conception of the nation and its foundations. One of the recurrent comic conflicts in *The Kingdom* is provided by the Swedish doctor Stig Helmer's (Ernst-Hugo Järegård) encounters with the Danish hospital staff. The most comic scenes involving contrasting national identities place Stig Helmer on the roof of the hospital, from where he can peer in the direction of Sweden. Here Helmer ceremoniously invokes a series of Swedish icons, which he affirms with a resounding 'yes', before going on to revile Danes. An example of the pronouncements in question is the following soliloquy, from *The Kingdom I*, Part 3:

> Tetra-Pak ... yes.
> Volvo ... yes.
> Pripps Blå ... yes.
> Björn Borg ... yes.
> Hepstars ... yes.
> I am here. I don't know how I got here. And what the hell am I doing here? Bloody Danes.

The foregrounding, for example, of brand name commercial products as symbols of national identity affords an *ironic* perspective on the very concept of national belonging. A personal identity that is importantly shaped by national culture appears to involve none of the fine-grained reflective evaluations that philosophers associate with human agency. Helmer's sense of self, it would appear, is not constituted by what Charles Taylor (1989) calls 'strong evaluation', for what we have here are trivial, rather than important choices. The implicit choice is between Volvo and some Danish car, between Björn Borg and some Danish sports star, and not, for example, between the untrammelled pursuit of erotic desire and the honouring of marriage vows. Von Trier and Arnfred foreground the trivial choices of weak evaluation and make them the basis for a nationally inflected personal identity. As a result, the very pursuit of personal identity in and through the national appears questionable, even laughable.

Conclusion

The theme of nation, I have argued, arises when the elements that are constitutive of banal nationalism are consistently flagged in the course of a narrative. This theme is typically topical in nature and, as a result, it tends to be subordinated to themes of the perennial type. The call for films about Denmark that characterises ongoing discussions of how to create and sustain a viable Danish national cinema is for the most part a call, not for thematisations of nation, but for films that simply incorporate the elements of a banal nationalism. Explicit thematisations of nation tend to involve one of two approaches: monocultural hyper-saturation and intercultural contrast. Thematisations of nation foreground the issue of target audiences, for the anticipated cognitive and affective responses of regional, national and international audiences will in many cases diverge. Thematisations of nation, particularly in the case of hyper-saturation, have a tendency to promote opacity in international contexts, for local, topical and nation-specific thematic elements are likely to be only partially comprehensible in other national contexts. The risks of opacity that accompany topical thematisations of specific nations in international contexts can, however, be somewhat mitigated by the more inclusive intercultural approach, which is by far the most common incarnation of the theme of nation.

Notes

1 I am grateful to Ulf Hedetoft and Roy Sellars for having brought this objection to my attention.
2 I interviewed these and many other Danish film-makers over a two-year period starting in 1997. References to remarks by Søren Kragh-Jacobsen and Erik Clausen below are similarly based on this interview project, which is forthcoming (Hjort and Bondebjerg 2001).

Bibliography

Agger, G. (1997) 'The "Sideplays" Aesthetics: On Popularity and Quality in a Danish Film Maker's Television Success', in M. Eide, B. Gentikow and K. Helland (eds), *Quality Television*, Bergen: Department of Media Studies.

Anon. (1998) 'Det Danske Filminstituts 4-årige handlingsplan', Danish Film Institute document.

Billig, M. (1995) *Banal Nationalism*, London: Sage Publications.

Bourdieu, P. (1987) *Distinction: A Social Critique of the Judgment of Taste*, trans. Richard Nice, Cambridge, MA: Harvard University Press.

Brinker, M. (1995) 'Theme and Interpretation', in C. Bremond, J. Landy and T. Pavel (eds), *Thematics: New Approaches*, Albany, NY: State University of New York Press.

Carroll, N. (1996) 'Film, Attention, and Communication', in *The Great Ideas Today*, Chicago, IL: Encyclopaedia Britannica.

Gellner, E. (1983) *Nations and Nationalism*, Ithaca, NY: Cornell University Press.

Greenfeld, L. (1993) *Nationalism*, Cambridge, MA: Harvard University Press.

Higson, A. (1989) 'The Concept of National Cinema', *Screen* 30, 4: 36–46.

—— (1995) *Waving the Flag*, Oxford: Oxford University Press.

Hjort, M. (1996) 'Danish Cinema and the Politics of Recognition', in D. Bordwell and N. Carroll (eds), *Post-Theory: Reconstructing Film Studies*, Madison, WI: The University of Wisconsin Press.

Hjort, M. and Bondebjerg, I. (2001) *The Danish Directors: Dialogues on a Contemporary National Cinema*, Bristol: Intellect Press.

Lamarque, P. and Haugom Olsen, S. (1994) *Truth, Fiction, and Literature: A Philosophical Perspective*, Oxford: Clarendon Press.

Lewis, D. (1969) *Convention: A Philosophical Study*, Cambridge, MA: Harvard University Press.

Taylor, C. (1989) *Sources of the Self: The Making of the Modern Identity*, Cambridge, MA: Harvard University Press.

III

FILM POLICY, NATIONALISM
AND THE STATE

8

CINEMATIC
NATION-BUILDING

Eisenstein's *The Old and the New*

Noël Carroll and Sally Banes

Introduction

If, as Benedict Anderson (1983) has suggested in his classic *Imagined Communities*, the idea of a nation is in large measure imagined retrospectively, the Soviet Union offers an interesting counterpoint – that of a nation imagined prospectively. The Soviet Union literally had to be invented. As is well known, cinema was expected to play a crucial role in this process. Surely it was for such a purpose that Lenin anointed cinema the premier socialist art-form. Many Soviet films of the 1920s were devoted to consolidating a tradition for the new nation, commemorating its revolutionary founding in historical spectacles, like V.I. Pudovkin's *The End of St. Petersburg* (1927) and Sergei Eisenstein's *October* (1927). But certain other films, like Dziga Vertov's *Man With A Movie Camera* (1929) and Eisenstein's *The Old and the New* (1929) (originally called *The General Line*),[1] looked primarily to the future, rather than to the past, in order to imagine what the Soviet Union could become. In this essay, we intend to look at the ways in which Eisenstein attempted in *The Old and the New* to contribute to the construction of the Soviet Union by means of what might be called 'cinematic nation-building'.[2]

Perhaps the most important feature of the future Soviet Union that Eisenstein envisions in *The Old and the New* is that it is a nation in which agriculture and industry, the countryside and the city are co-ordinated – turned into a smoothly operating, reciprocally functioning system in which each side of the equation adds to the other symbiotically. Undoubtedly, part of the inspiration for this ideal picture of the Soviet Union comes from Marxist theory. In *The German Ideology*, Marx and Engels noted the tendency of the rise of capitalism to exacerbate a division, even an antagonism, between town and country.[3] But, at the same time, Marx and Engels also predicted that the antagonism between town and country would be reconciled by the advent of communism and the co-operative development of machinery.[4]

In *The Old and the New*, this theoretical blueprint becomes virtually a storyboard for illustrating the imagined community into which Eisenstein hoped the Soviet nation might evolve. In the film, a part of which is explicitly notated as a dream (a wish-fulfilment dream), Eisenstein visualises a reverie derived straight out of the writings of Marx and Engels; he dreams of – imagines – a nation where town (industry) and country (agriculture) become as one, transcending (as the film's title suggests) the tsarist 'old' in favour of the Marxist 'new'.[5]

If abstract Marxist theory provides part of the background of *The Old and the New*, a more proximate cause of the thinking behind the film can be found in Soviet agricultural policies of the 1920s. One of the most pressing economic (and therefore political) issues the Soviet Union faced in the mid-1920s was the need to increase agricultural production and to modernise it. Increasing agricultural production would serve as a means toward modernisation inasmuch as agricultural surpluses could then be traded for foreign currency, which could then be used to purchase much-needed foreign technology.

Although some progress had been made under the New Economic Policy (NEP) (following the devastation of the Civil War), there were still major problems in the mid-1920s that needed to be addressed in order to integrate agriculture into the socialist economy. These included a regular, reliable supply of agricultural raw materials for industry and of provisions for a growing urban population, as well as foodstuffs for foreign trade to earn monies for industrialisation. However, as in tsarist Russia, the relationship between the peasants and the government was volatile; although they benefited from the Bolsheviks' reallocation of land, the peasants violently resisted the state's interventions, particularly taxation and repeated emergency requisitions of food supplies.

When Eisenstein began working on *The Old and the New* in 1926, there had been a good harvest for the first time in four years and, as a result of this and the relatively free-market situation during the NEP years, an economic equilibrium obtained between industry and agriculture as well as between the peasants and the state. The 'general line' of the Fourteenth Party Congress of December 1925 (for which Eisenstein's film had originally been named) called for the collectivisation of farming, but it was understood then that this would be gradual. In the fall of 1927, the party endorsed a plan to double grain production within ten years. And at the Fifteenth Party Congress of December 1927, agricultural collectivisation was named 'the main task of the party in the countryside'.[6] But this was soon followed by a massive grain crisis – due both to a lower harvest and to strong peasant resistance to state prices – and by more emergency requisitions. So by the time Eisenstein resumed work on *The Old and the New* in June 1928, there was a concentrated move by the state to speed up agriculture technologically, primarily through encouraging voluntary collectivisation and large-scale, mechanised crop production (rather than small-scale subsistence farming), for which the tractor was an essential component.[7] Thus, Soviet state policy had changed from primarily treating the peasant economy as a source for agricultural products to organising and socialising it to mesh with goals of increased production in the industrial sector, a goal that would soon find concrete expression in the first Five-Year Plan.

The Soviet government needed agricultural products not simply to feed the whole population but to use in the foreign-trade market to raise funds for capitalisation – that is, to get money to invest in industrialisation. Agriculture was to be a means to develop industry, which, in turn, would reciprocally contribute to the modernisation of agriculture through scientific planning, the breeding of both grains and livestock and the introduction of machinery. In this cycle of agricultural-industrial modernisation the tractor – which could replace inefficient strip cultivation of individual farms with large-scale co-operative crop production – played a central role. Erich Strauss notes that collectivisation was seen as the major means of modernising Soviet agriculture:

> a more effective force than the slow influence of education and example was needed. This was believed to be the mechanization of the main cropping operations ... thus the tractor became the symbol of this policy [of modernisation through co-operation] and the main agent of change.
>
> (Strauss 1969: 50)[8]

This theme of a nation built on the reciprocal co-ordination of agriculture and industry, to the mutual benefit of both – a link emblematised by the tractor – forms the basis of Eisenstein's film *The Old and the New*.[9]

Reconciling agriculture and industry visually

One of Eisenstein's abiding projects as a film-maker was the aspiration to break out of the photographic particularity of the cinematic image in order to generalise – in order to articulate abstract ideas and concepts. In his silent films, montage provided a major mechanism for achieving this end because by inducing the spectator to infer the relation between disparate shots, Eisenstein opened up the possibility of provoking the viewer to impute linkages of greater and greater abstraction, in order to make ongoing shot chains intelligible (Carroll 1973, reprinted in Carroll 1998).[10] As is well known, Eisenstein called his most ambitious attempts in this direction 'intellectual montage', and in *October* he pushed this line of experimentation to the hilt in the notorious 'Gods' sequence (in which he attempted to disprove the existence of God cinematically) (Carroll 1973).[11] Indeed, Eisenstein even supposed that he would be able to perfect the strategies of intellectual montage to the point where he could make a film of Marx's *Capital* (Michelson 1976 and 1989).

Though *The Old and the New* is most frequently cited by Eisenstein as an example of what he called 'overtonal montage',[12] notably with reference to the famous religious procession, it is, as well, an experiment in intellectual montage, one explicitly heralded by Eisenstein and Grigori Alexandrov (1988) as 'an experiment intelligible to the millions'.[13] In *The Old and the New*, Eisenstein is committed to clarifying for the plain viewer through montage an abstract social process – namely, the way in which agricultural production will make possible industrialisation, which, in turn, will abet even further agricultural production. Intellectual montage, that is, is put in the service of the Soviet policy of nation-building, articulating visually how enhanced agricultural output is connected to industrial modernisation, which then contributes to enhanced agricultural productivity, which then ... and so on. An underlying theme of *The Old and the New* is to make the ordinary audience conscious of an abstract causal relation – or, at least, a causal relation hopefully anticipated by Soviet planners – between agricultural productivity and industry.[14]

Intellectual montage becomes the means for cinematic nation-building in *The Old and the New* by proposing to viewers a series of what might be called instances of 'fantastic causation', which suggest impossible causal relations by juxtaposing shots of local agricultural activities and far-off industrialisation (Carroll 1981–2, reprinted in Carroll 1996). These juxtapositions can be rendered intelligible by inferring that they pertain to an abstract causal network, one belonging to the future Soviet Union, imagined as a nation where farm and factory are part of a single, co-ordinated process – one where town and countryside are thoroughly reconciled.

Three examples of this editing occur in the film: in the cream separator sequence; in Marfa's dream of the state collective farm; and in the 'marriage' sequence between the bull Fomka and his bride. In each of these sequences, interpolated into the edited array are shots of masses of water, pouring down the walls and over the locks of giant dams. These are, of course, hydro-electric plants, key elements in the industrialisation of the Soviet Union. Their inclusion in montage sequences ostensibly depicting local agricultural activities – such as cream separating – suggest that from such humble work, great industrial power-plants will come, exactly those of which Soviet planners dreamed. That is, this imagery implies that the work of the countryside can be harnessed and co-ordinated (causally) to the expansion of industry.

In the cream separator sequence, the imagery of dams first occurs after the liquid gushing from the mechanism splatters all over Marfa's face. An inter-title appears: 'It's thickened'. And then we see three shots of mountains of water cresting the wall of a hydro-electric plant. Ensuing shots of celebratory fountains shooting water upward follow, as do shots of the laughing, happy faces of peasants. As a result of the success of the cream separator, membership in the dairy collective increases. Inter-titles of the growing numbers of members, inter-cut with fountains spewing water, appear rapidly; '46, 48, 50' – and then we again see shots of the dam, taken from opposite directions, cascading into the array.

The imagery of the dam water in the cream separator sequence can be interpreted in two ways. Like the celebratory fountain imagery, it can be taken as a hyperbolic cinematic simile for the liquid flowing out of the cream separator –

as if the device produced oceans of milk. But it is also decipherable as part of a fantastic process of causation – from cream separators like these, mighty dams will emerge, thereby literalising the Soviet plan to transform agriculture into the basis for industrialisation.

This imagery of hydro-electric plants recurs in both Marfa's dream and Fomka's wedding. After saving the dairy collective's cash reserves, Marfa falls asleep on the money-box and dreams of acquiring a bull and, thereby, transforming the co-operative into a cattle collective. In her dream, through superimposition, a bull as large as Godzilla rises from the earth and dominates a field populated by a herd of cattle. Magically, the bull, somewhat unaccountably, seems to rain milk on the landscape. Then there are cuts to the cooling coils of a refrigeration machine, with milk spilling over and finally coating them. Inter-cut with the refrigeration coils are waves of white water, sometimes represented in reverse motion, as if the milk had gathered together in an immense torrent.[15] Yet this torrent does not look as though it belongs to a natural waterway, but more like water crossing locks. Finally, the shots of the dams from the cream separator sequence are also interpolated in the array, their repetition underscoring the importance for Eisenstein of linking the country and industry. Again, the cutting seems to move us from agricultural production to industrialisation.

As in the case of the cream separator sequence, these shots of dam water can be read equally as metaphors of plenitude or as parts of an imaginary causal process, one that links dairy production to industrialisation. Moreover, the theme of industry is clearly central to the cutting here, since this sequence of milk raining down from the sky segues into a sequence in an automated milk-bottling plant. Thus, we suggest that the best way to take the dam imagery is both in terms of metaphors of abundance ('rivers of milk') and images of fantastic causation (more milk makes for more industrialisation).

In the sequence of Fomka's wedding, the imagery of the dam appears for the third time. As the exuberant Fomka charges, in fast motion, toward his cow bride (so excited is he that he crosses the 180 degree line!) and as she opens her legs, there are shots of explosions followed by dam water. The shots are undoubtedly meant to symbolise a profusion of bull sperm, but, again, they also carry the implication of a relation between agricultural production and industry. Perhaps the explosion is doubly decipherable – not only as coitus, but as clearing the ground for a hydro-electric plant.[16] Compressing time drastically, what follows is a shot of Fomka's progeny, a row of at least eight calves – more milk and meat for further capitalisation.

The most obvious example of Eisenstein's use of intellectual montage to articulate the abstract plan to co-ordinate the farm with the factory comes in the finale of the tractor scene. As the tractor rushes toward the camera, in some prints an inter-title reading 'Forward' appears. Then there are three shots of fences – the fences, signalling privatisation, that appeared in the beginning of the film and that represent an impediment to agricultural productivity. Next the tractor crashes through the fences, expressing optatively the triumph of collectivisation. There ensue several shots of the tractor destroying the fences – Eisenstein evidently relishes this spectacle and wishes the audience to do likewise.

At last, there is a shot of a tractor wheel crushing a section of wooden fencing in a furrow. Thence, Eisenstein cuts to a steel factory, where the blast from the furnace seems figuratively to be ignited by the wheel of the tractor. After three shots of smelting, two shots depict a shower of molten sparks. Next a tractor is lowered from above, presumably from an assembly line. The cutting here unmistakably implies that by opening the fields to large-scale collective agricultural production, industrial productivity results causally. Or, at least, Eisenstein's 'unrealistic' juxtaposition of shots very strongly suggests such a thought.

Eisenstein continues the preceding cutting pattern several times – from shots of flaming steel to tractors swinging off the assembly line. Finally, one tractor is lowered toward the ground and, by means of a cut, it sets down 'magically' on farmland, where it proceeds to churn up the earth. If at the beginning of the shot chain, agricultural developments lead to increased industrial production, by the end of the sequence, industry's contribution to agricultural production is made apparent.

From tight shots of tractors plowing the earth, Eisenstein cuts to long shots of a group of tractors plowing together in an enlarging circle – what Eisenstein refers to as the 'merry-go-round' (Eisenstein and Alexandrov 1988: 255). If earlier shots of the film showed us multitudes of livestock, here we encounter multitudes of tractors – agricultural plenitude has been transformed into industrially produced plenitude (tractors everywhere), which, of course, will have momentous consequences for future agriculture.

The inter-title 'Forward' intervenes; the circularly moving tractors are now driving off the screen in a straight line. After the inter-title 'Onward', the tractors continue toward the camera, but they have just multiplied, as if by cell division, into three columns. Finally, Eisenstein pulls back for a very long shot, where we see not only columns of tractors, but other agricultural machinery. The image resembles nothing so much as a military parade – a revolutionary procession – displaying the newest agricultural hardware and celebrating the ultimate reconciliation of the farm and the city in which the countryside itself is becoming industrialised.[17]

In some prints, the parade is missing; the film cuts from the circular plowing to imposing silos and then to enormous piles of sacks of grain. This pattern also realises the planner's dream for the future Soviet Union, since this abundance of grain, seen in historical context, is now available for export where trade, in turn, would be a means to secure the badly needed foreign capital necessary for the further industrialisation of the future Russia, the imagined modern Soviet nation-state.

Through intellectual montage, in *The Old and the New* Eisenstein visualises existing plans for Soviet nation-building. By tracing processes of fantastic causation from agricultural activities to industry, Eisenstein attempts to make abstract economic planning intelligible, by cinematic means, to the millions. Perhaps one reason why the intellectual montage in *The Old and the New* could be more intelligible to the millions than much of the editing in *October* is that it is based upon visually suggesting causal relations, albeit fantastical ones, whereas the conceptual relations required to 'fill in' the 'Gods' sequence in *October* rely on ordinary viewers to mobilise ideas far less familiar to them than that of causation. But, in any case, it should be manifest that by editing in a manner that strongly suggests causal relations between country and city, Eisenstein discovered a way to deploy intellectual montage for the purposes of cinematic nation-building.

Along with the imagery connecting agriculture and industry, another major visual motif in the editing of *The Old and the New*, as already indicated, involves plenitude. Not only individual shots, but whole elaborate shot series are devoted to proliferating abounding herds of cattle and other livestock, as well as, by the end, an army of tractors. This theme of multiplication takes shape in contrast to a darkly opening introductory sequence about divisiveness among the peasants.

As is their custom, the brothers of a rural family divide their property in half. Eisenstein depicts this bifidisation process in great detail, illustrating with all sorts of cinematic devices – including not only cuts, but wipes – how the peasants take every piece of the house apart and criss-cross the land with a complicated fretwork of fences. This division between them is the source of their privation, and it is the problematic that the rest of the film promises to dispel, as ultimately the tractor smashes all the fences, unleashing the industrial and agricultural abundance described already. This movement from division to multiplication occurs in stages throughout the film, each agricultural breakthrough leading to more – more livestock, more grain, more tractors, all lovingly inventoried by Eisenstein's camera, which finds fecundity and multiplicity everywhere. The visual theme of multiplication radiates the prosperity of the imagined Soviet state through montage that not only attempts to show how agriculture and industry could be co-ordinated to attain this, but tries to instil enthusiasm in viewers to the point where they might be willing to participate in making this imagined abundance a reality.

Throughout *The Old and the New*, Eisenstein employs montage-in-the-single-shot, as well as editing, to make abstract Soviet economic policy visible.[18] Especially in the scenes at the state collective farm, by using a wide lens, Eisenstein articulates the backgrounds and foregrounds of many shots in such a way that the different temporal phases of the collectivisation/industrialisation process are co-present simultaneously. Thus, we will see cream separators in the background of shots with cattle in the foreground, or tractors at the back of, in front of, or in between cattle. The sequence – dairy collective (cream separator), cattle collective (bull-sire and/or harem), and automated collective (tractor) –

is, consequently, telescoped repeatedly into a single image, visually exhibiting for, and reminding the spectator of, the synergies upon which Soviet agricultural planners banked their hopes for the new Russian nation.

There is also an important visual motif in the film – which is the result of neither montage-in-the-single-shot nor montage between shots – that makes the point about the relation between agriculture and industry eminently apparent. It involves the visual equation of the bull Fomka and the tractor. When young Fomka 'grows up' to be a bridegroom, Eisenstein achieves this effect by quickly cutting together shots of successively larger bulls, thereby 'animating' the array. Likewise, the tractor Marfa acquires from the factory is constructed through animation. Moreover, when, in superimposition, that tractor enters its shed, it appears to go through the very doors that Fomka exited to meet his bride.

Fomka and the tractor are, in other words, treated as visual equivalents. As Fomka is poisoned by envious *kulaks*, the collective is acquiring the tractor; and as soon as Fomka dies, the tractor arrives, ready to take his place. The visual narration suggests an exchange of Fomka for the tractor, as if the death (sacrifice?) of the bull makes way for the appearance of the tractor. And this visual theme, of course, repeats in yet another register the recurring idea of Eisenstein's cinematic nation-building. That is, from bulls come tractors, or, more prosaically, from agriculture, industry, and then back again.

Marfa's story: reconciling agriculture and industry narratively

If through intellectual montage and related visual devices Eisenstein lays out an abstract plan for building the future Soviet nation, he also gives this scenario narrative substance, thereby literally bringing economic theorising down to earth. That is, Eisenstein fleshes out the intended relationship between agriculture and industry – between countryside and city – that is heralded in the editing in *The Old and the New* by creating a concrete embodiment of the collectivisation process in the experience of Marfa Lapkina, a case study that illustrates 'what is to be done'.[19]

In a departure from his practice in previous films of using mass heroes, here Eisenstein focuses on a particular hero – Marfa Lapkina, a peasant woman. Inter-titles explicitly state that Marfa stands for millions of peasants. On them the success of the Soviet Union depended, and, in turn, their future was in the hands of the new state. But Marfa is also an individual – a particularly intrepid one who, though a poor peasant in straitened circumstances, shows unflagging resourcefulness and dignity.

Marfa comes to see clearly, on a personal level, that she and her neighbours will only survive through co-operation for mutual aid; yet beyond this, she realises that the success of the community co-operative depends on the peasants' ability to reach out from the village to link their own agricultural production with modern urban and state industry. In other words, she understands not through abstract political theorising but directly from her own experience that the Soviet socialist model of collectivisation, on the one hand, and forging a *smychka* (union) between peasant and proletarian, farming and industry, on the other, together provide the only way out of poverty. And the fruit of her auto-didactic political consciousness is exemplary for the nation, since what Marfa makes happen on the local level – as she forms a village co-operative, which then collaborates with a group of city workers to their mutual benefit – is precisely what the Bolsheviks believed was needed in the Soviet state nationally, on a massive scale.

This union was also necessary at a more abstract macro-level: it was thought that agriculture in general needed to be linked to industrial mechanisation and scientific planning in order for the country as a whole to survive and flourish. In the film this desired union of agriculture and industry is finally secured allegorically in the coda, when Marfa and the male tractor-driver embrace, for the romantic ending of this story is the promise that countryside and city will live together, happily ever after – unlike the ending of Chaplin's *A Woman of Paris* (1923), against which Eisenstein is playing here.

Although Lenin is invoked many times in *The Old and the New* and the helpful district agronomist even looks like the Bolshevik leader, crucially it is an ordinary peasant woman, a 'little person', who is the representative hero of the film. This was in keeping with the tendency in Soviet art and literature at the time of the first Five-Year Plan – a period of cultural revolution as well as social construction. Inspired by Maxim Gorky, and in contrast to bourgeois writers who celebrated the actions of 'great men', Soviet writers during the late 1920s depicted 'little men' as important actors on the world stage; however small the actions of these characters, they were still 'great deeds', because they were essential to the overall functioning of society and, cumulatively, they added up.[20] Not yet the monumental heroic leader of the post-1932 Socialist Realist period, the 'little person' of Soviet fiction was an ordinary industrial worker or peasant, a small cog in the social machine who nevertheless was outstanding for his contribution to socialist construction.

Marfa is exactly the kind of 'little person' Gorky described, no longer to be pitied, as in so much pre-Soviet literature and art, but capable of raising herself and her neighbours to a full measure of 'human dignity' and realising her 'creative' potential.[21] It is in the details of Marfa's particularised story that Eisenstein dramatises the deplorable situation of the peasant masses and proposes a resolution. From a state of poverty, ignorance and separation, the peasants will reach an unheard-of level of prosperity, consciousness and co-operation by means of the union between agriculture and industry. But this does not happen magically, overnight. It is a process of economic growth and political awakening by successive stages; as Eisenstein puts it, 'From a separator to a pedigreed bull, from a bull to a tractor. To two, to ten, to a hundred!' (Eisenstein and Alexandrov 1929: 22). It is a process of nation-building through co-operation, unification and multiplication.

At the beginning of the film, we see the general situation (the old) that needs to be rectified (the new). Individual peasant families live in squalor – what Marx and Engels (1964: 65) called 'rural idiocy'. This was the legacy of poverty and illiteracy, as the inter-title tells us, left to the Russian peasant (and thus to the Russian nation) by the old order. In cramped and insanitary conditions, in chimneyless huts dimmed with smoke and puddled with rainwater, the peasants sleep indolently, right next to barnyard animals. The scene calls to mind Leo Tolstoy's play *The Power of Darkness*, a forceful and deeply disturbing outcry against the degradation and depravity of the Russian peasant in the late nineteenth century.[22] The scene raises the narrative (and political) question: can this situation be overcome?

As a farm is divided in half by two brothers, Eisenstein shows us that the peasants' problem is not only poverty and illiteracy, but the divisions between people, especially problematic in the privatisation of farming. To solve their problems, to emerge from their darkness, to escape poverty, the peasants must be brought together – and Marfa will be the instrument of that movement toward co-operation. The theme of co-operation (and ultimately of collectivisation) becomes as important for the narrative as the theme of the union between agriculture and industry is for the intellectual montage. Only with co-operation at every level of society will the new Soviet nation be realised.

Through editing and titling, Eisenstein narrows the focus from an undifferentiated group of peasants to 'one of many' – Marfa Lapkina. A typical 'poor peasant', she takes an inventory of her meagre belongings.[23] Depicted as alone in her barren courtyard, she has but a wooden plow, no horse, and only one emaciated cow. It's spring. However, without the right combination of animal and equipment, Marfa can't plow. She goes to the neighbouring *kulaks* to borrow a horse, but gets no help from them. As she fails in her attempts to use her cow to cultivate the field, and as we compare her struggle to those of her neighbours, she (and we) see the need for collaboration. Provoked by a sense of aloneness and frustration, Marfa pounds her fist against the inert plow. Eisenstein then cuts to her pounding her fist at a village meeting, where now she calls for positive, constructive action – for collectivisation. The ingenious matched-movement editing suggests that her indignation metamorphoses out of her frustration.

Marfa proposes that the village form a dairy co-operative – the Path of October *artel* – and she becomes its most vigorous supporter. In the face of her neighbours' scepticism, superstition and resistance to change, she steadfastly plans for – and takes actions to build – a better future. She defends the dairy co-operative's savings. And it is Marfa who has the idea to use the profits to buy a pedigreed bull; she herself goes off to the state farm to get the bull. Thus the dairy co-operative becomes a cattle co-operative. And again, it is Marfa who drives to the city to get the tractor, and who herself becomes a tractor driver. With the tractor, the *artel* can become a *kolkhoz* – a collective farm that works the land co-operatively. This local transformation is a segment of the general line – the strategy of building a Soviet nation.

As she moves, often overcoming setbacks, through these three key stages of rural economic development (dairy collective, cattle collective, collective farm), Marfa simultaneously moves through levels of political consciousness as well. By organising the dairy co-operative, she helps the villagers progress beyond individualised subsistence farming – and beyond competition and self-interest. Through the collective use of modern technology – the cream separator – the co-op can produce butter, which, since it doesn't spoil as quickly as milk, can be shipped to the city for trade. And when shared profits from that trade enable the co-op to buy the pedigreed bull Fomka, at the large state farm that produced him, Marfa sees the future: a marriage of agriculture and industry on a large-scale landscape, where not only is butter produced and, through genetic engineering, superior livestock are bred, but also a phalanx of tractors rolls through the fields. It is as if Marfa realises, seeing all these things together, that from cream separators both bulls and tractors can flow and that science and industry can enrich nature.

Finally, to procure a tractor for the co-operative, Marfa teams up with city workers to cut through the bureaucratic red tape that stands in the way of forming and fully automating a collective farm for crop production.[24] Where formerly Marfa was helpless in the face of the *kulaks'* obstructionism, uniting with the city workers helps her overcome the equally unyielding bureaucrats (who are visually equated with the fat but stingy *kulaks*).[25] This collaboration, this synergistic union of country and city, of agriculture and industry, is what is ultimately needed to cultivate the land properly – to help it reach its fullest potential. The land should be worked co-operatively for the common benefit (the peasants', the proletarians' and the nation's). The peasants advance from individualism to collectivism; from division to multiplication; from poverty to abundance.

Moreover, the wealth created by the *artel* is productive, since it is communal wealth that is plowed back into development – unlike the selfish, hoarded, individualised wealth of the *kulaks* who refuse to lend Marfa their horse and who poison Fomka. Metaphorically, we are shown through the optimistic story of Marfa and the Path of October dairy co-operative that the nation-state will flourish through collectivisation, despite the anti-social acts of corrupt individuals.

In trying to reinvent culture after the Bolshevik revolution, and especially during this period in the late 1920s, when the strategy of reaching mass audiences with avant-garde artworks had emerged as problematic, artists had to decide which elements of pre-Soviet culture to discard, which to preserve and which to rework and transform. *The Old and the New*'s fairy-tale traits are striking in this regard.

In some respects, Marfa's story resembles a traditional Russian fairy tale. The narrative has a conventional fairy-tale structure, in which the hero embarks repeatedly on trips to fulfil a quest, undergoes various trials, has visionary dreams, solves difficult problems and along the way encounters several magical helpers who help him attain his goal, in the form of a desired object (as well as meeting several hindrances and enemies) (Propp 1968). In fact, in accordance with the typical tripartite pattern, Marfa makes three trips: the first, to the *kulaks'* house, where she begs for a horse; the second, to the state farm, where she buys a bull; the third, to the bureaucrats' office, where she gets permission to get a tractor on credit. Though her first trip appears unsuccessful, in fact her failure to borrow the *kulaks'* horse leads her to a different and ultimately far better path – literally, since the Path of October dairy collective is formed as a result of her inability to plow.

Visually, Marfa's visit both to the *kulaks* and then to the bureaucrats is also reminiscent of a fairy tale, since they and the objects that surround them are huge – like fairy-tale giants – and she is minuscule. The cream separator, abundantly flowing with sustenance, recalls the various 'inexhaustible' magical objects of various folk-tales that produce endless cornucopiae of food and drink: 'the tablecloth that spreads itself', 'the decanter that does the catering' (Sokolov 1966: 425). Similarly, the tractor that can pull an apparently endless chain of wagons seems like a feat from a wonder tale. Finally, Marfa's story has a standard fairy-tale ending, alluding not only to the happiness of the hero, but to material abundance (often in the form of food or drink, as for instance in the tale-teller's stock conclusion: 'And I was there, I drank the mead and beer, it flowed over my moustache, but missed my mouth' (Sokolov 1966: 431)).[26] And this abundance, the film suggests, will be the bounty of the whole nation.[27]

Perhaps Eisenstein used the fairy-tale structure and imagery so familiar from oral folk culture as a deliberate strategy to make *The Old and the New* intelligible and attractive to, as he says, the millions. The use and reworking of popular folklore – the reinterpretation of fragments of tradition – is a recurring strategy of nation-building (Hobsbawm 1983). Other aspects of rural folk culture – notably, the wedding ceremony, though comically displaced here from humans to cattle – lace the film as well.[28] And the celebration of the tractor's arrival meshes traditional agrarian festivals with the revolutionary civic parades associated with the Bolshevik state ever since its beginning (von Geldern 1993). Thus does the sequence of the tractor's appearance in the village recapitulate the anticipated transit from the old (fertility rites) to the new (mechanisation); from rural idiocy to science; from agriculture to industry.[29]

Conclusion

Cinema is often complicit in consolidating national traditions. So many American spectacle films, for example, restage the putative founding tenets of the republic in ancient garb – the Jews standing in as transparent ciphers for our colonial forebears, rebelliously casting off the yoke of Egyptian tyranny (*The Ten Commandments*, 1956) or struggling against Roman domination (*Ben Hur*, 1959) in the name of freedom. In this way, a lineage is forged from the Declaration of Independence all the way back to the Bible. On the other hand, although he retools fragments of tradition in *The Old and the New*, Eisenstein is not primarily concerned with assimilating the past to the present, but rather the present to the future – he is preoccupied with imagining the Soviet Union to come and with encouraging viewers to participate in the task of nation-building.

If Eisenstein has any bible guiding him in this matter, it is the writings of Marx and Engels, which promised that with the advent of communism the countryside and the city would be reconciled. Through the co-operative use of machinery, the old, it is foretold, can be remade anew – and better. Though eschewing institutionalised Christianity and its theology, Eisenstein exploits the rhythms of redemption, making the peasants the chosen people and the Soviet Union the prophetic nation. The land plentiful in milk and honey becomes a nation abundant with tractors and overflowing with grain.

To this end, Eisenstein employs a full range of cinematic effects, ranging from intellectual montage to allegory. The ambitious editing fugues of *October* are made more accessible to the ordinary viewer by being rooted in causal processes – the recurring trajectory from agricultural production to industrialisation. On the narrative front, Eisenstein abandons his 'formalist' commitment to the mass hero (in what might be called the plotless film),[30] and focuses the story on a single figure, Marfa, who emblematises the ideal citizen of the future, collectivised Soviet state. Like the modifications in intellectual montage, this too is a gesture predicated upon making the film intelligible to the millions.

But by particularising the narrative centre of his film, Eisenstein has not forsaken the project of deploying the photographic resources of cinema for the purpose of making generalisations, since Marfa is an anagogical figure representing an entire class of future Russian citizens. In this manner, she prepares the way for subsequent Eisensteinian characters, notably Alexander Nevsky and Ivan the Terrible, who will also stand for all Russia, albeit in different ways.[31]

Notes

1   See Kepley 1974.
2   It might appear strange to speak of nation-building with respect to a communist state like the USSR, since insofar as it is Marxist, the Soviet Union should be committed to internationalism, not nationalism. However, as early as December 1924, Stalin had articulated the principle of 'Socialism in One Country', which, of course, entailed a policy of nation-building, especially (as this essay emphasises) in terms of economic development, see Service 1998:156–7.

A second caveat: throughout this essay, the authors should not be taken to be in sympathy with the policies they describe; these policies are discussed in order to clarify and to explicate Eisenstein's intentions and decision-making with respect to *The Old and the New*. We come not to praise, or even to criticise, but to explain.

3 See, for example, 'The Real Basis of Ideology', Marx and Engels 1968.

4 See, for example, Marx and Engels 1968: 40–1. Eisenstein makes this concern explicit both in the inter-titles of the film – for instance, the inter-title that reads 'And so the divisions between city and countryside are being erased' – and in his co-authored article 'An Experiment Intelligible to the Millions', where he speaks of the 'profound collaboration: the town and the countryside', see Eisenstein and Alexandrov 1988: 257.

5 James Goodwin points to Lenin's suggestive use of the need for dreaming in *What Is To Be Done?* There Lenin exclaims 'We should dream!', see 1993: 98–9. Maybe it is not too far-fetched to speculate that Eisenstein is taking Lenin seriously in *The Old and the New*. Moreover, since Eisenstein was familiar with Freud's theories, it is not surprising that his 'dream', like Marfa's in the film, should turn out to be a wish-fulfilment dream. The relevance of dreaming to *The Old and the New* is also discussed in Aumont 1987: 73–107. For our purposes in this essay, the relation between 'dream' and 'imagine' – as in *imagined* community – is especially pregnant.

6 Quoted in Davies 1980: 38.

7 Since the party's 'general line' regarding agriculture was in flux, the film was retitled *The Old and the New*.

8 Strauss points out that this approach did not originate with Lenin, but with Marx, who wrote in 1881 that '[the Russian peasants'] familiarity with the *artel* [handicraft co-operative] would greatly facilitate the transition from agriculture by individual plot to collective agriculture; [...] the physical configuration of the Russian soil demands combined mechanical cultivation on a large scale' (quoted in Strauss 1969: 51).

9 Eisenstein's film should not be understood as a brief in favour of Stalin's forced collectivisation of the countryside and the violent liquidation of the *kulaks*, which began in 1929. The film was conceived and completed before the killing began. Though the film is critical of the *kulaks*, it never – even remotely – recommends their individual destruction. Undoubtedly, *The Old and the New* celebrates collectivisation, but not the sort of forced collectivisation that led to the deaths of millions. In our exposition of *The Old and the New*, we have reconstructed Eisenstein's celebratory intentions, not because we endorse Soviet agricultural policy of the 1920s uncritically (we don't), but because our aims in this essay are interpretive.

10 For the best general overview of Eisenstein's theory of montage, see Bordwell 1993.

11 For an alternative interpretation of this sequence, see Bordwell 1993: 92. Also see Eisenstein 1988a: 161–80.

12 On overtonal montage, see Eisenstein 1988c.

13 Interestingly, there is a potential ambiguity in this essay as to whether the authors are referring to agricultural collectivisation as the experiment to be made intelligible to the millions or to the film itself, which is intended to depict/explain collectivisation. We think the authors mean both. (The term 'intelligible to the millions' did not originate with Eisenstein and Alexandrov in this article. The resolution passed by the December 1928 Conference of Sovkino Workers stated, in part: 'an essential part of any experimental work [should] be artistic *expression that is intelligible to the millions*' [emphasis in original]). Quoted in Trauberg 1988: 250–51.

14 One might mistakenly suspect that the relation of agriculture and industry would, perforce, be a theme in any film about collectivisation, and, in consequence, that we are making too much of Eisenstein's attention to this theme. It just comes with the territory, it might be said. But this is wrong. For example, in Dovzhenko's *Earth* (1930), also a film about collectivisation, there is scarcely a moment devoted to the relation between town and countryside. Thus, it seems fair to assume that the

emphasis on this theme in *The Old and the New* represents Eisenstein's special theoretical spin on the process of collectivisation.

15 Call this a socialist 'wet dream'.

16 This interpretation was first suggested in Carroll 1981–2: 185, n. 20.

17 Processions and parades were an integral part of the public iconography of the new Soviet state, see von Geldern 1993. Thus it is striking, in terms of the theme of nation-building we explore here, that the finale of *The Old and the New* is a parade – moreover, a parade in an agrarian setting, in the fields themselves, which supplies another link between country and city (where most revolutionary parades and processions took place).

18 See Bordwell 1993: 150–5 for a discussion of montage-in-the-single-shot (*mise-en-cadre*).

19 In 'For a Workers' Hit', written in 1928 (when he resumed work on *The Old and the New*), Eisenstein does not specifically mention the film, but shows that he was interested in 'how to elevate a particular case into a social epic', see Eisenstein 1988b: 1, 10.

20 Maxim Gorkii, 'On Little Men and Their Great Work', in his *O literature* (Moscow, 1955), quoted in Clark 1978: 191.

21 Eisenstein's Marfa is a more successful character, aesthetically speaking, than many of the 'little men' who populate the novels of the period. Katerina Clark (1978) notes the many problems with much of the literature of this period and concludes that the bulk of the industrial and construction novels 'represent a nadir in Soviet literature' (1978: 202). It should be noted that when Marfa visits the *kulaks*, Eisenstein literalises the idea that she is a 'little person', so tiny is she in the background of many of the shots.

22 Adaptations of classics for contemporary times (*peredelki*) were rife on the early Soviet stage – partly due to a shortage of new plays and partly as a way of renovating elements of the old culture that were deemed worth keeping. *Proletkult*, the organisation for revolutionary proletarian culture (for which Eisenstein had worked as a theatre director from 1921–24), was especially active in producing theatrical *peredelki*; Eisenstein's 1923 *Proletkult* production *The Wiseman*, based on Alexander Ostrovsky's *Enough Simplicity in Every Wise Man*, was a notorious example. The 'circusisation' both Vsevolod Meyerhold and Eisenstein used in their theatrical directing, especially in their *peredelki*, was employed first in Yuri Annenkov's 1919 Petrograd production of Leo Tolstoy's anti-alcoholism play *The First Distiller*, and several theatres staged Tolstoy's *Power of Darkness*, see von Geldern 1993: 115–16; Leach 1994: 52–4; and Rudnitsky 1988: 48–9. Perhaps the opening of *The Old and the New* can be seen as a cinematic *peredelka* of *The Power of Darkness* for Soviet times.

23 The Soviet government classified peasants into three categories: *kulak* (wealthy peasant), *serednyak* (middle peasant) and *bednyak* (poor peasant), see Davies 1980: 23. In *The Old and the New*, when the district agronomist first appears at the meeting where Marfa proposes forming the dairy co-operative, he specifically addresses the villagers (in an inter-title) as 'comrade poor and middle peasants'.

24 Earlier, in a reversal of the scene where two brothers divided up a farm, the city workers come to the country to help the co-operative build a cow shed.

25 Eisenstein depicts both the *kulaks* and the bureaucrats in terms of giganticism. In the early scene of Marfa's visit to the *kulak* compound, the wealthy peasants and their animals – often dominating the foregrounds of shots – dwarf Marfa like giants out of a fairy tale. Similarly, Eisenstein also uses close shots, wide-angle lenses, and montages-in-the-single-shot to exaggerate the bureaucrats' 'instruments' – typewriters, pencil-sharpeners, official stamps and such – until they, and some of the

bureaucrats who use them, appear oppressively immense. By making the *kulaks* and the bureaucratic 'machinery' *large*, Eisenstein literalises the rebus that they are *big* obstacles on the 'Path of October' to socialism.

Also, whereas the indolence of the *kulak* is indicated by his lazily imbibing *kvass*, the bureaucrats' decadence is marked by their ridiculously ostentatious, excessive smoking. The *kulaks* and bureaucrats are a fraternity of vice.

Eisenstein singles out *kulaks* and bureaucrats as leading impediments to the building of the new Soviet state. In this, bureaucrats are especially dangerous because bureaucracy would appear to be an ineliminable part of any modern state. Thus, in *The Old and the New* Eisenstein emphasises the need for the peasants and proletarians to work together against bureaucratisation, and he even comically alludes to the real campaign against this problem in the shot where a pen, an ashtray and two (bureaucratic) cigarettes rest on an obviously forgotten pamphlet entitled 'Fight Bureaucracy'.

26 Other conventional endings include: 'They lived happily ever after, in the enjoyment of their property', or 'Now they live there and eat their bread'.

27 Yet, in other ways, *The Old and the New* is a counter-fairy tale, for unlike the standard female characters in fairy tales, Marfa is never seen doing women's chores – such as cooking, spinning, weaving, or tending the oven (a symbol of female fertility) – within the household (though women did participate in farm chores in the tales as well), see Hubbs 1988: 48–9. It is true that she finds a love interest at the end of the film, but for the bulk of the film Marfa is concerned with agricultural production and with community organising. This aspect of Marfa as hero of the film contrasts with the conservative, superstitious peasant women in the village who resist change, and it also makes her an important role model for women spectators, whose political liberation was an integral part of the Soviet project, and an exemplar of the new Soviet woman for male spectators as well.

28 There is a connection in Russian folklore between human weddings and cattle. According to Sokolov (1966: 206) 'the bed for the newly married peasant couple was often made in the cattle shed, or not far away from the cattle shed, in the belief that the first sexual act of the young woman would exert a magical influence on the fertility of the cattle'.

29 Note, however that there are other elements of folk culture – those having to do with superstition and religion – that the film criticises, in line with the aggressively anti-religious policy of the Soviet Union at the time. The ecstatic religious procession in search of rain compares the celebrants to sheep but also recalls pre-Christian spells for rainmaking. When Fomka is poisoned by the *kulaks*, the women of the village revert to magic spells, carrying out a ritual exorcism against cattle plague that dates back to pagan times (and perhaps casting spells against local sorcerers who 'spoil' cattle as well). On rainmaking rituals, see Hubbs 1988: 255, n. 8, and on cattle disease exorcisms, see Hubbs 1988: 46. On 'spoiling' livestock, see Ivanits 1989: 109.

But both these incidents are framed as parts of a misguided belief system that contributes to the ignorance, poverty and degradation of the peasant and that hinders progress and co-operation. The cream separator, represented as a shining new icon of a scientific, modern faith, replaces the old Orthodox icons. (When the cream separator is first unveiled, it glows like a sacerdotal object, recalling a giant chalice.) Technology and scientific planning deliver the goods, where religion and superstition only delude and deceive. Eisenstein writes that the scientific breeding of better livestock will put 'an end to secret sorcery', and he envisions 'a hundred experimental guinea pigs' murmuring, 'We'll climb up to the heavens; we'll drive away all the gods' (Eisenstein and Alexandrov 1929: 143). The new Soviet state was intended to be a rational prodigy; its campaign against religion in the late 1920s derived not only from the classical Marxist idea that religion is the opiate of the people and keeps peasants in a state of degradation, but from the recent rise of religious observance and conversion among peasant youth that posed a threat to socialist nation-building. According to Sheila Fitzpatrick, in 1928 the Baptist 'Bapsomols' and Mennonite 'Mensomols' were said to outnumber the Komsomols, or communist youth, see Fitzpatrick 1978a: 20.

30 Eisenstein links films with a mass hero (i.e., the absence of an individual hero) to the absence of a plot in Eisenstein 1988e: 59–64.

31 Our descriptions and analysis of *The Old and the New* are based on our viewings of two different prints: one, released in video by Castle/Hendring, is held by the British Film Institute; the other is the London Film Society version.

Bibliography

Anderson, B. (1983) *Imagined Communities: Reflections on the Origin and Spread of Nationalism*, London: Verso.

Aumont, J. (1987) *Montage Eisenstein*, trans. L. Holdreth, C. Penley and A. Ross, Bloomington, IN: Indiana University Press.

Bordwell, D. (1993) *The Cinema of Eisenstein*, Cambridge, MA: Harvard University Press.

Carroll, N. (1973) 'For God and Country', *Artforum* 11, 5: 56–60.

—— (1981–2) 'Causation, the Ampliation of Movement and Avant-Garde Film', *Millennium Film Journal* 10/11: 61–82.

—— (1996) *Theorizing the Moving Image*, Cambridge: Cambridge University Press.

—— (1998) *Interpreting the Moving Image*, Cambridge: Cambridge University Press.

Clark, K. (1978) 'Little Heroes and Big Deeds', in S. Fitzpatrick (ed.) (1978b).

Davies, R.W. (1980) *The Industrialisation of Soviet Russia 1: The Socialist Offensive: The Collectivisation of Soviet Agriculture, 1929–1930*, Cambridge, MA: Harvard University Press.

Eisenstein, S.M. (1988a) 'The Dramaturgy of Film Form (The Dialectical Approach to Film Form)', in Eisenstein (1988d).

—— (1988b) 'For a Workers' Hit', in Eisenstein (1988d).

—— (1988c) 'The Fourth Dimension in Cinema', in Eisenstein (1988d).

—— (1988d) *Selected Works, Volume 1: Writings 1922–1934*, ed. and trans. R. Taylor, London/Bloomington, IN: BFI/Indiana University Press.

—— (1988e) 'The Problem of the Materialist Approach to Form,' in Eisenstein (1988d).

Eisenstein, S.M. and Alexandrov, G. V. (1929) 'Vostorzhennye budni [Enthusiastic Workdays]', *Rabochaia Moskva*, 22 February, section II, p. 22, reprinted in Eisenstein, *Izbrannyie proizvedeniia v shesti tomakh*, vol. 1, Moscow: Iskusstvo, 1964.

—— (1988) 'Eksperiment, ponyatnyi millionam', *Sovetskii ekran*, 5 February 1929, reprinted as 'An Experiment Intelligible to the Millions', trans. R. Taylor, in. R. Taylor and I. Christie (eds).

Fitzpatrick, S. (1978a) 'Cultural Revolution as Class War', in S. Fitzpatrick (ed.) (1978b).

—— (ed.) (1978b) *Cultural Revolution in Russia, 1928–1931*, Bloomington, IN: Indiana University Press.

Geldern, J. von (1993) *Bolshevik Festivals 1917–1920*, Berkeley, CA: University of California Press.

Goodwin, J. (1993) *Eisenstein, Cinema, and History*, Urbana, IL: University of Illinois Press.

Hobsbawm, E. (1983) 'Introduction: Inventing Traditions', in E. Hobsbawm and T. Ranger (eds), *The Invention of Tradition*, Cambridge: Cambridge University Press.

Hubbs, J. (1988) *Mother Russia: The Feminine Myth in Russian Culture*, Bloomington, IN: Indiana University Press.

Ivanits, L.J. (1989) *Russian Folk Belief*, Armonk, NY: M.E. Sharpe.

Kepley, V. (1974) 'The Evolution of Eisenstein's *Old and New*', *Cinema Journal* 14, 1: 34–50.

Leach, R. (1994) *Revolutionary Theatre*, London: Routledge.

Marx, K. and Engels, F. (1964) *The Communist Manifesto*, ed. Joseph Katz, trans. Samuel Moore, New York: Washington Square Press.

—— (1968) *The German Ideology*, Moscow: Progress Publishers.

Michelson, A. (1976) 'Reading Eisenstein Reading *Capital*', *October* 2: 27–38.

—— (1989) 'Reading Eisenstein Reading *Ulysses*: Montage and the Claims of Subjectivity', *Art & Text* 34: 64–78.

Propp, V. (1928) *The Morphology of the Folktale*, trans. Lawrence Scott, Austin: University of Texas Press, 2nd edn 1968.

Rudnitsky, K. (1988) *Russian and Soviet Theatre, 1905–1932*, ed. Lesley Milne, trans. Roxane Pennar, New York: Abrams.

Service, R. (1998) *A History of Twentieth-Century Russia*, Cambridge, MA: Harvard University Press.

Sokolov, Y.M. (1966) *Russian Folklore*, trans. Catherine Ruth Smith, Hatboro, PA: Folklore Associates.

Strauss, E. (1969) *Soviet Agriculture in Perspective*, New York: Praeger.

Taylor, R. and Christie, I. (eds) (1988) *The Film Factory: Russian and Soviet Cinema in Documents 1896–1939*, Cambridge, MA: Harvard University Press.

Trauberg, L. (1988) 'Eksperiment, ponyatnyi millionam', *Zhizn' Iskusstva*, 1 January 1929, reprinted as 'An Experiment Intelligible to the Millions', trans. R. Taylor, in R. Taylor and I. Christie (eds).

9

THE NATION VANISHES

European co-productions and popular genre formula in the 1950s and 1960s

Tim Bergfelder

Discourses on European cinema have traditionally focused less on the inclusive or cross-cultural aspects the term 'European' might imply, but on notions of national specificities, cultural authenticity and indigenous production contexts. In order to establish a national identity for a particular film culture, features which transcend or contradict these identity formations have been either neglected or marginalised, but also viewed as threatening. The globalisation of media industries and the concurrent blurring of cultural and national identities have frequently been perceived in apocalyptic terms, and as a marker of fairly recent, 'postmodern' developments against which a largely mythical film culture of the past, self-contained and part of an equally homogeneous nation, is imagined.

Yet at closer inspection, the history of European cinemas has always been characterised by two simultaneous yet diverging processes, namely the film industries' economic imperative of international expansion, competition and co-operation (often accompanied by a migration of labour), and the ideological project of recentring the definition of national cinemas through critical discourses and national film policy. Internationalising tendencies in cultural production have been viewed with suspicion by left-wing and conservative critics and politicians alike. For the former, globalisation has come to equal the advancement of (particularly American) capitalist hegemony, whereas for the latter internationalisation is seen to erode the cultural distinctiveness of a specific nation.

In this essay, my primary aim is not to discuss the validity (or otherwise) of such arguments. In my previous work I have argued that the standard definition of globalisation as a more or less exclusively American hegemonic enterprise has precluded a discussion of the potential reciprocities of such a process (Bergfelder 1997, 1999a and 1999b). I have suggested that a bipolar under-standing of the international film market ignores smaller-scale, but nonetheless important, interactions between a multitude of international players. I have also questioned the inherent cultural essentialism that informs many definitions of national cinemas, particularly in view of the influence that labour migration, exile, and diasporic communities have had on film production in Europe. Whatever one's position is with regard to the national and international dimensions of European film history, however, it is undeniable that the nearly constant dichotomy between these two dimensions has significantly determined the way in which European cinema has evolved and been perceived.

In this essay, my intention is therefore to show how these discourses (and their translation into film policy) have shaped, and have been negotiated by, international production initiatives in post-war European cinema. I will focus in particular on the practice of co-productions in the 1950s and 1960s. I shall look at the economic frameworks of post-war European film industries which facilitated and encouraged producers to move away from the idea of a national film culture, at the arguments and policies that were mobilised against this development, and at the specific generic formulae that were designed to compete in a marketplace which was becoming increasingly dominated by American interests. Popular genres of this period (among them the Euro-Western in its various transnational configurations, the spy thriller, the horror film, and the swashbuckler) were frequently dismissed by the critical establishment as bland and culturally vacuous imitations of pre-existing Hollywood formulae. In the second part of this essay I want to question this assumption, and I will suggest a number of ways in which these formulae relate, at least in part, to a long-established pan-European tradition of popular culture.

It is perhaps not surprising that pan-European production initiatives have featured only marginally in historical accounts of European cinemas. The American film industry's relatively unchallenged position as the market leader (at least in the Western hemisphere) almost throughout the history of cinema, has made it easy critically to dismiss the various attempts of European industries to create a pan-European film market or 'zone'. Indeed, neither of the two most influential initiatives, the 'Film Europe' project of the 1920s and 1930s and the call for a 'European cinema' in the late 1980s, have ventured far beyond their initial visions of a unified European industry and their idealistic rhetoric. 'Film Europe', initiated by producers and geared towards the popular as well as the international, came to an abrupt end in the early to mid 1930s, as a result of both the conversion to sound and increasingly nationalist political developments in Europe (Vincendeau 1989). The 'European cinema' of recent years, largely conjured up by cultural politicians, has, on the other hand, never been quite clear what its directions ought to be (apart from fending off Hollywood hegemony). It has become a byword, less for creative initiatives, than for a Byzantine process of subsidy allocation and distribution. The economic failure of these pan-European endeavours has further strengthened the argument for the national specificity of filmic texts, and reinforced an emphasis on culturally and nationally defined film industries. This, however, obscures a long tradition of shifting national alliances in European cinemas which do add up to a history of consistent transnational connections.

140

Since the days of the Lumière brothers, and later companies such as Gaumont and Pathé, industrial initiatives towards foreign distribution and production have determined the prevailing economic hegemonies across the continent. After the First World War and the increasing competition from Hollywood, such international activities accelerated and led to a wave of co-productions in the mid to late 1920s. The transactions between France, Germany and Britain in the context of the Film Europe project have recently been reassessed in their historical significance (Maltby and Higson 1999). However, there are many possible areas of economic interaction during this period which have not been sufficiently mapped (for example, the distribution and co-production patterns between Western and Eastern Europe). Even during the Second World War, an international dimension to film-making was evident (though decidedly less reciprocal) in German-occupied countries, where indigenous film industries were annexed as satellite outlets of the German UFA (for example, the French company Continental).

Beginning in the immediate post-war period, and accelerating from the mid 1950s onwards, most European film industries witnessed a decline in purely national productions, and a rise in bilateral, or multinational co-productions. In 1953, for example, of the 104 films produced by German companies, only fifteen had foreign involvement. These figures would fluctuate throughout the decade, but went drastically up in the early 1960s. Between 1963 and 1964 alone the number of co-productions more than doubled, and for the rest of the decade they consistently outnumbered purely indigenous films (Axtmann 1966: 26). Similar developments occurred in Italy and France.

In the face of declining audience figures and American distribution dominance (ensured by trade agreements in the immediate post-war years), co-production strategies provided for European film producers, at least in theory, an opportunity to boost productivity, to share production costs and to increase the number of cinema-goers. It would be a mistake, however, to assume a consistent or exclusively 'European' defence strategy against Hollywood behind this mode of production, at least as far as the film industries were concerned. In fact, many European producers of the 1960s preferred American co-operation over inter-European agreements where such co-operation was available. Thus, the Italian producer Carlo Ponti argued:

> The American film industry produces less films and needs more than ever before the co-operation of internationally minded producers, in order to fill the gaps in their home and international markets. We in Italy can no longer produce films for the Italian markets. The costs are too high, and we can't get our money back at the Italian box-office alone. We need American capital, we need the American market, and we need American companies to distribute our films globally.
>
> (Dost *et al.* 1973: 22)

Throughout the 1950s and 1960s, European co-production ventures were accompanied by, and often competed with, Hollywood's 'runaway productions', films which were shot on cheaper European locations with cheaper technical crews and studio facilities (Samuel Bronston's epics such as *King of Kings* (1961); *El Cid* (1961); and *The Fall of the Roman Empire* (1964), are examples of this mode of production). Countries such as Italy and Spain in particular benefited from these productions as their studios worked to full capacity (rented out to American and European companies) which in turn aided a boom in indigenous productivity and employment. In Germany and France, on the other hand, Hollywood expansion was mainly focused on the distribution sector which hardly benefited the indigenous production facilities. Thus, divergent economic interests between different European industries with regard to Hollywood intervention significantly determined attitudes towards European co-operation, and these interests weighed strongly against national and European cultural policies.

In the following pages, I will look at the ways in which European film industries responded to the possibilities of co-production. Throughout the 1950s and 1960s, the issue of European co-operation was widely and publicly discussed across national industries, and my analysis will draw to a significant degree on these debates.

The strategy of bilateral or joint production initiatives between European film industries resumed shortly after the war against the background of European integration policies and American competition (Hainsworth 1994: 13). From very early on, however, the European institutions' attitude towards commercial film production was rather ambivalently positioned between the drive towards economic liberalism and free trade, and on the other side the promotion and protection of national specificities. A document of the Organisation for European Economic Co-operation (OEEC) stated in 1960 that it was 'necessary to preserve national film production as a significant expression of national cultures' (Anon 1960: 1653), while a European Council directive in 1961 demanded the abolition of all quota regulations in member states of the EEC, thereby effectively undermining the intentions of the OEEC (Dost *et al.* 1973: 13).

While the newly formed pan-European institutions pursued both long-term cultural and economic goals, European film industries were more interested in concrete and immediate economic benefits. Regular discussions between the European industry (through its representative body CICE, or Committee of European Film Industries) and European political institutions took place throughout the 1950s and 1960s with the recurrent theme of defining the 'national film' against the economic necessity of international co-operation. During the same period, European co-productions were also regularly on the agenda at the meetings of FIAPF, the international association of film producers, of which the MPAA (Motion Picture Association of America) was the most powerful member. Understandably, the question of co-productions in this context concentrated particularly on the pursuit of American co-productions with Europe.

In 1949 France and Italy had been the first European countries to sign a co-production agreement, in order to boost production and to balance the quantity and steady influx of American imports. Between 1949 and 1964 alone, 711 films were produced under the French–Italian agreement, a number which since then has risen to 1,500 today. As Anne Jäckel has argued:

> the system worked well because co-producers came from countries with cultural affinities, a similar industrial and institutional framework, comparable schemes of incentives and markets which could claim, until the 1980s, a more or less equal potential. Such fruitful co-operation not only led the two countries to sign agreements with other partners, but encouraged other countries to follow their example.
>
> (Jäckel 1996: 87)

Except for France and Italy, co-production agreements between other countries initially developed, in fact, rather slowly, and on a cautiously bilateral basis, during the early 1950s. By the end of the decade, however, and particularly following the foundation of the EEC in 1957 with its directive of abandoning trade barriers between member states, most European film industries had established co-production agreements with each other. Furthermore, from 1957 onwards, the practice of relatively unregulated bilateral co-operation became increasingly replaced by joint arrangements between governments, setting out detailed contingency plans and guidelines for co-production. After the ratification of the Treaty of Rome, the nature of these arrangements depended to a great extent on EEC membership; for example the German–Spanish co-production agreement in 1960 was still coupled with strict and mutually protective contingency regulations, whereas the relationship between the German, French and Italian industries was free of such restrictions (Leitner 1960: 1654).

Co-productions were potentially lucrative, but they also involved, as an editorial in a German trade paper pointed out, laborious bureaucratic procedures for producers (Anon. 1963: 7). Although all of the co-production agreements were based on the assumption of equally shared investment, in practice the relation was more uneven, and frequently balanced at a 70/30 per cent share. The higher levels of state support in countries such as France, Italy and Spain, usually advantaged production partners from these countries, particularly over those from Germany. In an interview with a German newspaper, the producer Alexander Grüter complained, 'Cinema is still regarded by our government as a somewhat indecent institution. They have forgotten that film is a tough business and has nothing to do with sentimentality. There is far too much talk about culture' (Thomasius 1963: 8).

German producers faced considerable obstacles in entering into co-production agreements. Germany did not have the same 'cultural affinities' which existed between Italy and France, its industrial infrastructure was far more fragmented than in neighbouring countries, it lacked the financial incentives and state support schemes France and Italy could rely on, and it was hampered by Federal bureaucracy and cultural elitism among critics, who considered prestigious high literary adaptations as the benchmark of national German film production. During the boom period of European co-productions in the late 1950s and 1960s Germany contributed in terms of overall investment less than either Italy or France – though more than Spain (Schulte 1965: 10).

What Germany could provide from an outside perspective, at least up to the early to mid 1960s, was a sufficiently lucrative exhibition sector with still relatively sizeable audiences. A widespread strategy of German companies partaking in co-production was therefore the practice of 'desk production' where actual German involvement was minimal and difficult to trace, and largely limited to the negotiation of German distribution rights. The practice of minority involvement was frequently criticised in the German trade press. An editorial in *Film-Echo* in July 1960, entitled 'What does European film mean?' argued: 'Does a film with minority German involvement become a European film? No. It remains a foreign production. We think that we ought to take more care of the German film' (*FE* 1960: 836).

Representatives from the production sector, however, were less interested in the unconditional protection of the national film, nor were their motivations necessarily linked to idealistic concepts of European integration, or 'cultural affinities':

> In the age of political integration, co-productions are inevitable and necessary. Indeed they provide the only strategy to boost the cinema economically, and to secure a film's success at the box-office. Worries that the artistic input might suffer in purely economic considerations, might be justified. But much more important is to find the foundations for workable joint productions with any country in the world which is willing to co-operate and where co- or tripartite productions promise to be financially viable.
>
> (Axtmann 1967: 3)

Between 1949 and 1964, the total number of European co-productions (including bilateral, joint and tripartite productions) came to 1,091. The majority of these films were popular genre products, but it is worth remembering that the frameworks of co-production also aided the art cinema sector from the 1950s onwards, and benefited *auteurs* as diverse as Orson Welles, Federico Fellini, Pier Paolo Pasolini and Luchino Visconti. This does not necessarily mean that all industry sectors equally supported this development. Henri Back, secretary of the French Cinema Technicians Union, argued:

The producers are trying to form a European cinema. Their plan is the autofinancing of films at a European level. This, if it goes through, will enable them to film in any member country. Since conditions in both Italy and Germany are at a lower level than those obtaining in France, our studios will get the thick end of the stick.

(Back 1962: 215)

Similar sentiments prevented the British film industry from entering into co-production agreements. While British distributors and producers were largely in favour of developing stronger European ties and lobbied successive governments to that effect, the political establishment and film unions proved far more resistant, which reflected the British left's more general rejection of European integration during this period. In a particularly hostile article for the journal *Film and Television Technician* (affiliated with the British film technicians' union ACTT), the Labour MP Hugh Jenkins (and former Assistant General Secretary of British Actors Equity) condemned the 'incestuous Common Market' as 'Western European chauvinism' and 'continentalism', setting the tone for many subsequent debates on European co-production (Jenkins 1965: 4–5).

In the same journal, Sidney Cole, one of the founding figures of the ACTT, had earlier expressed his concerns about the free mobility of labour and increased American dominance, which he perceived would follow the integration of European film industries. In his reservations about the 'international' film, the spectre of a loss of cultural identity loomed large:

The kind of cosmopolitan film which has been made in great numbers in Europe in the last few years [involves] highbudgeted spectaculars with international casts, many of which might have been made on the moon for all the relation they bear to any recognisable specific European culture and tradition. [... This amounts to] the deathly elimination of the best kind of native film, that springs from the roots of a country and expresses something of the living reality of its people.

(Cole 1962: 4)

Compared to the large number of Anglo-American productions in the 1960s, explicitly declared co-production ventures between British and other European companies remained rare and limited in scope, and because of a lack in institutional support and guidelines, commercially risky. A co-production agreement between Britain and Germany was only signed in the early 1970s after Britain had joined the EEC. The Anglo-French agreement signed in 1965 has resulted, as Anne Jäckel has calculated, in on average one film per year since its inception (Jäckel 1996: 87). Anglo-Italian arrangements were slightly more common in the 1960s, and, since both markets were strongly dominated by US interests, were often coupled with American investment, as for example in the case of *Blow-Up* (1966). There are, however, a large number of 1960s British films whose national origins and business interests (including the crucial area of distribution) are far less easy to disentangle, and where a national label can only be applied haphazardly.

Obviously, the key factor for the success of European co-productions was to find generic formulae which had the widest possible appeal across national borders. The most successful co-production ventures in the 1950s were those between France and Italy in the area of costume melodramas and comedies, drawing on the combined box-office appeal of French and Italian stars. However, when Franco-German co-productions attempted to emulate a similar formula, the results were far less successful.

One problem with these co-productions had to do with the limited exportability of national stars. Thus, while a number of French stars were popular with German audiences (for example, Jean Marais, Gérard Philippe, Brigitte Bardot, and comedians such as Louis de Funès and Fernandel), the reverse was seldom the case. In particular, male German stars frequently only found acceptance abroad where they were typecast in villainous parts. Among the few German stars to become popular with French audiences was the Austrian-born Romy Schneider. A cycle of romantic costume melodramas between 1956 and 1958 about the tragic nineteenth-century Austrian empress Elisabeth ('Sissi') had made Schneider a top star in German-speaking markets, and the films also sold very well in other European countries, including France.

Schneider relocated to France in 1958, and appeared both in co-productions (*Ein Engel auf Erden/Madame Ange*, and *Christine*, both 1959) and in purely French films (*Katia*, 1960). These films drew on Schneider's established 'sweet girl' persona, but transferred it into a distinctly French context. Significantly, the German box-office revenues of these films were considerably below Schneider's previous German productions, and her subsequent transformation into a character actress in art films by Visconti (*Boccaccio 70*, 1962) and Orson Welles (*The Trial/Le procès*, 1962, a Franco-German-Italian co-production) met with almost complete rejection by German audiences (Gottgetreu *et al.* 1995: 378). Other top German stars with an established star image, such as Maria Schell (who by the late 1950s also appeared in French, Italian and Hollywood productions), Curd Jürgens, or O.W. Fischer experienced a similar indifference at the German box-office where their foreign or co-produced films did not conform to indigenous conventions or audience expectations.

Manfred Barthel who in the 1960s co-ordinated the marketing of the German production and distribution company Constantin argued in retrospect that 'co-productions only worked on the level of the adventure genre. Action was international. The perfect karate punch counted more than a subtle gesture, an exploding motor boat had a greater international appeal than the talents of a particular star' (Barthel 1986: 348). From the late 1950s onwards, action became indeed the dominant generic mode of European co-productions, particularly in those cases where more than two countries were involved. Histories of post-war European cinema often tend to perceive the popular generic output of the 1950s and 1960s as a continuous entity, yet the changes that occurred by the end of the 1950s were quite dramatic. Perhaps the most drastic shift can be observed in Germany, where the most popular genres of the 1950s (the rural-based 'Heimatfilm', the domestic melodrama and the women's film) had all but disappeared by the early 1960s, along with its most bankable indigenous stars. The typical cast of a 1960s co-production would normally be headed by an American actor in the role of the hero (frequently US tax exiles and former B-movie stars such as Lex Barker, Guy Madison, George Nader, or Rod Cameron), supported by a French, Italian or German leading lady, with the rest of the cast coming from a variety of countries. The genres that emerged in the 1960s marked a reorientation towards new audiences, away from the female and family constituencies of the previous decade towards particularly male adolescents. This also marked a distinctive shift from genres based on recognisable national specificities towards cosmopolitan chase stories.

When studying the generic patterns among European co-productions in the 1960s it is immediately apparent that, unlike 'classic' Hollywood genres (yet perhaps more like 1930s Hollywood B-serials), European popular films of this period conformed only vaguely to distinctive generic iconographies. Producers and audiences alike seem to have been guided instead by fairly general and broad categories. 'Adventure films', for example, a term commonly used by producers, distributors and exhibitors during the 1960s, constituted a rather fluid definition, and referred in turn to more or less short-lived cycles of Westerns, historical 'swashbuckler' movies, peplum films, biblical epics and exotic adventure films in a contemporary setting. With regard to the latter variant, the 'adventure' film would frequently overlap with spy thrillers, equally set in exotic locations.

Crime films, horror, costume melodrama and, later on in the decade, the sex film also rarely defined 'pure' genres, and were more often used as narrational components in hybrid combinations. Next to such 'straight' hybrids were innumerable genre parodies, drawing on the conventions of all the other major genres in circulation. One reason for the generic excesses of European co-productions of the 1960s has been identified by Christopher Frayling as a 'certain competitiveness between rival production companies working within a given genre, which in turn sometimes led to a type of internal pressure towards bizarre experimentation' (Frayling 1981: 73). While this may certainly be one explanation for the sometimes decidedly baroque generic manifestations in the 1960s, one could also argue that European producers revived and recycled a specifically 'baroque' European tradition of popular narratives which had its origins in the early decades of cinema, and even further back in the pulp fiction of the nineteenth century.

While many of the 1960s European action films clearly had correspondences with identifiable Hollywood genres, they drew almost as heavily on sources and conventions from European popular culture. Rather than simply imitating Hollywood blueprints, European co-productions of the 1960s frequently relied on the recognition value of well-known authors and fictional heroes from late nineteenth and early twentieth-century European adventure fiction. These included the Italian Emilio Salgari and his pirate and seafarer tales, the German Karl May and his entirely mythified Wild West, the colonial African adventures of Sir Henry Rider-Haggard, and the crime stories of Edgar Wallace and Sax Rohmer. In addition to these authors, co-productions of the 1960s also tapped into the vast resources of the European dime novel and comic strip markets. While certainly not in the first league of any national literary canon, these literary sources nonetheless constituted an international repertoire of youth-oriented fiction which had attracted wide circulation and successive generations of readers across Europe. Some of the most successful adventure film cycles of the 1960s combined the nostalgic appeal of old-fashioned 'boys' own' adventure yarns with a spectacular display of modern visual effects and stunt work.

Coinciding with the emergence of the various nationally defined art cinema movements across Europe (the French '*nouvelle vague*', the British Free Cinema, the Young German Cinema), it is easy to see why the co-produced adventure film cycles of the 1960s were greeted with critical resentment at the time. In their nearly unmediated recycling of narrative sources from the early part of the century, the adventure films were seen as eschewing the social and political reality of contemporary Europe, creating a temporally and spatially disjointed, and purely generic fictional universe. Moreover, the fact that several of the film cycles unquestioningly replicated the often colonialist and imperialist perspectives of their original sources (particularly in the adaptations of Edgar Wallace and Sax Rohmer), or alternatively mapped these perspectives on to the rhetoric of the Cold War (as in the various spy thriller cycles) confirmed to critics that these co-productions were not only escapist, but also essentially reactionary.

The problem with this kind of ideological reading is that it works on the assumption that because of the films' formulaic structures they conformed to the principles of narrative coherence and causality. I would suggest that this assumption significantly misinterprets the way in which the co-productions of the 1960s functioned. At closer inspection, these films do not resemble so much the paradigm of classical narrative cinema established by Hollywood in the late 1910s and subsequently adopted by national European cinemas, as the episodic serials of early European cinema. It is no coincidence that the co-productions of the 1960s regularly returned to, and remade, films from an earlier period, reviving in the process some of the most colourful villains of popular European culture.

Louis Feuillade's master criminal Fantômas (first introduced to audiences in 1913) resurfaced again in a new Franco-Italian series in the 1960s, starring Jean Marais and Louis de Funès. Dr Mabuse, the creation of the Luxembourg-born pulp novelist Norbert Jacques, and made immortal in the films of Fritz Lang, came back from the dead in six Franco-German-Italian ventures between 1959 and 1964. Sax Rohmer's oriental arch-villain Fu Manchu, who had found a temporary home in Hollywood B-serials in the 1930s and 1940s, equally returned back to European shores in the guise of Hammer star Christopher Lee, and threatened the world five more times in a series of Anglo-German-Spanish co-productions. Like their earlier cinematic incarnations, the 1960s remakes were essentially international chase stories, with an emphasis less on narrative consistency, but on a kaleidoscope of visual spectacles and on a multitude of generic attractions. Thus the 1960s Fantômas, Dr Mabuse and Fu Manchu series regularly combined elements of science fiction, crime and spy thrillers, comedy and horror against the scenic backdrops of the Middle East, South East Asia and Africa.

The 'master criminal' cycles provide an interesting link to the undoubtedly most successful 1960s adventure franchise of them all, the James Bond series. Technically speaking an Anglo-American production venture, the series had from the beginning much more in common with the conventions and characteristics of other European adventure films than with contemporary American genres. Robert Murphy has argued that Ian Fleming's fictional hero 'was in some ways an aberration, a throwback to the intensely patriotic heroes of Sapper, Dornford Yates and John Buchan ... when Britain was still the greatest world power' (Murphy 1992: 218). Yet if one considers the ubiquity of the literary adaptations of Edgar Wallace or Sax Rohmer among co-productions during the same period, Bond's roots in pre-Second World War boys' own literature may have been a very calculated move indeed. The James Bond films, aided by American investment, replicated the attractions of the European adventure film (foreign locations, special effects, stunt acrobatics) and retained their episodic structure and generic eclecticism on a gigantic and epic scale. The Bond villains easily found their way into the pantheon of their continental counterparts: Dr No became the double of Fu Manchu, while Ernst Stavro Blofeld, in his variety of disguises and in his mastery of electronic gadgets and televisual surveillance was clearly a cousin of both Mabuse and Fantômas. That the producers of the Bond films targeted not only the American, but also the European market, was evident not only in their adaptation of continental generic conventions, but also in their multinational casting, extensively using actors from France, Italy and Germany. The Bond series had perhaps the singularly most influential box-office impact in European markets during the 1960s, regularly outclassing purely American competition. While indebted to popular European genre traditions, the Bond series in turn inspired a boom of continentally produced secret agent cycles which often plagiarised the ingredients of the Bond films to the minutest detail. As Kim Newman has pointed out, 'if the European spy thrillers ever managed to struggle out of the shadow of Bond, it had more to do with moments of sex and sadism permissible in Europe than with expanse of budget or imagination' (Newman 1986: 51).

Analysing European adventure serials of the 1910s, Deniz Göktürk has argued that 'in their rapid succession of exotic locations these films enacted what Kracauer called the "shrinking of the world" for the tourist gaze' (Göktürk 1998: 181). A similar process in the perception of space can be observed in the various interconnecting sub-genres of the adventure film in the 1960s. Amidst increasingly international casts globe-trotting through convoluted global intrigues, the notions of national and cultural identity became dispersed or reduced to empty clichés. In the James Bond series, for example, Britishness constituted itself less as an identity or as a sense of place, but as an accumulation of consumer products, fashion accoutrements and self-mocking stereotypes. Despite their nostalgic references to old-fashioned narrative traditions, the popular genres of the 1960s suggested to their audiences the possibility of a cosmopolitan and classless identity in a new world, made accessible and commodified by tourism, leisure and lifestyle consumerism. Set against the political, social and economic pressures of national reconstruction in the first two post-war decades, one can gauge the escapist pleasures these genres provided for contemporary audiences.

In their decidedly low-brow appeal, the co-produced adventure cycles of the 1960s can hardly be seen to have connected with idealist aspirations for a European identity. In their multinational mode of production, and in their emphasis on exoticism over what Sidney Cole described as 'the roots of a country' and 'the living reality of its people', on the other hand, the films hardly contributed much to the notion of a nationally defined film culture. Yet from the late 1950s to the early 1970s, this generic framework and mode of production provided European producers with a successful formula to overcome the discrepancies and differences in national audience tastes across many parts of Europe, and in a consistent way which has rarely been achieved in European cinema either before or since. In its narrative malleability, the production category of the 'adventure film' was able to transform itself quickly according to changing film and audience trends by spawning successive cycles of sub-genres and hybrid combinations. Its generic eclecticism, its prioritisation of visual style over narrative coherence and, later on in the decade, its sexual explicitness, on the other hand, provided an alternative to the far more fixed and realist genre distinctions the standard Hollywood product offered during this period. Yet within its own parameters, this mode of production achieved a remarkable degree of standardisation among different European partners, ensuring that productions with varying national involvement still conformed to audience expectations in as many markets as possible.

However one may judge in retrospect the aesthetic merits of these films, it seems undeniable that the co-productions of the 1960s marked a significant moment in pan-European film production, and that they certainly deserve a more serious and thorough study than they have been granted until now. Christopher Frayling's ground-breaking study of the Spaghetti Western (Frayling 1981) and Kim Newman's work on Italian 'exploitation' genres (Newman 1986) are among the few exceptions where critics have attempted to approach this mode of production on its own terms, rather than seeing it merely as a negative foil either for the cultural triumphs of European art cinema, or for the greater technical and narrative accomplishments of Hollywood genres. However, even in Frayling's and Newman's studies, the primary goal is to contain these genres within a recognisably national (in both cases Italian) cultural context. What such an approach ignores, however, is that the success of these genres, and indeed the primary motivation for their production, rested precisely on their cross-cultural appeal.

For too long, film historians have been content with the rigid and ultimately self-defeating assumption that, in relation to the cultural, linguistic and national diversities in Europe, the 'internationalism' of Hollywood has always had a distinct advantage not only over national cinemas, but also over transnational initiatives within Europe. In this essay I have argued that the co-production ventures of the 1960s may certainly have emerged as a response to American pressures, but that they comprised, at least temporarily, a both culturally and economically viable strategy of pan-European co-operation.

Bibliography

Anon. (1960) 'Beispiel kulturwirtschaftlicher Förderung', *Film-Echo* 3, 12: 1653.

Anon. (1963) 'Wie entsteht eine Coproduktion?', *Film-Echo/Filmwoche* 13, 3: 7.

Axtmann, H. (1966) 'Die Exportsituation des deutschen Films', *Film-Echo/Filmwoche* 25, 6: 26.

—— (1967) 'Internationale Zusammenarbeit als zwingendes Gebot', *Film-Echo/Film-woche* 23, 6: 3.

Back, H. (1962) 'French Union Secretary's Warning on Common Market', *Film and TV Technician* December: 215.

Barthel, M. (1986) *So war es wirklich. Der deutsche Nachkriegsfilm*, Berlin: Herbig.

Bergfelder, T. (1997) 'Surface and Distraction', in P. Cook (ed.), *Gainsborough Pictures*, London: Cassell.

—— (1999a) 'Negotiating Exoticism: Hollywood, Film Europe, and the Cultural Reception of Anna May Wong', in R. Maltby and A. Higson (eds).

—— (1999b) 'The Internationalisation of the German Film Industry in the 1950s and 1960s', unpublished Ph.D. thesis, University of East Anglia.

Cole, S. (1962) 'Danger Ahead', *Film and Television Technician* January: 4.

Cook, P. (ed.) (1997) *Gainsborough Pictures*, London: Cassell.

Dost, M., Hopf, F. and Kluge, A. (1973) *Filmwirtschaft in der BRD und Europa*, Munich: Carl Hanser.

FE (1960) 'Was heisst Europäischer Film?', *Film-Echo* 6, 7: 836.

Frayling, C. (1981) *Spaghetti Westerns: Cowboys and Europeans from Karl May to Sergio Leone*, London: Routledge.

Göktürk, D. (1998) *Künstler, Cowboys, Ingenieure. Kultur- und mediengeschichtliche Studien zu deutschen Amerikatexten 1912–1920*, Munich: Wilhelm Fink.

Gottgetreu, S., Lang, A. and Vincendeau, G. (1995) 'Romy Schneider', in G. Vincendeau (ed.).

Hainsworth, P. (1994) 'Politics, Culture and Cinema in the New Europe', in J. Hill, M. McLoone and P. Hainsworth (eds).

Hill, J., McLoone, M. and Hainsworth, P. (eds) (1994) *Border Crossing. Film in Ireland, Britain and Europe*, London and Belfast: BFI/University of Ulster.

Jäckel, A. (1996) 'European Co-production Strategies: The Case of France and Britain', in A. Moran (ed.).

Jenkins, H. (1965) 'The First Fifty Days of Labour Rule', *Film and Television Technician* January: 4–5.

Leitner, E. (1960) 'Das deutsch-spanische Filmabkommen', *Film-Echo* 3, 12: 1654.

Maltby, R. and Higson, A. (eds) (1999) *Film Europe and Film America. Cinema, Commerce, and Cultural Exchange 1920–1939*, Exeter: University of Exeter Press.

Moran, A. (ed.) (1996) *Film Policy: International, National, and Regional Perspectives*, London: Routledge.

Murphy, R. (1992) *Sixties British Cinema*, London: BFI.

Newman, K. (1986) 'Thirty Years in Another Town: The History of Italian Exploitation', *Monthly Film Bulletin* 53, 624: 20–4; 53, 625: 51–5; 53, 626: 88–91.

Schulte, C.C. (1965) 'Coproduktionen sichern Europas Film', *Film-Echo/Filmwoche* 22, 1: 10.

Thomasius, J.W. (1963) 'Produzent sagt der Nachtausgabe: Höchste Zeit für Film-EWG', *Frankfurter Nachtausgabe* 24, 4: 8.

Vincendeau, G. (1989) 'Hollywood Babel: The Multiple Language Version', *Screen* 29, 2: 25–40.

—— (ed.) (1995) *Encyclopedia of European Cinema*, London: BFI/Cassell.

10

THE NEW SCOTTISH CINEMA

Duncan Petrie

Introduction

On 6 May 1999 the most fundamental reorganisation of the administrative apparatus of the British state took place with the election of the first separate Scottish Parliament in almost 300 years. While it is too early to predict the full implications of devolution for the continuing survival of the Union, this moment clearly marks the dawn of a new degree of national self-determination for Scotland. The outcome of the 1997 referendum can be related to developments in the 1980s. During that decade many Scots came to feel a profound sense of alienation from the British political process, with Margaret Thatcher's Conservative administration pursuing policies that seemed to represent the interests, and more crucially the political culture, of the south of England. Ironically this political dislocation was accompanied by a bold new affirmation of Scottish cultural creativity and self-expression, particularly in the fields of literature and painting and epitomised by writers like Alasdair Gray, James Kelman, Iain Banks and Liz Lochhead and artists such as Ken Currie, Peter Howson and Stephen Campbell. The 1990s witnessed, if anything, a broadening of this cultural renaissance with the explosion of a vibrant new generation of young writers spearheaded by Irvine Welsh, A.L. Kennedy and Alan Warner. The other sphere in which excitement began to be generated was film-making, providing the first glimmer of the possibility of an identifiably 'Scottish' cinema.

The justification for, or desirability of, a national cinema in a small European nation like Scotland is a complex issue. Scottish cinema has been, and can in some respects still be, regarded as part of a larger British national cinema which has itself struggled to survive in the face of the apparently unassailable dominance of Hollywood at the British box office. Yet, as John Hill (1992, 1999) has persuasively argued, only a national cinema can offer an alternative set of images and ideas and in doing so adequately address the preoccupations and experience of contemporary British cultural life. This concept of a national cinema also actively resists the essentialising and homogenising tendencies of discourses of 'nationalism'. And, as Hill notes, the 1980s saw the emergence of such a cinema in Britain reflecting:

a much more fluid, hybrid and plural sense of 'Britishness' than earlier British cinema generally did. In this respect, while the British cinema of the 1980s failed to assert the myths of 'nation' with its earlier confidence it was nevertheless a cinema that could be regarded as representing the complexities of 'national' life more fully than before.

(1999: 241)

This new diversity embraced not only the distinct voices and experiences of diasporic and immigrant groups, but also those of the culturally marginalised Celtic peripheries. Indeed for Hill, the advent of a distinctly Scottish or Welsh cinema offered the opportunity for a more complex interrogation of the discourses of nation and national identity than the traditionally Anglo-centric 'British' cinema had hitherto provided.

But the necessary conditions for a sustainable national cinema require more than the existence of a handful of films. What is needed are certain structures and institutions that can provide the resources to enable films to be produced on a relatively consistent and regular basis. Without this, there can be no national cinema, only isolated film-makers. In the early 1980s Scottish cinema was more or less equated with the work of Bill Forsyth. By comparison, the latter half of the 1990s has seen unprecedented levels of film production in Scotland, both features and short films. Many of those have been made with the assistance of an expanding number of indigenous sources of development and production finance. This has in turn created opportunities for the nurturing of a viable, if still fragile, infrastructure in Scotland, allowing film-makers to learn and practice their craft in their native country rather than accepting the inevitable move to London. Consequently it is this institutional conception of a national cinema which will be the focus of this essay, rather than the close analysis of a number of films articulating and addressing the cultural complexities of contemporary Scotland. While the latter is clearly an important and valid project, nevertheless for such 'Scottish' texts to exist in the first place requires the existence of the necessary environment. And to even begin to assess the virtues of particular Scottish films and film-makers we must first of all understand the institutional context, the resources, opportunities and constraints within which such cultural production has been realised.

The first steps

The number of feature films made either wholly or partly in Scotland increased dramatically in the 1990s from five productions in 1991 to an average of more than ten a year from 1994 onwards. A certain proportion of these films are foreign productions, attracted primarily by the location backdrops that the dramatic Scottish landscape provides. But the major upsurge in production activity has been spearheaded by a number of indigenous low budget features such as *Shallow Grave* (Danny Boyle, 1994), *Small Faces* (Gillies Mackinnon,

1996), *Trainspotting* (Danny Boyle, 1996), *My Name is Joe* (Ken Loach, 1988), *Orphans* (Peter Mullan, 1999) and *Ratcatcher* (Lynne Ramsay, 1999). In addition, several international productions have embraced Scottish subject matter – from the Oscar-winning Hollywood epic *Braveheart* (Mel Gibson, 1995), to the innovative *Breaking the Waves* (Lars von Trier, 1996), a modest Danish/Swedish/French co-production – and are important contributions to the current diversity of cinematic representations of Scotland. Statistics compiled by the publicly funded agency Scottish Screen demonstrate the prevailing range of production. Of a total number of sixty-one films made in Scotland between 1991 and 1997, twenty-five can be considered as wholly or partly 'Scottish', fourteen originated from elsewhere in the UK, nine were North American, eight European, one a British/European co-production and four were from elsewhere in the world.[1] While a viable national cinema is necessarily rooted in indigenous forms of cultural expression, these can exist within an industry which also services outside productions drawing upon local technicians, services and facilities. Indeed such overseas interest in Scotland as a location or production base plays an important part in cultivating a thriving infrastructure.

Such a possibility of a distinct Scottish cinema was until very recently completely unimaginable. From the teens onwards the British film industry, including all the major studios and the head offices of most of the distributors and exhibitors, was firmly consolidated in and around London. For a long time, the only viable form of indigenous film production in Scotland was the sponsored documentary. The first Films of Scotland Committee was set up by the Scottish Office to provide funding for a programme of seven films projecting aspects of contemporary Scotland for the 1938 Empire Exhibition in Glasgow. In 1954 a second Committee was established but this time proved to be somewhat more tenacious, surviving some twenty-eight years and helping to generate the production of more than 150 films sponsored by private business and public bodies. The sources of sponsorship proved to be a major determinant on subject matter and many of the films were made to promote tourism, Scottish industry and the Arts.[2] But the Films of Scotland Committee's existence did provide a continuity of work which allowed the independent production sector in Scotland to expand and develop. It provided contracts for established companies and created opportunities for the formation of an array of new independents.

Many of the new companies were run by ambitious film-makers such as Bill Forsyth, Charlie Gormley, Murray Grigor and Mike Alexander, who were keen to move beyond the confines of the sponsored documentary. And as the form became more and more subsumed by television, so the desire to move into cinema fiction grew. The first small opportunities were provided by the Children's Film Foundation and Films of Scotland, resulting in a number of short dramas from Scottish independents including *Flash the Sheepdog* (1967), *The Big Catch* (1968), *The Duna Bull* (1972), all made by the director/cameraman team of Laurence Henson and Edward McConnell, and *The Great Mill Race* (Robin Crichton, 1975). But Scottish film-makers wanted more substantial opportunities to expand their creative horizons and in 1977 a conference was organised by the Association of Independent Producers (Scotland) and the Scottish Arts Council to address the problem of the restricted opportunities available to Scottish film-makers. 'Cinema in a Small Country' led to a submission to the Secretary of State for Scotland urging the setting up of a working party to inquire into and report on the means of ensuring that Scottish film-makers make the fullest possible contribution to the cultural life of Scotland (Bruce 1996: 75–6). The event did not directly effect a change in the current situation, but it did help galvanise the film-making community, allowing their desires to be collectively articulated in a forceful manner and signalling the need for change.

Such cultural arguments were given greater symbolic weight by the emergence of two individual writer/directors whose work caught the critical imagination and provided evidence of the possibility of a distinctly Scottish cinema. The breakthrough came rather modestly in the form of a trilogy of autobiographical films by Bill Douglas recounting his rather harrowing experiences growing up in Newcraighall, a mining village outside Edinburgh, in the 1940s and 1950s. Financed on tiny budgets from the British Film Institute and shot in an austere black and white style, *My Childhood* (1972), *My Ain Folk* (1973) and *My Way Home* (1978), garnered critical acclaim at film festivals around the world and drew comparisons with the work of such international film artists as Alexander Dovzhenko, Carl Th. Dreyer, Robert Bresson and Satyajit Ray. Douglas' achievement was immediately complemented by two wry contemporary comedies by the Glasgwegian film-maker Bill Forsyth. *That Sinking Feeling* (1979) is a truly independent production produced for a meagre £6,000 with the participation of members of the Scottish Youth Theatre. This was followed by *Gregory's Girl* (1981), a charming and insightful examination of teenage obsession set in the Scottish new town of Cumbernauld. The film enjoyed an extended cinematic life as a result of its inclusion in a popular 1982 double bill with the Oscar-winning *Chariots of Fire* (Hugh Hudson, 1981). In their very different ways the achievement of Douglas and Forsyth was to be claimed as home-grown Scottish auteurs who could be taken seriously.

One of the financial backers of *Gregory's Girl* was Scottish Television who also provided funding for other local feature productions during this period including *A Sense of Freedom* (John Mackenzie, 1981), *Ill Fares the Land* (Bill Bryden, 1983) and *Comfort and Joy* (Bill Forsyth, 1984). The direct involvement of a major broadcaster in cinema production at this time was a relatively novel event. But all this changed dramatically in 1982 with the arrival of Channel 4, heralding a new relationship between cinema and television in Britain. The Channel's first Chief Executive, Jeremy Isaacs, was a Scotsman who had produced *A Sense of Freedom* and, according to one source, had also been instrumental in persuading STV to support Bill Forsyth (Gormley 1990). The Channel's innovative commissioning policies have undoubtedly provided a life-line for British cinema, supporting over 300 film productions in sixteen years. But more importantly, from a Scottish perspective, what Channel 4 also ushered in was a greater diversity with regard to the range of films (and television programmes) which could be made and the kinds of cultural experience and identity which could be represented – i.e. the new progressive national cinema celebrated by John Hill. As John Caughie has argued:

> At the most obvious level, it has created the conditions for an expanding independent production sector. This in turn has created not only more, but more diverse films and programmes and representa-tions. Perhaps even more importantly for the development of a film culture, it has allowed the work of the independent sector, and of a whole range of cinematic forms and national cinemas, to be seen.
>
> (1990: 21)

The Channel 4 effect helped generate the economic and cultural conditions which led to a number of feature films being made in Scotland, telling distinc-tively Scottish stories. During its first year of operations, five features set in Scotland were commissioned and broadcast by the Channel. This first group included *Hero* (Barney Plats Mills, 1982), the first feature made in the Gaelic language, *Living Apart Together* (Charlie Gormley, 1982), *Scotch Myths* (Murray Grigor, 1982), *Ill Fares the Land* and *Another Time, Another Place* (Mike Radford, 1983). However, this rapidly appeared to be something of a false dawn, with only one major commission during the next six years, Charlie Gormley's *Heavenly Pursuits* (1986). But the decade ended with a second mini-wave of Scottish productions including *Play Me Something* (Timothy Neat, 1989), *Venus Peter* (Ian Sellar, 1989) and *Silent Scream* (David Hayman, 1990), all three projects developed by the British Film Institute with significant finan-cial support from Channel 4. These were complemented by *The Conquest of the South Pole* (1989), a feature fully funded by the Channel which was also the feature debut of Gillies Mackinnon, soon to become one of the most prolific directors in British cinema throughout the 1990s.

While Channel 4 created unprecedented creative opportunities for Scottish film-makers, it did not create the conditions for a viable and sustainable Scottish cinema. The basic problem was one of continuity. In some years several projects might be realised, while in others – 1987 and 1988 for example – no Scottish films were commissioned. One of the reasons behind this was that Channel 4 had no special brief to promote Scottish cinema and Scottish projects had to compete with the rest of the British independent production sector in chasing what were actually quite limited funds. It was also increasingly rare for Channel 4 fully to fund any feature and so other sources of production finance became more and more crucial. The BFI were helpful in this respect but again their *raison d'être* was British cultural film-making in its broadest sense. What was required was a different kind of institutional intervention geared towards the nurturing of a continuity of Scottish feature-film production.

New institutions/new opportunities

This is exactly what has happened in the 1990s with the emergence of a range of important indigenous institutional sources of film finance that collectively were to transform the sector by nurturing the first green shoots of a distinctly Scottish film industry. The institution most consistently active in the promotion of a Scottish cinema has been the Scottish Film Production Fund (SFPF), initially set up in 1982 by the Scottish Film Council and the Scottish Arts Council. The ability of the SFPF to make a real impact was initially hampered by the limitations of its budget, a mere £80,000 in the first year of operations and memorably described by Ian Lockerbie, the first chair of the Fund, as 'a state of penury' (Lockerbie 1990: 175). During its first decade the SFPF concentrated on granting a small number of modest awards to the development of feature projects, including *Living Apart Together*, *Every Picture Tells a Story* (James Scott, 1984), *Play Me Something*, *Venus Peter*, *Silent Scream* and *Blue Black Permanent* (Margaret Tait, 1993). The fund also supported documentary productions and graduation films of Scottish students at the National Film and Television School. Among those to benefit were Gillies Mackinnon, Michael Caton-Jones and Ian Sellar, all of whom quickly made the break into features.

But by the late 1980s the fund had begun to increase significantly. In 1989 the funds available were £214,000, by 1994 this had risen to £340,000 and 1996 saw a peak of £735,000. This dramatic rise was the result of subventions from a range of bodies including Channel 4, BBC Scotland, STV and the Gaelic Television Committee, Comataidh Telebhisein Gaidhlig (CTG), established in 1990 by the Scottish Office to administer a new fund to promote minority language production. As the fund's resources increased so did its ability to play a more effective role in achieving its objectives. One of the major developments from the early days of the fund has been an enhanced role in the realm of feature films, from the £25,000 invested in *Living Apart Together* to the provision of more than £130,000 towards the development and production of *Prague* (Ian Sellar, 1992). The latter investment generated a certain amount of controversy with critics attacking the decision to invest such a high proportion of the money available in a single production, and one whose content seemed to be only tangentially relevant to Scotland (McArthur 1993).[3] With increasing funds the SFPF was also gradually able to contribute to a greater number of feature projects. The majority of these have been in the low budget range (between £1 million and £3 million) and include *Shallow Grave* – the success of which did much to launch the idea of a new Scottish cinema – *Small Faces*, *The Near Room* (David Hayman, 1997), *Carla's Song* (Ken Loach, 1997), *The Life of Stuff* (Simon Donald, 1998) and *Orphans*. Development finance was also given to the substantially higher budget *Rob Roy* (Michael Caton Jones, 1995), backed by United Artists. In 1997 the Scottish Film Production Fund was merged into a new agency, Scottish Screen, created by integrating the existing public bodies involved in film including also the Scottish Film Council, Scottish Screen Locations, the Scottish Film Training Trust and the Scottish Film and Television Archive. At present Scottish Screen is able to assist the development of more than twenty new feature projects a year. While some of these will fail to be realised as feature films, this funding is a crucial element in the nurturing of a Scottish cinema, allowing a significant number of projects to reach a stage of fruition where potential investors can be realistically approached.

But the ability to develop feature projects in Scotland cannot in itself realise an indigenous film industry. Developed screenplays remain pipe dreams unless they can attract production finance and in this context Scottish projects have had to fight for the same limited resources alongside their English, Welsh and Northern Irish counterparts. The broadcasters have remained perhaps the major source of British film finance, particularly Channel 4 who, in addition to investing in several of the feature films developed by SFPF/Scottish Screen, also fully financed the production of *Trainspotting* to the tune of £1.7 million. But the problem for a distinctively Scottish cinema is that British broadcasting is largely controlled and run from London. The Scottish broadcasters have either been reluctant or unable to become substantially involved in film finance. After a flurry of investments in the early 1980s STV has only made one other signifi-cant contribution to a Scottish feature, *The Big Man* (1990) adapted from the novel by William McIlvanney by writer/director David Leland. BBC Scotland has made a modest but important contribution in recent years, *Small Faces* representing its first foray into feature-film production followed by the period drama *Mrs Brown* (John Madden, 1997), a film made ostensibly for the small screen but which also found a substantial audience in the cinema, and *Ratcatcher*, co-financed with Pathé Pictures. But being a 'regional' office of a 'national' broadcaster, BBC Scotland must defer major commissioning decisions to head office in London. And as the Corporation's priorities are clearly aimed at maintaining a certain status within the broadcasting ecology, so BBC Scotland has unsurprisingly concentrated its energies on producing drama specifically for television.

But fortunately for Scottish producers, new indigenous sources of produc-tion finance have emerged in the 1990s, allowing a greater continuity of work made primarily for the big screen. The Glasgow Film Fund was set up in 1993 by the Glasgow Development Agency, Glasgow City Council, Strathclyde District Council and the European Regional Development Fund, and adminis-tered by the SFPF. Ostensibly a local initiative to promote local economic activity, the GFF explicitly geared its remit to stimulate film production in the Glasgow area to the cinema, in that the projects the fund will invest in must be budgeted at over £500,000 and intended for *theatrical* release. This approach can also assist projects in the difficult process of raising money from other sources to complete the financing. As Andrea Calderwood, former head of BBC Drama notes:

> at the under £2 million budget on which many British films are made, the investment of around £150,000 per film available from the Glasgow Film Fund can make a significant difference to whether a film can be made on a feature scale, either providing top-up finance to a broadcaster's budget, or representing a respectable contribution which a producer making a film in Glasgow can propose as part of a co-production finance deal.
>
> (1996: 194)

The first award made by the fund was to *Shallow Grave*. Although set in Edinburgh, the majority of the film takes place indoors and was shot in a temporary studio constructed in an industrial unit in Glasgow. The film was a major critical and commercial success, earning more than £5 million at the British box office. From this auspicious start the fund has made an important contribution to an impressive number of subsequent projects including *Small Faces*, *The Near Room*, *Carla's Song*, *The Slab Boys* (John Byrne, 1997), *Regeneration* (Gillies MacKinnon, 1997), *The Life of Stuff* (Simon Donald, 1998), *My Name is Joe*, *Orphans*, *The Acid House Trilogy* (Paul McGuiggan, 1999) and *The Debt Collector* (Anthony Nielson, 1999).

Even more significant than the Glasgow Film Fund for the upsurge in Scottish film production has been the existence of national lottery finance. The Government decided that the new resource would not be solely administered by a UK (i.e. London-based) agency but rather would be devolved to the Arts Councils of England, Scotland, Wales and Northern Ireland. The Scottish lottery panel was established in 1995 and in the first two years of operations some £12 million were awarded to a range of projects with the average grants to features being between £500,000 and £1 million. Consequently almost all the major Scottish films to be made since then have directly benefited. The list includes *Stella Does Tricks* (Coky Giedroyc, 1997), *The Slab Boys* (which also received funding from the Arts Council of England), *Regeneration*, *The Winter Guest* (Alan Rickman, 1998), *The Life of Stuff*, *My Name is Joe*, *Orphans*, *The Acid House Trilogy*, *This Year's Love* (David Kane, 1999), *Ratcatcher*, *Gregory's Two Girls* (Bill Forsyth, 1999) and *My Life So Far* (Hugh Hudson, 2000). Not every project backed by the lottery has been realised, the most high profile of these being an adaptation of Alasdair Gray's prize-winning novel *Poor Things*, ironically the very first lottery award made to a feature project in Britain in August 1995.[4]

The significance of short films

Another major development in Scottish production in the 1990s has been the increase in the number of short films being made, constituting a significant secondary tier of activity. Once again the major player in this has been the Scottish Film Production Fund/Scottish Screen. In 1990, Ian Lockerbie expressed regret that so few short films had been supported by the fund, the primary reason given being the lack of opportunities for such work to find an audience. By the mid 1990s however, the Fund was involved in four separate short-film schemes with various funding partners and in 1996 some twenty-two short films were produced in Scotland with some kind of public support (Scottish Screen 1998). The longest running and most successful of the schemes is 'Tartan Shorts' which began in 1993 as a collaborative exercise between the SFPF and BBC Scotland. The scheme involves the production of three short films a year of around fifteen minutes in length. The initial budgetary ceiling stood at £30,000 but this has since been raised to around £60,000 with lottery support, the average lottery contribution being in the range of £15,000. The scheme is designed to cultivate new talent and is aimed explicitly at writer/director/producer teams who have yet to make the break into feature films. The resulting work is originated on film (in most cases 16mm) and is distributed internationally to film festivals in addition to being broadcast by the BBC. 'Tartan Shorts' got off to a spectacular start when one of the first three films produced, *Franz Kafka's It's a Wonderful Life* (1993), written and directed by Peter Capaldi, won the Oscar for best short film. In the six years the scheme has been running, films made under the auspices of 'Tartan Shorts' have won more than forty international awards among them. The most significant films in this context are *Fridge* (Peter Mullan, 1995) and *Gasman* (Lynne Ramsay, 1997), both of which helped to pave the way for the respective film-makers to make their debut features.

The success of 'Tartan Shorts' helped the SFPF to establish two similar initiatives in 1996 with different funding partners. 'Gear Ghearr' is effectively a Gaelic language version of 'Tartan Shorts' run with a similar remit and budgetary levels although only two films a year are made under this scheme. The funding partners are BBC Scotland and the CTG. After helping to finance the SFPF feature film, *As An Eilean* (Mike Alexander, 1993), the first Gaelic language feature since the Film on Four production of *Hero*, the CTG has concentrated its contribution to television drama and 'Gear Ghearr'. 'Prime Cuts', on the other hand, is a scheme backed by Scottish Television and British Screen and involves the production of five shorts productions of around 5–7 minutes made on a budget of up to £23,000. Again the work is originated on film and intended applicants are film-makers with some (non-broadcast) experience. Collectively these programmes have substantially increased the visibility of Scottish production in the international arena, just as they have provided invaluable professional experience to a great number of up and coming film-makers in Scotland.

STV were also involved, with the Scottish Film Council, in establishing the 'First Reels' scheme. A lower budget initiative than those noted above, 'First Reels' provided entry-level opportunities to aspiring film-makers via small grants of between £500 and £4,000 to assist the production and completion of their projects. These awards effectively functioned as catalysts for the productions, helping pay for film stock and post-production. The film-makers consequently had to rely heavily on the generosity of the industry, particularly the workshop sector, for expertise and equipment, and their own pockets. But the scheme did allow some extraordinary work to be produced, including Peter Mullan's first two shorts, *Close* (1993) and *A Good Day for the Bad Guys* (1994), kick-starting his career as a writer/director and paving the way for *Fridge* and then *Orphans*. The portfolio of short-film schemes administered by Scottish Screen took a major blow in 1998 with the withdrawal of STV from 'Prime Cuts' and 'First Reels', demonstrating the fragility of a system dependent on the continuing collaboration of key institutional partners. But the damage was partly rectified by yet another new scheme aimed at aspirant film-makers at the very beginning of their careers. 'Cineworks', a collaboration between Scottish Screen, the Lottery and the Glasgow Film and Video Workshop, provides production awards of up to £10,000 and £15,000, or completion funding up to £5,000 and successful projects also receive support, advice, training, production offices and discounted equipment and stock.

The existence of these various schemes constitutes a crucial element in the development of a Scottish film industry. Collectively they provide a vital mechanism for career development for new film-makers by way of an identifiable and structured path from 'First Reels' to 'Prime Cuts' and 'Tartan Shorts'. This model has not met with universal approval and has been criticised by Colin McArthur (1994b) as imposing a particular aesthetic hegemony on aspiring film-makers which privileges the conventional narrative feature to the detriment of any possible alternatives. This is part of a more complex and sustained critique by McArthur of the funding policies of the SFPF and Scottish Screen which will be explored below. What is indisputable is that the increased activity in the short-film sector has provided a vital continuity of work for numerous technicians, actors, equipment rental and post-production facilities houses among others, helping to sustain the individual careers and businesses which are vital components in the building of a viable infrastructure in Scotland.

Economics vs. culture

The developments examined above have created the economic means by which films can be funded and produced in Scotland. But the creation of a Scottish 'national cinema', particularly given the role played in this by public sources of funding, must be concerned with more than questions of economics. How these initiatives relate to the rather thorny but pressing question of cultural need must also be addressed. As noted above, a sustained line of criticism has been levelled at the SFPF and other bodies by Colin McArthur. At the heart of McArthur's attack lies the accusation that the policies of the Scottish Film Council and the Scottish Film Production Fund have embraced an economic conception of film as primarily a commodity at the expense of important cultural considerations. In other words the kind of cinema envisaged, and arguably being realised, is not appropriate to the needs of Scotland:

> The absence of cultural analysis in the discourses of the SFC and SFPF has meant that they have both been unequipped to think of alternatives to the industrial model, or to recognise the problems relating to national culture and identity that the industrial model might create.
>
> (1993: 31)

At the heart of the problem lies the impulse by the agencies concerned to conceive of projects on the kind of scale which locks them into a particular set of constraints affecting both form and content. The emphasis is placed on the creation of a cinema rooted in narrative-based storytelling derived from Hollywood film practice, coupled with an emphasis on market-driven production strategies. This not only drives up costs but also fails to address the more pressing cultural and social questions to which an indigenous Scottish cinema ought to be committed. Indeed the bigger the budgets, the greater the necessity that films 'work' internationally, the less they are able to address the specificity of the national culture concerned. As a more appropriate alternative, McArthur has elaborated the case for the necessity of a 'low budget, aesthetically austere, indigenously-oriented' cinema under the label (somewhat unfortunate for a rallying cry) 'Poor Scottish Cinema'.[5] Using the subsidised workshop sector as a facilitator, and restricting budgets to a maximum of £300,000, McArthur proposes funding conditions which would inspire filmmakers to look to alternative aesthetic strategies and production methods – touchstones include individual auteurs like Bill Douglas, Chris Marker, Robert Bresson, Dušan Makavejev and Derek Jarman and 'movements' such as Italian Neo-Realism, the French *nouvelle vague* and Brazilian *Cinema Novo*. The products of a McArthurian 'Poor Scottish Cinema' would also, by necessity, have to display a sense of the contradictions of Scottish culture, society and history. The resulting national cinema would consequently 'be manifestly rooted in the society from which it comes' (McArthur, 1994a: 124).

McArthur's critique has drawn rather vigorous responses from some of the prime movers in the agencies concerned. Describing 'poor cinema' as 'an ultimately defeatist interpretation of low budget film-making', Eddie Dick (director of the Scottish Film Production Fund between 1994 and 1997) rejects McArthur's proscriptivism and the idea that aesthetic austerity should be a necessity for Scottish cinema rather than a choice. Dick advocates a cinema which can be both austere and flamboyant, which can incorporate both low-budget innovation and ambitions to work on a larger canvas. While McArthur had built his critique partly on the observation that the kinds of film-funding policies in Scotland had failed to address culture, so Dick's rebuttal charges McArthur with a neglect of the economic:

By definition, poor cinema accepts economic poverty as a given. Poverty is not a condition which we should accept, glorify or aspire to. We should be doing everything to eradicate it. ... Poverty doesn't free the cultural imagination, it ensnares it.

(1994: 20)

The McArthur/Dick debate raises some central questions about the relationship between culture and economics in the process of the development of cinema in a small country. For McArthur the key is establishing certain strategic priorities which promote particular kinds of cultural film-making and allow the greatest number of film-makers access to public funding. While this is laudable as an ideal, it fails to address certain key issues concerning both the material costs of production and the expectations of audiences. While McArthur has argued that the policies of the Scottish film funding agencies have inflated budgets, it is certainly the case that on very low-budget productions various deals are struck in order to reduce costs that may be acceptable in localised situations but have certain economic implications on a wider level. Eddie Dick uses this as a riposte against McArthur's suggested maximum budget of £300,000 for 'Poor Cinema' features:

what he is suggesting would not lead to a sustainable film industry. This is because, in most instances, the budget level he wants production limited to is based on deferrals, low wages or often no wages at all for the work force involved in production.

(1994: 23)

The issue also holds for short films. If everyone concerned were paid at a comparable rate for regular television drama or feature production then the cost of a 'Tartan Short' would be double the current figure.

Of course such budgeting is based on the assumption of a particular kind of production process and end product. One individual film-maker associated with a very different approach to making films, and cited approvingly by McArthur, is the producer James Mackay. Mackay's reputation is primarily built on a series of innovative experimental productions he made with Derek Jarman including *The Angelic Conversation* (1985), *The Last of England* (1987), *The Garden* (1990) and *Blue* (1993), all of which cost a fraction of the average low-budget British production. Mackay received support from Scottish Screen and the lottery for his latest production, *Daybreak*, a collaboration with writer/director Bernard Rudden whose first film, *The Hunger Artist*, attracted a great deal of critical praise. But while it is important that a space exists for such unorthodox work to be funded properly, not every film-maker has the creative abilities of a Derek Jarman or even a Bernard Rudden. At every level the crucial question is the relationship of production to audiences and it is important to acknowledge that audiences have certain aesthetic and technical expectations about what

164

constitutes a legitimate feature film, even a low-budget one. The danger of restricting Scottish production to minimally budgeted works is that audiences might be alienated altogether.

The argument that for a national cinema adequately to address important cultural questions it must necessarily be a poor or dependent cinema has been articulated elsewhere by John Hill (1992) and Paul Willemen (1994). But Hill's (1997) sense of a successful national cinema offering an alternative to Hollywood is one drawing upon an integration of the aesthetic strategies, cultural preoccupations and support mechanisms of European 'art' cinema and British public-service broadcasting. Such a version of poverty or dependency necessarily embraces the kind of projects and budgets (between £1 and £3 million) supported by the agencies and broadcasters mentioned above. It also necessarily embraces the importance of films reaching an audience. From the 1980s most British films have been differentiated from Hollywood products by being distributed in line with an expanded concept of 'art cinema', embracing diverse strands of distinctively British production including the gritty realism of Ken Loach, the aesthetic formalism of Peter Greenaway or Terence Davies and the heritage cinema of Merchant-Ivory:

> In this respect, the adoption of aesthetic strategies and cultural refer-
> ents different from Hollywood also involves a certain foregrounding of
> 'national' credentials. The oft-noted irony of this, however, is that art
> cinema then achieves much of its status by circulating internationally
> rather than nationally.
>
> (ibid.: 247)

The success of films like *Trainspotting*, *My Name is Joe* and *Orphans* can be seen very much in this context. At the same time, the involvement of broadcasters ensures that these films will also reach a sizeable domestic audience on television, a medium which, despite concerns about the proliferation of new channels and a concomitant 'dumbing down' of content, continues to engage with the diversity and complexity of contemporary cultural life.

The need for innovation within the bounds of the feature film is as pressing as ever and Colin McArthur's argument for certain forms of innovation is incontrovertible. But while low-budget experimental production can facilitate unorthodox approaches to form and content, aesthetic frontiers can also be challenged on higher budgets as Peter Mullan and Lynne Ramsay have recently demonstrated. A certain diversity of production does seem to be the most appropriate strategy in relation to both cultural and economic arguments. This is also beginning to be recognised at the level of funding policy, with the Scottish Arts Council announcing a new funding scheme in 1999, Twenty First Films, aimed at stimulating precisely this kind of production. The scheme will provide up to 75 per cent of the production costs, from lottery funds, for projects with a budget of up to £500,000. The major difference between this initiative and Colin McArthur's position is that it will complement rather than replace the existing funding mechanisms available in Scotland.

Conclusions: a devolved British cinema?

This essay has argued that the 1990s have witnessed the emergence of a distinct Scottish cinema, generated by a significant increase in production finance dispensed and administered by a small number of key organisations. This has enabled more and more feature productions to be developed in Scotland and a considerable proportion of production finance to be raised from Scottish sources. But other sources of money have also continued to play a vital role, limiting the extent to which this is simply a Scottish phenomenon. Channel 4 were a major investor in *Shallow Grave*, *Trainspotting*, *Carla's Song*, *The Slab Boys*, *The Winter Guest*, *Stella Does Tricks*, *My Name is Joe*, *Orphans*, *The Acid House Trilogy*, *The Debt Collector* and *Gregory's Two Girls*, while BBC Films contributed to *Prague*, *Small Faces* and *Regeneration*. Scottish productions rely heavily on securing deals with British distributors and being shown in cinemas across the United Kingdom, Scottish cinema-going representing only 10 per cent of the UK total audience figures. Some of the principal figures in the new Scottish cinema are effectively British or even international film-makers, working on a range of different kinds of productions. In the last decade Gillies Mackinnon may have directed three Scottish features, *The Conquest of the South Pole*, *Small Faces* and *Regeneration*, but he has also made films in Liverpool, London, the United States, Ireland and Morocco. The team responsible for *Shallow Grave* and *Trainspotting* has also moved on to more international concerns with *A Life Less Ordinary* (1997) and *The Beach* (2000). One of the more recent projects backed by the Scottish lottery fund, *This Year's Love* (David Kane, 1999), is a romantic comedy set in Camden featuring three Scottish protagonists among its ensemble cast. And despite their Scottish subject matter, *Carla's Song* and *My Name is Joe* are also very much part of the distinctive oeuvre of the English director Ken Loach. In this sense the new Scottish cinema still needs to be seen in the context of the wider British cinema. The new Scottish cinema is a distinct and meaningful entity, but as yet its status should be understood in terms of a devolved British cinema rather than full independence.

Moreover, the sustenance of this nascent Scottish cinema will be largely dependent on its finding an audience, for it is films like *Shallow Grave* and *Trainspotting* which keep the flame alive, and indeed allow other films to fail. The profitability of *Shallow Grave*, which earned £5 million at the domestic box office alone, allowed the Glasgow Film Fund to recoup its initial investment of £150,000 and expand its subsequent contribution to Scottish production. In the next five-year period the GFF supported ten films, including investments of some £250,000 in both *The Near Room* and *Orphans*. If there has been an institutional shortcoming affecting Scottish cinema it has been the more general problem of distribution which has hit the British film industry. While production levels remain buoyant, the figure of 128 in 1996 representing the highest number of films produced in Britain in a year since 1957, this was mitigated by the alarming recognition that many of these films were likely to struggle to find a distributor in what is their own home market. Indeed, of the seventy-eight films produced in 1995, twenty-four had still failed to appear two years later (Thomas 1998). Several recent Scottish films have struggled to find distribution. *The Near Room* waited for two years before being picked up, while *The Slab Boys* and *The Life of Stuff* were given only very minimal cinema releases. *Orphans* also experienced problems when Channel 4, who had provided a major part of the production budget, declined to handle the film through their own distribution arm. Luckily it was picked up by the small independent Downtown Pictures and opened in Britain in May 1999. But the significance of the distribution crisis has yet to be properly recognised. It is perhaps instructive that the annual publication *Scottish Screen Data*, an otherwise invaluable source of statistical information on Scottish film and television, should concentrate on production and exhibition while omitting any information relating to the distribution of Scottish films. But if a number of films continue to fail to find adequate distribution then the legitimacy of public-funding mechanisms like the lottery and Scottish Screen may be brought into question, threatening the healthy but vulnerable green shoots of the new Scottish cinema I have alluded to in this essay.

And finally, what of the films themselves? My express purpose here was to explore the material conditions for the creation and sustenance of a Scottish national cinema rather than to engage critically with the products generated by these conditions. But I will take this opportunity to make a few preliminary remarks about the new Scottish cinema. All of the films supported by the various agencies examined in this essay fit John Hill's expanded concept of the 'art film'. Some can clearly be identified as 'auteurist' works in the European tradition (*Small Faces, Carla's Song, My Name is Joe, Orphans, Gregory's Two Girls* and *Ratcatcher*), while others can be related more to generic traditions in British cinema and television (*The Near Room, Stella Does Tricks, Regeneration, The Debt Collector*). Collectively the predominant concerns of recent Scottish cinema has been contemporary, urban and masculine. Almost all of the films have been set in the present or the recent past, further distancing these films from the Hollywood vision of Scotland represented by *Braveheart* and *Rob Roy*. The city has featured even more strongly than in the films of the early 1980s, effectively burying the traditional Scottish cinematic with picturesque mountains and lochs, remote magical islands and lonely windswept shores. The engagement with masculinity, particularly a complex, vulnerable and damaged masculinity, can be seen as a concerted effort to critique and move beyond the Glasgow 'hard man' stereotype.

While the new Scottish cinema appears on the surface to be predominantly male dominated in narrative and production terms, this masks some significant developments. Some of the films, including *Stella Does Tricks* (written by A.L. Kennedy and directed by Coky Giedroyc), *The Winter Guest* (written by Sharman MacDonald) and *Ratcatcher* (written and directed by Lynne Ramsay) engage in important ways with female experience. In addition to Ramsay, an increasing number of young women film-makers are making interesting short films including Morag Mackinnon (whose *Home* won the 1999 BAFTA award for best short film), Aileen Ritchie and Hannah Robinson. There are also more female producers, most notably Frances Higson, producer of *Orphans* and of Peter Mullan's previous short films, while some of the high-profile institutional gate-keepers are also women, including Jenny Attala, the film officer at the Scottish Arts Council and Barbara McKissack, BBC Scotland head of drama, whose predecessor Andrea Calderwood is currently head of production at the London-based Pathé Pictures.

These developments bode well for the future, suggesting the continuing development of a culturally diverse and aesthetically vibrant Scottish cinema. Contemporary Scottish experience is both urban and rural, masculine and feminine, anglophone and Gaelic. But Scotland is also heterogeneous in ethnic terms and it is important that Scottish cinema in due course embrace the distinctive experiences of Scottish Jews, Italians, Poles and Asians. As a popular form capable of addressing the complex hybridity of contemporary national identity, the cinema has an important role to play in maintaining the cultural health of a newly devolved Scotland.

The issues raised in this essay are explored in more detail in Petrie, D. (2000) *Screening Scotland*, London: BFI.

Notes

1 Figures from Scottish Screen 1999.

2 For more details on both phases of the Films of Scotland Committee, see Hardy 1990, Chapters 3 and 7, Blain 1990 and Bruce 1996.

3 While I want to avoid a debate about the pros and cons of the film's subject matter here, it is worth noting that the SFPF investment in *Prague* represented a mere 6.5 per cent of the final £2,000,000 budget.

4 The substantial sums of money released through the mechanism of the lottery have helped to stimulate production to unprecedented levels. But the administration of this fund has also generated the greatest amount of controversy. The initial panel charged with administering the new money was effectively the sitting board of the Scottish Film Production Fund. But following a bitter and acrimonious public dispute between Bill Forsyth and the board over allegations of corruption, the Scottish Arts Council established its own panel in 1997. The dispute arose out of the (inevitable) dilemma of having a selection panel which makes decisions affecting major investments towards feature production consisting of professional Scottish film-makers who effectively depend on all available sources of film finance for their livelihood. The subsequent reporting of the incident in the Scottish press highlighted objections made by Forsyth and other film-makers to the process but also specifically to the awards made to *Regeneration* and *The Life of Stuff*, produced respectively by panel members Allan Shiach (also the chair) and Lynda Myles. Ironically, two years

later negotiations are taking place for the return of administrative responsibility for lottery money to Scottish Screen.

5   This is developed principally in McArthur 1993 and at greater length in McArthur 1994a.

Bibliography

Blain, N. (1990) 'A Scotland as Good as Any Other?: Documentary Film, 1932–82', in E. Dick (ed.).

Bruce, D. (1996) *Scotland the Movie*, Edinburgh: Polygon.

Calderwood, A. (1996) 'Film and Television Policy in Scotland', in J. Hainsworth, J. Hill and M. McLoone (eds).

Caughie, J. (1990) 'Representing Scotland: New Questions for Scottish Cinema', in E. Dick (ed.).

Dick, E. (ed.) (1990) *From Limelight to Satellite: A Scottish Film Book*, London/Glasgow: BFI/SFC.

—— (1994) 'Poor Wee Scottish Cinema', *Scottish Film* 10: 19–23.

Gormley, C. (1990) 'The Impact of Channel 4', in E. Dick (ed.).

Hainsworth, J., J. Hill and M. McLoone (eds) (1996) *Border Crossing: Film in Ireland, Britain and Europe*, Belfast: IIS/Queen's University.

Hardy, F. (1990) *Scotland in Film*, Edinburgh: Edinburgh University Press.

Hill, J. (1992) 'The Issue of National Cinema and British Film Production', in D. Petrie (ed.).

—— (1997) 'British Cinema as National Cinema: Production, Audience, Representation', in R. Murphy (ed.).

—— (1999) *British Cinema in the 1980s*, Oxford: Clarendon Press.

Lockerbie, I. (1990) 'Pictures in a Small Country: The Scottish Film Production Fund', in E. Dick (ed.).

McArthur, C. (1993) 'In Praise of a Poor Cinema', *Sight and Sound* 3, 8: 30–2.

—— (1994a) 'The Cultural Necessity of a Poor Celtic Cinema', in J. Hainsworth, J. Hill and M. McLoone (eds).

—— (1994b) 'Tartan Shorts and the Taming of the First Reels', *Scottish Film* 9: 19–20.

Murphy, R. (ed.) (1997) *The British Cinema Book*, London: BFI.

Petrie, D. (ed.) (1992) *New Questions of British Cinema*, London: BFI.

Scottish Screen (1998) *Scottish Screen Data 1996*, 3rd edn, Glasgow: Scottish Screen.

—— (1999) *Scottish Screen Data 1997*, 4th edn, Glasgow: Scottish Screen.

Thomas, N. (1998) 'UK Film, Television and Video Overview', *BFI Handbook 1998*, London: BFI.

Willemen, P. (1994) 'The National', in P. Willemen, *Looks and Frictions: Essays in Cultural Studies and Film Theory*, London: BFI.

IV

THE PRODUCTION OF
NATIONAL IMAGES

11

INDONESIA

The movie

Martin Roberts

If nation-states are widely conceded to be 'new' and 'historical',
the nations to which they give political expression always loom
out of an immemorial past, and, still more important, glide into a
limitless future. It is the magic of nationalism to turn chance into
destiny. With Debray we might say, 'Yes, it is quite accidental that
I am born French; but after all, France is eternal'.

(Benedict Anderson, *Imagined Communities*, 1991: 11–12)

The golden snail

In the summer of 1996, I visited Taman Mini 'Indonesia Indah', a heritage park
on the outskirts of Jakarta which presents a miniature representation of the
nation of Indonesia.[1] Allegedly inspired by Madame Tien Suharto's visit to
Disneyland in the early 1970s, the park was one of the major cultural initiatives
of the Suharto regime after its seizure of power in 1965–67, and as such has
attracted the attention of a number of Indonesia scholars (Anderson 1990b;
Pemberton 1994b; Errington 1998a). What first caught my eye when I arrived
at the park, however, was a giant shell-like structure which proved to be one of
its more recent additions: the Keong Emas (Golden Snail) IMAX theatre. The
theatre, I was to discover, houses a 1,000-seat auditorium containing what is
claimed to be the world's largest IMAX screen (21.5 m. × 29.3 m.),[2] as well as
being – to my knowledge – the only IMAX theatre to include its own VIP
lounge. For double the usual entrance fee of 3,000 Rp. (around $1.25 in
1996), indeed, the visitor can watch films from a lounge adjacent to the projection booth, in comfortable seats with side-tables previously graced by the likes
of Vice-President George Bush (1984), King Hussein of Jordan (1986) and
Princess Diana (1989). A visitor's book in the lobby outside records the signatures and comments of some forty-four heads of state who have visited the
theatre since its official opening by President Suharto on 20 April 1984.[3]

In addition to American IMAX films (*To The Limit* (1989) was playing when I
visited), the Keong Emas' main attraction are a series of three films depicting
the nation of Indonesia, its geography, people and culture: *Indonesia Indah*

(*Beautiful Indonesia*, 1984), *Anak-Anak Indonesia* (*Indonesian Children*, 1988) and *Indonesia: Untaian Manikam Di Khatulistiwa* (*Indonesia: A String of Emeralds on the Equator*, 1991). The films were commissioned especially for screening at the Keong Emas from MacGillivray-Freeman, a Los Angeles company which has been a pioneer in the development of IMAX films since producing *To Fly* for the National Air and Space Museum in Washington, DC, in 1976.[4] Like Taman Mini, the Keong Emas and its films were an initiative of Mrs Suharto and funded by her Our Hope Foundation (Yayasan Harapan Kita).[5] In 1992, a coffee-table book about the films was published, in which it was claimed that by 1991 over six million people had seen them.[6]

The arrival of an IMAX theatre in a theme park on the outskirts of Jakarta, along with shopping malls, multiplexes and Planet Hollywood, at first sight looks like a straightforward example of the much-discussed globalisation of North American popular culture (Iyer 1988; Barber 1995). The IMAX film format has from its inception had a global dimension: originating in experiments with multi-screen projection at the world's fairs of Montreal (1967) and Osaka (1970), it has established itself over the past three decades as a popular entertainment format around the globe, with the Keong Emas being only one of 150 such theatres worldwide.[7] The fact that the majority of the 200 or so IMAX films produced to date have been American-made seems to add weight to the arguments of critics of American global cultural imperialism. The 'Indonesia Indah' films themselves reproduce many of the familiar tropes of IMAX film-making, and are typical examples of a genre of IMAX film known as the destination or tourism film, a number of which have also taken the form of portraits of nations.[8]

The globalisation of North American popular culture, however, also entails a corresponding Javanisation of global cultural forms, and their adaptation to suit local cultural contexts and agendas. This is most immediately apparent in the transformation of the standard-issue IMAX theatre into a Golden Snail, a metamorphosis which (the book-of-the-films explains) is an allusion to an episode from a popular Javanese folktale, reproduced in a mural in the theatre's main lobby. More generally, both the Keong Emas project and Taman Mini itself are symptomatic of the very local cultural and political agendas of the New Order regime, most notably the project of national self-imagining begun by the Suhartos in the 1970s with the construction of Taman Mini itself. The 'Indonesia Indah' films are in many ways a continuation of that project, and much of what has been written of Taman Mini applies equally well to the films. Like Taman Mini, they are characteristic of the 'official nationalism' whereby the New Order sought to construct 'Indonesia', both for its own citizens and the world at large, as an imagined community, albeit a hierarchical community in which a Javanese centre presides over a regional periphery (Pemberton 1994b; Errington 1998a). Like Taman Mini, they present not so much a model *of* as a model *for* the nation (to use Geertz's classic distinction), an idealised 'Indonesia' which says more about the fantasies of the New Order than the contemporary realities of the nation itself (Geertz 1973: 93).

Yet if the park and the films share a common ideological project, the films are, after all, films, raising the question of how they differ from the park – how, for example, they relate to the history of film-making in Indonesia and its role in the construction of Indonesian national identity. The work of Benedict Anderson and others, valuable as it has been, has to date ignored this question, focusing rather on the role of print media and architectural monuments (notably Taman Mini) in relation to Indonesian nationalism. Scholars of Indonesian cinema, on the other hand, have argued that popular cinema in Indonesia has occupied a key position in relation to the emerging national consciousness since the country achieved independence in 1949 (Said 1991; Heider 1991 and 1994; Sen 1994).[9] Focusing on the 'Indonesia Indah' films thus provides an opportunity to bring these two bodies of work together, and to reflect further upon the role of cinema in the construction of national cultural identities.

The fact that the films were made by an American company using a film technology developed by a company based in Toronto, Canada, may explain why they are not mentioned in any of the English-language studies of Indonesian cinema which have been published over the past decade. The films thus raise questions about the criteria by which national cinema itself is defined, showing how as film-making becomes an increasingly *trans*-national affair, it becomes difficult to locate films within convenient national categories. Yet even though the 'Indonesia Indah' films may not qualify as 'Indonesian cinema' in the usual sense, the fact that they were commissioned and funded as an official cinematographic portrait of the nation makes them at the very least relevant to discussions of the relationship between cinema, nation and state.

In what follows, I discuss the 'Indonesia Indah' films from the perspective of three different contexts within which they can be situated: the national, the transnational and the regional. I begin by situating the films within the historical context of film-making in Indonesia and the Suharto regime's policies with regard to cinema in the 1970s. I then turn to the films' transnational dimension, notably their packaging of Indonesian culture in the global IMAX format. The regional context, thirdly, is concerned with colonialism and its postcolonial aftermath, particularly with regard to the role of cinema in this context. I conclude with some general reflections on the significance of the Keong Emas and its films, and their relation to the recent political changes within Indonesia itself.

The spirit of national unity

Cinema in Indonesia was from the outset made by outsiders. As Vincent Monnikendam's film *Mother Dao The Turtlelike* (1995) shows, it originated in the colonial propaganda films made by the Dutch in the first quarter of the century. The film usually mentioned as the first Indonesian film, *Loentoeng Kasaroeng* (*Enchanted Monkey*, 1926), was made by Heuveldorp, a Dutchman, and Kruger, a German (Said 1991: 16). *Pareh* (*Rice*, 1934), an ethnographic film which could be considered an antecedent of the 'Indonesia Indah' films, was made by Indonesian-born Chinese film-makers, the Wong brothers, for Java Pacific Film, a Dutch-owned company operated by Albert Balink and Mannus Franken. At this point, film production in what was still the Dutch East Indies was largely a Chinese monopoly, and the nation-state of Indonesia did not yet exist. Not until the Japanese occupation (1942–46) did film begin to be associated with an emergent national consciousness, which would culminate in the declaration of a sovereign nation-state of Indonesia in 1945. The years following independence (1950–56) saw a massive influx of American, Chinese and Indian film imports which inhibited national film production. The period of Guided Democracy after the election of Sukarno (1957–65) was marked by an increasing politicisation of the film industry, leading to a boycott of American film imports in 1964. This policy was overturned after General Suharto's seizure of power – Krishna Sen (1994: 49) notes that in 1967 alone, nearly 400 American films were imported – and over the following decade the film industry was transformed into one of the largest of the Suharto family's media monopolies. The late 1970s saw the production of *Janur Kuning*, the first of several big-budget feature films about Suharto himself and his role in the rebellion against Dutch rule (1946–49) which led to Indonesian autonomy. As Sen comments:

> Perhaps the most important reason for the Suharto propaganda films was that the regime felt that new efforts were needed to justify Suharto's long and repressive control over the country. According to Abbas Wiranatakusumah (producer of *Janur Kuning*), by the end of the 1970s the time had come to remind the people, especially the younger generation which did not know the nationalist movement and did not remember 1965, that 'Pak Harto' had served the country well in the past.
>
> (1994: 102)

She continues, however:

> One needs to ask why in the late 1970s was there this urgency to 'educate' the community, particularly the younger generation? Why did this project of rekindling 'the spirit of national unity' involve the centrality of Suharto in a way that put him apart from and above military officers of the 1945 generation as a whole? Part of the answer may lie in the way in which, in the late 1970s, the first serious student criticism of the President himself coincided with the fairly widespread criticism of the Suharto government from amongst prominent members within the military itself.
>
> (1994: 102)

One of the characteristics of the IMAX film format has been its 'educational' pretensions, as the presence of IMAX theatres in science museums and their popularity as destinations for school trips attests. The day I first visited the Keong Emas, indeed, most of the audience consisted of pre-teen Indonesian schoolchildren. The Keong Emas films, then, which date from the same period as the Suharto propaganda films, can be seen as part of the government's project of the time of 'educating' the population, especially the young, about the nation, 'rekindling the spirit of national unity', and broadening the appeal of the Suhartos themselves as custodians of the national heritage.

In spite of their individual differences, the three films share a common ideological project: that of acknowledging the nation's diverse regional and ethnic cultural traditions while affirming their unity within the modern nation of Indonesia, a principle embodied in the national motto, *Bhinneka Tunggal Ika* (Unity in Diversity).[10] Regional folk cultures are accordingly framed by national symbols, emblems and messages: the national anthem, *Indonesia Raya*, and other songs; the national flag; national monuments such as the ninth-century Buddhist temple, Borobudur; national fauna (the orang-utan, the Komodo dragon) and flora (including the *Rafflesia*, a giant parasitic flower ironically named after the former British governor of Java).[11] The incorporation of regional diversity within national unity is most clearly enacted at the end of *Indonesia Indah*, when children representing the nation's twenty-seven provinces, dressed in regional folk costume, stand in a circle around an ornamental lake while singing a hymn of national unity. The treatment of religion follows a similar pattern: while foregrounding the centrality of Islam (the religion of 90 per cent of the population), the films also acknowledge the country's Hindu, Buddhist and Christian traditions, and emphasise the harmony between religions: during a sequence on the Pope's visit to Indonesia, for example, the voice-over notes that the pontiff 'was very much impressed by the interreligious harmony in the country' (*Indonesia: Untaian Manikam Di Khatulistiwa* 1992).

Indonesia Indah (1984), the first film, focuses primarily on Bali and Java and covers the traditional Indonesian arts and culture most familiar to Westerners: dance, *batik*-making, the shadow puppet (*wayang kulit*) and theatrical (*wayang wong*) performance of the Hindu epics the Mahabharata and the Ramayana, Borobudur, the *kecak* 'monkey dance' in Bali. *Gamelan* music is prominent in the soundtrack. At the same time, the film emphasises Indonesia's modernity, from the urban metropolis of Jakarta to nationally popular sports such as soccer or badminton. Throughout, the unifying theme of the dance is used as a means of tying together traditional and modern, regional and national. The film is the most visually experimental of the three, at times multiplying the image within the frame and using lenses to create visual special effects.

Anak-Anak Indonesia (1988), the second film, is largely an idealised portrait of Indonesian children shot in Sumatra and Kalimantan (Borneo). Children feature prominently in each of the three films, in part, perhaps, because their youth symbolises that of the nation itself, in part because children are undoubtedly a primary target of the films' ideological message mentioned earlier. Composed mainly of Disneyesque vignettes of happy children playing and learning, and lacking the visual effects of the earlier film, *Anak-Anak Indonesia* is arguably the least impressive film of the series. It is, however, the only one of the three to feature the archipelago's rich marine life, through an extended underwater sequence reminiscent of MacGillivray-Freeman's IMAX-3D film *Into The Deep* (1994).

Indonesia: Untaian Manikam Di Khatulistiwa (1991), the third film, focuses on ten provinces from Riau (central Sumatra) to Irian Jaya (west New Guinea) and seems to have been designed primarily with a view to promoting regional tourism. Traditional festivals and colourful local events are juxtaposed with adventure tourism: folk dances, an island cycle race, or an elephant soccer game are interspersed with sequences of rock-climbing, white-water rafting, caving, game fishing, a wildlife park. Modernity and tradition often collide in the same frame, as in a shot of sky-divers parachuting into a circle of chanting *kecak*-dancers in Bali. A segment on East Timor is devoted to the popularity of soccer among Dili's teenage girls.

Transnational geographic

One way of looking at the 'Indonesia Indah' films, I have suggested, is from the national perspective, in terms of their place within the cultural agendas and policies of the Suharto regime in New Order Indonesia. Another way is from the transnational perspective, which takes account of the fact that the films are IMAX films made by American film-makers and is concerned with their transcultural dimension, the dialectic of global and local, outside and inside perspectives, within them. This process partly involves a kind of formatting of 'Indonesia' in accordance with the visual conventions of IMAX films, but also, less obviously, in terms of local cultural meanings.

The IMAX film-makers unsurprisingly make the most of the archipelago's spectacular physical geography, with extensive helicopter footage of volcanoes, lakes, coastlines and the terraced landscapes of rice-fields. Animal and marine life, popular IMAX subjects, receive similar treatment, from Komodo dragons lunging at the camera to coral reefs and shoals of tropical fish. Fish-eye lenses, kaleidoscopic effects, multiple images within the frame, point-of-view shots of rapid forward motion, vertiginous aerial views, extreme close-ups of large animals are all standard items of the IMAX visual repertoire. Time-lapse photography, a familiar visual trope of large-format films such as *Koyanisqaatsi* (Godfrey Reggio, 1983), *Powaqaatsi* (Reggio, 1988) or *Baraka* (Ron Fricke, 1992), is much in evidence in sequences of racing cloudscapes, rush-hour traffic, ant-like factory workers.[12] Collectively, such elements constitute the global dimension of the 'Indonesia Indah' films.

But the film's transcultural dimension also works in the other direction, with the American film format at times being 'Indonesianised' in ways that may escape a Western audience but not an Indonesian one. A case in point is the

178

analogy between the white screen of the movie theatre and that of the shadow-puppet theatre, and the Indonesian cultural association of the 'shadows on a silver screen' of the cinema with those of the *wayang kulit*. In the IMAX films, the analogy is made explicit in the sequence of an actual *wayang* featured in *Indonesia Indah*, but the analogy extends beyond this. Critics of Indonesian cinema have noted that it draws extensively on the tropes of the *wayang*, from narrative structures to the use of stock characters. Discussing the film *Serangan Fajar* (1982), for example, Krishna Sen notes that the film:

> opens with the vision of a rumbling mountain covering the expanse of the cinemascope screen, evoking a *wayang* opening, with the *gunungan*, the mountain-shaped symbol of the universe, casting its trembling shadow across the white screen on which the story or *lakon* is to be played out by the leather puppets.
>
> (1994: 100)

Each of the 'Indonesia Indah' films, similarly, either opens with or includes during its opening sequence the gigantic image of the *gunungan*, one of the country's many active volcanoes. The appearance of the familiar *wayang* characters of Rama, Sita and Hanuman later in the film will come as no surprise to an Indonesian audience. The giant IMAX screen thus becomes a kind of super-*wayang* screen and exemplifies how the films are as much an Indonesianisation of the American film format as the reverse.[13]

One of the most paradoxical aspects of the films – to a Western viewer, at least – is how the image of Indonesia they project, while ostensibly an 'authentic', 'inside' view, is also strangely familiar. To such a viewer, indeed, the mysterious, exotic Indonesia of shadow puppets, chanting *kecak* performers, masked Balinese dancers and *gamelan* music in *Indonesia Indah*, in particular, are by now staples of Indonesian tourism, with a long history in the pages of *National Geographic*, *Travel and Leisure* and innumerable coffee-table books. It was perhaps to be expected that the American film-makers would reproduce the Western cultural mythology of Indonesia; yet even so, it could be objected, *wayang kulit*, *batik*-making, or *gamelan* music are living cultural traditions within Indonesia, and are closely associated by Indonesians with their national identity.

A distinction made by Benedict Anderson is useful here. One of the processes in the New Order's construction of national identity, he has explained, was the appropriation of cultural monuments such as Borobudur as icons of nationhood. The significance of, for example, Borobudur today, Anderson might suggest, is less as a Buddhist sacred site than as a national symbol of 'Indonesia'. What is true of cultural monuments is true of cultural practices: while, for example, shadow-puppet theatre or *batik*-making have been practised by the Javanese and Balinese for centuries and long predate Indonesia as a nation, in the 'Indonesia Indah' films they are, so to speak, appropriated and turned into signs of nationhood. If, then, for a Western audience the films reproduce a familiar, touristic image of Indonesia, for Indonesians they provide a kind of national identity kit, a repertoire of what it means to be Indonesian. The construction of cultural sign systems is one of the characteristics of tourism, and one of the more troubling implications of the films is that in turning everyday cultural practices into signs of nationhood, they reify those practices and, in a certain sense, place Indonesians outside their 'own' culture, looking in. In short, they turn them into tourists as well.

Colonial phantoms

The nation-state itself, as Anderson has suggested is a model: by the early twentieth century, concepts such as 'nationalism' and 'revolution' had become internationally known models, 'there, so to speak, for the pirating' (1991: 156), available to those aspiring to nationhood. The same is true of the institutional media by which nations were constructed: Anderson has focused in particular on the role of the census, the map and the museum. Postcolonial nation-states such as Indonesia, Anderson argues, inherited and were modelled on the infrastructure of the colonial states as censuses, maps and museums had already defined them, and adopted these institutions themselves in their construction of postcolonial nationhood. Indonesia is a case in point: from Aceh in northern Sumatra to Irian Jaya in western New Guinea,[14] the nation's borders correspond to those already established by the colonial state (with the exception of East Timor, annexed in 1976).

As Shelly Errington has shown (1998a: 194–9), Taman Mini not only reproduces this national model but does so using the very institutional media by which the colonial state itself had been constructed: the map of the nation is reproduced in the miniature archipelago of islands in its central lake; the customary houses of the nation's provinces reproduce the major ethnic groups as defined by colonial ethnography; and as a kind of inventory of national icons and emblems, the park as a whole reproduces the model of the museum. The 'Indonesia Indah' IMAX films can be seen in similar terms. In constructing 'Indonesia', the film-makers' first impulse is to get above it, and the extensive use of aerial footage reproduces the bird's-eye-view perspective of the map which was central to the conceptualisation of the colonial state (Anderson 1991: 170–8). *Indonesia: Untaian Manikam Di Khatulistiwa* even opens with a map showing the ten provinces we will be 'visiting' in what follows. The provinces in question are symbolised by a shot showing still images of the customary houses of each region, but the houses are not actual houses filmed on location in the provinces themselves but their 'typical' models from Taman Mini – an interesting example of the continuity between the park and the films. Third, the films reproduce the 'museum' model of nationhood, as does Taman Mini, in the images of Borobudur and modern national monuments such as the Monas national monument in central Jakarta.

One cultural institution which also appears to have been a model for Taman Mini is the colonial exhibition, inaugurated in Amsterdam in 1883 and which reached its apotheosis in Paris in 1931 (Norvindr 1996). The Amsterdam exhibition popularised the now notorious tradition of the 'ethnographic village', in which indigenous subjects from the colonies were displayed as living museum exhibits to European audiences (Hinsley 1991); it included a Javanese village.[15] Taman Mini's staging of the cultures of Indonesia's indigenous societies – the Batak, the Dayak, the Dani and others – does not directly reproduce the ethnographic village model, using mannequins rather than human subjects, but it reproduces the ethnographic museum display which is the colonial exhibition's twentieth-century descendant (Karp and Lavine 1991). The Indonesian park's replicas of Borobudur also recall those of the Bayon at Angkor-Wat which were one of the star attractions at French colonial exhibitions.

The colonial exhibition was itself an offshoot of the world's fair, which began with the Great Exhibition in London in 1851 and has continued to the present. The New York World's Fair of 1964–65, in particular, appears to have been the prototype for Taman Mini, which reproduces a number of its details in addition to the familiar structure of exhibition pavilions grouped around a central lake (Mattie 1998).[16] The New York fair included an Indonesian pavilion, whose exhibits – shadow-puppet theatre, a *gamelan* orchestra, dance performances, *batik*-making demonstrations and even movies – anticipate much of the subject-matter of *Indonesia Indah*.[17]

Part colonial exhibition, part postcolonial world's fair, Taman Mini exemplifies how the relations between the New-Order state and its provinces have reproduced within the borders of the nation itself those of the imperial powers in relation to their colonies (and later, ex-colonies): the exploitation of natural resources, cheap sources of labour, compulsory transmigration, imperialism (East Timor) and, following independence, tourism. This continuity is true of cultural institutions, as Taman Mini and the 'Indonesia Indah' films make clear. In the days of the colonial exhibition, travel to the colonies was restricted to a select minority of imperial subjects: the ethnographic villages of colonial exhibitions thus brought the colonies from the periphery to the centre for display to audiences unable to travel there themselves. After decolonisation, the trajectory reverses. The colonial exhibition is, so to speak, globalised, with tourism displacing it as the primary medium for the display of exotic cultures: whereas Parisians in 1931 visited the Bayon at Angkor-Wat virtually, in the giant life-sized replica reproduced at the Colonial Exhibition, their contemporary counterparts visit its model, now restored for touristic consumption, on location in Cambodia.

Cinema and photography have occupied a key position in the colonial project since their invention (Tobing Rony 1996). The photographs and *actualités* films of the colonies brought back by European photographers and film-makers for viewing by metropolitan audiences served a purpose similar to the colonial exhibitions. In the postcolonial age of tourism, colonial cinema becomes tourist cinema, depicting the world not of the colonies but as remade by tourism, a world of exotic foods, colourful costumes and performances reminiscent of the colonial exhibitions of Amsterdam and Paris. This is the kind of cinema which might have been shown at the Indonesia pavilion of the New York World's Fair of 1964–65, and which is shown at its successor, Taman Mini, in the 1980s. If Taman Mini, in its evocation of the colonial exhibition and the world's fair, recalls the colonial phase of global history, the IMAX films clearly correspond to its postcolonial, touristic phase, in which the trajectory from periphery to centre is reversed, and the provinces are viewed less as colonies than tourist destinations. While Taman Mini symbolically brings the provinces to the Javanese centre, the IMAX films symbolically *take us there*, in the process promoting actual tourism to the provinces concerned.

In light of the preceding discussion, it becomes interesting to compare the 'Indonesia Indah' films with Dutch colonial propaganda films of the Dutch East Indies of the kind anthologised in Vincent Monnikendam's film *Mother Dao The Turtlelike*.[18] The Dutch films were made for consumption at home, and appear to have been intended to legitimate the colonial project and naturalise the idea of the colonial state as an extension of the imperial one. The second and third IMAX films, in particular (which focus on islands outside Java and Bali) are also filmed for a metropolitan (Javanese) audience and shot on location in the exotic territories of the Outer Islands. They too serve to naturalise the metropolitan state's authority over these territories. The relation of centre to periphery in this case, is, however, the postcolonial one of tourism. The Dutch colonial films emphasise labour and productivity; colonial subjects are shown, above all, working, producing and processing raw materials for the imperial centre, always under the watchful eye of their white-suited colonial superiors. In the IMAX footage of the provinces of Sumatra, Kalimantan, Sulawesi and Irian Jaya, by contrast, the focus is emphatically on play, in the form of colourful local festivals, folk dances – all of which, of course, are favourite spectacles for tourists. The provinces are depicted above all as a kind of adventure playground packed with exciting and fun leisure activities, from white-water rafting to watching elephants playing soccer. If work seems curiously absent from these provincial lives, it may be because the tourist industry is fast becoming one of the few remaining sources of income available to indigenous societies; the performance of cultural rituals for tourists has itself become a new form of work.

If the advent of mass tourism has, in part, turned the world into a postcolonial exhibition, it could be said that through the 'Indonesia Indah' IMAX films, the New Order symbolically turns the nation itself into Taman Mini. What is ultimately most troubling about both the park and the films is that they show how in the contemporary world, tourism has become one of the dominant modes for articulating national identity. A visit to Borobudur, an icon of nationhood, becomes a ritual way of affirming one's national identity. The outcome of the New Order's project of national self-imagining has been to turn its citizens into tourists.

The IMAX Borobudur

One of the characteristics of tourism as a system of representation, according to Dean MacCannell, is 'staged authenticity' (1976: 91–107). Taman Mini is a case in point, and its staging of the authenticity of its exhibition pavilions or its miniature replicas of Borobudur as if they were the real thing is, to this extent, eminently touristic (see Pemberton 1994b). The 'Indonesia Indah' IMAX films appear to take the staging of authenticity a step further than the park in several respects. To take the example of Borobudur: in contrast to the miniature replicas outside, first of all, the IMAX Borobudur almost reproduces the scale of the original monument; better yet, while admittedly 'only' an image, it is nevertheless an image of the *actual* Borobudur.[19] The image is a record of the camera's (authentic) presence at the real Borobudur: the indexical quality of the cinematographic image offers a superior experience of authenticity to the merely iconic replicas of Borobudur outside.[20] The camera functions as a kind of proxy: it was there *on our behalf*, so to speak, and through it we can, in imagination, feel as if we are there too.

What is true of 'Borobudur' is true of 'Indonesia' in general: the indexicality of film – the fact that the camera was *there* – makes the exhibition pavilions of the park outside pale into inauthenticity by comparison. The authenticity the camera seems to deliver is illusory, of course, but it is a powerful illusion nonetheless: while the folk dances the camera records are, in their way, as staged as those regularly held at the park itself, their authenticity is guaranteed by the fact that they are performed by the people who *actually* live there. This principle of actuality – the actual Borobudur, actual Bali, an actual Komodo dragon – is ultimately what makes the 'Indonesia Indah' films seem like an improved version of Taman Mini.

Claiming modernity

Benedict Anderson has suggested that one of the ways in which the New Order sought to legitimate its political authority was by the claiming of tradition, in the form of the appropriation of historical monuments as icons of national identity (1990b: 175–83). Both Taman Mini and the 'Indonesia Indah' films include much evidence of this claiming of tradition, of course, from Borobudur to all the other emblems of Indonesianness they put on display. It is equally clear, though, that they are as much about the claiming of modernity (or in the case of the IMAX films, perhaps, postmodernity) as about claiming tradition. The appropriation of (post-) modern global cultural forms as well as local, traditional ones – deciding that Indonesia should have its *own* world's fair, its *own*

IMAX theatre – are as much acts of national self-definition as claims to tradition: ways of staking a claim to being a (post-) modern nation-state, a legitimate player on the global stage.

From this perspective, the Keong Emas' VIP lounge begins to make more sense. Bringing the world's statesmen and women to the theatre, while ostensibly to show the 'traditional' Indonesia, also becomes a ritual proclamation of modernity. What better way to say to the world's leaders: our nation has its roots in a traditional, ancient past, yet *we too are modern*. Both the architecture of the Keong Emas itself and the images on the screen embody the same message. What is ultimately striking about this message is that it is addressed either over the heads of ordinary Indonesians themselves, from the Suhartos to the world's leaders, or at best from the top down, from the state to the people. It is, in other words, the discourse of official nationalism, in contrast to the resurgent popular nationalism of Sukarno which has recently, after thirty years, overthrown it.

A peculiar sense of temporality

> Yet might not the park itself one day stand as an unintended monument to an era strangely devoted to 'tradition', to a bygone time founded upon a peculiar sense of temporality? Or as an unintended museum to the New Order past which might be called a museum because everything in it would be, indeed, old?
>
> (John Pemberton, 'Recollections from "Beautiful Indonesia"', 1994b)

Concluding his analysis of what he calls the 'peculiar sense of temporality' which pervades the Suhartos' cultural projects, a kind of self-inscription into a future history not yet realised, John Pemberton looks forward, in a similarly future-anterior mode, to a time when Taman Mini and similar projects will have become simply relics of a bygone age of Indonesian history known as the New Order. Writing in 1994, Pemberton may not have suspected that the future would come so soon. Five years on, with Suharto deposed and a fragile democracy debating whether to appoint the daughter of his former rival, Sukarno, as the nation's president, Taman Mini and the 'Indonesia Indah' films are being rapidly overtaken by history. As the Indonesian army withdraws from East Timor in the wake of a UN-sponsored independence vote and its subsequent devastation by pro-Jakarta militias, with long-running separatist movements in Aceh and West Irian continuing to gain ground, ethnic wars continuing between Dayak headhunters and Madurese transmigrants in West Kalimantan,[21] Christians and Muslims in Ambon, and at the time of writing, a return to mass student protests in Jakarta, the integrity of the nation itself is in question, with some predicting that its future lies in a confederation of more or less autonomous states. Against such a background, the 'Indonesia Indah' of Taman Mini and the Keong Emas' IMAX films looks increasingly like a colonial fantasy.

The repercussions of these developments for film-making in Indonesia are not clear. While the nation's fledgling democracy may facilitate a more critical re-examination of the New Order by Indonesian film-makers, another outcome may be the increasing emergence of post-national regional cinemas which document their own cultural realities, in contrast to the centralising view of the 'Indonesia Indah' films, as postcolonial cinemas have been doing elsewhere in the world since the 1950s.

As history widens the temporal divide between Taman Mini and the present, it seems likely that, as Pemberton anticipated, it will come to be seen as a museum of a different kind, the Museum of the New Order, and the nation it once imagined. In the ruins of this museum, in the coming century, the future historian may still be able to visit the old Keong Emas IMAX theatre with its films of 'Indonesia Indah', its VIP lounge and its visitor's book, whose yellowed pages still bear the fading signatures of the world's leaders and their friends, the Suhartos.

Acknowledgements

I would like to thank Alec Lorimore, Vice President of Film Production and Development at MacGillivray Freeman Films, for kindly agreeing to lend me videotape copies of the three 'Indonesia Indah' IMAX films discussed in this article. I am also indebted to Benedict Anderson, Shelly Errington and John Pemberton, whose writings on Taman Mini and Indonesia were the starting-point for many of my reflections on the Keong Emas IMAX theatre and its films. Special thanks to John Pemberton, whose article on Taman Mini first brought it to my attention and inspired me to go there.

Notes

1　The term 'heritage park' has become common in the recent literature on tourism to describe parks which differ from those of the Disney variety in their focus on cultural history and goal of educating rather than just entertaining their visitors. On heritage parks, see Kirschenblatt-Gimblett 1998.

2　Figures for the exact size of the screen are inconsistent. The frontispiece to Philip Hayward and Tana Wollen's book *Future Visions* (1993) lists its size as 21.5 × 28.3m, but the official book on the theatre, *Indonesia: Untaian Manikam Di Khatulistiwa* (1992: 180), lists it as 21.5 × 29.3m. The latter book notes that the screen was listed as the world's largest in editions of the Guinness Book of Records from 1985–92.

3　The official book on the theatre and its films reproduces a selection of comments by these dignitaries, as well as by Indonesian tourists. After watching *Indonesia Indah* in 1985, British Prime Minister Margaret Thatcher commented: 'A wonderful occasion; we wouldn't have missed it for anything. Many congratulations'. Her husband, Dennis, added: 'A very beautiful film with high taste and creativity' (*Indonesia: Untaian Manikam Di Khatulistiwa* 1992: 186).

4 MacGillivray-Freeman's website (www.macfreefilms.com) notes that the company has produced twenty-seven IMAX films in all, including the *Indonesia Indah* series, since 1976.

5 E.N. Sudharmono 1992: 8–9. On Harapan Kita's role in the building of Taman Mini, see Anderson 1990b: 176 and Pemberton 1994a: 152–5.

6 *Indonesia: Untaian Manikam Di Khatulistiwa* 1992: 182.

7 A recent article in a supplement commemorating the opening of the British Film Institute's new IMAX cinema in London claims that ninety-eight of these theatres were built between 1996 and 1998, with 100 more planned to open in the next two years. See *The BFI London IMAX Cinema 1999: 4.*

8 On genres of IMAX film, see Wollen 1993: 19, 22. In addition to Indonesia, IMAX films have been made about Japan (1984), Switzerland (1991) and Mexico (1996).

9 For a short introduction to Indonesian cinema and its history, see Hanan 1996. Heider's study of Indonesian cinema takes an anthropological approach to popular cinema; Sen's provides a detailed institutional history of the political and economic issues which have shaped the Indonesian film industry from the 1950s to the present.

10 The Indonesian national motto, ascribed to the poet Empu Tantular (Sudharmono 1992: 8).

11 Bastin (1999: 20) explains that the giant parasitic plant discovered in Bengkulu (Sumatra) by Dr. Joseph Arnold and Raffles around 1818 was assigned the generic name of *Rafflesia* by Robert Brown. On Raffles, see Barley 1999.

12 On global documentaries and Ron Fricke's film *Baraka* in particular, see Roberts 1998.

13 An interesting exploration of the affinities between shadow-puppet theatre and cinema is ShadowLight Productions' *Wayang Listrik: Electric Shadows of Bali* (1998), an experimental form of *wayang kulit* which:

> expands on its traditional roots by adding ideas from the world of cinema: a giant screen, multiple light sources, and cinematic perspective, brought alive by a cast of several actors and puppeteers. The effect is an extraordinary kind of epic theater which combines the power of shadows, the scale of film and the immediacy of live performance.
>
> (ShadowLight Productions 1998)

ShadowLight's web site is at: www.shadowlight.com.

14 On the colonisation and history of the struggle for independence in Irian Jaya, see Sharp 1977.

15 A website devoted to the 1883 exhibition notes that it included 'a Javanese village … inhabited by real natives, as well as a Javanese compound with a pagoda, (and) a bridge made of bamboo' (parallel.park.org/Netherlands/pavilions/world_expositions/ index_2.htm). It was in a similar Javanese village, sixteen years later, that the French composer Claude Debussy is reputed to have first heard a *gamelan* orchestra at the 1889 Exposition Universelle in Paris.

16 I have been unable to confirm whether the Suhartos actually attended the New York fair, but a number of Taman Mini's features suggest that they at least knew of it. The Indonesian park includes a scaled-down replica of the Unisphere, the giant stainless-steel sculpture of the globe which was the New York fair's central symbol. Taman Mini's cable cars and monorail also closely resemble those of the New York fair.

17 *Official Guide: New York World's Fair 1964–65* 1964: 144, 168. Ironically, the Indonesia pavilion closed prematurely during the summer of 1965 (Nicholson 1989: 82), possibly because of the political events which were to culminate in General Suharto's rise to power.

18 In what follows, I am comparing the IMAX films to the historical Dutch films, not Monnikendam's contemporary reassemblage of them in *Mother Dao The Turtlelike*, which is meant as a critique of the colonial regime, contrary to the intentions of the original films.

19 On the history of Borobudur's reincarnation as national icon and tourist attraction, see Anderson 1990b and Errington 1998b.

20 I realise that I am departing from the semiotic orthodoxy here, according to which a photographic image is usually categorised as an *icon* (graphic image of its object) in contrast both to the *index* (which involves a causal relation between signifier and signified) and the *sign* (in which the relation is arbitrary). The problem with this model is that it fails to differentiate adequately between the photograph and the replica, both of which are 'iconic'. To view a photographic, or cinematographic image as indexical is to emphasise its analogical dimension, as the result of a visual *imprint* on the film itself. Inasmuch as photography and film record something before which the camera was actually present, they differ from replicas.

21 On the resurgence of headhunting among the Dayak and their ethnic war with Madurese transmigrants in Western Kalimantan, see Parry 1998.

Bibliography

Anderson, B. (1990a) *Language and Power: Exploring Political Cultures in Indonesia*, Ithaca, NY: Cornell University Press.

—— (1990b) 'Cartoons and Monuments: The Evolution of Political Communication under the New Order', in Anderson 1990a.

—— (1991) *Imagined Communities: Reflections on the Origins and Spread of Nationalism*, 2nd edn, London: Verso.

Barber, B. (1995) *Jihad vs. McWorld*, New York: Times Books.

Barley, N. (ed.) (1999) *The Golden Sword: Stamford Raffles and the East*, London: British Museum Press.

Bastin, J. (1999) 'Raffles the Naturalist', in Nigel Barley (ed.).

BFI London IMAX Cinema, The (1999), special supplement sponsored by BFI London IMAX Cinema, 8 June 1999.

Dissayanake, W. (ed.) (1994) *Colonialism and Nationalism in Asian Cinema*, Bloomington, IN: Indiana University Press.

Errington, S. (1998a) 'The Cosmic Theme Park of the Javanese', in Errington 1998c.

—— (1998b) 'Making Progress on Borobudur', in Errington 1998c.

—— (1998c) *The Death of Authentic Primitive Art and Other Tales of Progress*, Berkeley, CA: University of California Press, pp. 188–227.

Geertz, C. (1973) 'Religion as a Cultural System', in *The Interpretation of Cultures*, New York: Basic Books.

Hanan, D. (1996) 'Indonesian Cinema', in Nowell-Smith (ed.).

Hayward, P. and Wollen, T. (eds) (1993) *Future Visions: New Technologies of the Screen*, London: BFI.

Heider, K.G. (1991) *Indonesian Cinema: National Culture on Screen*, Honolulu, HI: University of Hawaii Press.

—— (1994) 'National Cinema, National Culture: The Indonesian Case', in Dissayanake (ed.).

Hinsley, C.M. (1991) 'The World as Marketplace: Commodification of the Exotic at the World's Columbian Exhibition, Chicago 1893', in Karp and Lavine (eds).

Indonesia: Untaian Manikam Di Khatulistiwa (1992), Jakarta: Gramedia.

Iyer, P. (1988) *Video Night in Katmandu, And Other Reports from the Not-So-Far East*, New York: Random House.

Karp, I. and Lavine, S.D. (eds) (1991) *Exhibiting Cultures: The Poetics and Politics of Museum Display*, Washington, DC: Smithsonian Institution Press.

Kirschenblatt-Gimblett, B. (1998) *Destination Culture: Tourism, Museums, and Heritage*, Berkeley, CA: University of California Press.

Mattie, E. (1998) *World's Fairs*, New York: Princeton Architectural Press.

MacCannell, D. (1976) *The Tourist: A New Theory of the Leisure Class*, New York: Schocken Books.

Nicholson, B. (1989) *Hi, Ho, Come to the Fair: Tales of the New York World's Fair of 1964–65*, Huntington Beach, CA: Pelagian Press.

Norvindr, P. (1996) 'Representing Indochina: The French Colonial Phantasmatic and the Exposition Coloniale de Paris', in P. Norvindr, *Phantasmatic Indochina: French Colonial Ideology in Architecture, Film, and Literature*, Durham, NC: Duke University Press.

Nowell-Smith, G. (1996) *The Oxford Dictionary of World Cinema*, Oxford: Oxford University Press.

Official Guide: New York World's Fair 1964–65 (1964) New York: Time Inc.

Parry, R.L. (1998) 'What Young Men Do', *Granta* 62: 83–123.

Pemberton, J. (1994a) *On the Subject of 'Java'*, Ithaca, NY: Cornell University Press.

—— (1994b) 'Recollections from "Beautiful Indonesia": Somewhere Beyond the Postmodern', *Public Culture* 6, 12: 241–62.

Remembering the Future: The New York World's Fair from 1939 to 1964 (1989) New York: The Queens Museum.

Roberts, M. (1998) '*Baraka*: World Cinema and the Global Culture Industry', *Cinema Journal* 37, 3: 62–83.

Said, S. (1991) *Shadows on the Silver Screen: A Social History of Indonesian Film*, trans. Toenggoel P. Siagian, Jakarta: The Lontar Foundation. (*Profil Dunia Film Indonesia*, Jakarta: Grafitipers, 1982.)

Sen, K. (1994) *Indonesian Cinema: Framing The New Order*, London: Zed Books.

—— (ed.) (1988) *Histories and Stories: Cinema in New Order Indonesia*, Clayton: Monash University.

ShadowLight Productions (1998) 'Wayang Listrik Performance Tour', online, email: shdw@sirius.com, 24 August 1998.

Sharp, N. (1977) *The Rule of the Sword: The Story of West Irian*, Victoria, Australia: Kibble Books.

Sudharmono, E.N. (1992) 'Preface', *Indonesia: Untaian Manikam Di Khatulistiwa*, Jakarta: Gramedia, 1992, pp. 8–9.

Tobing Rony, F. (1996) *The Third Eye: Race, Cinema, and Ethnographic Spectacle*, Durham, NC: Duke University Press.

Wollen, T. (1993) 'The Bigger the Better: From Cinemascope to IMAX', in Hayward and Wollen (eds).

12

NOTES ON POLISH CINEMA, NATIONALISM AND WAJDA'S *HOLY WEEK*

Paul Coates

During the Elevation of the Host one man in church remains standing.
Later, another asks him why he did not kneel.
'Because I'm not a believer.'
'Then why did you come to church?'
'I can't stand the communists.'

(anon.)

Romanticism, Polishness and the imagined community

Benedict Anderson has described 'the nation' as an 'imagined community' forged through a *visualisation* of like-minded others in a process allegedly linked to the dissemination of print vernaculars from the sixteenth century onwards. This national self-conceptualisation involves the generation of rhetorics of nationhood by small would-be (bourgeois) (Anderson 1983: 74) elites seeking to persuade both themselves and others of their power, inspire self-confident action and intimidate prospective opposition. The concept of nation, so often the phantasmal power-base of the bourgeois intelligentsia's contestation of aristocratic establishments, becomes in the Polish case an opposition to institutions imposed by foreign powers. This early-modern *imaginary* visual self-definition may be piquantly juxtaposed with the actually visual, late-modern one permitted by a new technology as revolutionary as printing had been: that of cinema. Socialism's claim to speak for 'the people', and post-war Poland's status as a *soi-disant* socialist society, raise the question of whether the use of actual, rather than mental, images renders the process any more genuinely 'popular', or whether the struggle for the means of image-transmission remains one between elites. In the end the socialist's dream of a unity of populace and elite materialises ironically, if briefly, in their 'anti-socialist' nemesis, the Solidarity movement (and, in cinema, in Andrzej Wajda's *Człowiek z żelaza* [*Man of Iron*], 1981).

189

In the first instance, during the period of the formation of 'nation-states', the hyphenation both embodies and seeks to combat unease over its components' possible disjunctiveness. Whereas rulers could once imagine communities in terms of what could be realistically defended – or seized – from neighbours, ignoring the will of prospective new subjects, as of the late eighteenth century they seek to legitimate such incorporations as the liberation of imagined fellows (speakers of the same language, members of the same 'race', fellow opponents of oppression). Linking statehood to 'the nation' masks the alien features of a state that projects itself not as an apparatus but as the natural – organic – outgrowth of a particular people. The state may bring a unity of law, but the deeper, vaguer unities of 'culture', 'society', 'language' and – yes – 'nation' put flesh on its bones, serving as the naturalising disguise of the arbitrariness of state formations and as a block on the possible fissiparous hatching of further 'nations' within them. If the state is perceived as alien, of course, this may be the consequence of actual invasion or simple invasiveness, as its burgeoning bureaucratic centralisation and tax-gathering outreach into distant communities (feudal tithes to local lords being long gone) define it as inherently foreign. This sense of its alienness may also respond to the inevitable dissonance between romantic dreams of unity and the unfortunate violence required to actualise them. Projecting 'the state' as a bad father may render bearable the lack of any immediate audience for the romantics' own utopian, intensely subjective work, with the ideology of 'inspiration' both combating and reflecting the feared futility and arbitrariness of speech *vis-à-vis* a void, it being directed not to any known group – a class, one's peers – but to the putatively classless nation (itself perhaps an idealisation of growing market anonymity into 'community'). Writers take the existence of such communities on faith: faith in the existence of an audience for messages in bottles. Earlier rhetorics of 'the sublime' are reconjugated into a 'beyond' which becomes this-worldly and yet unattainable, the invisible systems, networks and grids of which one knows oneself to be part stimulating both fear of encroachment and the romantic longing for engulfment.

Internal exile in one state while communing with the nation in the dream of a different one, a *nation*-state: this romantic condition is central, of course, to the self-conception of two centuries of Poles subjected to the invasions that absolutised a nation-state split that elsewhere was only partial, 'Polish' state apparatuses being by definition the creatures of alien rulers. Following the partitions of the late eighteenth century, in the early nineteenth century the voice of 'the nation' excluded from imposed state structures migrated mediumistically into singular individuals, the Romantic poets described as 'seers' (*wieszcze*): Mickiewicz, Słowacki, Krasiński. Between the lines of their work 'the nation' (as represented by the gentry [*szlachta*] elite imagining a unity that belied its actual past chronic disunity) spoke to itself *sotto voce*, in the allegorically disguised, 'Aesopian' language that would typify two centuries of Polish cultural production. Such nationalism is as revolutionary as it is conservative. In the second half of the twentieth century, meanwhile, in everyday Polish discourse the nation-state disjunction would be overlaid with one between 'Polska', the Slavic term designating Poland as a geographical entity, and the 'Polonia', the appropriately deracinated Latin word for millions of émigré Poles. In a complex manoeuvre of compensation and self-castigation, those native Poles who looked to the Paris-based Instytut Literacki's publications for untainted exemplars of national culture often simultaneously sustained a sense of their own worthiness by deriding the linguistic incompetence of 'the Polonia' (usually Americans whose technological superiority was as embarrassing as their financial aid was welcome). Local intellectuals compelled to speak indirectly could disavow disempowerment by viewing themselves as descendants of Mickiewicz's Konrad Wallenrod, the apparent traitor who rose through enemy ranks so as to be able to lead them to their doom. More plausibly, they may have argued that at least they had their fingers on the pulse of events. Within the sphere of Polish cultural production, meanwhile, different products had a different status. Whereas writers still publishing only domestically could be deemed compromis-ingly accommodating to the censor's demands, film-makers dependent on local resources for both materials and sites of dissemination could expect greater understanding. In periods of extreme repression their films may have been banned or – in the technologically advanced twilight of the Soviet empire – have suffered the distribution condition of books, circulating privately as '*samizdat*' video-cassettes, or may even have taken the form of co-productions of restricted local relevance, but cyclical thaws nourished hopes of eventual national distribution. My concern in the following piece will be with the ques-tion of whether or not a 'nationalist' discourse can be said to have existed in a public sphere monopolised by socialist discourse (gentry-based romantic 'class-lessness' differing from state-sponsored worker-peasant 'classlessness'). I shall also consider some of the effects of the collapse of the official state discourse in 1989, particularly as manifest in the fashionability of treatments of 'the Jewish question' (my test case will be Andrzej Wajda's *Holy Week* [*Wielki tydzień*, 1996]). The imbrication of art and politics in a would-be totalitarian system renders some degree of socio-political scene-setting necessary.

'Nationalism', 'Socialism', 'Heroism'

After 1947, when stage-managed elections returned the Soviet-sponsored PPR (Polish Workers' Party) and Stanislaw Mikołajczyk – the last significant pre-war Polish leader still on Polish soil – fled the country, discourses of nationalism became subject to ban in Poland. Wladyslaw Gomułka, the first governing Party leader, who had pursued relatively independent policies for several years, was placed under house arrest, not to recover power until the upheavals of 1956. In Jerzy Andrzejewski's 1947 novel *Ashes and Diamonds* (*Popiół i diament*) – in the view of some, inspired by a suggestion by Party ideologue Jakub Berman (Kąkolewski 1998: 27–30) – Maciej Chełmicki, the young AK (Home Army)

191

partisan who mistakenly assassinates workers rather than the newly installed Party leader he is charged with removing, is termed a 'fascist' by a grieving soldier. Under the binary mentality of the 'struggle for peace', 'he who is not with us is against us'. And yet, ten years later, after the 'Polish October' and Gomułka's reinstallation as Party First Secretary, Andrzej Wajda could film Andrzejewski's novel with a Chełmicki who was no 'fascist' but at worst misguided. The imprint of post-war Polish history's conjunctural freezes and thaws is apparent not only in the differences between Andrzejewski's 1947 text and the classic 1958 film he scripted with Wajda, but also in the disparity between that script and the various unfilmed versions of the intervening Stalinist period, all of which render Chełmicki a socialist realist 'positive hero' who undergoes an ideological change of heart.[1]

If the Soviet Union had found it possible to incorporate nationalist and even quasi-religious motifs into Stalinism, reconjugating Bolshevik internationalism into 'socialism within one country', no such latitude would be allowed its new satellite states. The Stalin who had annihilated the resolutely internationalist, Luxemburgist pre-war KPP (Polish Communist Party) would hardly extend leniency to Polish patriots who, following National Socialism's defeat, considered communism the new enemy. During Poland's Stalinisation the real-life Maciek Chełmickis were shot or jailed, regardless of whether they continued fighting in forests or surrendered. And yet, ironically, the pilloried nationalist rhetoric had become paradoxically part-otiose, the pre-war nationalities question having been virtually 'solved' by Hitler's elimination of the one major minority (the Jews), Stalin's annexation of another (the Ukrainians, those subjects of the Sienkiewicz novel *Ogniem i mieczem* (*By Fire and By Sword*) recently filmed by Jerzy Hoffman, 1999), and the Western Allies' 'transfer of the German populations and elements of German populations that remain in Poland' under Article 13 of the Potsdam Agreement. Within the Soviet empire as a whole, meanwhile, nationalism persisted in sharp communal demarcations with immediate neighbours. Where 'good fences make good neighbours', the best fence is an entire country. Leading Poles' appearances in films by the Hungarians Jancsó, Makk and Mészáros mattered less than their absence from those of the Czechs and Slovaks, those direct neighbours and practitioners of a realism so often qualified in Polish discourse by the dismissive adjective *mały* (little), while Wajda's only Soviet-block co-productions were with the former Yugoslavia, that black sheep of the socialist family. Equally pointedly, his adaptations of Russian literature were of nineteenth-century, pre-Soviet texts, co-produced either in Yugoslavia (*Siberian Lady Macbeth* [*Sibirska Ledi Magbet*], 1961–2) or France (*The Possessed* [*Les Possédés*], 1987).

The ideological shifts of post-war Poland suggest that 'nationalism' is no unitary discourse but comprises various, possibly detachable components, some of which can go underground while others remain visible, abbreviated into metonymies or mere markers of the place of the buried, the repressed that always returns, albeit through upward leakages of varying strength. If socialism forbids some (such patriotic emblems as the crowned eagle), others remain compatible with it and persist. Meanwhile, wartime instances of anti-Semitic nationalists aiding Jews because local priests or New Testament ethics required succour of neighbours indicate the complexity of Polish nationalism's relationship with religion – a question to which I will return in my final section and which also suggests that no one of us has a single, unified 'ideology'. The primary element of nationalist discourse to survive into post-war Poland – perhaps because most politically neutral – was the idea of 'the heroic'.

For the thoroughgoing socialist, heroism belonged to Labour and was of safe Soviet provenance. Literary theorist and Newspeak-analyst Michał Głowiński has argued that this conception of heroism typified a socialist realism that never put down Polish roots (Głowiński 1991: 21), but *Man of Iron*'s recycling of the iconic worker, albeit to different ends, qualifies Głowiński's generalisation. Like the Solidarity whose activists' terminology sometimes echoed that of the Party they opposed – and when it did not, was threatened by the incoherence proverbially characteristic of Wałęsa – Wajda the *bricoleur* was constrained by the political language of his formative years: the parody of socialist realism in *Man of Marble* (*Człowiek z marmuru*, 1976) bespeaks near-affectionate youthful intimacy with it, awareness of how, although distant, risible, almost camp, it is also close.

For the nationalist, meanwhile, heroism involved Polish fidelity to the cause, often at great cost, and overlapped with Conradian, gentry codes of honour. 'Heroism' here has the traditional epic and martial connotations, while the time-lag between the war's end and its realistic cinematic treatment testified both to deep-seated, slow-healing trauma (lending maturity to the reckonings when they *did* come) and to the insuperable obstacles to its fair representation thrown up by Stalinism. In what came to be known as the Polish School (a term first proposed as an ideal in 1954 by Aleksander Jackiewicz, but not actualised until after 1956, following the return to power of the man identified with 'the Polish road to socialism', Gomułka) the discourse of heroism would be ironised, be it in the bitter, tragic mode of Wajda or the blackly comic one of Andrzej Munk (*Eroica*, 1957; *Zezowate szczęście* [*Bad Luck*], 1960). Weighing heroism's fatal price renders this cinema apparently compatible with official socialist discourse. But late 1950s Party activists would remain suspicious even of a film like *Ashes and Diamonds*, despite its description by sixty-eight of ninety-nine cinema-goers polled by the *Polityka* weekly as 'a condemnation of counterrevolutionary activity' (Gębicka 1998: 136). Party resolutions would castigate the School's lack of images of what they termed 'the joint struggle against Hitlerism of the Polish and Soviet soldier' (Gębicka 1998: 137). Thus the filmmakers' critique of heroism is no simplistic, ideologically correct denunciation of a key element of nationalist discourse: here, as later, the finest Polish cinema would be ironic, tortured, dialectical, activating the ambiguity of the word *bohater*, which can designate both the morally positive 'hero' *and* modern narrative theory's morally neutral (and hence possibly blank or ambiguous)

193

'protagonist'. Interrogations of a traditional male epic hero whose resistance had left Poland still occupied after the war relocated heroism in women: just as Colonel Netzer, leader of the Warsaw Uprising's 'Kryśka' group, contrasted the heroism of 80 per cent of his male fighters with the total dedication of the girls, so Wajda's *Kanał* (1956–57) shows a girl dismissing her wound as 'nothing' before her stretcher blanket slips to reveal her loss of a leg. The privileging of women, however, is the other face of male 'feminisation': stoical endurance of the status of history's object rather than subject. In Wajda's trilogy an ethos that identifies Poland's future with socialism grapples and clashes with one fascinated by the defeated, but perhaps not defunct gentry codes that inspired the Uprising's soldiers. The phantom limb still aches, and a nationalism complexly underlies and is interwoven with the socialism. Eric Rhode pinpoints the contradiction when he remarks – of *Ashes and Diamonds* – that 'the Polonaise may be butchered by an indifferent pianist, yet it still remains Chopin's Polonaise' (Rhode 1966: 186). Wajda's later work would be weakest when deeming self-division and doubt incompatible with heroism, yielding the flat iconic heroes of *Man of Iron* or *A Love in Germany* (*Eine Liebe in Deutschland*, 1984), or the more academic recreations of the gentry's lost world (a polemical sub-strand of *Ashes and Diamonds*) found in *Birchwood* (*Brzezina*, 1970) or *The Young Girls from Wilko* (*Panny z Wilka*, 1979).

For the directors of the Polish School heroism is ironised by its mortgaging to the visual image, the requirement that the hero look the part, that theme of Andrzej Munk's picaresque *Bad Luck*. This irony fosters doubling and its richest focus is perhaps in the work of Zbigniew Cybulski. In Wojciech Has' *How to be Loved* (*Jak być kochana*, 1962) he plays Wiktor, the ironically named supposed assassin of a German occupier, whom the Gestapo hunt and a woman, Felicja, conceals. Out of love for him she sleeps with German soldiers, buying their silence as he lies hidden in the next room: the hero is compelled unheroically to tolerate abuse of the female he traditionally exists to defend. Felicja's is the true, secret heroism, and Has pointedly contrasts it with the mere image Wiktor later purveys. As a girl sings 'The Poppies of Monte Cassino' (the song that accompanied the commemoration of dead fellow partisans in *Ashes and Diamonds*) Felicja enters a bar where he boastfully retails wartime exploits to a quietly mocking, incredulous young audience. Neither has found the love they sought in different ways. In *Ashes and Diamonds*, meanwhile, which Has' film glosses, Cybulski had been called Maciek and was doubled by a young resistance fighter named Marek, who appears in a defiant cameo. Marek's single-minded heroism renders him less interesting however than the tragic hero Maciek, torn between budding love and the military code that enforces assassination of a Communist leader. A decade after *Ashes and Diamonds* Wajda would resurrect Cybulski and his heroism under the sign of absence, for *Everything for Sale* (*Wszystko na sprzedaż*, 1968) was precipitated by the death of the actor, which haunts it. In this film-about-a-film a director seeks a substitute for him and thinks he has found one in Daniel Olbrychski. But Olbrychski refuses to assume Cybulski's mantle, becoming himself heroic in his refusal; as if in dialogue in his turn with *How to be Loved*, Daniel verifies the legends surrounding his predecessor: the story of a wartime excursion to Berlin to find better roses proves true. He then accuses the director, Wajda's own stand-in, of opposing the dead actor. If Cybulski represents both fantasist and hero, self-mythologiser and living legend, *How to Be Loved* insists on the fantasy while the *de mortuis nil nisi bonum* of *Everything for Sale* underwrites the legend. Apparently defunct heroism persists, transformed, in Olbrychski's fiery-eyed integrity: no wonder he would shortly play the lead in Jerzy Hoffman's film of Sienkiewicz's patriotic *The Deluge* (*Potop*, 1974). In one episode of *Eroica*, meanwhile, by Wajda's great counterpart Andrzej Munk, POWs' morale is upheld by the legend of the man who escaped. We then see him concealed by men who feed him and the sustaining legend. Munk's irony does not so much puncture heroism as the need for traditionally heroic images: after all, the man who consents to this living death is extraordinary, his self-sacrifice perhaps the greatest – because unobtrusive – heroism. In a dialectic of visibility and the invisible, these films inculcate distrust of their own medium, the image: the hero always has a double, is always as dead as alive, giving blood transfusions to an image-vampire, be it unofficial, oral legend (*Eroica*) or official visual icon (the statues and posters of shock-worker Birkut in Wajda's *Man of Marble*).

In the last instance the socialist state's public sanctioning of images or emblems with primarily patriotic associations concedes the failure of its own ideological project – a development always on the cards in a Poland whose fitting for socialism Stalin had likened to the saddling of a cow. One glaring example was Wojciech Jaruzelski's reintroduction of the interwar four-cornered hat for the army shortly after the imposition of martial law in 1981, while his post-martial law civic renewal organisation was significantly termed the *Patriotic Movement for National Regeneration*. Before socialism enters its late 1980s twilight, however, patriotism is available for mobilisation by dissenting Party factions; it does not yet represent a desperate final governmental dice-throw. Thus in the late 1960s Mieczysław Moczar played up his own Resistance credentials in coded opposition to the increasingly beleaguered Gomułka government, whose subsequent appropriation of Moczar's 'patriotic' anti-Semitism gave the measure of his success. So if the debate about Wajda's *Lotna* presented the bizarre spectacle of Zbigniew Załuski, an officer of the Polish People's Army, *defending* the romantic values the interwar cavalry embodied against directorial mockery, apparently oblivious to romantic nationalism's hatred of the Russian ally, the explanation lay in his allegiance to the Moczar faction and its nativist rhetoric (Przylipiak 1991). The authorities themselves would appropriate other elements of nationalist rhetoric, avidly sustaining the bugbear of a (West) German revanchism eager to recapture Silesia. The 1960s' inauguration of a cycle of large-budget films of works by Henryk Sienkiewicz, the late nineteenth-century novelist whose trilogy is a cornerstone of Polish patriotism, surely indicated how badly the socialist project had begun to falter once the hopes of the Polish October had guttered in the decade's 'small stabilisation' – namely, stagnation. The mid 1960s would see Skolimowski lambaste the triumph of a non-socialist materialism among a self-enriching 'red bourgeois' elite: *Hands Up!* (*Ręce do góry!*, 1968, premiere 1985) registers the emptying of patriotic symbols by a generational and careerist reduction of wartime experiences to drunken party games. It thus echoes that most penetrating of Polish patriotic works, Stanisław Wyspiański's *fin-de-siècle* play *The Wedding* (*Wesele*), which critiques intellectuals' surrender of responsibility amidst alcoholic inertia. That play would be filmed by Wajda in the early 1970s, but the startling exercise in *mise-en-scène* disappointingly lacked the political resonance of the original – or of Skolimowski's banned film. The string of historical epics and Sienkiewicz's adaptations begun in the 1960s marked socialism's cynical attempt to deploy nationalist sentiments to cloak its own ideological bankruptcy, to legitimate itself by demonstrating ostensible liberal tolerance and the will and ability to provide lavish entertainment spectacles. In the early 1970s they represented, in a sense, the cinematic equivalent of the 'consultations' Party First Secretary Edward Gierek had promised after the Gdańsk unrest of December 1970: the token presence of something whose reality the Party could not stomach and had every reason to fear.

A film like Jerzy Hoffmann's *Deluge*, however – his second Sienkiewicz adaptation, his more recent *By Fire and By Sword* proving so popular as to make Wajda postpone release of his own *Pan Tadeusz* – hardly threatened the authorities: only allegorical reading could make Sienkiewicz's work say anything of Poland's struggle against its primary bugbear of the last two centuries, Russia. Kościuszko – probably Poland's pre-eminent national hero – was a fixture of interwar, not post-war, cinema, as was the Polish-Russian struggle in general (e.g. Ordyński's *Ten from Pawiaki Prison* [*Dziesięciu z Pawiaka*], 1931, or Lejtes' *The Young Forest* [*Młody Las*], 1934). And when a film dealing with turn-of-the-century Polish anti-Russian terrorism finally did surface – Agnieszka Holland's *Fever* (*Gorączka*, 1980) – it was during the liberal last gasp of the Gierek regime, and in any case was by no means nationalistic: Holland's unremittingly sardonic, Dostoevskian view of the terrorist cell's disintegration recalls the sub-plot of Andrzejewski's canonised *Ashes and Diamonds* (an element omitted from the 1958 film). Moreover, since the traditional primary sustainer of national self-consciousness had been poetry rather than prose narrative, the literary adaptations central to Poland's post-war cinematic narrative production, which, as elsewhere, were usually prose-based, touched both contemporary reality and nationalist themes only obliquely. Thus the spark for the student demonstrations of 1968 came from the theatre – from a production of Mickiewicz's *Forefather's Eve*, whose poetic prologue depicts the Russian steppe as a site of brooding imminent horror – rather than from the seemingly more popular artform, cinema. It seems as if only revolts from above – from the gentry, as in the nineteenth and mid twentieth centuries, then the student elite in the late 1960s – take their cue from cultural production, and that they derive from traditionally 'higher' artforms. Indeed, Polish cinema's symbiosis with the theatre has lacked the aesthetic conservatism of the comparable English one. Theatre's patent audience-accountability required close attunement to public demands: demands less for entertainment than for derision of the authorities, those paradoxically self-contradictory and patently absurd top-down sponsors *both* of an *un*popular 'popular' generic production aimed at swamping the works that questioned its own activities, *and* of those questioning works themselves. Thus the theatrical form that most fruitfully fed the post-1956 flowering of Polish cinema was the cabaret that specialised in such mockery and launched such figures as Cybulski and Skolimowski. The nationalism of intellectuals expressed itself in the recovery of the interwar absurdist theatre of Gombrowicz and Witkacy, allegorically read as reflecting ludicrous established orders – an example of which was very near-to-hand.

A test case: before the ghetto wall: *Holy Week*

For much of the last 200 years the discourse of Polish nationalism has been interwoven with that of Roman Catholicism, a linkage sealed in the well-known coinage *Polak–Katolik* (Pole = Catholic) and the eventual election of a Polish Pope who would ardently support the Solidarity trade union. In the seventeenth century the Black Madonna of Częstochowa was thought to have halted the Swedish invader. Poland was often dubbed Europe's antemurale; a bastion against such infidel hordes as the Turks Jan Sobieski III turned back at Vienna in 1683. When unbelieving 'Eastern' armies (T.S. Eliot's 'hooded hordes') again entered 'European' space in 1920, repulsing their own prior invasion by Jozef Piłsudski, their last-ditch defeat by the Polish army was dubbed 'the miracle on the Vistula'. The post-war state's official atheism, of course, prompted efforts to separate the 'Polish' from the 'Catholic', a project whose unfeasibility at the time (the Church's post-1989 self-enrichment is proving more effective in alienating the population) caused a complex crab-dance between Party and Episcopate.[2] No communist critique of nationalism animated state efforts to disconnect 'Polishness' from Catholicism, however. The state's own febrile anti-German propaganda deemed nationalist aversions less lamentably ineradicable than possibly useful, a way of presenting 'Soviet friendship' as the guarantee of Poland's post-war Silesian acquisitions (Stalin's annexations of swathes of interwar Eastern Poland, roughly compensated by those new territories, remained unmentionable). In the post-enlightenment scenario, the decline of religious observance promotes the sense of nationhood to the position of cementing communal identity. In pre-1989 Poland, however, the suppression and absorption of religious identity by a national one, long under way elsewhere, was arrested by the Catholic Church's status as sole alternative to governments imposed from abroad.

Although a Catholic country, before 1795 Poland was deeply tolerant of difference, as in the case of its laws for the protection of Jews. As Eva Hoffman notes, however, after the final partition 'to the nationalist thinker, the prospect of a Jewish subculture in Poland pursuing its own beliefs education and civic institution' – a subculture such as had flourished earlier – 'was becoming unacceptable, even intolerable' (Hoffman 1998: 144). Polish–Jewish relations became more fraught. That fraught condition, symbolised by the Ghetto Wall – both the visible one and the invisible one, the 'wall inside people's heads' – dominates Andrzej Wajda's version of Jerzy Andrzejewski's *Holy Week*, first published in 1946 but not filmed until fifty years later (1996). It may be taken as a footnote to the series of films made up of *Samson, The Promised Land* and *Korczak*,[3] and is far from simply exploiting the theme's topicality since 1989. Indeed, in a sense it marks his work's coming full circle to, and expanding, the moment of Jasio's rejection of his Jewish friend, a refugee from the Ghetto, in *A Generation (Pokolenie,* 1954), and constitutes that brief scene's necessary expansion. The scene's importance for *A Generation* is marked by its use of film's two largest close-ups, one of Jasio and one of Avraham, images which both test the veracity of Jasio's comment on his friend's appearance and stress the intensity of the relationship and moment of fatal choice. In the background, Polish women intone a hymn: the Stalinist critique of religion is both present and de-emphasised by relegation to the soundtrack. On the explicit level of diegesis, *A Generation* would toe the standard Party line on the Home Army. The hero's mother wonders whether to classify them as Germans, police or rats seeking Jews to blackmail, and the hero Stach himself tells them to go and fight the Germans. They are bourgeois armchair soldiers, contemptuous of the militant communist young. *Holy Week* however, side-steps the question of political affiliation, though the lack of any hints of possible communism in Julek – the brother of Jan Malecki, the former lover of the Jewish Irena Lilien – combines with Jan's nationalism and the religiosity of Anna, Jan's wife, to suggest his connection with the majority organisation, the AK, to which Wajda himself had belonged. The apparent depoliticisation surely means his AK membership in fact goes without saying.

Holy Week evokes the double-bind whereby mere observation provokes guilt, while abandonment of the observer's position catapults one towards death. Wajda himself has said:

> it is not a question of the guilty and the innocent but rather that that terrible crime took place before our eyes. That we watched it in a sense, and so did I, though I wasn't living in Warsaw at the time but in the provinces – but I too saw the extermination of that Ghetto after a fashion.
>
> (Wajda 1997)

The distance between Jan Malecki's household and Warsaw's centre corresponds both to Wajda's own during the uprising, and our own temporal one. The very first images broach the theme, as two people later identified as the Jewish Professor Lilien and his daughter Irena watch a dejected group shuffle through a forest, prodded by a German soldier. As the group passes the camera a closer shot reveals the yellow stars on their backs. The camera's move towards them mimics their attraction upon the Professor, who feels he belongs with them and, ignoring his daughter's stifled, despairing remonstrations, moves forwards to join them. The price of vacating the observer's position becomes drastically clear as he falls and is kicked. The incident glosses the opening title spelling out the German prohibition on leaving the Ghetto, a capital offence both for Jews and for Poles aiding them. After citing numerous incidences of wartime anti-Semitism, Tomasz Gross makes the following comment on this prohibition: 'if the Poles had helped the Jews on the same scale as they engaged in conspiracy the risk involved in helping Jews would have diminished radically' (Gross 1998: 51). Whatever the rights and wrongs, however, by following this title with a scene originally located much later in Andrzejewski's story Wajda lays out his theme: what it means to watch a crime, and how people react to the sight in different ways. Irena's frozen observation of the incipient Ghetto rising a few scenes later leaves her oblivious to safety, as nearly hypnotised by the vision, dream and fear of community as her father was; she has to be bustled into a doorway by her old lover Jan – now married to a Polish girl – who decides to take her home. For all his cowardice, self-doubt, reluctance and mixed feelings – spelled out extensively in Andrzejewski's text – Jan too crosses the line separating observer from observed and so finally suffers the fate of the observed: death.

Jan Malecki's death is followed by the appearance of motorcycled German soldiers, faceless, impersonal. Wajda's perspective on these Cocteau-like 'messengers of death' may just be open to description as 'Jewish'. Consider Eva Hoffman's eloquent evocation of Jewish survivors' experiences of the Holocaust's sweep through their Eastern Polish village of Brańsk:

> The German soldiers in Brańsk had frightening, hard faces – everyone agrees on that – but they existed at such a remove of power and terror that they were hardly individuals; they were embodiments of an abstract force. ... It is possible that the Nazis were beyond hate, trans-ferred to the realm of psychological trauma, of numbing and wordlessness.
>
> (Hoffman 1998: 245)

Poles, however, those merely human neighbours, could be freely hated for their betrayals. Wajda's perspective may of course simply reflect aesthetic weakness and stereotyping, but its possible overlap with a 'Jewish' one may indeed help bridge the festering gulf between the two cultures, indicating that the effort to transcend the pre-1989 official state perspective on 'the Jewish question' by filming a pre-1989 text is not necessarily fatally self-contradictory.

Holy Week dramatises the irrevocable separation of Jews and Poles *during a particular period* by the disaster the Nazis visited upon the former. National

Figure 12.1 *Holy Week.* The Ghetto Wall, I: Jan Malecki recognises his old love Irena
Lilien near the Ghetto Wall
Source: Image by Renata Pajchel, courtesy of Heritage Films

Figure 12.2 *Holy Week.* The Ghetto Wall, II: Jan Malecki's brother Julek uses the
infamous Carousel to scout the wall for possible entrances
Source: Image by Renata Pajchel, courtesy of Heritage Films

Socialism may indeed have envisaged an eventual Polish arrival at the same destiny, but 'the Final Solution of the Jewish question' came first. Andrzejewski's early statement of the separating effects of one person's happiness and another's sorrow fittingly furnishes Wajda's final title. The disparity pervades the dialogues of Irena and Jan, the latter's words stumbling repeatedly over the incommensurability of the former lovers' suffering. Structuring the story around Holy Week renders the gap ironic, tragic and all-but unbridgeable, rooted in two communities' divergent readings of the crucifixion of Jesus. Anna, the work's religious conscience, the venerator of a dead Jew's statue in a scene Wajda moves to the film's end, is the closest to Irena, and not just because the women flank Jan as beautiful onetime lover and plain wife. Anna alone is allowed to recount a loss comparable to Irena's, her family's decimation by the Nazis. Her belief apparently unlocks dimensions inaccessible to her pusillanimous husband, and her religious awareness of 'last things' recognises death's ever-nearness. Her ideal Catholicism knows no separation from its neighbour's suffering. Thus to deem her kissing of Christ's image 'quelque chose d'obscène' (Axelrad 1996: 57), a way of eclipsing the Ghetto's sufferings, is to ignore the work's final focus on Irena's departure into its smoke, as well as the way Christ's own Jewishness short-circuits any facile transcendence. The Good Friday end leaves us in a darkness not yet known to precede a resurrection. Wajda's ending, which modifies Andrzejewski's, may be problematic but Axelrad's 'obscenity' is far too strong. Here, as in *Korczak*, the last word is that of the inter-title that underlines the limitations of the observer's position: at a certain point images give out, others pass out of sight. One can only imagine what one cannot see, one's effort aided by the written word, the Andrzejewski text privileged at the end. As so often in cinema, be its allegiances Brechtian or not, the inter-title is an admonition, the sign of our need to learn – in this case, of the Polish need to learn more of the neighbour whose place is now an absence. Only the mind's eye – not that of flesh – can still follow the neighbour separated by her suffering. It alone can see through walls.

Notes

1   For a penetrating analysis of these unfilmed scripts, see Lubelski (1994).
2   The project may have been unfeasible, but it is interesting nevertheless that the nightmare of a possible loss of identity preoccupied the most radical film-makers of the late 1970s and early 1980s, perhaps reflecting fear of reinforcement of the state's seductions and threats by those of postmodernity. Thus in Wojciech Marczewski's *Shivers* (*Dreszcze*, 1980) a boy who begins as a good Catholic is seduced into Stalinism by a female instructor, while Kieslowski's *Blind Chance* (*Przypadek*, 1981) casts Party and dissident activists as versions of the same person.
3   I consider these films in my article 'Walls and Frontiers: Polish Cinema's Portrayal of Polish–Jewish Relations' (Coates 1997). For more on *Holy Week*, see Coates (forthcoming) 'Observing the Observer'.

Bibliography

The research for this essay was supported in part by a grant from the Carnegie Trust for the Universities of Scotland.

Anderson, B. (1983) *Imagined Communities: Reflections on the Origins and Spread of Nationalism*, London: Verso.

Appignanesi, L. (1999) *Losing the Dead*, London: Chatto.

Axelrad, C. (1996) 'La semaine sainte: Quelque chose d'obscène', *Positif* 423 (May): 57.

Coates, P. (1997) 'Walls and Frontiers: Polish Cinema's Portrayal of Polish–Jewish Relations', *POLIN: Studies in Polish Jewry* 10: 221–46.

—— (forthcoming) 'Observing the Observer'.

Gębicka, E. (1998) 'Partia i państwo a kino. Przypadek "Szkoły polskiej". O ideologicznym stylu odbioru filmów i jego konsekwencjach', in E. Nurczyńska-Fidelska and B. Stolarska (ed.).

Głowiński, M. (1991) *Marcowe gadanie: komentarze do słów 1966–1971*, Warsaw: PoMost.

Gross, J.T. (1998) *Upiorna dekada: trzy eseje o stereotypach na temat Żydów, Polaków, Niemców i komunistów 1939–1948*, Cracow: Universitas.

Hoffman, E. (1998) *Shtetl: The Life and Death of a Small Town and the World of Polish Jews*, London: Secker and Warburg.

Kąkolewski, K. (1998) *Diament odnaleziony w popiele*, Warsaw: von borowiecky.

Lubelski, T. (1992) *Strategie autorskie w polskim filmie fabularnym lat 1945–1961*, Cracow: Uniwersytet Jagielloński.

—— (1994) 'Trzy kolejne podejścia', *Kwartalnik filmowy* 6: 176–87.

Nurczyńska-Fidelska, E. and Stolarska, B. (eds) (1998) *'Szkoła Polska' – Powroty*, Łódź: Wydawnictwo Uniwersytetu Łódzkiego.

Przylipiak, M. (1991) 'Spór o "Lotna"', *Gazeta Gdańaze* 5–6 January.

Rhode, E. (1966) 'Andrzej Wajda', in E. Rhode, *Tower of Babel: Speculations on the Cinema*, London: Weidenfeld and Nicolson.

Wajda, A. (1997) Interview preceding *Wieczór Andrzeja Wajdy (An Evening of Andrzej Wajda)*, broadcast in Poland 26 April by Canal+.

13

DEEP NATION

The national question and Turkish cinema culture

Kevin Robins and Asu Aksoy

> He on the other hand – the thought has just occurred to him for
> the first time – has never lived in a true commonwealth, but
> rather in his ideal image of a state. Later he intends to follow this
> line of thought further and see where it leads.
>
> (Christa Wolf, 'No Place on Earth')

Christa Wolf's short novel, 'No Place on Earth' (1998), stages a fictional
encounter between the German Romantic writers Heinrich von Kleist and
Karoline von Günderrode, both of whom are individuals in conflict with society.
In the case of Kleist, his difficult relationship is with Prussia and the Prussian
authorities. He has come to experience Prussia as a country to which 'he is
attached against his will' (1998: 229):

> The first time he crossed the border, he says, he realised that his native
> land looked better and better to him the farther away from it he got;
> that he was gradually ceasing to be weighed down by a self-imposed
> obligation to his country which he could never live up to ...
>
> (1998: 229)

Across the border, Kleist is able to think things which were previously impossible. He thinks beyond the question of his obligations to the state, to consider
the matter of its responsibilities towards him. And '[i]f the state rejects the
demands I place upon it, let it reject me as well' (1998: 230). 'To be sure, he
says, he finds many of this world's institutions so unsuited to his needs that it is
impossible for him to participate in the labour of maintaining or developing
them further' (1998: 231). Now he is able to think beyond his old ideal image
of the state and to raise the question of what it would be to live in a true
commonwealth. That night, it was in December, when he crossed the border,
Kleist felt as if he were 'stepping into a new life' (1998: 230).

'To possess a culture', says Tzevtan Todorov (1997: 3), 'means having at our
disposal a pre-arrangement of the world, a miniature model, a map of sorts,

which permits us to orient ourselves within it'. Taking this general definition as a starting point, Todorov then moves on to identify two characteristics of culture:

> each individual is a participant within multiple cultures and every culture is subject to change. Indeed, it is because of the diversity of cultures that change is unavoidable: the culture of the group is bound to change, because culture does not exist in isolation, because groups are numerous, because the individuals within each group are numerous.
>
> (1997: 6)

'But', Todorov goes on to observe, 'this inevitable change within the culture of the group is perceived by the individual as a menace and it generates resistance' (1997: 6). Very commonly, as we all know too well, communities – and particularly, it seems, national communities – work to resist change, and do this by disavowing the diversity that is their condition of possibility. In the context of what Todorov describes as 'an ultimately insurmountable tension between the need for stability and the need for change' (1997: 6), they seem to gravitate more easily towards the static and regressive option.

In this chapter we are concerned particularly with this tendency towards the denial and repression of diversity – what Katherine Verdery (1993: 43) regards as the national desire to 'institut[e] homogeneity or commonality as normative' – and with its connection to the fear and inhibition of change in the national community. How this denial works itself out – with what degree of compulsion and compulsiveness – will of course vary in different national and historical contexts. The focus of our discussion here will be on modern Turkish culture and identity, which we think illustrates in an especially clear way what is at issue (the Turkish case is striking, but not exceptional). We are particularly interested here in the ways in which the logic of cultural denial and repression affects the community's relation to knowledge. How does the nation know itself? What does it do with and to what it knows? It is in this context that we shall be concerned with cinema – with cinema as a mechanism, we suggest, for at the same time knowing and not knowing the nation. Finally, we shall very briefly come to touch on the possibilities, in the specific case of our Turkish example, for a 'true commonwealth' that would return change to the culture.

Their ideal image of a nation

The Lebanese historian, Georges Corm, has characterised the Ottoman empire in terms of an astonishing complexity of identity – multi-cultural, multi-confessional, multi-lingual. 'Everywhere in the Balkans, and in Anatolia', he observes:

> [ethnic and religious groups] have lived intermixed lives over long centuries, on the same soil, in the same towns, though often practising

the same way of life. ... Without exaggeration, one may speak of
Balkan civilisation for Eastern Europe and Arabo-Ottoman civilisation
for Asia Minor, both of them sharing many traits in common, being
complex syntheses of European, Greek, Slavic, Turkish, Armenian and
Arab cultures.

(Corm 1992: 51–2)

But during the course of the nineteenth century, the Jacobin model of the
nation-state rose to prominence, demanding 'the collapse of those complex
ensembles and with them their ways of life and a cultural cosmopolitanism that
has today faded from people's memories' (ibid.: 52). The various ethnic groups
of the empire claimed the right to exist in the form of independent states; and,
finally, after the traumatic events of the First World War and the 'War of
Liberation' – when the Ottomans were at last condemned to become 'a people
who do not exist' (Goodwin 1998: xiii) – the Turkish nation-state, too, was
forced into existence.

This induced birth of a Turkish nation provides, in our view, some important
insights into the processes through which national cultures are instituted. The
necessarily expedited formation of the Kemalist state allows us to see, in a
particularly intense expression, the collective processes that work towards the
normalisation of cultural homogeneity and against cultural diversity and change.
These are the obscure and unconscious mechanisms of what we shall call the
'deep nation'. The 'deep nation' is the name we give to the most fundamental
aspect or level of belonging in any group. It is what Daniel Sibony characterises
as the primordial aspect of the group – the basic 'appeal just to be together and
to survive as a group' (1997: 247). This is grounded in what Freud identified in
the mythological scene of the murder of the father, which provides the sons
with a reserve of shared guilt that henceforth ties them to a communal 'law'.
The truth of this Freudian myth resides in the idea of a 'shock of origination' –
a shock that is never 'really past' – an act of symbolic violence through which
the group comes to have the experience of existing and existing together (of
existing as existing together). It is the deep nation that provides the grounding
for what is imagined as the ontological nation, affording the energy and tenacity
that inform its act of imaginary closure.

In addressing the question of the deep nation, we are concerned with how it
is that a group exists together and holds together. We suggest that there are two
binding mechanisms, both of which are crucial for understanding the nature of
the ties of national belonging. First, there is a fundamental mechanism of
repression, linked to what Daniel Sibony refers to as the group's 'point of
silence'. What binds the group is its commitment to remain silent about the
violent and arbitrary nature of the originary act of symbolic institution: the
group comes into existence as '*a collection of people who are resolved to stay silent
about the same thing* – to protect that thing, and to protect themselves from it,
by means of it' (ibid.: 248, Sibony's emphasis). This silence is the condition of

membership, and whoever threatens to evoke or expose this point of silence is threatened with exclusion from the group. This constitutes the defensive core of the deep nation, functioning to hold the group together through time, and denying the possibility of change through the disavowal of internal differences. The second mechanism involves the positive valorisation of the group – for the group has to imagine itself as the kind of community that is worth belonging to and worthy of loyalty. In establishing the terms of both inclusion and exclusion – in 'making sure that "not just anyone" can be a member' – the group works 'to ensure its love of itself' (ibid.). It is this mechanism that ensures the conditions of possibility for the idealisation of the group's own self – the uncontaminated ground on which it is possible to construct the ideal image of the nation.

In the Turkish example, we suggest, with its twentieth-century instantiation of the violent origination and symbolic institution of a national culture, the workings of the deep nation have been particularly apparent and significant. (The notion of the 'deep nation' is also meant to resonate with what Turks now call the 'deep state' [*derin devlet*] – the corrupt and repressive state implicated in mafia business and authoritarian politics.) Now, of course, we recognise that the broader social and cultural experience of modern Turkey is more complex, and cannot be analysed simply in terms of these basic group dynamics. We shall confront this complexity a little later in our argument. But, for the moment, we want to stay with the deep nation perspective, because it most certainly does engage with the prevailing logics at work in the narrower domain of the 'official' nation-building project. What the early Republican nation-builders confronted – in the wake of the more or less 'traumatic' events surrounding the end of the Ottoman empire and the institution of the new Turkish Republic – was a dual imperative. On the one hand, it was a matter of finally killing off the imperial past – which would amount to the erasure of the multicultural legacy of the Ottoman empire. And, on the other, there was the necessity to valorise the new national ideal in the heart of a dead empire where 'the notion of national identity, let alone the veneration of the national past, had no popular roots' (Keyder 1993: 24). Both of the key identity mechanisms of the deep nation – the denial or disavowal of difference, and the narcissistic idealisation of the collectivity – were mobilised in the cause of imagining the new Kemalist nation. And the mobilisation of both has always been deeply problematical for the Turkish people.

Consider first the repression. The social engineering of the Kemalists sought to bring into existence 'new Turks', who would be defined by their difference from the Ottoman population. There was, as Hugh Poulton observes, an absolute rejection of the Ottoman past, which came to be regarded as 'the dark age' (1997: 114). The Ottoman experience was regarded as alien and non-Turkish. The Kemalist innovators instituted a radical programme of 'reforms' – the abolition of the caliphate and the disestablishment of the state religion, dissolution of religious brotherhoods (*tarikats*), proscription of male religious headgear, language reform (the purging of Arabic and Persian influences), the introduction of the Latin alphabet, the reform of the calendar, and so on – amounting to a large-scale cultural evacuation. As Ayşe Kadıoğlu says, the Republican elites thus 'started a tradition of discontinuity with the past which culminated in a state of amnesia imbued in the psyche of the "new Turks"' (1998: 10).

This programme of purification was directed against the multicultural legacy of the Empire, intended to eliminate the communities of identification that were increasingly perceived as compromising the cultural unity of the new Turkish nationalism. The old complexity of religions, ethnicities and languages was replaced by the modern and uniform space of the monochrome Republic. Islam was rejected as a meaningful element of social and cultural life (as should be apparent from the 'reforms' listed above). The cultural presence of groups such as the Laz, Bosnians, Georgians, Jews, Tatars, Yoruks, Azeris, Circassians, Pomaks or Albanians was obscured – and, of course, the most consequential repression was that of Kurdish identity (White 1999). And, most violently of all in the early days, was the expulsion, exchange and massacre of the Greek and Armenian populations of the empire – events which, as Çağlar Keyder says, were 'covered up in official discourse as much as in the national psyche ... the principal event of the nationalist struggle was repressed in the collective memory of all participants' (1997: 44). The imagined community of new Turks had its more or less traumatic origins in acts of cultural repression and then the silence of a cover up.

But what were these new Turks? At the moment that the Ottomans began to be a people who do not exist, the Turks were also a non-existent people. The Kemalist revolution had instituted a modern nation-state, and it was then confronted with the task of drawing up the blueprints for a community of modern Turks who would be its citizens – its ideal citizens, the kind of people whom its leaders would be happy to represent. The new Turks were henceforth to be both a rational and a national people, suddenly unrelated to the superstitious and cosmopolitan people who had come before them. The initial inspiration for this new model people came from Europe and the Western principles of 'civilisation'. Atatürk was fundamentally a modernist and a Westerniser, and 'to make Turkey catch up with the West and assume its "rightful place" as a modern civilised state and society was always his aim' (Poulton 1997: 97–8). Western and Western-style cultural innovations were intended to elevate and enlighten the new Turkish nation. But there was also the need to connect this Western graft to something local – something local that had nothing to do with Ottomanism. As Levent Köker observes, modernist nationalism was complemented by a traditional form of new Turkish nationalism:

> The former laid stronger emphasis on the scientific-technical progress of the Turkish nation together with a process of creating a Turkish consciousness in order to exploit the gains of progress in the interests

of the nation, while the latter laid strong emphasis on the role of religion and customs somewhat dismissed by the modernists.

(Köker 1997: 70)

In one respect, this latter kind of nationalism was about the need for a culture – in the form of private religious beliefs – that would compensate for the upheavals of rapid modernisation. And, in another, it was the familiar and conventional and predictable invention of tradition, turning the 'heritage' of Anatolia into a purified and idealised 'folk' culture. Like all nations, Turkey had to become modern and traditional at the same time.

The elite set out its ideal image of the nation, but it was never an easy ideal for the Turks to live with. Throughout the history of the Republic, it has proved to be a source of unproductive tensions and discomforts. For one thing, there has been the difficulty of actually reconciling, first the Western and the traditional components of the national culture, and then the Turkish/Anatolian and Islamic elements within the latter. The need for 'synthesis' has been constantly articulated, but the conditions for fusion have never seemed achievable. The consequence has been the frustrating inability to achieve consensus on what the national culture actually is – that is to say, which elements 'essentially' belong and in what proportions. The Kemalist blueprint was very sketchy. Some have subsequently sought to resolve uncertainties through programmatic elaborations. Others have thought it better to keep quiet in case their accounts should disturb the doctrines – and the silences – of the 'official' culture. But perhaps the most problematical aspect of Republican nationalism has been its vague connection to reality – precisely its transcendent idealism. Kemalism was an ideology that originated in the urban centres, among those unfamiliar with, and generally uninterested in, the peasant realities of Anatolia. And on the basis of this cultural distance they were able to think of themselves as the governors of an ideal and homogeneous – ideal because homogeneous – people (*halk*). For them, the Turkish nation existed as 'a unified, solidaristic totality devoid of class divisions and conflicts, sanctified as an eternal entity to be represented and protected by the state' (Köker 1997: 68). Their expectation and exhortation was that the actually existing Turkish people should themselves acknowledge and conform to this fiction and ideal.

The fundamental perversity of the deep nation lies in how it comes to act for the people in spite of the people – or even for the people against the people. It invents the ordered image of a people, and then mobilises this image against their own disorderly existence. Thus, the logic at the heart of the Kemalist project worked on behalf of an ideal people – 'new Turks' – against the actual people, with their primitive religious brotherhoods or disturbing Kurdish identities. In the earliest days of the Republic, this illusion of instituting a unified and inclusive new nation could almost be sustained by the Kemalist will to civilisation. Because the less than ideal people of the Anatolian countryside lived very far removed from the urban bases of the elites, their real cultures and ways of life did not significantly challenge the modernising projections of the elites. The problem would only arise if ever their embodied reality came face to face with their imaginary reality. It would be a consequence of the irruption of their socio-historical presence into what we might call the psycho-mythological logic of the deep nation. And, of course, it was inevitable that that encounter would eventually occur. It is at this point that we are called upon to introduce a greater complexity into our account of the social and cultural experience of modern Turkey. At this point, we move from the deep processes mobilised to secure the imagined community to the more complex realm of historical encounter, contingency and openness. We are concerned with what happens when what was originally conceived almost in terms of a pure ontological nation encounters the empirical nation. The question is then raised of how the deep nation can deal with the real heterogeneity of ordinary Turkish life. And also, of course, of how the people in all their complexity may act out the logic of the deep nation (this, as we shall suggest later, is a real issue to be addressed in the Turkey of the 1990s).

The Republican ideal nation was a very patent fiction of the elites. As Hugh Poulton notes, 'much of the countryside continued to live according to traditional, usually folk-Islamic, values' (1997: 121). The story of modern Turkey is officially told in terms of the progressive expansion of the Kemalist principles of modern nationhood. But it could also and better be told in terms of the continuous erosion of the imagined community of 'new Turks'. In one respect, this more complex account would be a history of the migrations that have brought the disorderly periphery into the urban strongholds of the Republicans. It would be about the development of the huge *gecekondu* areas (squatter settlements) which transformed the cities, creating new encounters and confrontations and a new urban culture (Robins and Aksoy 1996). It was in the perceived and feared disorder of the *gecekondu* that the new migrants from the countryside developed the music and culture of *arabesk*, which seemed to represent such an affront to the values of Kemalism (Stokes 1994). And, as Martin van Bruinessen says, 'the increased mobility of which their presence in Istanbul was a symptom [also] brought the message home that there was a "Kurdish reality" that sooner or later would have to be recognised' (1998: 42). This alternative narrative would also have to take account of rural and religious migrations into media spaces, particularly as a consequence of the development of commercial television in the 1990s, sustaining a new popular culture – including *arabesk* – that dramatically outpaced the 'official' output of the state broadcaster TRT (Robins and Aksoy 1997), and also worked to normalise and render ordinary the image of the 'dark face' of Islam (Öncü 1994). And we would have to take account, too, of the development of the new population of 'European Turks' (de Tapia 1994), whose culture is now bringing back home another kind of Turkish reality.

These complex realities have challenged the premises of the Kemalist nation, giving rise to new discourses of difference and multiculturalism (Robins 1996).

We do not have the space here to go into what has been achieved. The point of the present discussion is to stick with the deep nation, which tenaciously survives, whatever the complexities thrown up by contemporary social processes. Turkey is, as Zafer Şenocak says, a 'master of repression' (*Verdrängungskünstler*) (1994: 83). It is possible for Turkey to become a society that recognises its multiplicity of cultures and acknowledges its consequent susceptibility to change. But first it would have to release itself from the mechanisms of denial and idealisation that have long sustained a culture of uniformity and closure. Turks would have to recognise how debilitating the deep nation has been for their cultural and creative life. They would have to reflect on the experience of a nation that closed itself to experience.

In the following section, we shall move on to consider what is at issue with respect to one particular domain of cultural production. Turkish cinema provides an interesting illustration of our general argument: on the one hand, among those who like to invoke the 'seventh art', it has been expected to play its part in projecting the ideal image of the nation; on the other, as popular culture, watched by the new urban migrants, it has responded commercially to the unofficial forces in the culture (*arabesk*, for example).

In certain areas of popular cinema – in popular melodramas, for example – themes of class conflict and of urban/rural opposition have found a certain expression (Erdoğan 1998). But where this has been the case, it has generally been in spite of strong countervailing forces that have inhibited and often repressed the creative treatment of social issues. In the following discussion, it is this latter aspect of Turkish film culture that we shall be concerned with particularly. Şerif Mardin has put forward the argument that 'the Turkish republic created a void in the setting and practice of intellectual production' (1997: 77). And what we might call the void effect has certainly been apparent in Turkish cinema history. We may consider it in terms of how the deep nation exerted its pressure on cinema – and art cinema, particularly – at once demanding a national cinema and making impossible the conditions of its production.

Turkish national cinema? What is Turkish?

Invariably accounts of Turkish cinema have been structured in terms of the progressive emergence of a distinctive national cinema. 'A nation has to develop its own cinematography, its own film language, by relying on its own visual culture, narrative traditions, and capacity for artistic experiments', claims Yusuf Kaplan (1996: 661). And, he goes on, 'Turkish film-makers have proved that they are beginning to discover a distinctive way of story-telling which will enable them to create a truly national cinema'. When, in 1996, the Centre Georges Pompidou staged a monumental retrospective of Turkish cinema, it was providing an overview of the long and often difficult trajectory through which this modern national cinema had come into existence. And Mehmet Basutçu's *Le cinéma turc* (1996), the monumental survey catalogue produced to accompany the Paris screenings, endeavoured to give substance to the idea of a national film industry and culture that had evolved to creative maturity. To institute a national cinema is presented as an entirely self-evident aspiration. Does not a national cinematic *oeuvre* affirm the very existence and reality of a nation? Can a nation be a nation without its own national cinema?

So, has a Turkish national cinema come of age in the 1990s? We say not. What we are going to argue now is that this national cinema template is actually deeply problematical for thinking about cinema made in Turkey. We have two simple arguments to make. The first, which we shall develop most fully, brings us back to our central theme of the deep nation – to the question now of the deep nation's influence on the development of cinema culture in Turkey. As we indicated in our introduction, this can be posed in terms of cinema's relation to knowledge, where we are interested in the conditions under which film-makers have been able to know and represent the social and cultural realities of their country. In the following, we shall be concerned with how the deep nation has worked to inhibit cinematic knowledge. And we shall argue that, through its particular combination of repressive and idealistic dynamics, deep nationalism actually worked to obstruct the formation of the kind of national cinema that the political and cultural nation could aspire to celebrate as a 'truly national cinema'.

Turkey came into existence as nothing more than a state, having then to give itself substance through the creation of a nation and a national culture. It should be a unitary and integrative culture:

> The nation was supposed to express a homogeneity deriving from ethnic unity, and this unity would be expressed in a single voice. Hence, the collectivist vision implied its authoritarian implementation because it called for a cadre of interpreters and expressers to know and represent the unique voice of the nation.
>
> (Keyder 1997: 42)

Film-makers were necessarily among those called upon to know and represent in the cause of building the ideal image of the nation. But, more than artists in other fields, they were confronted in their efforts by a fundamental dilemma. The principles of the Kemalist nation had only been thinly formulated, and film-makers were expected to give thickness and substance to these founding ideals. But, precisely because the basic principles remained so unelaborated, there was always then the possibility – in fact the probability, as it turned out – that any cinematic engagement with actual Turkish society might involve misinterpretations or betrayals of the Kemalist national project. On the one hand, there was the need to give visibility and sense to the actual social realities of modern Turkey. And, on the other, the imperative to defend the basic principles of Kemalism – principles which gained their authority and credibility precisely by invoking an ineffable source of authority (in this respect they were like the dogmas of any religious doctrine). Inevitably, in this authoritarian context of production, the interpreters of Turkish reality existed in a tense and uneasy relation with the legislators of Kemalist ideology.

It was a relation in which the latter called all the shots. It would not be an overstatement to say that the aspiring Turkish national cinema was grounded in a regime of severe censorship. The regulations that were introduced in 1939 (and which lasted until 1986) put film censorship in the hands of the Interior Ministry, implemented through a commission whose members were drawn from state departments, including the police and the military. The practices of the commission were particularly harsh, involving the scrutiny of projects at the script stage, as well as the inspection of the final product (which meant that film-makers were bound to internalise the rules of censorship, not least for economic reasons). And central to its mission was both the protection and projection of the national culture: Turkish censorship spoke the language of nationalism. So, as well as proscribing films which were 'harmful to the order and security of the country', or which 'made propaganda on behalf of political, economic or social ideologies that are damaging to the national regime', the censors were also on the lookout for anything that fell into the vague and expansive category of being 'contrary to public decency, morality and national sentiments' (Özön 1995: 252). The censorship commission established itself as one of the firm guardians of Turkish national identity.

Film censorship provides a crucial index of the closure of the reflective sensibility of the Turkish nation. The acts of the censors tell us a great deal about the limits of the national imaginary: on the basis of what could not be afforded access into the national space of cultural and political reflection, we can see how the official nation could and wanted to imagine itself. In their decisions about what could be produced and distributed in Turkey, the censors worked ardently on behalf of the ideal image of their state and nation. The focus of their concerns changed over time. In the early days, a central issue concerned the representation of the Anatolian people. Thus, in 1956, they found it necessary to prevent a documentary film on the Hittites, made by Istanbul University, from being shown at the Berlin Film Festival, because the film made it seem as if Anatolia had not progressed over four thousand years: 'This film shows that the primitive plough depicted in Hittite reliefs is the same as those used in Anatolia today' (Özön 1995: 274). In 1964, it was the turn of Metin Erksan's *Susuz Yaz* (*A Summer Without Water*), which was refused official permission to participate at the same festival – though, it was unofficially exhibited, and won the Golden Bear award – because, as the head of the censorship commission later expressed it, the film 'depicted rural life in Turkey in a "grotesquely" exaggerated way' (Onaran 1994: 112). Anatolia could only be seen in an ideal light. Thus, Metin Erksan's first film *Karanlık Dünya: Aşık Veysel'in Hayatı (Dark World: The Life of Aşık Veysel*, 1952), was a problem because the wheat it depicted in the fields of Anatolia was too short (suggesting unproductivity) – these scenes were cut, and, Erksan tells us, images of mechanical harvesters were also added at the request of the censors (from an American documentary) (MTTB 1973: 33). These are just three examples from the many. As Nijat Özön notes, the line was always and everywhere clear and insistent: 'Turkish land is not unproductive', 'Turkish peasants do not go around in bare feet', 'Turkish peasants do not wear torn clothes' (1995: 141).

Later, as the political climate of Turkey began to become more polarised, the focus shifted to deal with more serious social and political issues, with the issue of class becoming particularly sensitive. Yilmaz Güney's film *Umut* (*Hope*, 1971), which depicts poverty and class exploitation in the south-eastern city of Adana, was banned outright in Turkey. And, when the film was taken illegally out of the country to be screened at the Cannes Film Festival, Güney was sentenced to seven years imprisonment. The scenario of Yavuz Özkan's *Maden* (*The Mine*, 1978), which portrayed the hardship and struggles of Turkish coal miners, was refused many times by the commission, which regarded it as a 'film promoting discord, corrupting family life, and harmful to national customs and morals' (Makal 1996a: 141). The films of Erden Kıral in the late 1970s and early 1980s provoked the wrath of the censors for their portrayal of poverty in the south east. After a viewing of his film *Hakkâri'de bir Mevsim* (*A Season in Hakkâri*, 1983), which depicted the isolated lives of peasants in a Kurdish frontier village, the censorship commission claimed that 'the dialogues weakened the authority of the state, and that the subject matter, which had been given a subversive treatment, was harmful to the integrity of both the state and the nation' (ibid.: 141). The fractures in the nation were becoming ever more apparent and dangerous, but still the censors demanded a cinematic image of national harmony and unity.

The censorship system always worked towards the objective of instituting a singular vision of the Turkish nation. Through its more or less repressive – and sometimes paranoid – practices, this system defended the Republican ideals in their pure and elaborated form – defended them from the inevitable challenges and compromises that must arise as a consequence of any artistic engagement with the changing socio-historical realities of Turkish society. (According to this censorious dogma, the filming of Atatürk's life would be deeply problematical because the image interposed by an actor would undermine the mythic standing of the father of the Turks.) The censors defended the deep nation, the mute bond of the nation. The consequence, of course, was to institute a void in the creative and cultural heart of that nation. And while the censors were content to secure this empty space, film-makers (and other cultural producers) were anxious to fill it with some content. What is Turkish? they began to ask. What should a national Turkish cinema look like?

Attempts to formulate positive proposals for a national cinema in Turkey began to take off in the mid 1960s. One development was the critical movement that called itself *Yeni Sinema* (New Cinema), which initiated the Turkish Cinémathèque in 1965, as well as a new journal for critical debate (Görücü 1997–98). This movement was highly critical of what it considered to be the parochial way in which Turkish cinema was developing, judging it according to the criteria of European art cinema and the culture of international festivals (Erdoğan 1998: 263). *Yeni Sinema* advocated the development of a more 'universal' cinema – invoking the exemplary models of the French *nouvelle vague* cinema and the wave of 'third cinema' in developing countries. But the ideas of these new-wave critics failed to win the support of Turkish film-makers, who seemed more concerned to promote local values. A contrary movement emerged, led by the film director Halit Refiğ, seeking to elaborate the principles of a locally sensitive and distinctive national cinema (*Ulusal Sinema* – '*ulusal*' is the modern Turkish word for 'national').

Refiğ's counter-position put great emphasis on what made Turkish society different from Western societies – it was said that Turkish society had a different social structure and also a different 'soul' (Makal 1996b: 160). The *Ulusal Sinema* movement aimed to draw on cultural elements from the Ottoman period, and also on the style and motifs of popular Anatolian culture, such as miniature paintings and folk tales (Dorsay 1986: 120), with the aim of elaborating an idiosyncratic and particularistic popular cinema in Turkey. The imperative, according to Refiğ, was for Turkish film-makers to find inspiration in their own 'history and people' (quoted in Scognamillo 1997–98: 52); to find 'a language that is right for the country' (quoted in Özön 1997–98: 57). But *Ulusal Sinema* was not only involved in debating with the Westernisers of *Yeni Sinema*. It was also in dialogue with yet another group that had its sights set on creating a properly indigenous film industry and culture. *Millî Sinema* ('*millî*' is the Ottoman Turkish for 'national') shared many of its concerns, but its own emphasis was on providing a specifically religious orientation in Turkish national cinema. In the words of the influential director Yücel Çakmaklı, 'a national [*millî*] cinema identity could only be achieved by producing films that reflect Anatolian realities, which [he maintained] embody the beliefs, national character and traditions of Muslim Turkish people ...' (quoted in Diriklik 1995: 21). The sources of inspiration for the new – pious and spiritual – cinema were to be found 'in the Turkish-Islamic morality of the Anatolian people, and in Turkish-Islamic works of art' (ibid.: 77). From this perspective Islamic culture and tradition constituted the fundamental reference point for the national identity.

What was taking place in cinema, then, was a debate around the meaning of national culture. The impact of this debate was not extensive (*Ulusal Sinema* involved few film-makers, and was short lived; *Millî Sinema* had a more lasting influence, but exclusively in religious circles, giving rise in the 1980s to the so-called 'White Cinema'). The key point, however, is that the debate was focused around a sense of deficit in national culture. As Halit Refiğ put it, in a roundtable discussion organised by the film society of the National Students Association (*Millî Talebe Birliği*):

It is necessary to think of national [*millî*] cinema within the context of 'National [*Millî*] Culture'. But we do not have an environment in which the cinema industry could contribute to such a development because, for some time now, our state has not had a clear and explicit policy for 'National Culture'.

(MTTB 1973: 91)

National culture is something the state denies its people:

> In order to continue as a nation we need to have a national conscious-
> ness. In order to ... protect our society from external and internal
> dangers, to maintain its unity and protect it from disintegration, we
> need to have a national consciousness. In cinema, this consciousness
> will be possible only through the existence of a conscious National
> Cinema. In the present circumstances, the state provides no support in
> this area. On the contrary, the state has an institution called censor-
> ship.
>
> (ibid.: 93)

The solution that offers itself, through the debates on national cinema, is in terms of some kind of synthesis of Turkish, Ottoman and Islamic elements – in a sense, it is an anticipation of the idea of a 'Turkish-Islamic synthesis' that developed in conservative circles in the 1980s (see Poulton 1997: 181ff.). It has been in the sterile idea of synthesis that the ideal image of the nation has found its most comfortable articulation.

At this point we come, more briefly, to the second argument that we want to make concerning Turkish cinema. And it is simply that the national agenda has always been a wrong agenda. Of course, it is possible to tell the story of Turkish cinema in terms of the development of a national cinema. But in that case, the story must then be one of a cinema culture caught between, on the one hand, the censorships and repressions of the deep nation, and, on the other, its compensatory idealisations of a harmonious and indivisible people. It is possible to tell the story of how Turkish cinema culture has lived with the deep nation – how it has struggled to reflect the unity of the Turkish nation. But what we want to argue here is that the story of cinema in Turkey can also be told – and can better be told – the other way round. It can be told in terms of the progres-sive disordering of the ideal of the Kemalist nation, which may be regarded as a productive disordering. It can be told in terms of creative efforts to weaken and loosen the grip of the deep nation in the Turkish imagination. We are suggesting an openness to the possibilities of cultural unbinding and pluralisa-tion as an alternative to the shallow illusion of national cultural integration and synthesis.

Indeed, we would argue that since the early 1980s it has become increasingly difficult to regard cinema culture except in terms of clouding the nation. Since then, the Turkish cinema scene has been characterised by a proliferation of what are characterised as 'personal identity' themes – all of which go very much

215

against the grain of the national imagination. These films have frustrated many critics. Thus, according to Emin Alper and Zahit Atam, 'we are again and again faced with the same thing: the non-existent problems of non-existent people, the counterfeit pains of decaying environments ... prostitutes, lesbians, homosexuals, transsexuals, transvestites, dwarves ... marginal themes, subjects and people' (1995–96: 38). But perhaps we might better regard these 'non-existent' people as now representing the actual people who have been occluded in the image of an ideal Turkish people (the people that Kemalism was against are now returning to haunt the people it wanted to be for). And we might be concerned with how, again and again, they have brought with them to the screen the problems – of both material life and cultural life – that were supposed to be non-existent in the life of the Turkish nation.

What we should also note is that these films have also involved a transformation of imaginary space – from the nation to the city. In the imaginary space of the nation, it is possible to declare and assert the ideal – which is to say, the illusion – of cultural homogeneity and unity. But this is not at all possible in the imaginary space of the city. The city can only be conceived as a place of difference, a meeting place, a place of encounter. It is significant, then, that many of the more interesting recent films made in Turkey have moved from a national to an urban focus. In Yavuz Turgul's *Eşkiya* (*The Bandit*, 1996), we see how the village ideal is finally transformed in the mill of the city (Özsoy, 1998). Mustafa Altıoklar's *Ağır Roman* (*Cholera Street*, 1997) is staged in a poor but cosmopolitan *mahalle* (a local urban community), comprised of Turks, Roma (gypsies), Greeks and Armenians. In Ferzan Özpetek's *Hamam* (1997), the old Ottoman Turkish bath becomes the focus for an exploration of sexual identities. Istanbul – the Ottoman and cosmopolitan city – comes back into the frame, providing a new kind of symbolic map with which to explore the experiences of Turkish society. The urban focus begins to provide the possibility for a new mobility in thinking about Turkish cultures.

> True: accidents are departures, and departures are accidents.
> (Orhan Pamuk, *The New Life*)

Yesim Ustaoğlu's remarkable film *Güneşe Yolculuk* (*Journey to the Sun*, 1999) tells the story of Mehmet Kara, an urban migrant from Tire, which is in the Aegean region of Turkey. He is working for the municipal water authority as a detector of leaks under the asphalt of Istanbul (a long brass ear trumpet is the tool of his trade). At the end of a pleasant evening spent with his girlfriend, Arzu, Mehmet is walking home, when he gets caught up in a brawl of right-wing nationalist youths leaving a football match. Mehmet and another passer-by, the Kurdish Berzan, are pursued by the youths, but manage to escape. Subsequently, they become friends. Berzan is curious to know where Mehmet is from, thinking that Mehmet, too, must be a Kurd (because of his dark skin). Berzan, who sells music cassettes from a street barrow, gives a Kurdish cassette to Berzan as a present.

Later, Mehmet is riding on a minibus. A stranger gets on, but immediately jumps off, leaving his bag, which turns out to contain a gun. The police suspect Mehmet of owning the gun, and they have found the cassette on him. Putting what they think is two and two together, they treat him as a Kurdish suspect, interrogate him, beat him up, and, a week later, finally let him go. Mehmet discovers that his lodgings have a red cross daubed on the door, as a warning to quit the place; and then, when he returns to work, he discovers to his amazement that the job of water detecting is no longer his. Berzan temporarily finds him a place and a job with Kurdish friends, but again the red cross appears on his door, and he is forced to move on again. He ends up living with Berzan, working as the lowest of the low, paid to scavenge on the municipal rubbish dump.

Then Berzan is found dead after having been interned by the police, following a Kurdish demonstration in support of hunger-striking prisoners. He had once told Mehmet of his eternal desire to return to his native village. Mehmet resolves to take him back to be buried in that distant village called Zorduç. And so the film begins its journey to the sun, part road movie – Mehmet travelling the width of the country with Berzan's coffin – and part migration in reverse. We see images – unfamiliar on Turkish screens – of burned out villages in the south-east, with red crosses painted on the doors of targeted houses. Towards the end of the journey, the film is intercut with bleak

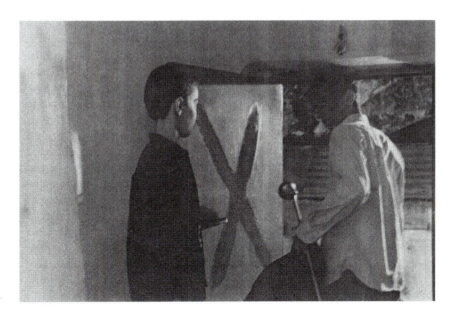

Figure 13.1   Journey to the Sun

documentary footage of the military occupation, showing sinister and menacing tanks guarding a dismal, rainy town square. Finally, having experienced the Kurdish ordeal, Mehmet reaches his destination in Zorduç. And what Mehmet, the erstwhile water detector, finds there is a god-forsaken place that is now submerged beneath a vast lake, as a consequence of a new government irrigation scheme. The reality of the Kurdish village has thus been covered over. Mehmet floats Berzan's coffin into the lake, to a watery grave. As Yesim Ustaoğlu herself remarks in an interview:

> This is the story of a transformation. When, in the final scene, along with Mehmet, we bid farewell to Berzan, sending his coffin into the water, we also meet another Mehmet. It is a Mehmet who has accomplished a responsibility, who gives hope, who has matured.
>
> (Baydar 1999)

Güneşe Yolculuk is about being a Turk. Mehmet is a migrant like countless others, having travelled to Istanbul with the expectation of being an ordinary Turk, just another member of the homogenised nation. We see the warmth of Mehmet's friendships, with Berzan and with Arzu. But the film is about a tense Turkey in the 1990s – a society which is struggling to know itself – to overcome its modern history of unknowing. It is concerned with the need to overcome the logic of the deep nation as it exists in every Turk, and with the imperative to achieve cultural awareness and lucidity about the difficult complexities of contemporary Turkish society. At its heart is the question of how it could come to be that, in this ideal nation, some of its members could come to be regarded as 'black Turks' – and what needs to be done when such a reality has occurred. Mehmet – his family name Kara, actually means 'Black' – tries his hardest to be an ordinary Turk – his final, desperate gesture comes when he sprays his hair blonde, from an aerosol can that he had pulled out of the rubbish dump. But, whatever his efforts, he is rejected and abused by the state and the people to which he thought he had the right to belong.

And so *Güneşe Yolculuk* becomes a film about releasing oneself from being a Turk (a post-national and counter-national film). It poses the question that a national community (and cinema) can never pose: the question of change and the conditions of possibility for change. It is the fundamental question that Maurice Dayan (1990) articulates in terms of 'becoming undone from oneself' (*'se défaire de soi'*), of moving from the 'passion of identity' to the possibility of 'becoming-other' in the most radical sense. As he journeys to the sun, Mehmet crosses a border, and when he crosses that border – a symbolic border – he finds that he is then able to imagine possibilities that were never available to him before. Towards the end of his journey, he is in a train carriage, sitting opposite a young soldier on military service in the south-east. They begin to talk:

Figure 13.2   Journey to the Sun

Soldier: Where are you travelling to?
Mehmet: Zorduç.
Soldier: Is that where you're from?
Mehmet: (nodding his head) Uh, uh.
              Where are you from?
Soldier: Tire. Do you know it?
Mehmet: Yes. I had a friend from Tire. Mehmet, Mehmet Kara.

Mehmet has confronted the other whom he might once have become. He has stepped outside of himself, and has assumed a new relation to identity and to knowledge. Stepping across the border – the border within – Mehmet, like the fictional Kleist, stepped into a new life.

At the time of writing this article, *Güneşe Yolculuk* had won many awards at international film festivals, and had been widely praised outside Turkey. But, even though it had, after some delay, been finally cleared for exhibition by the Ministry of Culture, it had not been released for distribution in Turkey. This was no doubt partly due to reticence among Turkish film distributors, given the difficult political climate occasioned by the trial of the PKK leader, Abdullah Öcalan. But one must suspect, from the lack of apparent interest among film critics and reviewers in Turkey, that the problem resided in a more general evasion of the critical issues raised by the film – the problem of the culture of silence in contemporary Turkish society.

219

Bibliography

Ahmed, A.S. and Donnan, H. (eds) (1994) *Islam, Globalisation and Postmodernity*, London: Routledge.

Alper, E. and Atam, Z. (1995–96) '1990'lı yıllar ve Türk sineması, *Görüntü* 4: 29–38.

Basutçu, M. (ed.) (1996) *Le cinéma turc*, Paris: Centre Georges Pompidou.

Baydar, Y. (1999) 'Yeşim Ustaoğlu'yla *Güneşe Yolculuk*', *Milliyet* 17 April.

Bozdoğan, S. and Kasaba, R. (eds) (1997) *Rethinking Modernity and National Identity in Turkey*, Seattle, WA: University of Washington Press.

Bruinessen, M. van (1998) 'Shifting National and Ethnic Identities: The Kurds in Turkey and the European Diaspora', *Journal of Muslim Minority Affairs* 18, 1: 39–52.

Corm, G. (1992) *Conflits et identités au moyen-orient (1919–1991)*, Paris: Arcantère.

Dayan, M. (1990) 'L'impossibilité de se défaire de soi', *Nouvelle Revue de Psychanalyse* 41: 257–78.

Diriklik, S. (1995) *Fleşbek: Türk Sinema-TV'sinde İslamî Endişeler ve Çizgi Dışı Oluşumlar*, vol. 1, Istanbul: private publication.

Dorsay, A. (1986) 'An Overview of Turkish Cinema from its Origins to the Present Day', in G. Renda and C.M. Korpeter (eds).

Erdoğan, N. (1998) 'Narratives of Resistance: National Identity and Ambivalence in the Turkish Melodrama between 1965 and 1975', *Screen* 39, 3: 259–71.

Gay, P. du and Hall, S. (eds) (1996) *Questions of Cultural Identity*, London: Sage.

Goodwin, J. (1998) *Lords of the Horizons: A History of the Ottoman Empire*, London: Chatto and Windus.

Görücü, B. (1997–98) '*Yeni Sinema* dergisi üzerine bir inceleme', *Yeni Sinema* 4: 89–106.

Kadıoğlu, A. (1998) 'Republican Epistemology and Islamic Discourses in Turkey in the 1990s', *The Muslim World* 88, 1: 1–21.

Kaplan, Y. (1996) 'Turkish Cinema', in G. Nowell-Smith (ed.).

Keyder, Ç. (1993) 'The Dilemma of Cultural Identity on the Margin of Europe', *Review* 16, 1: 19–33.

—— (1997) 'Whither the Project of Modernity? Turkey in the 1990s', in S. Bozdoğan and R. Kasaba (eds).

Köker, L. (1997) 'National Identity and State Legitimacy: Contradictions of Turkey's Democratic Experience', in E. Özdalga and S. Persson (eds).

Makal, O. (1996a) 'Le cinéma et la vie politique: le jeu s'appelle "vivre avec la censure"', in M. Basutçu (ed.).

—— (1996b) 'Le mouvement du "cinéma national"', in M. Basutçu (ed.).

Mardin, Ş. (1997) 'Projects as Methodology: Some Thoughts on Modern Turkish Social Science', in S. Bozdogan and R. Kasaba (eds).

MTTB (1973) *Millî Sinema Açık Oturumu*, Istanbul: Milli Türk Talebe Birliği Sinema Kulübü.

Nowell-Smith, G. (ed.) (1996) *The Oxford History of World Cinema*, Oxford: Oxford University Press.

Onaran, A.Ş. (1994) *Türk Sineması*, vol. 1, Ankara: Kitle Yayınları.

Öncü, A. (1994) 'Packaging Islam: Cultural Politics on the Landscape of Turkish Commercial Television', *New Perspectives on Turkey* 10: 13–36.

Özdalga, E. and Persson, S. (eds) (1997) *Civil Society, Democracy and the Muslim World*, Istanbul: Swedish Research Institute.

Özön, N. (1995) *Karagözden Sinemaya: Türk Sineması ve Sorunları*, vol. 2, Ankara: Kitle Yayınları.

—— (1997–98) 'Yeşilçam 1965: Kırılma Noktası', *Yeni Sinema*, 4: 56–65.

Özsoy, E. (1998) '*Eşkiya* ve *Ağır Roman*', *25.Kare* 22: 3–5.

Poulton, H. (1997) *Top Hat, Grey Wolf and Crescent: Turkish Nationalism and the Turkish Republic*, London: Hurst.

Renda, G. and Korpeter, C.M. (eds) (1986) *The Transformation of Turkish Culture: The Atatürk Legacy*, Princeton, NJ: Kingston Press.

Robins, K. (1996) 'Interrupting Identities: Turkey/Europe', in P. du Gay and S. Hall (eds).

Robins, K. and Aksoy, A. (1996) 'Istanbul between Civilisation and Discontent', *City* 5–6: 6–33.

—— (1997) 'Peripheral Vision: Cultural Industries and Cultural Identities in Turkey', *Paragraph* 20, 1: 75–99.

Scognamillo, G. (1997–98) 'Türk Sinemasında Tartışmalar/Polemikler/Kuramlar', *Yeni Sinema* 4: 43–55.

Şenocak, Z. (1994) *War Hitler Araber? Irre Führungen an den Rand Europas*, Berlin: Babel Verlag, Hund and van Uffelen.

Sibony, D. (1997) *Le 'racisme' ou la haine identitaire*, Paris: Christian Bourgois.

Stokes, M.A. (1994) 'Turkish Arabesk and the City', in A.S. Ahmed and H. Donnan (eds).

Tapia, S. de (1994) 'L'émigration turque: circulation migratoire et diaspora', *L'Espace Géographique* 23, 1: 19–27.

Todorov, T. (1997) 'The Co-Existence of Cultures', *Oxford Literary Review* 19, 1–2: 3–17.

Verdery, K. (1993) 'Whither the "Nation" and "Nationalism"?', *Daedalus* 122, 3: 37–46.

White, P. J. (1999) 'Citizenship under the Ottomans and Kemalists: How the Kurds were Excluded', *Citizenship Studies* 3, 1: 71–102.

Wolf, C. (1979) 'No Place on Earth', in P.A. Herminghouse (ed.), *Ingeborg Bachman and Christa Wolf: Selected Prose and Drama*, New York: Continuum, 1998.

14

FRAGMENTING THE NATION

Images of terrorism in Indian popular cinema

Sumita S. Chakravarty

> There is hardly an anomaly more anomalous than the stranger. He
> (sic) stands between friend and enemy, order and chaos, the inside
> and the outside. He stands for the treacherousness of friends, for
> the cunning of enemies, for fallibility of order, penetrability of the
> inside.
>
> (Zygmunt Bauman, 'Modernity and Ambivalence')

The popularity of the subject of terrorism in the Hollywood cultural machine in
recent years suggests that we have entered a new phase in the ongoing drama of
the nation. Fears of the fragmented nation are no longer the unique preoccupation of third world intellectuals and politicians, but have struck at the heart of
the first world itself, as the recent spate of Hollywood films dealing with
terrorism suggests. *Arlington Road* (1999), *The Siege* (1998), *Executive
Decision* (1996), *Naked Gun* (1988), *Die Hard* (1988), *Die Hard 2* (1988),
Under Siege (1992), *Passenger 57* (1992), all show how both internal and
external forces threaten the lives of ordinary Americans and that American
national identity, perhaps for the first time in its cultural history, can no longer
be taken as a given.[1] Concurrently, at the other end of the artistic and
geographical spectrum, the 1999 Human Rights Film Festival held in New York
recently featured a film called *The Terrorist* by Indian cinematographer-turned-
director, Santosh Sivan. Inspired by the assassination of former Prime Minister
Rajiv Gandhi by a female suicide bomber, this feature film is a laboured attempt
at a psychological portrayal of the modern-day terrorist and the culture of
violence in which she is caught. Coupled with the almost routine media reports
of terrorist acts in different parts of the world, the spectacularisation of terrorist
violence, in an ironic twist, is now a constitutive part of the global imaginary.
What this tendency makes evident is that we now need a theory of fragmentation and *its* cultural imagining to supplement Benedict Anderson's theory of
nationally imagined communities. Hollywood's forays into an area that is
marked by anguish and fear and its processing of the putative thrills of terrorism
as action drama may be said to capture the antithetical emotions that attach to

the subject and the intense debates generated within nations which see them-selves as besieged by internal and external enemies.

New terms have arisen to describe this situation: tribalism, sub-nationalisms, neo-nationalism, new ethnicities, fundamentalism, separatism, neo-revivalism, neo-racism, neo-ethnicism and the like.[2] At a time when the world seemed to be entering an era of full-blown globalisation, it is localisation in all its varied forms that has thrust itself centre-stage. For the years before the turn of the century are witness to the unexpected resurgence of sometimes extremely narrowly defined group identities based on religious, ethnic or regional affilia-tions.[3] Many regions of the world are marked by separatist movements, examples being the former Soviet Union and the former Yugoslavia, Canada, Indonesia, China or India, to name a few. Nor have the supposedly invincible multi-ethnic nations such as the United States been immune from their internal enemies, as America's phase of nationalist 'innocence' was shattered by the Oklahoma City bombing of April 1995.

This new phase of nationalism requires us to rethink and update Benedict Anderson's metaphor of 'imagined community'. Clearly, we are in a third stage of nationalism: if the first emanated from Western Europe and the second from the decolonising world, the most recent phase is highly uneven, with no clear moral or political centre, and with goals ranging from the ultra chauvinistic to the more traditional strivings for a designated nation-space. If earlier stirrings of nationalism could be related to broad world-historical movements such as the transformative stages of capitalism or the end of colonialisms, today's sub-nationalisms refuse to fit a pattern, affecting the affluent United States and impoverished Russia alike.

Not surprisingly, a host of studies have sought to keep pace with these devel-opments, and nationalism as a theoretical or scholarly enterprise is enjoying a boom.[4] While these studies, like their predecessors of the previous decade, make no mention of the cinema, the reverse is not true, for the problematic of 'nation' has emerged as a salient mode of understanding the cinema. Not only are the cinemas of the world differentiated on the basis of national origin, but the film medium may be said to approximate most closely what Eric Hobsbawm identified as the tension contained within nationalism itself, namely, the cultural singularity evoked by the concept (the 'nation' as a collectivity linked by ties of a common history, place of origin and language) and the reality of nations/nation-states in the contemporary world as inevitably diverse and plural (1990: 14–45). Hobsbawm makes two other observations that have a bearing on my subsequent argument. He draws a distinction between the *making* of nations and the *maintaining* of nations, seeing these as essentially different ideological processes. And he points out that popular expressions of national feeling cannot be read off from official or elite pronouncements. He stresses that 'the view from below' is 'exceedingly difficult to uncover' (1990: 11).

Extending Hobsbawm's historical insights to the cinema, I want to argue that

223

as an audio-visual medium, film's thrust is primarily towards 'nation' in its early and original formulation (that of an ethnic unit with identifiable characteristics), and only secondarily (ideologically) towards the *political* entities that are recognised as nationally designated spaces, where the emphasis is on unity and sovereignty. The question then arises: In what precise ways is popular cinema an expression of a nation-group? The answers to this question pull in several directions, showing that the complex analytical issues raised here are no less difficult to resolve than in academic nationalism itself. On the one hand, commercial cinema's mass appeal provides precisely a sense of 'the view from below', a glimpse of the fears, hopes and aspirations of ordinary people that is behind many of our everyday assumptions of the natural fit between cinema and nation. On the other hand, it would seem that what makes many mainstream cinemas 'national' is their (broad) identification with official versions of national priorities, of which maintaining nation-state unity is key. Against these twin tendencies, and nodding in both directions, the visual medium of film alternately problematises and forecloses meaning. But in order to make this point, we need to turn to Benedict Anderson's thesis of nationalist development via the literary medium. Despite the widespread recourse to his notion of 'imagined community' in the literature on national cinemas, it is arguable that the medium of film and the institution of narrative cinema in its mainstream forms may actually be resistant to nationalist imaginings, given that 'the nation' is always mediated by its 'fragments', that is, by individuals whose particularities of dress, speech and lifestyle locate them within specific regional, social and cultural configurations. Because in dominant cinema the hero usually belongs to the majority community, his presence on screen renders invisible all those others whose incorporation into the national mainstream dominant cinema undertakes to bring about in the first place.[5] I am not suggesting that films therefore cease to be nationalist or wide-ranging in their appeal, merely that the conjoining of cinema and nation cannot be guaranteed in advance.

Imaging the nation?

In Benedict Anderson's classic study of nationalism, the agent of nationalist creation is the written word, spread through the mechanisms of print-capitalism and given impetus by the writing of nationalist novels. Anderson argues that the shift from a hierarchical social order to a nationalist horizontal order is brought about by notions of simultaneity shared by people who feel connected to the same social space without knowing one another. He gives the example, among others, of a tale by the Indonesian communist-nationalist Mas Marco Kartodikromo, in which a young man finds a newspaper account of a destitute man dying on a street. Anderson writes:

> Finally, the imagined community is confirmed by the doubleness of our reading about our young man reading. He does not find the

corpse of the destitute vagrant by the side of a sticky Semarang road, but imagines it from the print in a newspaper. Nor does he care the slightest who the dead vagrant individually was: *he thinks of the representative body, not the personal life.*

(1983: 37, italics added)

Anderson makes the point that it is through these written works that a sense of belongingness among a people is created and disseminated. In the cinema, such a sequence would provide viewers with a host of information that may or may not invite the sense of community that creates national feeling: as an iconic rather than symbolic medium, the cinema divides and differentiates as much as it connects.

Hence while there are recognisable nationalist novels, it is arguable that the idea of a national cinema is an oxymoron. What is the nature and impact of a nationalist film, and which films can lay claim to such a distinction? Even a random choice of examples reveals how contradictory is the idea of nationalism in film, for images both anchor and 'liberate' the signifier. D.W. Griffiths' *Birth of a Nation* (1915), although a landmark film, is considered racist and divisive and was greeted with protest by African-Americans when it was first released. *Gone with the Wind* (George Cukor, 1939), a historical epic, also builds its nationalism on the back of a profound national trauma. Eisenstein's political cinema of collective heroism and solidarity is more internationalist than nationalist in inspiration. Examples of films of national liberation struggles, such as *Battle of Algiers* (Gillo Pontecorvo, 1966), may more aptly be called anti-colonial films, since the opposing sides are so clearly marked. An Australian film like *Gallipoli* (Peter Weir, 1981) on the other hand, an example of Australia's own struggles to forge a national identity, exploits the distinctiveness of the Australian landscape and the bush myth to enforce the mateship ethic that virtually shuts out the non-white and female population.[6] In the feature film, in mainstream or revolutionary traditions, it is the individualised hero-figure, set apart though interacting with, the broader socioscape, who typifies the collectivity or imagined community. In the Cuban nation-building film, *Memories of Underdevelopment* (Tomás Gutiérrez Alea, 1968), the disaffected bourgeois hero is presented as the outsider against whose self-exiled stance the nationalist goals of the Cuban Revolution take on force and meaning. Through an intricate blend of the documentary and the fictional, the film succeeds in creating a Cuban nationalist image through the perspective of a Cuban who is simultaneously insider and outsider, and whose ambivalent state of mind is expressed through voice-over. Because the film does not mark Cubanness in any simple, or easily readable way, *Memories of Underdevelopment* puzzled many commentators in the metropolis and was perceived as critical of the Revolution.[7] In India, with its bifurcated cinematic tradition (more on that below), Satyajit Ray's *Pather Panchali (Song of the Little Road*, 1955) and Mehboob's *Mother India*

225

(1957) have vied for alternative definitions of Indianness, with strong adherents and apologists in both camps. If the former signalled the birth of a 'truly' Indian cinema to foreign critics and audiences, it equally was the precursor for the regionalist impetus; the latter's overt mythologising-feminising of the nation and its now-cult status among Indian audiences worldwide have served to define it in the popular imagination with India, although the story focused on a struggling peasant woman who was visibly from northern India.[8]

What the above examples are meant to show is that in narrative cinema a sense of collective identity can only be mediated and dramatised through the particular, and the imaginative leap from the latter to the former is never automatic. (That is why the question of how representative a film is of its cultural-national origins is always waiting to be posed, and numerous studies of audiences have found that the issue of 'realism' in visible fictions (John Ellis' term) continues to be a dominant axis of reception even in our so-called post-structuralist times.) Distinctions of gender, class, ethnicity and region draw attention to themselves as constituents of a putative national identity, and potentially, as breakaway fragments. By its very nature, then, the fiction film can only present fragments of the nation and project them as evidence of the whole. The story of a couple, family or group represents/re-presents the whole of which they constitute a part. Thus the 'nation' as an entity is always eclipsed in cinema and has to be reconstituted by viewers through its screen absence. It is the absence which marks the fullness of the nation. The fragment is therefore both the nation's source of fear and its object of desire, its threat and its promise. Outlaw figures come to be romanticised, even when they are demonised, as is the terrorist in *Arlington Road*. Thus the paradox of cinema may well be that while its form of exhibition and viewership, and hence its address is collective, its narrative organisation and visual dynamics privilege the concrete and specific, the face in the crowd, the personal and singular.

With this paradox in mind, we can mention briefly some recent tendencies in world cinema in which nationalisms are increasingly expressed through region-alisms and localisms. In the case of British national cinema, for instance, apart from Scottish and Irish films as distinct sub-national entities, a film like *A Letter to Brezhnev* (Chris Bernard, 1985) makes use of a highly specific Liverpool dialect, identifiable as such only to insiders. Films like *My Beautiful Laundrette* (Stephen Frears, 1985) and *Young Soul Rebels* (Isaac Julian, 1991) articulate the Asian and black experience in Britain. In France, the trend towards regional cinema is reflected in film-makers going outside Paris to make their films and in the emergence of *cinéma beur*, films that focus on the lives of second-generation North African immigrants to France. The category of 'national cinema', then, may be more a term of convenience, one that orients foreign audiences rather than reflects the social realities of the nation-group so designated.

Mainstream/marginal, national identity and cinematic discourse

Such reconsiderations are particularly moot for a country like India, with its staggering internal diversity and tensions. For if the dialectic of inclusion and exclusion is built into the processes of film as a medium, one of the key questions for a 'national' cinema is how to incorporate individual identities into group identities, and this is always a matter of particular inflections and narrative strategies for particular historical and social contexts. For instance, what a Christian character/cinematic body signifies in Egyptian cinema for Egyptian audiences would be very different from what a similar character would signify for audiences in India, and within India, in Kerala as opposed to Calcutta. How, then, is the nation-group signified in Indian mainstream cinema, given its recent history of anti-nationalist violence and fissiparous tendencies? And how is the internal dissident (doubly inscribed as such through cinematic 'alienation') re-absorbed into the social body? In an essay entitled 'Modernity and Ambivalence', Zygmunt Bauman uses the spatial images of inside and outside to comment on the way people constitute their social worlds, and notes: 'There are friends and enemies. And there are strangers'. He points out that while friends and enemies are locked in philosophical opposition and hence form the very basis of sociation:

> (A)gainst this cosy antagonism, this conflict-torn collusion of friends and enemies, the stranger rebels. The threat he carries is more awesome than that which one can fear from the enemy. ... And all this because the stranger is neither friend nor enemy; and because he may be both.
>
> (1990: 145)

The stranger who is *either/or* and *neither/nor*, belongs to the category of the undecidable and functions in many ways as the Derridean *supplement*. Bauman's conception puts a curious and contemporary spin on 'the stranger' encountered earlier as the fellow-citizen in Anderson's evocation of the Indonesian nationalist novel. It throws light on one of the dilemmas haunting cinematic evocations of the nation in the age of terrorism and internal separatist movements, and is particularly relevant to an understanding of India's post-independence history and continued engagement with constructions and reconstructions of the nation through cinema.

Following Bauman, one can pose the question, 'Who is the stranger, the undecidable element, in the Indian cinematic imaginary?'. For if, as I have argued above, the cinema subsumes the plural in the singular, the iconic as the symbolic, it is continually belying its promise of representation, to be equally imagined by all the different groups that inhabit a social space. Around the cinema, as a result, have emerged discourses which seek to define how groups relate to each other in society, the issue of majority and minority representation, and the like. These issues are also at the heart of the long history of the Indian cinema and its protean forms. Here the question of national identity and its mainstream expression through Bollywood, the role of the state in promoting alternative (high cultural, aesthetically based) articulations of Indian identity, the production of films in numerous Indian languages as an assertion of regional identities, and the highly taboo subject of the representation of communal discord and violence as a threat to the nation's fragile sense of unity, have all been (and continue to be) matters for debate. It is instructive to revisit this history briefly, broadly conceived in three stages, in order to inflect it retrospectively in terms of 'the separatist threat'.

What emerges in any kind of historical overview is the differential investment in ideas of nationhood on the part of film personnel, nationalist leaders and governing bodies representing the Indian state, and the varied publics frequenting the cinema. Historians of Indian cinema in its pre-independence phase have associated it with a nation-building agenda, a cultural and ideological space where forms of Indianness were constructed and expressed in opposition to British domination.[9] Yet it is also the case that none of the nationalist leaders took any interest in this cinema, considered it marginal to the independence movement, and saw it as a foreign imposition. After independence in 1947, there was no official recognition of the Bombay cinema as a cultural organ of the Indian nation-state. Rather, attempts were made to revive and promote the classical arts. No matter: the mainstream cinema had developed various strategies for 'managing' tensions within Indian society. In particular, its self-imposed ideological task has been to incorporate various others into the body politic through what I have called, in a previous work (1993), processes of 'imperso-nation': ethnic or religious difference as a kind of lived masquerade which when peeled off, always could be counted on to reveal an essential Indianness comprised of a core of fraternal or civilisational, and patriotic values.

Given that the partition of India in 1947 had rendered the Indian Muslim as 'the undecidable', he whose loyalty to the motherland could not be counted upon and needed to be ritually re-affirmed, the popular film's mythic function served to fulfil this task. In film after film, too numerous to name, the iconic Muslim figure sentimentally voiced and upheld the values of a community or the nation-in-microcosm.[10] If naming Pakistan, the 'rogue state', was *taboo*, the Muslim figure could function as the *totem* – following Marvin and Ingle's (1999) use of these terms – that reaffirmed the integrity of the nation-group, and this structure has held steady till as recently as the mid 1990s.

If mainstream cinema's narrative organisation assigned marginal but highly coded roles to minority figures, and subsumed the discourse of nationhood in visual dynamics of disguise and role-playing, its own status for official culture was as impersonator and hijacker of the nation's artistic traditions. The second stage of nationalist definition, therefore, can be said to begin in the early 1960s when a host of institutions (a national film archive, a film institute and a film finance corporation) were created for the development of an art cinema to contest the hegemony of the mainstream film. Ironically, it was Bombay cinema's flirting and skirting of the nation's internal differences, its homogenising tendencies, that provided one strong rationale for state patronage of the alternative cinema. Reflecting a mood of national self-confidence implicit in an openness to self-critique, regionalism in cinema was not perceived as a threat to national unity but as its cultural apotheosis, with regional productions connoting authenticity, non-commercial values and seriousness of artistic purpose. Regional film-makers were seen as promoting the broader aims of a pluralist national culture in bringing audiences face to face with the social realities of different areas of the country. Like west Bengal's Satyajit Ray and Mrinal Sen, regional film-makers made films in their own languages and sought audiences in their native states, encouraging the development of a cinematic consciousness that would override the 'cheap' tastes inculcated by the popular all-India film. An essentially *auteur*-driven impulse was mapped on to the various constellations of national/regional, art/commerce, public/private, socialist/capitalist and marginal/mainstream. These various pressures were brought to the surface when so-called 'serious' filmmakers tackled 'sensitive' subjects, as in the case of the first film – *Garm Hawa* (*Hot Winds*, 1975) that dealt with partition (as the splitting off of the Muslim-dominated regions of the country into Pakistan is referred to in India) and explored both ethnographically and subjectively its effects on a Muslim household. Made by a Bombay-based director in Urdu and released in theatres nation-wide, the film reflects the dilemmas and ideological tensions underlying the regional/national dialectic in India. For while in its ethnographic thrust, it could qualify as 'regional' (the film shows a Muslim family from Agra), its subject-matter put it under national jurisdiction. After an initial ban and numerous bureaucratic snares, the film opened to critical acclaim and public enthusiasm, going on to win a prize for 'National Integration'. The film's success lies in its subtle negotiation of the gaps that structure cinematic discourse and reception in India, for it builds upon decades of schematic but sympathetic representations of the Muslim character in the mainstream cinema, presenting its Muslim hero not as 'the undecidable', a denizen who lives in India and 'desires' Pakistan, but as the nation's embodiment of the ideal (secular) male citizen. While his relatives leave one by one, the hero himself pays the ultimate price of attachment, that of blood sacrifice, through his daughter's suicide and his son's willingness to work for a better India by merging in a human stream under a blood-red banner.

Against the inscription of the 'stranger' as 'friend' (citing Bauman's categories above) through much of Indian film history in both mainstream and alternative guises, the cinema of the 1980s and 1990s signals a departure that marks the third stage in the narrativisation of the nation and its internal Others. The past two decades have seen the most severe challenges to Indian nation-state unity, as new breakaway movements surfaced (as in the Punjab) or older internal tensions took a virulent turn (as in the north-east and most ominously, in Kashmir). Terrorist acts by militant Sikhs reached their acme with the assassination of Prime Minister Indira Gandhi in 1984 by her own bodyguards, in reprisal for the storming of the Sikh sacred site, the Golden Temple in Amritsar. Succeeded by her son, he too succumbed to a terrorist attack by a suicide bomber, this time protesting Indian involvement in the Tamil separatist movement in Sri Lanka. In the early 1990s, terrorism in Kashmir escalated to such an extent that at one point it was felt that this state would be lost to India. Hence Naipaul's characterisation of India in that period as 'a million mutinies now'. In keeping with the violence in political culture and its threat to everyday life, the Bombay film industry itself entered a new phase as links were found between film personnel and terrorist and mafia elements in the Middle East (as in the case of the actor Sanjay Dutt) and Bombay was rocked by terrorist attacks in 1994. Concurrent with these developments has been the rise of Hindu fundamentalism, justifying itself as a response to a (Hindu) nation under siege, and culminating in its own act of violent destruction of the Babri Masjid in Ayodhya and in ensuing communal riots (these form the backdrop of Mani Ratnam's film, *Bombay*, discussed below). In 1993, the documentary film-maker, Anand Patwardhan, explored Hindu and Muslim fundamentalisms in his film, *Father, Son and Holy War* and advanced the thesis that these sentiments are linked to ideologies of masculinity and male fears of emasculation. In the dominant cinema, meanwhile, the era of 'sex and violence' had arrived. The 1980s saw the mutation of megastar Amitabh Bachchan from idealist to outlaw, and when the public tired of Bachchan, a new generation of male stars readily fitted the bill. The Bombay film exploited the public rage against 'the system' to portray corrupt politicians, corrupt bureaucrats and murderous bosses and street gangs. Recently, the vengeful female has emerged as a new hero, 'the system' in her case including patriarchy itself.[11]

India's internal divisions, never entirely absent from the social unconscious, have increasingly been thematised in terms of the above scenario, and terrorism itself has been the subject of several recent films. References to Pakistan in the popular cinema (unheard of in previous decades) are now surreptitiously or overtly worked into the stories: in *Maachis* (*Matches*, 1996), one member of a terrorist group is teased by the leader for having fallen in love with a Muslim girl 'when he was across the border' and for composing ghazals in remembrance of her; in *Border* (1998), devoted to India's intermittent but protracted war with Pakistan, it is the pain and loss inflicted by the war on both sides that is stressed; in *Sarfarosh* (*Betrayer*, 1999), a celebrated poet is revealed to be a Pakistani agent plotting destruction within India; in *Khal Nayak* (*Anti-Hero*, 1996), the protagonist in police custody for having killed a politician, is questioned and his activities linked to 'elements abroad'. *Maachis*, made by the respected Bombay writer-director, Gulzar, and devoted to Sikh militancy and terrorism in the Punjab in the 1980s, is perhaps the only film that presents the conflict from the disaffected group's viewpoint, indicative of the internal and external censorship prevalent in dealing with such issues. Set in the Punjab and Himachal Pradesh area, it portrays the politicisation and alienation of a young Sikh male (and later, his fiancee), his life as a terrorist centred around guns and bombs, and his capture and death at the hands of the police. The film does not condone terrorist violence or lend credence to the claims of Sikh ethnic difference or separatism, but it does deflect blame from the Sikh community to 'the Indian state', symbolised variously by government functionaries, political leaders, and above all, the police and intelligence services. The reasons for Sikh militancy are not economic or cultural, but rather personal and emotional: the protagonist is enraged when his best friend is falsely accused by the police of harbouring a terrorist in his house and is subjected to brutal treatment in prison. Thus 'innocent people' are shown as caught between Sikh separatists on the one hand and ruthless policemen and uncaring politicians on the other.[12] When Kirpal, the protagonist, joins a terrorist organisation run by Sanatan (Om Puri), he finds that the latter too has no specific ideology to guide him, but has himself turned to violence when his family was massacred by the police in an earlier fight. Terrorism is a matter of the heart, the resort of lonely souls who kill because their loved ones were killed. When Kirpal asks Sanatan if he is fighting for a separate homeland, the leader denies having any such aim and points to the common historical and cultural roots of all of India's major religious groups – Hindus, Muslims and Sikhs. But the path of violence, once chosen, is irrevocable and creates its own brutalisations, as weak or unwilling members of the group are eliminated in turn. Both Kirpal and his fiancee die in the end, as do virtually all the other characters in the film.

Re-visioning India as nation

It is against this 'structure of feeling' in contemporary India, in which violence and terror are rendered at once threatening and routine, that Mani Ratnam's 'terrorism' trilogy takes on meaning, quite apart from the fact that Ratnam is arguably the most influential film-maker in India today. A Tamil film-maker who has worked his way into the all-India market, he brings about interesting convergences between the traditional divides of regional and national, artistic and commercial, serious and frivolous cinema. Using popular melodramatic forms to pose questions of identity and citizenship, *Roja* (1992), *Bombay* (1995) and *Dil Se* (*From the Heart*, 1998) stage fantasmatic encounters with the other, played out at the borders and interstices of social life and consciousness: the space between civil society and the state in *Roja*, between Hindus and Muslims in *Bombay*, and between the terrorist and the non-alienated, 'benign' individual in *Dil Se*. All three films allude to actual groups or events (Kashmiri militants in *Roja*, the Ayodhya stand-off and Bombay communal riots in

Bombay, a terrorist plot involving a female suicide bomber reminiscent of the Rajiv Gandhi assassination in *Dil Se*) as dramatic backdrops for tales of passion and ineluctable desire. In a sense, these films may be said to reverse the scenario familiar in earlier Bombay films, where the locus of desire is never outside the community (the nation-group writ small) itself. In the Mani Ratnam trilogy, however, desire leads to 'the outside', the danger zones of national self-awareness, those nebulous regions hitherto unrepresented but now rendered seductive and compelling. This is particularly true of *Dil Se*, but *Bombay* and *Roja* also focus on isolation and new configurations of liminal identity: Roja the child-woman who, crazed with grief when her husband is kidnapped by terrorists on a visit to Kashmir, single-handedly tries to take on the Indian state; the transgressive Hindu/Muslim couple in Bombay whose immersion in each other virtually shuts out the surrounding world; in *Dil Se*, the protagonist's obsessive love of the 'stranger' culminating in the embrace of a bomb-induced death. If terrorism in different guises is a looming presence in these characters' lives, it is also a means of interrogation of national ideals gone awry, and of evoking the faces and voices of the estranged who must be brought back into the cultural mainstream. In focusing, however obliquely, on the communal or terrorist Other, the films suggest that the nation is problematic if not compromised and needs to be rethought. For the films do not explore the polarities between friends and enemies (nations and their terrorists), but rather the linkages, through the theatrics of violence, between dominant and subordinate, friend and foe, the nation and its would-be fragments. The latter entities end up mirroring each other, for terrorist violence is spawned by state violence and oppression. In each film, the male heroes are caught between these warring factions, beaten and abused by both, so that their declaration of an Indian (read secular) identity foregrounds an identity that is under erasure and in crisis. Thus in *Roja*, when Rishi Kumar is in terrorist custody and tortured by his captors, he insists on mouthing, 'Jai Hind!' (Hail, India!) and rescues a burning flag with his body. In *Bombay*, the hero, Shekhar Mishra, refuses the communally inflamed designation of 'Hindu' or 'Muslim' during the Bombay riots and calls himself an 'Indian' instead. In *Dil Se*, the hero's national belongingness only goes as far as his professional affiliation: he is a radio reporter for All-India Radio. But if such alignments are expressed under duress, it is the seductiveness of the stranger (not love of the national mainstream) that propels these films' narrative energies and photographic powers.

Critics of *Roja* and *Bombay*[13] (*Dil Se* flopped at the Indian box-office[14] and has not merited much critical commentary, while the former were among the top ten hits in the years of their release and were widely reviewed) have faulted these films on their stereotypical portrayals of the Kashmiri militants and the Muslim community respectively, and their 'vulgar' appeals to patriotism and Indian national identity. But such critiques (which themselves seem to conflate the 'separatist', pro-independence Kashmiri Muslim with the Indian Muslim *per se*) focus exclusively on 'realist' criteria, and tend to ignore the more cinematic dimensions of these films, primarily their investment in the narrative and visual allure of the marginal, brought to a head in *Dil Se*, in which the hero totally abandons himself to his passion for the beautiful and enigmatic stranger-cum-terrorist. The issue then is less the presumed reinvigoration of a prior patriotism, and more a shift in the nationalist discourse itself towards the margins and their incorporation into the national body through idealised visions of romantic love and empathy. Of course, Mani Ratnam is no radical: even if the film censor board were to pass a 'realistic' and sympathetic portrayal of Kashmiri separatism (a highly unlikely scenario), the evidence of these films makes it unlikely that Mani Ratnam would suggest that the territorial integrity of the Indian nation-state is open to negotiation or violation.

Mani Ratnam's terrorism trilogy, then, does not sever the ties that bind the nation to its fragments, but problematises those ties by exploring the culture of disaffection, mediated and filtered through the exigencies of internal and external censorings[15] and the conventions of entertainment cinema with its emphasis on music, spectacle, and romance. Ironically, these latter elements, which form the basis of spectatorial address and constitute the vehicle for the films' more serious concerns, are usually dismissed rather than foregrounded by critics. Yet it is important not to foreclose meaning production on narrowly defined ideological premises, since films are multiaccentual and polyvocal. As Shohat and Stam state:

> If spectatorship is on one level structured and determined, on another it is open and polymorphous. The cinematic experience has a ludic and adventurous side as well as an imperious one; it fashions a plural, 'mutant' self, occupying a range of subject positions. One is 'doubled' by the cinematic apparatus, at once in the movie theater and with the camera/projector and the action on screen. And one is further dispersed through the multiplicity of perspectives provided by even the most conventional montage. Cinema's 'polymorphous projection-identifications' (Edgar Morin) on a certain level transcend the determinations of local morality, social milieu, and ethnic affiliation. Spectatorship can become a liminal space of dreams and self-fashioning. Through its psychic chameleonism, ordinary social positions, as in carnival, are temporarily bracketed.
>
> (1996: 165)

Such a stance goes far in explaining the gap between critical and public reception of these films. For while it is true that the films under consideration posit Indian terrorism as a futile exercise in self-alienation and show the inherent recuperability of the terrorist, they also refashion the nation-space itself into a liminal space of dreaming. It is here, I contend, rather than in the traditional visual paraphernalia of flags, maps or buildings, that the films do their ideological work of re-affirming the nation. Moreover, the appeal of the new India is not constituted on moral or ideological grounds but on the level of the experiential and sensuous. Song and dance sequences powerfully evoke the pleasures of an essentially fluid, joyful and globalised world in which viewers are invited to participate, while the world to which the terrorists belong is essentially closed and claustrophobic, rule-governed and predictable. Terrorism or separatism in these films is essentially atavistic, out of sync with a multiethnic, multicultural ethos shaped by transnational influences. Moreover, if terrorism or communalism entraps the spirit, making its adherents have the proverbial lean and hungry look of a Casca, the secular heroes are fun-loving and erotic figures. This contrast is tellingly communicated in *Dil Se*: in a scene, the hero playfully asks the enigmatic stranger he has fallen in love with to name what she likes least about him and she replies, 'Your laughter, your sense of fun, your constant chatter'. In reply, the hero states that he both likes and dislikes the sadness in her eyes which give him no clue as to her deeper (read real) self. In a long song-and-dance sequence against a desert backdrop that precedes this conversation, the movements involving the protagonists are a *mélange* of Martha Graham and modern dance, jazz and aerobics, fashion advertising, Latin American and Middle Eastern hip and belly thrusts, rock music video and the like. The effect is bizarre, and yet, strangely compelling: presented as reverie, this love tango connotes the world of passion to which the terrorist denies herself membership. In *Bombay*, the first song in which the Hindu hero's call of love is reciprocated by the Muslim heroine takes place in a visually stunning landscape rendered movable and sentient by swirling camera movements. Cut off from the world, it is this mythic Eden that sets the tone for the inter-communal entity, which is then recreated at will at different points in the narrative. Thus neither the real space of village nor city harbours the liminal space that is occupied by this emergent unit and rendered palpable through hybrid musical compositions. In the narrative sequences, the home of the romantic couple contrasts with the tense atmosphere in both the Narayan Mishra and the Bashir Ahmed households, the parents (or the fathers) only able to become playful and accommodating once they start living in their children's home. Romantic and playful memories of each other also underscore the virtual absence of family members as Roja struggles to free her husband from his captors. It is as though these characters feel the need to start afresh and have no models of interaction with a larger social world against which to define themselves.

However, this 'mythic' transcendence of what might be called the 'old' nation-family is effected through a hermeneutic of exoticisation and alterity. It is here that Bauman's category of the stranger (here, the terrorist or communal other), becomes useful again, for what is most puzzling about the stranger is that he/she is an anomaly, and fits no schema. In the films under consideration, the desire to locate the stranger is compelling: *Roja*'s Rishi Kumar voices his scepticism to his captors, 'You are Kashmiris? Whose independence are you fighting for?'; In *Dil Se*, the hero, Amar Verma, tells the Assamese 'terrorist' he interviews for his radio story, 'You look like the rest of us. Absolutely normal ...

and yet ...'. But the films draw a thin line between this desire to interpret the other and fetishisation as a hermeneutic strategy, especially with regard to Shailabano in *Bombay* and Meghna in *Dil Se* (Manisha Koirala appearing in both roles). These characters are primarily sumptuous objects of the spectatorial gaze, the latter conflated with that of the hero. Entrapped and distanced by the mechanisms of looking, the stranger remains a stranger whose claim to our consideration is as an exotic entity. The disaffected Other tied to place and purpose is now the exoticised Other in a transnational marketplace of substitutable imaginaries.

Conclusion

Nationalism – the integrity of the nation-state and the imagined belongingness of its citizens – is predicated on its dreaded Other, namely, the enemy within, the dissident, the terrorist. A nation manages a precarious peace by negotiating between its desire to tolerate and even encourage difference and diversity, and setting the limits beyond which claims of difference become unrecognisable. Paradoxically, the cinema foregrounds particularity and resists as a result any easy conflation with nationalist agendas. In India, this paradox has fed into at once formulaic and utopian representations of the national community as an interplay of mainstream and marginal ethnicities. This essay has tried to show how the popular cinema in India has sought to accommodate a recent rise in separatist or independence movements within India's borders. The focus has been on Mani Ratnam's 'terrorism trilogy' in which trangressive couples embody an inclusion in a new globalised national imaginary purveyed through a visual language of exotic abandon, as well as the terror of the unassimilable stranger. These films reflect a national obsession with a hermeneutics of the stranger, but it is the stranger fetishised and distanced, even when romantically appropriated.

Notes

1   The assumption and conviction on the part of scholars and popular film reviewers alike that 'national identity' concerns belong to other (read third world) nations is evident in the fact that the term 'national cinema' was used exclusively for these others up to the 1990s, and it is only in the last few years that American film historians have turned the lens on the local product.
2   For an account of these tendencies in the post-Cold War world, see Miyoshi 1996.
3   Perhaps it is this 'extremism' in its early manifestations that led Yugoslav writer Danilo Kis to a bitter denunciation of nationalism in 1973, leading to his subsequent exile in Paris, see Kis 1992. I am grateful to Bronwyn Jones for making this essay available to me.
4   The list of books on nationalism published in the 1990s is far too long to include here. What is interesting in the context of my discussion is that several of them address the new forces of ethnic revivalism and this is reflected in their titles, see Watson (ed.) 1990; Smith (ed.) 1992; Conner 1994; Van Horne (ed.) 1997; Kellas

1998. Following upon Nairn 1977, Chatterjee 1993, the idea of fragmentation may well be the emergent paradigm in studies of nationalism. For studies of India's separatist rumblings in particular, see Ludden (ed.) 1996 and Nandy 1994.

5 But see how Robert Stam and Ella Shohat enumerate the various ways in which Hollywood films stirred nationalist (and imperialist) imaginings in the colonial era. They write: 'The fiction film also inherited the social role of the nineteenth-century realist novel in relation to national imaginaries'. But they also point out, further on, that filmic chronotopes are deployed 'to the advantage of some national and racial imaginaries and to the detriment of others' (1996: 153–4). An awareness of this tension marks their excellent essay.

6 For an early discussion of the construction of Australian national identity, see Bertrand 1984.

7 See Chanan 1985.

8 There are more studies of *Mother India* than of any other single film of the Bombay cinema, see Thomas 1989 and Roy 1998.

9 See Baskaran 1981 and Rajadhyaksha 1986.

10 An interesting version of this narrative and ideological ploy can be found in Ketan Mehta's *Mirch Masala* (*Hot Spices*, 1984) in which it is the old Muslim gatekeeper who emerges as the only 'virile' protector of female honour when a chilli factory is besieged by a lecherous colonial functionary.

11 See Gopalan 1997 and Virdi 1999.

12 For a totally different (and humorous) take on the subject of terrorist activity in India, see Nandy 1995.

13 See, in particular, Niranjana 1994, Vasudevan 1996 and Rajadhyaksha 1996.

14 However, *Dil Se* was reported to have hit the British top ten list by the London-based reporters for the *Indian Express*, 4 September, 1998. The same article stated that 100,000 cassettes of its musical soundtrack had been sold.

15 For an account of the trouble that Mani Ratnam ran into with *Bombay*, see Pendakur 1996.

Bibliography

Anderson, B. (1983) *Imagined Communities: Reflections on the Origins and Spread of Nationalism*, London: Verso.

Baskaran, T. (1981) *The Message Bearers: Nationalist Politics and the Entertainment Media in South India, 1880–1945*, Madras, Cre-A.

Bauman, Z. (1990) 'Modernity and Ambivalence', in M. Featherstone (ed.).

Bertrand, I. (1984) ' "National Identity"/"National History"/"National Film": The Australian Experience', *Historical Journal of Radio and Television* 4, 2: 179–87.

Chakravarty, S. (1993) *National Identity in Indian Popular Cinema, 1947–1987*, Austin, TX: University of Texas Press.

Chanan, M. (1985) *The Cuban Image: Cinema and Cultural Politics in Cuba*, London: BFI.

Chatterjee, P. (1993) *The Nation and its Fragments*, Princeton, NJ: Princeton University Press.

Conner, W. (1994) *Ethnonationalism: The Quest for Understanding*, Princeton, NJ: Princeton University Press.

Featherstone, M. (ed.) (1990) *Global Culture: Nationalism, Globalization and Modernity*, London: Sage.

Gopalan, L. (1997) 'Avenging Women in Indian Cinema', *Screen* 38, 1: 42–59.

Hobsbawm, E. (1990) *Nations and Nationalism Since 1780*, Cambridge: Cambridge University Press.

Kellas, J. (1991) *Politics of Nationalism and Ethnicity*, 2nd edn, New York: Macmillan, 1998.

Kis, D. (1992) 'Danilo Kis on Nationalism', in M. Thompson (ed.), *A Paper House: The Ending of Yugoslavia*, New York: Pantheon Books.

Ludden, D. (ed.) (1996) *Contesting the Nation: Religion, Community, and the Politics of Democracy in India*, Philadelphia, PA: University of Pennsylvania Press.

Marvin, C. and Ingle, D. (1999) *Blood Sacrifice and the Nation: Totem Rituals and the American Flag*, London: Cambridge University Press.

Miyoshi, M. (1996) 'A Borderless World?: From Colonialism to Transnationalism and the Decline of the Nation-State', in R. Wilson and W. Dissanayake (eds).

Moran, A. (ed.) (1996) *Film Policy: International, National and Regional Perspectives*, London: Routledge.

Nairn, T. (1977) *The Break-Up of Britain: Crisis and Neonationalism*, London: New Left Books.

Nandy, A. (1994) *The Illegitimacy of Nationalism*, Dehli: Oxford University Press.

—— (1995) 'The Discreet Charms of Indian Terrorism', in A. Nandy, *The Savage Freud and Other Essays on Possible and Retrievable Selves*, Princeton, NJ: Princeton University Press.

Niranjana, T. (1994) 'Integrating Whose Nation?: Tourists and Terrorists in *Roja*', *Economic and Political Weekly* 15 January.

Nowell-Smith, G. (ed.) (1996) *The Oxford History of World Cinema*, London: Oxford University Press.

Pendakur, M. (1996) 'India's National Film Policy: Shifting Currents in the 1990s', in A. Moran (ed.).

Rajadhyaksha, A. (1986) 'Neotraditionalism: Film as Popular Art in India', *Framework* 32/33: 21–67.

—— (1996) 'India: Filming the Nation', in G. Nowell-Smith (ed.).

Rajchman, J. (ed.) (1995) *The Identity in Question*, New York: Routledge.

Roy, P. (1998) 'Figuring Mother India: The Case of Nargis', in P. Roy, *Indian Traffic: Identities in Question in Colonial and Postcolonial India*, Berkeley, CA: University of California Press.

Shohat, E. and Stam, R. (1996) 'From the Imperial Family to the Transnational Imaginary: Media Spectatorship in the Age of Globalization', in R. Wilson and W. Dissanayake (eds).

Smith, A. (ed.) (1992) *Ethnicity and Nationalism*, Leiden, NY: EJ Brill.

Thomas, R. (1989) 'Sanctity and Scandal: The Mythologization of Mother India', *Quarterly Review of Film and Video* 11, 3: 11–30.

Van Horne, W. (ed.) (1997) *Global Convulsions: Race, Ethnicity and Nationalism at the End of the Twentieth Century*, Albany, NY: State of New York University Press.

Vasudevan, R.S. (1996) '*Bombay* and its Public', *Journal of Art and Ideas* 29.

Virdi, J. (1999) 'Reverence, Rape – and then Revenge: Popular Hindi Cinema's "Woman's Film"', *Screen* 40, 1: 17–37.

Watson, M. (1990) *Contemporary Minority Nationalism*, London: Routledge.

Wilson, R. and Dissanayake, W. (eds). (1996) *Global/Local: Cultural Production and the Transnational Imaginary*, Durham, NC: Duke University Press.

Part V

THE RECEPTION OF
NATIONAL IMAGES

15

MIMETIC NATIONHOOD

Ethnography and the national

Scott MacKenzie

In recent years, the body of critical works which examine national cinemas has expanded greatly. However, far less attention has been paid to whether the category of 'national cinema' can be as easily applied to minor, third, alternative or aboriginal cinemas.[1] There are many reasons for this. One of the key descriptive categories to emerge from both industrialisation and colonialism is that of 'nation' and certainly, one of the tensions underlying the notion of the 'national' is its historical trajectory as a first-world concept intrinsically tied to colonialism and Euro-centrism. That said, a growing number of groups within cultures that are not typically considered 'nations' now invoke 'nationhood' in order both to address and challenge the dominant public sphere. Here I am thinking of 'first nations', 'aboriginal nations', or 'queer nations', all of which fall outside the modernist vision of the nation-state. I am also thinking of the growing number of critiques which point to the fact that discourses of 'nationhood' often elide questions of gender and sexuality (Bruce 1999; Hall 1999; Waugh 1999). Because of these exclusions, hierarchies and elisions, the invocation of 'nationhood' on the part of alternative and minority groups often functions as an inverted mirror-image of the structure of typical, late-modernist nationhood.[2] This mirror-like, mimetic image of the 'nation' is often appropriated by minority groups to challenge the precepts of the dominant public sphere. In this light, what I wish to explore in the following pages is the efficacy of applying categories such as 'national identity' or 'national cinema' to ethnographic film and video production, specifically in West Africa (Ghana), Latin America (Brazil) and – in order to provide a first-world example of a nation which often invokes the discourses of (post-) colonialism – Québec.

While there are a variety of contrasting theoretical approaches to the questions raised by nationalism and national identity, 'modernists' such as Benedict Anderson (1991), Ernest Gellner (1983) and Eric Hobsbawm (1992) more or less agree that the concepts of national identity and the nation arise with the advent of industrialisation, the formalisation of an official, 'state' language, the homogenisation of local cultures into 'high' cultures, and the emergence of the centres of power around which the contemporary nation-state are based. 'Perennialists' such as Anthony Smith grant that the current formation of the nation-state is distinctively different from the occurrences of 'ethno-symbolic' group formation which precede industrialisation, centralisation and widespread literacy (Smith 1999). It is therefore difficult, in the first instance, to address the production of visual culture both by and about aboriginal and colonised groups in terms of 'nationalism' and 'national identity', at least in relation to the ways in which the terms are currently understood.

Eric Hobsbawm has argued that the concept of the nation can only be understood in light of its intrinsic connection to modernity. He writes:

> The basic characteristic of the modern nation and everything connected to it is its modernity. This is now well understood, but the opposite assumption, that national identification is somehow so natural, primary and permanent as to precede history, is so widely held that it may be useful to illustrate the modernity of the vocabulary of the subject itself.
>
> (Hobsbawm 1992: 14)

For instance, as Hobsbawm points out, in the Brazilian context, the word *nación*, before 1884, meant ' "the aggregate of the inhabitants of a province, a country or a kingdom" and also "a foreigner" ' (ibid.: 14). This former definition is far more applicable to present-day aboriginal cultural formations than the first-world conceptualisation of the nation that currently holds sway, while the latter definition has little or no present-day currency.

If the term 'nation' had a substantially different meaning in pre-modern times, it can also be understood in a variety of often conflicting ways in postcolonial ones. As Anthony Smith notes (1991: 106–10), present-day post-colonial nations are often built upon frameworks that are remnant of the colonial powers, which raises the question whether or not the nation, as the West understands it, is a valid form of self-representation for the post-colonial state. Indeed, it is the post-colonial recasting of the 'nation' – the hybridisation of indigenous and Western European cultural and political formations – which frequently provides the former colonies with their political and cultural frameworks. In the Latin American context, the hybridised *ethnie* of much of the population – the *mestizo* in Mexico, for example – is a salient example of this process.

In order to examine how conflicting notions of national identity are understood at these points of contact between the coloniser and the colonised, I wish to examine the notion of mimesis and how it relates to questions of national representation in ethnographic endeavours. What interests me here is how colonised or otherwise oppressed groups can adopt through mimesis the trappings of nationhood in a series of both positive and negative ways in order to comment on, reinforce, or critique the (post-) colonial nation-state.

Mad masters and the mimetic faculty

Nature creates similarities. One only need think of mimicry. The highest capacity for producing similarities, however, is man's. His gift of seeing resemblances is nothing other than a rudiment of the powerful compulsion in former times to become and behave like something else. Perhaps there is none of his higher functions in which his mimetic faculty does not play a decisive role.

(Walter Benjamin, 'On the Mimetic Faculty', 1986: 333)

In *Mimesis and Alterity*, Michael Taussig offers a highly peculiar example of the mimetic faculty. A photograph depicts a Nigerian mud sculpture of a white man in a pith helmet, with one fist raised in the air (Taussig 1993: 239).[3] It is hard to imagine why this totem was built and what exact function it served; nevertheless, it offers an eerie example of the art of the colonised 'other' staring back in 'white face'. Why would Nigerians want to build a totem to white invaders? To answer this question, one must re-examine the often binary debates between 'coloniser' and 'colonised' and 'self' and 'other', so as to explore the mimetic interchange that often plays itself out in culture, through film, and more recently, through video.

The role played by mimesis and mimetic power in political resistance and in the construction of national identities in both the first and third-world orders is complex, for the mimetic faculty blurs simple distinctions between 'us' and 'them'. For instance, in the colonial and post-colonial contexts, is mimetic ritual an oppressive or emancipatory process? Who engages in mimetic activity and what is their relationship to institutional, cultural and state power? How do these issues relate to the question of national identity? In the following pages, I address the question of mimesis, drawing on debates within cultural anthropology and from a number of examples in visual ethnography which problematise 'mimesis', 'mimetic power' and the 'mimetic faculty'. A shift seems to have taken place in the supposed global village: in the colonial past, mimesis was often used to subvert, scare and destabilise the coloniser; in the post-colonial world, with the advent of video technology and the 'new' world order of globalisation, the camera itself often becomes the instigator of mimetic practice. This shift points to the new ground that resistance is fought upon: resistance politics seem increasingly to relocate their focus to the realm of representation. Furthermore, the kinds of representations which are produced through this relocation are most often intrinsically tied to the concepts of national identity and nationhood.

Mimetic resistance is apparent in many of the rituals that developed within the colonised world. The totem described above is one example; another is the Hauka possession ritual. As Michael Taussig points out, the Hauka 'begun among the Songhay people in 1925; [the participants] would dance and become possessed by the spirits of the colonial administrators' (1993: 240). The ritual itself is therefore intrinsically tied to the history of colonialism.

One of the key figures to document this ritual is the French film-maker and anthropologist Jean Rouch. In many ways, Rouch's work rewrote the principles of ethnographic film-making in the 1950s and also greatly influenced France's *nouvelle vague* (Marie 1979). Rouch's *Les Maîtres fous* (France, 1954/released 1957),[4] a 'trance film', documents the Hauka possession of Ghanaians mimicking colonialists, frothing at the mouth, and eventually sacrificing a dog, drinking its blood, boiling it and eating it.[5] As the film begins, we are introduced to various Ghanaian workers. The workers, who are described as 'normal' in every way, depart for the weekend, in order to partake in the yearly possession ritual. Rouch documents each step of the process: the admittance of new members, the purging of the sins of the returning members, and the possession itself. At first, the film seems to uphold the construction of otherness that is so often found in ethnographic cinema: viewers watch a bizarre set of practices that seem totally alien to their own frames of reference, but are explained away by an authoritative voice-over; indeed, the film was attacked by African intellectuals upon its release for these very reasons (Cervoni 1996; Hennebelle 1996; Mayet-Giaume 1996; Rouch 1996).

But then a dramatic shift takes place, which throws into question any straightforward reading of Rouch's ethnographic practice. Halfway through the film, Rouch compares the Hauka to the ritual pageantry of the British colonial soldiers. Taussig outlines the effect of this juxtaposition:

> A man possessed by a Hauka spirit stoops and breaks an egg over the sculpted figure of the governor ... that presides over the day's event of Hauka possession. Cracked on the governor's head, the egg cascades in white and yellow rivulets. Then the film is abruptly cut. We are transported to a big military parade in the colonial city two hours away. The film hurls at us the cascading yellow and white plumes of the white governor's hat as he reviews the black troops passing. Those of us watching the film in a university lecture hall in New York City gasp.
>
> (Taussig 1993: 242)

On a formal level, this moment functions as a synthesis of Sergei Eisenstein's theory of intellectual montage and Walter Benjamin's notion of the 'dialectical image'.[6] This radical juxtaposition brings out the latent meanings in these images of first and third-world rituals; meanings that are typically left repressed and unspoken. The images of possession suddenly make sense, while the colonial pageantry seems denaturalised, its traditional signification of divine right turned into a parody of ritual.[7] Denaturalisation, in this context, can be seen as a non-fictional counterpart to the self-reflexive distanciation (*Verfremdungs* or *V*-effect) proposed by Bertolt Brecht in his theory of the Epic Theatre, combined with the stripping away of aura which Benjamin postulated as an outcome of the advent of photographic reproduction.[8]

The rest of the film takes on a dramatically different tone, as both the Hauka possession and the British pageantry seem to explode with heretofore unrecognised meanings. Following Benjamin's thesis on the philosophy of history, these

244

meanings are not 'constructed' on the part of the film-maker, but are related to the repressed or *ur*-histories of both the colonialist and Hauka realities.[9]

After the cut to the British ceremony, the role of the mimetic faculty in the Hauka ritual comes to the forefront. Each of the participants in the trance plays out a role derived from the British colonial hierarchy. There is the wicked major, the general, the general's wife and many others, all of whom perform roles derived from the British hierarchy. André Bazin refers to this sequence of the film as a sort of *commedia dell'arte* (1983: 186). Indeed, the nature of the 'stock character' in *commedia dell'arte* and the key function played by repetition and variance is easily apparent in the Hauka ritual.[10] Eventually, the participants come out of the trance and resume their day-to-day existence. As the film ends, we see the workers back at work in their subjugated roles, with Rouch's sardonic voice-over pointing to the fact that by acting out the roles of the colonialists, the Ghanaians stay sane, exorcising their white demons in the process. It is interesting to note that the power of mimesis lies not only in the editing of the film: the practice of the Hauka was so despised by colonial governments that practitioners were jailed.

Les Maîtres fous offers interesting insights into the mimetic faculty, both in terms of ritualised practice and the mimetic power of the cinema itself. Images which at first are unintelligible, showing the practices of a culture which Western audiences cannot immediately understand, are given a very specific colonial context halfway through the film; the Ghanaians are mimicking the often fearful and merciless power to which they are subjugated on a daily basis. The reference to the British colonial context (the marching bands, etc.) is not present to give the viewers a familiar frame of reference; the British pageantry does not explain away the Hauka. The flowing plumage and the running egg are present because they are part of the rituals themselves. The people of Ghana adapt the European ritual to their own ends and, in the process, recontextualise the symbols of the coloniser's world, demonstrating both the pomposity and cruelty of the naturalised colonialist rituals. It is this act of denaturalisation the colonialists feared and despised, as Taussig writes:

> The British authorities in Ghana banned the film. The reason? According to Rouch they 'equated the picture of the Governor with an insult to the Queen and her authority'. But what was the insult? It turns out to be exactly that moment ... where the mimetic power of the film piggybacks on the mimetic power of African possession ritual.
>
> (Taussig 1993: 242)

Colonialism, a concept that had been naturalised as an outgrowth of 'progress' and 'civilisation' is recontextualised into ritual, while 'untranslatable' ritual is transformed and re-constituted through the colonialist presence. Significantly, both Western colonialist pageantry and non-Western ritual are seen as escapes from the real, yet it is the non-Western ritual that, according to the voice-over, preserves the sanity of the people of Ghana.

The Hauka demonstrates how the explosive underpinnings of mimesis can emerge and recontextualise or reframe the meaning of a practice that is both a part of, and critique of, national identity within the colonial experience. Much the same way that the mimetic practice of the Hauka recontextualises the colonial experience for the people of Ghana, the juxtaposition of the Hauka ritual with colonial ceremony shocks the viewer into seeing connections they have not seen before; not only does the experience make the viewer aware of the relationship between the supposedly impenetrable cultural practice of possession and Western oppression, it also points to the more irrational elements of the colonialist ceremony.[11] *Les Maîtres fous*, then, functions as an indictment of 'old' world colonialism; in the 'modern' world, mimetic practice is seen unambiguously as resistance.

In *Ritual and Process*, Victor Turner contends that status reversal, similar to the kind found in *Les Maîtres fous*, is a type of ritual performed by the structurally inferior, or the permanently weak and marginalised members of a society. Turner defines ritual status reversal in the following manner:

> At certain culturally defined points in the seasonal cycle, groups and categories of persons who habitually occupy low status positions in the social structure are positively enjoined to exercise ritual authority over their superiors; and they, in their turn, must accept with good will their ritual degradation.
>
> (1969: 167–8)

Turner contends that there are two contrasting social models in each human society: the structured, typically hierarchical, model of:

> jural, political, and economic positions, offices, statuses and roles, in which the individual is only ambiguously grasped behind the social persona. The other is of society as a communitas of concrete idiosyncratic individuals, who ... are regarded as equal in terms of shared humanity.
>
> (ibid.: 177)

Most societies oscillate between structure and communitas; structure is the ordering principle, while communitas lends itself to social mobility, fluidity and individual idiosyncrasy. Each society consists of members who are structurally inferior and structurally superior social agents within the social structure. For Turner, status reversal, which he sees as connected to cyclical patterns of ritual or calendrical rites, do not provide the structurally inferior with access to power. Instead, status reversal temporarily grants the structurally inferior the fantasy of structural superiority. Role reversal realigns these opposing parts of the social structure. Mimetic power, then, is a force of stabilisation in culture, but the temporary power it grants the disenfranchised is planned and illusory. The structurally inferior can gain power within their grouping, but this power is on the margins of culture, reversed only during the proper calendrical period. Indeed, the structurally inferior exist as a group precisely because of their marginality. Turner summarises the process in the following way:

> [T]he masking of the weak in aggressive strength and the concomitant masking of the strong in humility and passivity are devices that cleanse society of its structurally engendered 'sins' and what hippies might call 'hang-ups'. The stage is then set for an ecstatic experience of communitas, followed by a sober return to a now purged and reanimated structure.
>
> (ibid.: 185)

There are many similarities between this theoretical description of mimetic practice and the Hauka ritual documented in Rouch's film. Yet, there are also some glaring differences, as we shall see.

Rouch's film raises interesting questions about Turner's theory of mimesis. It is true that the Hauka possession ritual absolves the sins of the participants (indeed absolution is the first part of the practice itself), and the ritual also preserves the stability of the social structure, as Rouch points out in his final voice-over about the maintenance of Ghanaian sanity. For Turner, role reversal and mimesis are processes of social regeneration. Mimesis is part of a social structure's larger ritual pattern, and does not constitute an act of transgression or resistance on the part of the mimics. If the social structure of Ghana were defined only in terms of the indigenous people of the area, then the cyclical pattern of status reversal and mimesis proposed by Turner could function. But, in the case of the Hauka possession ritual, the structurally superior group that is mimicked and has its social position reversed (admittedly unwillingly), is an invader from the outside; it is a group that is not a part of the local cultural practices. Therefore, instead of promoting social stability, mimetic practice promotes social instability and has a destabilising effect on the colonialists' attempt to naturalise their hierarchical position. The practitioners of the Hauka in Ghana understood all too well the latent meanings of the pomp and circumstance of their colonial masters. This reason, above all others, is why the practitioners were jailed. The practitioners of Hauka possession took the symbols of colonialist power and turned these representations of oppression into a liberating force. They did this by taking colonial symbols and making them 'foreign', 'incomprehensible' and 'other' to the British themselves. The difference between the Hauka ritual, addressed in *Les Maîtres fous*, and the examples given by Turner, is that all of Turner's examples come from *within* one culture, not from the subjugation of one culture by another. It seems, then, that the recuperative power of mimicry takes hold if the reversal takes place within one social structure. When more than one culture is involved, and when it is not the structurally superior and inferior who perform mimicry, but instead, members of the subjugated culture mimicking aspects of the super-imposed, subjugating culture, it is cultural instability that ensues, not recuperation. In the colonial world, mimesis denaturalised a power system that seemed, most of the time, to be utterly hegemonic.

Simulating authority

In exploring the effects of mimesis on colonialism, and of the mimetic strategies adopted in the face of colonialism, Roger M. Keesing's work (1992) on mimetic power and political resistance in the Solomon islands offers some relevant avenues of inquiry. Keesing offers a strikingly different view of the power of mimesis. Carrying out his research among the Kwaio of the Solomon islands, Keesing is interested in questions of resistance and cultural autonomy. Tracing the history of the Kwaio people and their colonial subjugation, Keesing contends that part of the colonialist agenda was to impose British cultural standards on to the culture which they were invading, while concurrently labelling the cultures of the indigenous peoples as brute, savage, and uncivilised. Keesing writes that:

> [t]he ideological edifice and artifice on which British colonialism was built, in the Solomons and in other parts of the world, rested on the premise that a rule of law and order, rationally ordered accounting to the higher canons of 'civilisation', was benevolently introduced to replace what had been uncivilised and anarchic and irrational.
>
> (1992: 228)

This system became naturalised, and the colonisers offered some of the indigenous people an emulative role to play in the new, official culture, setting up an elite within the colonised culture. This gave the indigenous people the paradoxical incentive to access power which kept them powerless. Some Solomon islanders became *simulated* officials:

> Part of the process of colonial domination has been to instill in a stratum of the indigenous population simulacra of the manners, languages, styles, and values of the colonial élite. I say 'simulacra' because the 'natives' are permitted within certain bounds to emulate, one might say mimic, the ways of those who rule them: but always with a distance and deference that preserves the bounds of their subalternity.
>
> (ibid.: 230)

The power of colonialism, then, was twofold: the British could maintain power by offering simulated or emulative power to indigenous people, and the British could also keep power over the members who did not accept this offer by branding them as brute, and 'other', outside of the culture the British had imposed and created. Some of the people of the Solomon islands were complicit with the colonialist endeavour, became Christian, and took on the simulated position of power as members of the native élite. Others, like the Kwaio, remained 'pagans' and were branded as such by their newly colonised compatriots. The Kwaio, instead of choosing the sanctified, simulated, mimetic patterns endorsed by the structurally superior British, developed their own oppositional strategies through the use of mimesis. This took mimesis out of the realm of sanctified ritual and placed it in the domain of oppositional politics, as Keesing notes: '[t]o emulate without this deference, to presume equality, was *transgression*, a challenge to white supremacy and colonial domination' (ibid.: 230).

The question the Kwaio were faced with was the following: which type of strategy of resistance would work against the colonialist power? Keesing argues that the power of non-sanctifying mimesis was the strongest form of resistance that the Kwaio had. He believes this for two reasons: (1) It allowed the Kwaio to demystify the cultural systems of the British, and in doing so; (2) it enabled the Kwaio to fight the British with their own forms of communal and cultural exchange. Keesing writes that the Kwaio demystified British symbols of power and civilisation in the following way:

> Kwaio appropriations of the categories, logics, and semiology of colonial rule progressively stripped away the mystifications of this ideology by portraying the colonial presence as what it was: an act of invasion, an appropriation of lands, an imposition of an alien cultural system, a rule by force and not by law – since the British did not follow their own laws and moral codes – or by consent.
>
> (ibid.: 229)

This process of demystification to some extent denaturalised the British system. Furthermore, transgressive mimesis worked as a means of appropriating the British system and making it work to the Kwaio's own ends:

> If one wants to challenge colonial assertions of sovereignty, one must do it in a language of flags and ancestors-on-coins in place of Kings. ... A recognition that if counterclaims are to be recognised and effective, they must be cast in the terms and categories and semiology of hegemonic discourse, is politically astute, not blindly reactive.
>
> (ibid.: 236–7)

Unlike Audre Lorde's oft-quoted statement that one cannot dismantle the master's house with his own tools (1984: 110–13), Keesing is proposing that not only can this be done, but in the process of mimetic appropriation, indigenous peoples can transform the systems of power and make them, to some extent, their own. Keesing concludes by stating:

> All this is to say that the reactive process is a highly complex dialectical one in which the categorical structures of domination may be negated or inverted – hence doubly subverted – as well as reproduced in opposition. Even when they appear to be appropriating the structures and categories and logics of colonial discourse, subaltern peoples progressively but ulti- mately radically transform them, in the very process of transgression and in their deployment in a counterhegemonic political struggle.
>
> (1992: 238)

Mimetic power that is not sanctioned by the structurally superior can bring about violent conflict and drastic change within a culture; it is not part of the social structure itself, and that is where its power lies. What Keesing points to here is that the clash of cultures, where one culture appropriates the other and uses its own naturalised systems against it, can lead to the denaturalisation of the 'inherent' rights to power held by the colonialists; this has the potentiality of leading to a dramatic shift in power. Finally, Keesing's argument points to the fact that mimetic power is not always recuperative.

Mimesis in the first world, or, 'where the rich eat the rich'

It should be clear by now that mimetic practices do not have an *a priori* polit- ical or ideological disposition; rather, the political consequences of mimesis are relational. What transpires when these kinds of mimetic representational strate- gies, even in jest, are relocated into the first world? To examine this question in light of the application of post-colonial discourse to first-world contexts, I wish to turn to Pierre Falardeau's video *Le Temps des bouffons* (Québec, 1985–93), which addresses the mimetic practices of a group of bourgeois French and English Canadians celebrating the colonialist past in the Beaver Club, a private club in Montréal located in the Queen Elizabeth II hotel. Falardeau saw this video as, to borrow Jean-Luc Godard's phrase, a *'ciné-tract'*, and therefore wanted the tape in the hands of the people (read: the working-class, disenfran- chised francophones), so that they could see these mimetic images of national identity as the deception he understood them to be. Two thousand copies of the video were released at a retail price of $9.95. Piracy and illegal copying were encouraged by Falardeau; this action led to 2,000–4,000 bootleg copies entering into circulation, in an attempt to short-circuit 'official' systems of distribution (Falardeau 1999: 108). In undertaking this kind of distributional subterfuge, Falardeau was able to expand greatly his audience. In essence, Falardeau's tape is a grass-roots video, which has a long tradition in Québec and Canada, both as a state-sponsored means of enpowerment and as a radical alter- native practice designed to challenge the state.[12]

Le Temps des bouffons begins with a scene from Rouch's *Les Maîtres fous*, taken from the possession ritual.[13] In a voice-over, Falardeau summarises the Hauka possession ritual and its relationship to the colonial endeavour. He then cuts to footage surreptitiously shot at the Beaver Club and provides a voice-over account of the mimetic practices of the participants:

> We're in 1985. Each year, the colonial bourgeoisie assembles at the Queen Elizabeth Hotel for the Beaver Club banquet. Here, there are no possessed, just possessors. At the table of honour, with their false beards and their paper hats, the lieutenant governors of the ten provinces, businessmen, judges, shopping centre Indians, Negro kings with white skin who speak bilingual.
>
> (Falardeau 1994: 14)

Falardeau's juxtaposition of sound and image takes a realist video image and turns it into a surreal pageant of the history of colonialism in Québec. At the video-taped party, the powers-that-be in Québec are seen eating, drinking and dancing, all the while dressed in the 'traditional' garb of the time of the Conquest in 1759. Each nationality is represented as a stereotype and both coloniser and colonised seem quite happy to be playing a version of himself or herself from times past. As Falardeau notes in his sardonic voice-over:

> In Ghana, once a year, the poor imitate the rich. Here, this evening, the rich imitate the rich. Everyone in their place. ... The English bourgeois are disguised as the English bourgeois; the bilingual collaborators are dressed as bilingual collaborators, smiling and satisfied; the Scots take out their Scottish skirts; the Indians put a feather in their ass to be aboriginal. The Québécois are disguised as musicians and waiters. The immigrants? Like the Québécois, as waiters. Plaid shirts and sagging sashes. The only things missing are snowshoes and cans of maple syrup. ... *Alouette, gentille Alouette!*
>
> (Falardeau 1994: 16)

Le Temps des bouffons inverts the process undertaken by Rouch in *Les Maîtres fous*. For Falardeau, thanks to Rouch, the Hauka ritual is, ethnographically speaking, understandable, and can be summoned to denaturalise the supposedly innocuous, and therefore natural, practices found in the Beaver Club. Here, mimesis fundamentally alters national identity, as what constitutes the shared culture which forms a nation is staged without reference to the systems of power which underlie the performance. Falardeau therefore suggests that the francophones participating in the celebration are unwittingly celebrating their own colonial status. Here, national identity, founded on shared myths of the past, becomes not an empowering force, intrinsically tied to a cultural group's self-realisation; instead, it functions as a way of obliterating the historical struggles which underlie the foundation of Québec and Canada and replace them with an innocuous notion of the 'traditional'. Falardeau denaturalised a seemingly harmless mimetic practice built around the notion of the founding of Canada and demonstrated how this mimetic vision of national identity elided and obliterated historical reality. By introducing ethnographic practices to the analysis of national identity, Falardeau attempted to position spectators as ethnographers capable of analysing their own place in history from a vantage point outside of their day-to-day existence. Essentially, Falardeau was challenging the audience to demystify the banal (but not so innocent) mimetic processes of the participants at the Beaver Club itself. *Le Temps des bouffons* therefore demonstrates how mimesis is not only a function of the disparity between first and third-world cultures; the video demonstrates that mimesis is a universal practice, engaged in by both the empowered and the disempowered in the often uneven relationship between different national cultures. Furthermore, it demonstrates how the myths which surround all national cultures do, to a great degree, involve a mimetic relationship with an imagined past. Finally, *Le Temps de bouffons* points to a very different kind of mimetic practice. The Hauka mimicked the colonisers; the participants at the Beaver Club celebration mimicked their own colonial image of themselves.

Ethnography and the simulation of the national

What role does self-mimicry play in the postcolonial world? To consider this question, I would like now to consider the ethnographic videos of Vincent Carelli, who is part of the *Centro de Trabalho Indigenista* in São Paulo, Brazil. Carelli's videos inadvertently address mimetic power in colonised cultures in the post-colonial world. I use the term 'inadvertently' for the simple reason that unlike Rouch's *Les Maîtres fous*, Carelli's videos presume to address the positive cultural aspects of the advent of video technology in indigenous culture; the camera itself is of central importance. Yet, it seems that the presence of this equipment brings about a far more complex set of problems than justice can be done to by a simple argument which posits that getting technology into the hands of the people is *a priori* a positive political goal. In Carelli's videos, the video camera becomes the instigator of mimetic ritual. One is left wondering whether or not the mimetic actions evoked in these videos come from inside or outside the culture being documented, or if the production of these videos instigates a strange amalgamation of the 'outside' and the 'inside', where the video itself becomes the mimetic ritual.

In *Video in the Villages* (1989), *The Spirit of TV* (1990) and *Meeting Ancestors: the Zo'e* (1993), Vincent Carelli documents the Waiãpi Indians' documentation of themselves, for themselves, on video. Carelli, with the help of the Brazilian government, undertook this project in order to set up an archive of the traditions, cultures and images of the Indian inhabitants of the Brazilian Rain Forests.[14] It is important to note that these videos are *not* the ones that

252

Figure 15.1 Waiãpi Indians watching themselves on television in Vincent Carelli's *The Spirit of TV*

the Waiãpi keep in their process of archival self-documentation, but are made by Carelli for a Western audience. The footage is kept by the Waiãpi, but it is not edited into the concise formats that are distributed in North America. The North American versions are made in order to raise funds and keep grant agencies happy; Carelli contends that there are no political effects generated by these videos whatsoever. Furthermore, he contends that it is impossible for video images to politicise viewers.[15] This strikes me as an overly naive view to hold of the political import of images. After all, if images are so ineffectual, why would the Waiãpi's self-documentation seem like an important endeavour to Carelli?

These videos (both Carelli's 'Western' versions and the Waiãpi's self-documentation), produced a strange effect within the Waiãpi culture. The Waiãpi began to mimic their imaginary view of their past traditions, in order to produce a 'true' document of their past; this is taken to its extreme in *Meeting Ancestors: The Zo'e*, where the chief of the Waiãpi visits an 'untouched' tribe in a search for mythic origins. *Video in the Villages*, the first video in the series, documents an eerie cultural effect: the Waiãpi videotape images of themselves performing a traditional dance ritual, and then, when they see the images played back, restage their ritual performance, in order to make it look more 'savage' and 'Indian'. To achieve this effect, they add more body paint and remove their Western clothes. Yet, in the process, they cease to document their culture *as it exists*, and begin to engage in a mimetic ritual, although unlike the Hauka or the transgressive mimetic practices of the Kwaio, the Waiãpi mimic their imaginary view of themselves. This imaginary view is as much a Western one as it is an Indian one. The Waiãpi restage their traditional performance, mimicking their imaginary view of what 'savageness' is.[16] This imaginary view of savageness corresponds to what they imagine the Western viewer will deem to be 'savage-looking'. In essence, they consciously engage in the process of self-mimicry critiqued by Falardeau. In a sense, they are colonising their own image, in order to retrieve what they believe has disappeared from their rituals because of colonisation. In this video, the Waiãpi also revive a piercing ceremony that has not been practised in twenty years. Ron Burnett cites the voice-over, scripted by Carelli, as the Waiãpi 'reinvent' piercing, as evidence that the video-maker believed he was capturing an historical moment: 'We never imagined that the video would be a catalyst for nose piercing ceremonies which had not been done for twenty years' (Burnett 1995: 173). Both the examples of the restaged savageness and of the return to body piercing raise questions about mimetic power. What is the relationship between these images and the culture that is under self-reconstruction? Patricia Aufderheide, a proponent of the video project, believes that it affords the Waiãpi a certain autonomy: 'Using video reinforced an emerging concept of "traditional" in contrast to Brazilian culture – a concept that had not, apparently been part of [the culture's] repertoire before contact but that had practical political utility' (Aufderheide 1993: 588). This strikes me as highly problematic. If 'traditional' did not exist as a category in the Waiãpi's culture prior to the presence of the video cameras, then where did this concept come from? Even if we turn to the 'perennialist' model of national identity, we can see that the 'traditional' is a concept that exists as a past-oriented phenomena. In this post-colonial video world, what is authentic and what is a simulated reconstruction of an idealised past? Through the presence of video technology, the Waiãpi are engaging in a mimetic process, whereby they are both reconstructing the myths of the past, and adjusting their own self-image (that of 'savageness') to conform to what their imaginary ideal of Indian existence is. It is important to note that they are not documenting their own culture, but recreating it through video. The question, of course, is why?

In *The Spirit of TV*, Chief Wai-Wai, the head of the Waiãpi, who is also the head storyteller responsible for preserving the group's history from generation to generation, is happy to have the Waiãpi's stories on tape, as this preserves them for all time; at the same time, the videos make him and the oral tradition he keeps alive superfluous. Yet, getting one's history from a videotape is not the same as having it passed on through an interactive oral tradition. These reconstructions of rituals change the nature of their symbolic functions within the community, as the ritual dance and body-piercing no longer reflect or demonstrate communal bonding, or even what takes place within the community; instead they are the Waiãpi's mimetic representations of themselves, as much for imagined others as for themselves. The images are directed, as the people in the video state, at other Indian tribes and are also supposed to scare Western viewers with their savageness. So, in *Video in the Villages*, *The Spirit of TV* and *Meeting Ancestors: The Zo'e*, the past and present and imagined image of the future are all fused into the video image. The question which remains is how will the culture survive, or more appropriately, transform itself when image production is fundamentally changing the culture itself? While in *Les Maîtres fous* this fusing of the coloniser and the colonised raises questions about the naturalised existence of the colonialist power, in Carelli's videos, the tapes themselves question the future existence of the culture, even though the tapes are supposed to preserve the exact culture they are changing. Furthermore, the mimetic faculty, which is traditionally used by the oppressed, the marginalised, the structurally inferior, to seize power from the oppressor, is now used by the oppressed to mimic their own representations, creating in the process a highly bizarre *doppelgänger* effect.

Conclusion

What do these different examples demonstrate about the relationship between mimesis and national identity? Traditionally the mimetic faculty played a desta-bilising role in colonial cultures. When true mimetic power falls into the hands of the structurally inferior, as is the case with the Hauka ritual and the transgres-sive mimesis of the Kwaio, instability and the possibility of a profound shift in the social structure ensues. But for this oppositional political stance to emerge, there must be an audience for the mimetic act, even if that audience (in the case of the Kwaio and the Ghanaians, the British) does not particularly wish to see the performance. As Falardeau demonstrates in *Le Temps des bouffons*, mimesis – especially self-mimicry – can as easily be an act of colonialisation as it can be an act of resistance. In the case of the Waiãpi, it seems that they have turned the mimetic faculty back on to themselves, mimicking their past, in order to regain a symbolic power they once seem to have had when their historical traditions were strong. Yet, it seems that video production diffuses this power, as the mimetic act supersedes the desire to document culture accurately. Yet, paradoxi-cally, the videos represent themselves as the true document of the Waiãpi culture. Furthermore, the mimetic image becomes a patronising one in the West, as the discourse which often surrounds these videos is one of conde-scending paternalism. By this, I mean that Carelli and others believe that their presence with video cameras has somehow instigated the retrieval of tradition and perpetuation of an indigenous form of 'national identity', whereas it strikes me that, in the case of the Waiãpi, the power of mimesis is to supplant the ability of the culture to document itself. In the modern world of globalisation, nationalism and assimilation, all that seems to remain in both Falardeau's and Carelli's videos are simulacra of a mythical past.

Acknowledgements

This is a greatly revised and expanded version of an article of mine entitled 'Mad Priests and the Mimetic Faculty: Ethnographic Film, Post-Colonialism and the (New) World Order', which originally appeared in *Cinéaction* (1994) 33. Research for the present essay was funded by the Social Sciences and Humanities Research Council of Canada.

Notes

1 Key exceptions here are Hjort 1996 and Willemen 1989.

2 While the current essay focuses on ethnographic film and video, questions of sexuality and nationhood have been foregrounded in many recent feminist and queer films and videos. For example, Brenda Longfellow's *Our Marilyn* (Canada, 1987) questions the construction of the female body-as-image, and as image-of-nation, through the analysis of the 'American Marilyn' (Marilyn Monroe) and the Canadian Marilyn (Marilyn Bell, the first woman to swim across Lake Ontario). John Greyson's *The Making of 'Monsters'* (Canada, 1990) humorously deconstructs both Canadian national identity and masculine hetero-identity (both of which are embodied by hockey in the video) in the pseudo 'making of' video about queer bashing in Toronto, which features Georg Lukács and Bertolt Brecht (played by a cat-fish) debating the use of realist and anti-realist techniques as means of political representation.

3 The image is reproduced from Blackburn 1979. The photograph was taken by Herbert M. Cole in 1967 and published in *African Arts* in 1969.

4 The exact date of release of Rouch's film is not entirely clear. Completed in 1954, the film was released and withdrawn and re-released by Rouch with great frequency. For a history of the film's production and releases, see Stoller 1992: 145–60; for Rouch's own account of the making of the film, see Rouch 1995.

5 Other key 'trance films' include Margaret Mead's and Gregory Bateson's *Trance and Dance in Bali* (US, 1952) and Maya Deren's unfinished *Divine Horsemen* (US, 1947/released 1985). For a critical examination of the 'trance film', see Russell 1999: 193–237.

6 For a more thorough discussion of the relationships between Walter Benjamin's and Sergei Eisenstein's notions of montage, see Wees 1993: 32–57.

7 The cinema's ability to perform this kind of parodic inversion has a long tradition. See, for instance, Charles Ridley's *Swinging the Lambeth Walk* (UK, 1940), which denaturalises and parodies the militarism of Nazi Germany by re-cutting Leni Riefenstahl's *Der Triumph des Willens* (*Triumph of the Will*, Germany, 1935). Ridley accomplishes this denaturalisation through montage and sound/image juxtaposition. As Jay Leyda notes, the re-editing of Riefenstahl's film 'to the rhythm of a popular English tune ... happily deflated the ritual' (Leyda 1964: 55).

8 On the effects of the Epic Theatre, Brecht writes:

> Once the content becomes, technically speaking, an independent component, to which text, music and setting adopt 'attitudes'; once illusion is sacrificed to free discussion, and once the spectator, instead of being able to have an experience, is forced as it were to cast his vote; then a change has been launched which goes far beyond formal matters and begins for the first time to affect the theatre's social function.
>
> (Brecht 1964: 39)

In Rouch's work, which often blends the fictional and the non-fictional, we can see the development of an ethnographic distanciation technique, similar to the kind postulated earlier in the writings of both Benjamin and Georges Bataille in the 1920s. Benjamin's own account of the alienation (*Verfremdungs*) effect illustrates quite well the process of denaturalisation found in Rouch's film:

> The task of Epic Theatre, according to Brecht, is not so much the develop-
> ment of actions as the representation of conditions. This presentation does
> not mean reproduction as the naturalists understood it. Rather, the truly
> important thing is to discover the conditions of life. (One might say just as
> well alienate them.) This discovery (alienation) of conditions takes place
> through the interruption of happenings.
>
> (Benjamin 1969b: 150)

9 See Benjamin 1969a.

10 Clubb summarises the plots of *commedia dell'arte* in the following way:

> The plots in which these characters meet were built of condensed and
> recombined structures from the repertory developed in regular comedy,
> stories of crossed love, mistaken identity, disguises of sex and status,
> runaway wives and children, adventurous rescues, madness, apparent death,
> reunion of separated families, clowning, ingenious tricks, ridicule of jealous
> husbands and lustful old men, mocking of masters by servants, witty extor-
> tion, gulling, and unlimited opportunities for mayhem, erotic play and
> coarseness.
>
> (Clubb 1995: 131)

The parallels between these kinds of themes and many of those found in the Hauka ritual are quite striking.

11 For more on the 'dialectical image' and anthropological inquiry, see Taussig 1993: 240–2. For a thoroughgoing analysis of Benjamin's notions of the 'dialectical image' and *ur*-histories, see also Buck-Morss 1989.

12 See MacKenzie 1996 and Marchessault 1995b.

13 For reasons unknown, the footage that Falardeau appropriates from *Les Maîtres fous* is black and white, while Rouch's original film is colour.

14 For an overview of the 'Video in the Villages' project, see Carelli and Gallois 1992.

15 Or, to be more precise, Western viewers. The Waiãpi, Carelli contends, can and do use these images to political ends. Carelli made these points at a screening of his works at the *Cinéma Parallèle* in Montréal, on 12 November 1993.

16 For more on the effect of the Western construction of savageness on Indian self-identity, see Taussig 1987: 317–19.

Bibliography

Anderson, B. (1991) *Imagined Communities: Reflections on the Origin and Spread of Nationalism*, 2nd edn, London: Verso.

Armatage, K., Banning, K., Longfellow, B. and Marchessault, J. (eds) (1999) *Gendering the Nation: Canadian Women's Cinema*, Toronto: University of Toronto Press.

Aufderheide, P. (1993) 'Latin American Grassroots Television: Beyond Video', *Public Culture* 5, 3: 579–92.

Bazin, A. (1983) 'Jean Rouch: *Les Maîtres fous*', in A. Bazin, *Le Cinéma français de la Libération à la Nouvelle Vague (1945–1958)*, Paris: Cahiers du cinéma/Éditions de l'Étoile.

Benjamin, W. (1969a) 'Theses on the Philosophy of History', in W. Benjamin, *Illumina-tions: Essays and Reflections*, trans. Harry Zohn, New York: Schocken.

—— (1969b) 'What is Epic Theatre?', in W. Benjamin, *Illuminations: Essays and Reflec-tions*, trans. Harry Zohn, New York: Schocken.

—— (1986) 'On the Mimetic Faculty', in W. Benjamin, *Reflections: Essays, Aphorisms, Autobiographical Writings*, trans. Edmund Jephcott, New York: Schocken.

Blackburn, J. (1979) *The White Man: The First Responses of Aboriginal Peoples to the White Man*, London, Orbis.

Bordwell, D. and Carroll, N. (eds) (1996) *Post-Theory: Reconstructing Film Studies*, Madison: University of Wisconsin Press.

Brecht, B. (1964) *Brecht on Theatre: The Development of an Aesthetic*, trans. John Willett. New York: Hill and Wang.

Brown, J.R. (ed.) (1995) *The Oxford Illustrated History of Theatre*, Oxford: Oxford University Press.

Bruce, J. (1999) 'Querying/Queering the Nation', in K. Armatage, K. Banning, B. Longfellow and J. Marchessault (eds).

Buck-Morss, S. (1989) *The Dialectics of Seeing: Walter Benjamin and the Arcades Project*, Cambridge, MA: MIT Press.

Burnett, R. (1995) 'Video Space/Video Time: The Electronic Image and Portable Video', in J. Marchessault (ed.) (1995a).

Carelli, V. and Gallois, D.T. (1992) 'Vidéo dans les villages: l'expérience Waiãpi', *Lumières* 32: 41–51; trans. V. Carelli and D.T. Galois 'Video in the Villages: The Waiãpi Experience', in F. Roy (ed.) (1993).

Cervoni, A. (1996) 'Une confrontation historique en 1965 entre Jean Rouch et Sembène Ousmane: "Tu nous regardes comme des insectes"', *CinémAction* 81: 104–6.

Clubb, L.G. (1995) 'Italian Renaissance Theatre', in J.R. Brown (ed.).

Eaton, M. (ed.) (1979) *Anthropology-Cinema-Reality: The Films of Jean Rouch*, London: BFI.

Falardeau, P. (1994) *Le Temps des bouffons et autres textes*, Montréal: Les Éditions des Intouchables.

—— (1999) *Les bœufs sont lents mais la terre est patiente*, Montréal: VLB Éditeur.

Gellner, E. (1983) *Nations and Nationalism*, Ithaca, NY: Cornell University Press.

Hall, C. (1999) 'Gender, Nations and Nationalisms', in E. Mortimer (ed.).

Hennebelle, G. (1996) 'L'éthique du cinéma ethnographique', *CinémAction* 81: 76–9.

Hjort, M. (1996) 'Danish Cinema and the Politics of Recognition', in D. Bordwell and N. Carroll (eds).

Hobsbawm, E.J. (1992) *Nations and Nationalism Since 1780*, 2nd edn, Cambridge: Cambridge University Press.

Hockings, P. (ed.) (1995) *Principles of Visual Anthropology*, 2nd edn, Berlin: Mouton de Gruyter.

Keesing, R.M. (1992) *Custom and Confrontation: The Kwaio Struggle for Cultural Autonomy*, Chicago, IL: University of Chicago Press.

Leyda, J. (1964) *Films Beget Films: A Study in the Compilation Film*, New York: Hill and Wang.

Lorde, A. (1984) *Sister Outsider: Essays and Speeches*, Freedom, CA: Crossing Press.

MacKenzie, S. (1996) '*Société nouvelle*: The Challenge for Change in the Alternative Public Sphere', *Canadian Journal of Film Studies* 5, 2: 67–83.

Marchessault, J. (ed.) (1995a) *Mirror Machine: Video and Identity*, Montréal/Toronto: CRCCII/YYZ Books.

—— (1995b) 'Reflections on the Dispossessed: Video and the "Challenge for Change" Experiment', *Screen* 36, 2: 131–46.

Marie, M. (1979) 'Direct', in M. Eaton (ed.).

Mayet-Giaume, J. (1996) 'La polémique autour des *Maîtres fous*', *CinémAction* 81: 80–2.

Mortimer, E. (ed.) (1999) *People, Nation and State*, London: I.B. Tauris.

Rouch, J. (1995) 'Our Totemic Ancestors and Crazed Masters', in P. Hockings (ed.).

—— (1996) 'Jean Rouch parle des *Maîtres fous*', *CinémAction* 81: 83–4.

Roy, F. (ed.) (1993) *Amerindians in View*, Montréal: Vidéo tiers-monde.

Russell, C. (1999) *Experimental Ethnography: The Work of Film in the Age of Video*, Durham, NC: Duke University Press.

Smith, A.D. (1991) *National Identity*, London: Routledge.

—— (1999) 'The Nation: Real or Imagined?', in E. Mortimer (ed.).

Stoller, P. (1992) *The Cinematic Griot: The Ethnography of Jean Rouch*, Chicago, IL: University of Chicago Press.

Taussig, M. (1987) *Shamanism, Colonialism, and the Wild Man: A Study in Terror and Healing*, Chicago, IL: University of Chicago Press.

—— (1993) *Mimesis and Alterity: A Particular History of the Human Senses*, London: Routledge.

Turner, V. (1969) *The Ritual Process: Structure and Anti-Structure*, New York: Aldine.

Waugh, T. (1999) 'Cinemas, Nations, Masculinities' (The Martin Walsh Memorial Lecture, 1998) *Canadian Journal of Film Studies* 8, 1: 8–44.

Wees, W.C. (1993) *Recycled Images: The Art and Politics of Found Footage Films*, New York: Anthology Film Archives.

Willemen, P. (1989) 'The Third Cinema Question: Notes and Reflections', in J. Pines and P. Willemen (eds), *Questions of Third Cinema*, London: BFI.

16

FROM NEW GERMAN CINEMA TO THE POST-WALL CINEMA OF CONSENSUS

Eric Rentschler

A new cinema for a new Germany?

Germany has enjoyed a privileged status in discussions about national cinema. No other cinema, in fact, has lent itself so consistently and productively to investigations into the relations between film and nationhood. New German Cinema, most critics would agree, constitutes the most recent chapter in this national cinema's compelling and controversial saga. Dozens of books and hundreds of articles in many languages celebrate New German Cinema's achievements. In the early 1990s, lavish exhibitions in Frankfurt and Berlin commemorated its hallmarks and, in so doing, certified its status as a thing of the past. I would like to consider the continuation of this story, to account for what has come in the wake of New German Cinema. German films, between sixty and seventy features a year in fact, are still being made, watched and talked about. How does one speak of national cinema in Germany today and how does this discourse relate to the ways in which people once spoke of a previous epoch's national cinema?

This is no easy matter for we have at present no convincing paradigms or even useful catch phrases. Is post-New German Cinema simply to be situated within an unchartable (*unübersichtlich*) landscape, a site without signposts, a post-histoire locus where all is familiar, foregone and forgettable? The cultural landscape in Germany, claims Jürgen Habermas, is 'a desert of banality and bewilderment' (Habermas 1985). The scene he describes is moribund and amorphous, divested of the topical impetus and utopian resolve which once energised the New German Cinema. The German film industry's present self-estimation, however, bears no trace of Habermas' cultural discontent. 'German film is on the move', rejoices a perky pamphlet that appeared after a dramatic (albeit ephemeral) box-office breakthrough in 1997. During the first quarter of that year the success of four movies (*Jenseits der Stille/Beyond Silence, Knockin' on Heaven's Door, Rossini* and *Kleines Arschloch/Little Asshole*) yielded an unheard-of 37 per cent German share of the domestic film market.[1] Above all

260

the comedies of the mid 1990s have, in the upbeat phrases of lobbyists, 'reawakened spectator interest for German films and also created a demand for other kinds of genre films. Young actors and actresses provide strong points of identification and new directorial talents bring fresh air to movie screens and television monitors' (Amend and Bütow 1997: 9). Such high spirits about a national film revival have nothing in common with Habermas' grim prospects; at best they confirm his ironic assertion that 'The German "sense of being special" is regenerating itself hour by hour' (1997: 81).

How are we to describe, much less comprehend, German national cinema in the 1990s? Beyond Habermas' less than precise cultural topography, another perspective poses itself, although its approach is not altogether unrelated. Its impetus is as tempting as it is predictable and obvious, especially for a former American friend of the New German Cinema like myself. In this scenario I look back at the alternative cinema of Fassbinder, Herzog, Kluge, Wenders, von Trotta, Sanders-Brahms and others with an ardent nostalgia, regarding the popular cinema that has replaced it with a marked disdain and a bitter sense of loss. To do this is to remain the captive of former enthusiasms, which even in the past prompted serious critical objections (e.g., about these films' negotiations of history, gender and otherness). We know that 'New German Cinema' above all constituted a potent mythical construction, replete with a heroic historical narrative driven by hero-directors, an international co-production of domestic supporters and foreign enthusiasts which played an essential role in the legitimation and continuing existence of an otherwise unpopular minor cinema. More tempered responses to the dynamics of this myth-making process (much less to the workings of new German films) were common already in the early 1980s. To embrace this myth uncritically today means potentially to ignore past insights as well as perspectives that have subsequently surfaced – a decided drawback for any film historian. Let my point of departure, therefore, be one that avoids dismissiveness and nostalgia without denying my own critical bias. I want to begin with a simple question in the hope that it might lead to less obvious conclusions: What factors and determinations have produced present-day German conceptions of a national cinema?

To answer this question I will need to rehearse the strong tension between New German Cinema and the cinema that now stands for Germany in media representations, to analyse how New German Cinema came apart and how recent German cinema came into being. In the process I want to consider shifting constructions of a national cinema and the ways they have assumed shape in relation to a host of determinants. Finally, I would like to discuss these quite divergent conceptions of national cinema in terms that take us beyond previous impasses and that perhaps might afford us more analytical forms of historical understanding.

Frontlines

'Something or other was simply not right about German filmmakers and their actors. A collective plague had left them incapable of representing conflict' (Schwanitz 1995: 230). The litany is familiar; the critique related in Dieter Schwanitz's novel, *Der Campus*, is alternately sharp ('simply not right') and fuzzy ('something or other'). Journalists, cineastes and intellectuals at large have frequently rebuked German film-makers for ignoring the nation's social problems and political debates. Contemporary productions, they tell us, studiously and systematically skirt the 'large' topics and hot issues: the messy complications of post-wall reality, thematics like right-wing radicalism, chronic unemployment, or the uneasy integration of the former GDR into the Federal Republic. And, to be sure, prominent directors like Sönke Wortmann insist that their priorities as film-makers lie elsewhere. Questioned about the lack of German reality in German films, Wortmann becomes snappish: 'Germany, as it really is. ... If I want to see that, I'll switch on the evening news' (Vahabzadeh 1998).

Contemporary German cinema, writers like Georg Seeßlen, Andreas Kilb and Kraft Wetzel have been saying for more than a decade, is vapid and anaemic, devoid of substance, conviction and deeper meaning. Projects nowadays, maintains insider Reinhard Hauff, have no dialectical volition, no driving passion, no compelling justification:

> In the case of most films it works like this: someone finds subsidy money and a well-disposed tv editor, he then finds a producer who sorts out the rest of the financing, and before you know it you have yet another German film. Another German film without any real dramatic or emotional conflicts.
>
> (quoted in Seeßlen 1995: 211)

Domestic fare is dominated by a formula-bound profusion of romantic comedies, crude farces, road movies, action films and literary adaptations. This cinema is above all star-driven, peopled with the familiar faces of Katja Riemann, Til Schweiger, Joachim Król, Maria Schrader, Martina Gedeck and Meret Becker.[2]

In the 1980s only a handful of German films, almost without exception comedies featuring television stars (Otto Waalkes, Didi Hallervorden, Gerhard Polt and Loriot), various instalments of *The Super Noses* (*Die Supernasen*) and *Three Crazy Jerks* (*Zärtliche Chaoten*) and features starring Mantas and Trabis, would become box-office hits. During the next decade comedies would constitute the most prominent factor in German cinema's public profile. In representative features like *Makin' Up* (*Abgeschminkt*), *Talk of the Town* (*Stadtgespräch*), and *Super-woman* (*Das Superweib*), we find young upscale urbanites working in a sector of the culture industry. The protagonists – attractive, successful and around thirty – run up against the reality principle and confront the responsibilities of the adult world. The narratives occupy the liminal space between a bohemian everyday and a bourgeois existence; in this regard they represent post-1968 panoramas. As Karl Prümm puts it, new German comedies 'move between the makeshift student life style that one is loathe to give up and the fixed professional security that one aspires to, but dislikes, between rundown communes and well-appointed penthouses' (1996: 122). These films focus on identity crises which are in fact pseudo-crises for they have no depth of despair, no true suffering, no real joy. With their triangulated desires and mismatched partners, their schematic constellations and formulaic trajectories, these yuppie comedies of errors follow strictly codified patterns.

Domestic diversions that stay close to home, they play it by the (German) book. Recent German films, claim critics, are out of touch with the world at large and the larger world. And perhaps for that reason they do not travel well no matter how strong their domestic appeal. (*Maybe, Maybe Not*, the signal German success of the 1990s, had a painstakingly prepared American release whose returns were decidedly meagre. Tom Tykwer's *Run, Lola, Run* (Lola rennt, 1998) fared very well in the United States, but even this great exception was a resounding flop in France.)[3] Over the last decade new titles from the Federal Republic have all but vanished from the New York Film Festival, the catalogues of US distributors, and North American arthouse programmes.[4] Despite its resonance at home, the new German genre cinema, in the mind of its detractors, is bland and provincial, infantile and harmless.[5] Ideological opponents castigate this cinema for its lack of oppositional energies and critical voices, seeing it as an emanation of an overdetermined German desire for normalcy as well as of a marked disinclination towards any serious political reflection or sustained historical retrospection.

While deploring the present state of affairs, commentators (especially those of an older generation) frequently hold up New German Cinema as an object of comparison and a positive alternative, fondly recalling its stylistic idiosyncrasy, narrative subversion and political rebellion. German films of the 1960s and 1970s – e.g. Jean-Marie Straub's and Danielle Huillet's *Unreconciled* (*Nicht versöhnt*, 1965), Volker Schlöndorff's *Young Törless* (*Der junge Törless*, 1966), Alexander Kluge's *Yesterday Girl* (*Abschied von gestern*, 1966) and Rainer Werner Fassbinder's *The Marriage of Maria Braun* (*Die Ehe der Maria Braun*, 1978) – seen from this nostalgic vantage point, militated against collective forgetting, taking leave of a problematic national past by constantly problematising that past's presence, turning against mindless escapism and crude commercialism, insisting that films need not only serve as pliers of distraction but rather might operate as time machines and critical vehicles.

A body of films conscious of its own status as a part of German film history, New German Cinema coalesced as a collective and, in crucial regards, a programmatic endeavour. Films, in the understanding of the generation born shortly after 1945, the cohort that instigated the student movement, did not just tell stories and orchestrate effects; they interrogated images of the past in the hope of refining memories and catalysing changes. At some point, Fassbinder was fond of saying, films must cease just being films and stories and come alive, so that spectators take pause to ponder their own persons and question their own lives. New German Cinema was challenging and unsettling, which in part explains why it found such a modest domestic following. It was taken seriously abroad because it was spurned at home; it was a curious cultural ambassador which at its best spoke for the nation by speaking (indeed: acting out) against it. Critics who fondly look back at the new German film generally have a far dimmer view of recent productions from the Federal Republic.

The New German Cinema, on the other hand, gets little respect from people who champion the films of Rainer Kaufmann, Dominik Graf, Doris Dörrie, Sönke Wortmann, Katja von Garnier, Joseph Vilsmaier, Helmut Dietl and Detlev Buck. These industry partisans reject the *Autorenkino*'s arrogance and introspection, its artistic indulgence, intellectual pompousness and economic incapacity. For most German taxpayers, New German Cinema generated strained seriousness and sensory deprivation, films that appealed to minds rather than to emotions, that sought to enlighten rather than to entertain. For the average viewer new German features were slapdash and soporific, irritating and downright hard to look at, prone to protracted long takes and confusing plot lines, to under-narrated stories, unappealing characters and unsatisfying conclusions. New German Cinema's richness, its adherents were fond of saying, lay in its diversity. In the minds of its assailants, however, this diversity remained an empty assertion. How rich could a cinema be if it had no gripping stories or sympathetic figures, if it denied its viewers pleasant evenings in the dark?[6]

The supporters of today's mainstream film-makers applaud a German cinema that has a much lighter touch and is far more user-friendly. This new cinema cultivates familiar genres and caters to popular tastes. At no price do its purveyors wish to come off as rarefied or esoteric, to challenge or disconcert their public in the manner of the new German militia. Rather than intervening or speaking out, self-avowed professionals like Dörrie, Graf and Wortmann engross and accommodate. They want the cinema to be a site of mass diversion, not a moral institution or a political forum. Quite empathically, the most prominent directors of the post-wall era aim to please, which is to say that they consciously solicit a new German consensus. In this sense the cinema they champion is one with a decidedly affirmative calling.

From *Autorenfilm* to the designer world

In current discussions, then, there is a marked divide between the New German Cinema and its successor, what I am calling the German Cinema of Consensus. Let us consider more carefully some of the key factors that have made for their quite different assumptions and operations.

The waning of the cinema of authors

Since its institutionalisation in the wake of the Oberhausen Manifesto, the German *Autorenkino* proved to be a precarious entity, invariably in crisis and frequently under attack. The death of Fassbinder in June 1982 vanquished the all too rarely realised hope that New German auteurs might mediate between the personal and the popular, the radical and the accessible, the alternative and the mainstream. In the words of critic Manfred Etten:

> Fassbinder's life and work was a model which seemed to embody and 'realize' the founding myths of New German Film. The loss of this model makes it poignantly clear that these myths no longer are in effect. By dint of his mere presence he constantly reminded people what New German Film as a whole (perhaps) might have become. In this sense Fassbinder was not only the calling card of New German Film, but also its guilty conscience.
>
> (Etten 1992: 5)

Fassbinder, claimed Wolfram Schütte, was the heart of New German Film, 'the pulsating, vibrating core'. With his death this heart had 'now stopped beating' (Schütte 1992: 73).

The demise of New German Cinema was in any case overdetermined and, in most observers' minds, long overdue. Fassbinder's passing coincided with the arrival of Friedrich Zimmermann and a shift in government film politics. By the early 1980s, New German Cinema had by and large lost its small audience and its counter-public sphere. Outside of festival exposure and obscure television screenings, its presence was limited to an ever dwindling number of exhibition sites. With a CDU/CSU/FDP coalition firmly in power by March 1983, the new Minister of the Interior (whose charge included administering federal film subsidies and the annual state film prizes), Zimmermann (CSU), declared war on the *Autorenfilm*, insisting on popular movies that would appeal to the average German taxpayer.[7] Outraged by an irreverent portrayal of Christ's return to the modern world, Zimmermann and his followers denounced Herbert Achternbusch's *The Ghost* (*Das Gespenst*), denying the director a final instalment from a 1982 state film prize. This intervention (the object of a decade-long court battle) was perceived as an outrageous act of censorship, as the first of many radical changes in government policies regarding public film subsidy.

Zimmermann's programme catalysed widespread endeavours among producers to make German films commercially competitive and to recapture the confidence of domestic audiences. Upcoming directors, particularly graduates from the Munich Academy for Film und Television, openly eschewed the counter-cultural strategies of their elders. 'Much more than by New German Film', opined Doris Dörrie, 'I've been influenced by the films of the "New

American Cinema" – Scorsese, Cassavetes and Rafelson' (Nolden 1989). Dominik Graf, another successful Munich graduate, railed against the limited appeal of a rarefied 'art gallery cinema' and advocated a higher level of professionalism: 'I think we often tend to forget audiences when we make films and let our own preferences and egomania guide us rather than worrying about technical expertise' (Rhode 1990). Attempting to create accessible and commercially viable movies, young German film-makers thoroughly acquainted themselves with genre cinema's patterns of recognition. Reinhard Münster's resolve of 1984 was widely followed: 'When I watch a classical film, I can only learn something. It would be inappropriate to say that I'm going to make something altogether new when there are models out there which I can use as a point of departure' (Schmidt 1984: 41). Characterising this new generation of film-makers in 1988, Alexander Kluge remarked:

> They believe in Spielberg and so on, and not at all in politics. They believe completely in a professional fantasy: some day having a huge budget with three assistants. It's a strange idea, but very common. They think a real director must be recognized with a telephone call from Hollywood or somewhere, and he mustn't do anything political. They find politics boring. They believe that one shouldn't fight.
>
> (Liebman 1988: 38)

Epigonal endeavours of various hues – e.g., Peter F. Bringmann's *The Snow Man* (*Der Schneemann*, 1985), Roland Emmerich's *Joey* (1985), Hajo Gies' *Schimanski – On the Killer's Track* (1985) and Peter Timm's *Fifty Fifty* (1988) – painstakingly duplicated Hollywood formulas in a studied attempt to craft popular German films.

Even prominent practitioners of the *Autorenkino* resigned and bid the model adieu. What hope was there in a culture of short attention spans and disposable images, Wim Wenders reflected, for a cinema of emotional investment and social concern, for penetrating films, 'which have a soul and a discernible inner core, which emanate a distinct identity?' (Wenders 1991). 'In a society addicted to amusement', lamented producer Günter Rohrbach, 'one that is less and less able to take time for sensitive stories, does there remain any hope of survival at all for a type of film which relies precisely on this sort of sensitivity?' (Roth 1989: 11). The continued existence of the *Autorenfilm*, its detractors claimed, had been mainly a function of narcissistic artists, credulous subsidy boards, indulgent television editors, and leftist film reviewers. Angry and disinclined observers insisted that this cinema had been kept alive artificially by a state welfare system. Early in 1991, Wenders said that the historical existence of the authorial design had reached its end (Wenders 1993: 42). The respected media expert Klaus Kreimeier went further; he wondered in fact whether this model might have been a fundamental mistake, inappropriate to the workings and co-operative imperatives of the film medium itself. German film authors, in their quest for self-expression, had assumed an untenable and unrealistic stance. Their emphasis on control was egocentric and autistic; so often people presumed competence in areas where they possessed little or no expertise. The *Autorenkino*'s *mélange* of arrogance and amateurism, in Kreimeier's harsh condemnation, might well be the reason for cinema's decline in Germany over the last decades (ibid.: 23).

New formations in film subsidy arrangements

Without question, the dramatic shifts in the nature of German film subsidy since the early 1980s have influenced the content and shape of productions, diminishing the possibility for political interventions and the presence of alternative perspectives and formal experiments. Four major developments are crucial in this regard:

- The transformation of cultural subsidy into an almost exclusively economic one (the primacy of commerce over art).
- The greater power of television officials on film boards and the decisive influence of TV programming priorities on subsidy decisions.
- The increasing centralisation and consolidation of film finance as television and film subsidy sources collaborate with regional media initiatives (e.g., the co-operations between the Filmstiftung Nordrhein-Westfalen with both public and commercial TV stations (ZDF, WDR, Pro7, Sat.1, and RTL), or the interactions between the Bavarian State Film and Television Fund, Bavaria studio and Pro7).
- Arrangements between film academies, television stations, and commercial producers. Diploma films are less likely to be sites of experimentation and risk; rather, young directors are encouraged to work under the sway of commercial imperatives and industry priorities already in their inaugural features.

The model that ensured the continuing existence of *auteur* film-makers and a public sphere for alternative perspectives is on the wane. Questions of *Wirtschaftlichkeit* (commercial potential) generally outweigh all other concerns. Or, put differently, 'those parties who prefer to speak of film as a disposable property are the ones who by and large determine the drift of contemporary discussions' (Weingarten 1990). Given these dynamics, it is easily apparent why difficult films that explore the darker sides of German reality rarely are produced.

The transformation of cinema within the public sphere

Bestandsaufnahme. Utopie Film (Taking Stock: The Utopia Film), an extensive pamphlet edited by Alexander Kluge, appeared shortly after Zimmermann came into power (Kluge 1983). Kluge and his collaborators fully recognised the endangered status of alternative film-makers. With the proliferation of cable networks and media consortia, of electronic software and satellite television, this status had become even more precarious. The so-called 'new media' have fostered technological change and economic opportunity. In the process these heavily capitalised industrial forces remould perceptions of space and time, reprogramming human senses in a round-the-clock barrage of prefabricated meaning and patterned experience. New German Cinema, which over the years had encouraged experimentation and militated against the powers of exclusion, amnesia and repression, was reduced to an anachronistic outpost in a radically transformed public sphere.

The crisis situation addressed in *Bestandsaufnahme* and experienced throughout the 1980s and 1990s was of course hardly singular to Germany. It was felt throughout the world by a host of national film industries, which, overwhelmed by American blockbusters, transnational distributors and decreasing market shares, took desperate recourse to popular domestic counterventures or regional self-help initiatives (e.g., the GATT-Manifesto or European co-productions). The crisis was more one of cinema than of film, a function of dramatic changes in the institutional spaces, social callings and material forms assumed by mass-produced sights and sounds. No longer items necessarily encountered in a public forum at a fixed time, films increasingly circulate in a variety of formats (video-cassettes, laser discs, DVDs, digital texts), readily available commodities at the consumer's constant disposal. In a world where audio-visual software proliferates in constantly new and advanced packages, individual films transmute into

> temporary constellations of particles from our galaxy of images which assume a fleeting shape before our eyes on the screen and then flit back into the galaxy of images, reappearing later perhaps as television images, raw material for commercials, as magazine photos or music videos.
>
> (Kreimeier 1992: 10)

And as single films cease to be main attractions, the institution of cinema must constantly consider how it might maintain a viable profile against competing forms of leisure-time diversions.

Changes in exhibition and distribution

Cinema has become one outlet in an exponentially expanding field of audio-visual providers.[8] In 1980, Wolf-Eckart Bühler had characterised the three major sites of German film exhibition: 'The McDonald-cinema of the urban movie center chains'; 'the Peter Stuyvesant-Kino of the new progressive film freaks'; 'the Suhrkamp-cinema of the communal celluloid catacombs' (Bühler 1980: 473). During the next decade, the big city cine-centres would increasingly come under attack for their small screens, substandard technical facilities and exorbitant prices. Few German films would find their way into such houses; they – along with art films and alternative productions – unreeled instead in *Programmkinos*. By the mid 1980s many *Programmkinos* had cut back their initially ambitious programmes, showing a more limited array of films and taking fewer risks. Communal cinemas, an important locus for independent and alternative endeavours, struggle to keep alive despite smaller turnouts and government budget cuts. Old cinemas are being torn down today in numerous urban locations. In their place arise technically advanced multiplexes with large screens, luxurious seating, state-of-the-art projection and sophisticated sound systems, as well as a host of other enticements including restaurants, bars and entertainment centres.

Five major American distributors now play a leading role in Germany: Warner, UIP, Columbia, Buena Vista and Fox. (In the last several years Polygram has likewise become a strong player.) These companies have come to recognise that German films, professionally packaged and appropriately marketed, can play well in German cinemas. Buena Vista released *Dressing Down* (*Abgeschminkt*), *Nobody Loves Me* (*Keiner liebt mich*), *Talk of the Town* (*Stadtgespräch*), and *Maybe, Maybe Not* (which sold 6.5 million tickets in 1995). During the illustrious first quarter of 1997, *Knockin' on Heaven's Door*, another Buena Vista release, screened in one of every four big city cinemas. Backed by the majors, modest-scale German productions (albeit a very small number of them) were able to gain a substantial public profile. The recent breakthrough of German comedies is unthinkable without the investments of the major companies. Popular film genres and visible stars coupled with the marketing ploys of American distributors: this gathering of forces above all generated the German film boom of the 1990s.

Different experiential priorities for the trend- and tonesetters of a younger generation

Altogether different interests are to be found among spectators of the German 'New Age', an era of programme changes and identity shifts. No longer does one flee to the cinema in search of heightened experiences and alternative perspectives as one had in the 1970s: 'Cinema – that could be a drug'. Peter Handke noted in his diary, *Das Gewicht der Welt* (*The Weight of the World*): 'My moviegoing has become an addiction: after almost every film lethargy and hopelessness ... and nonetheless a day later I once again feel anxious when "my movie time" nears'. That was 1977. Eight years later, Rainhald Goetz, at work on texts like *Krieg* (*War*) and *Herz* (*Heart*) notes: 'Friday, October 26. Work on *War*. Walk. News from Malta. Home, work on *Heart*. Later at the Mathäser Cinema, *Conan the Destroyer*, cracks me up, go out afterwards to a disco with the crowd, get really smashed'. Here, claims Helmut Schödel, 'ends the dream of cinema. Disco, cinema, writing – it's all one big simulation game, part of a culture of gigantic spectacles in which the single event loses its importance' (Schödel 1989).

A new tone and a new mobility came into play during the 1980s, claimed cultural critic Bernd Guggenberger, in his psychogram of a younger generation's sensibility (Guggenberger 1987).

> The 'New Wave' of this newest youth has no representative *Zeitgeist*, but instead attitudes and gestures, postures and poses whose common denominator often seems to be the lack of one – or rather the most common one of all: 'anything goes!' A pluralism of styles and a blend of moods, mixed media and passing erotic encounters – these elements characterized the signature of an epoch.
>
> (ibid.: 82)

According to Guggenberger, the cardinal sins for this 'Joy-Stick Generation' were 'reflection' and 'commitment': 'Anything except too much identity!' (ibid.: 83). Culture yielded to the cool tour, a space wont to a free-floating narcissism and a hypertrendy *mise-en-scène*: 'Nowhere do gazes cross and eyes meet', Guggenberger elaborates:

> One doesn't talk or laugh, is neither happy or excited; one has nothing to communicate – except perhaps that uncertain 'message' which body language and (preferably black) clothing suggest. ... The new heroes are beautiful and inert, sullen and introverted. Their preferred expression is a well-calculated gesture with just the right blend of 'come on' and turn off.
>
> (ibid.: 78)

This new sensibility, in keeping with the proclivities of the New Cinema of Consensus, favours velocity over repose; one is mobile and unfixed, ever in transport, responding to the rhythms of the *Zeitgeist*. It is a world of show and simulation, everything a bit unreal, flashy and bright with no dark shadows. In this signal culture *Sein* is Sign. And here *Dasein* means Design, which is art out of the icebox, beauty without the good – high quality, low affect (ibid.: 17). The best personality is none whatsoever; rough edges only spoil a smooth appearance (ibid.: 22). One is not really there at all, one just pretends to be present. The post-political motto of Guggenberger's designer world is either: 'We've seen through the world, why should we bother changing it?' or 'We've seen through the world, how could we ever manage to change it?' (ibid.: 26).

The world that Guggenberger depicts is, to be sure, one of comforts and privileges common to a decided minority of young Germans. This small world and its circumscribed view, however, is the commanding perspective of recent German comedies. This new age of precise superficiality and precious tristesse characterises innumerable recent German films set in the current scene's trendy hangouts and peopled by its flashy movers and shakers. Elegant sitting rooms, glitzy restaurants, well-heeled characters decked out in ensembles by Cerutti or Versace or dessous from La Perla grace balanced frames, tasteful compositions redolent of advertising spreads in pages of the German *Vogue* or *Schöner wohnen*. Denizens of these post-1968 fantasies have stopped making sense and searching for sensuality. Their motto is nonstop nonsense (ibid.: 28), to be *abgeklärt* and mobile, to remain cool without freezing (ibid.: 29).

Martyrs and men in motion

'The discourses in circulation about film, as well as wider cultural discourses in the nation-state', Stephen Crofts has pointed out, 'clearly affect industry and audiences, and also inform – and are articulated within – film texts' (1998: 387). We have talked about the factors that have produced quite different conceptions of German cinema. It is now time to consider the fantasy scenarios and master narratives of these two cinemas.

Critical discussions about New German Cinema in the main privileged three central preoccupations: (1) America and Hollywood as objects of post-war German love/hatred; (2) National Socialism and its legacy of shame; and (3) the political malaise of the Federal Republic as experienced by the post-war generation. Angry young men (and to a degree, women), revolted against a collective past, especially the Nazi experience as well as the Adenauer era. To a large extent, the focus was on a critical cinema fuelled by an overdetermined Oedipal rage which reacted to the abuse of film under Hitler and the medium's affirmative status during the 1950s. This cinema challenged the nation's will-ingness to forget the past and get on with business as usual, to follow the dictates of Allied occupiers and to become a Cold War bastion. The work of Fassbinder and his cohorts surveyed a traumatic past and the wreckage (both physical and psychic) that remained in the present, seeking as well to spell out the precarious terms of post-war German reconstruction. It also generated a positive project, a desire to construct a better Germany and to reconceive cinema, to rewrite German history and to renew German film history. It was a cinema of disenchantment, in equal measure a function of critical fury and utopian resolve, of negative will and reformist design.

New German Cinema was renowned abroad for its demonstrations of stunted identities and reduced personalities, of outsiders, underdogs and over-reachers. Its narratives typically featured vulnerable protagonists, captives of situations that they do not comprehend or control. Kluge's Anita G. in *Yesterday Girl* (*Abschied von gestern*, 1966) and Herzog's Kaspar Hauser in *Everyone for Oneself and God against All* (*Jeder für sich und Gott gegen alle*, 1974) provide paradigms for this cinema of German martyrs. Their life stories serve as didactic parables in the form of station dramas. These films constituted allegories of a post-war generation's collective destiny, forging a master narra-tive in which immature subjects are cast on to dangerous ground and into a realm of fear and loathing. These figures (orphans or products of disfunctional families) desperately wish for a secure living space and an authentic identity. Misunderstood, abused, and tormented, they confront anachronistic institutional structures whose functionaries are indifferent and brutal. Typically these tales have a lethal conclusion or an open ending: their negativity nonetheless intimates that a less tragic outcome would be thinkable in a different world.

The haunted and homeless protagonists of New German Cinema often sought refuge in America and its mass culture. The United States became an insistent site of self-reflection and identity formation, if indeed an unreliable and unstable source of sanctuary (as films like *The American Soldier* [*Der amerikanische Soldat*], 1970, *The American Friend* [*Der amerikanische Freund*], 1977 and *Stroszek*, 1977, bear out). The world of fitness centres, shopping malls, rock-and-roll records and mass-produced images evoked by Wim Wenders, however, is no longer experienced as foreign in today's German cinema. This is in keeping with a Federal Republic for which these commodities and experiences are facts of everyday life. In those few instances where recent films make overt forays into political settings, the malaise of the present is less the function of a German authoritarian legacy that refuses to go away. Repeatedly the Cinema of Consensus presents characters whose primary sense of person and place is rarely an overt function of their national identity or directly impacted by Germany's difficult past. Instead of German tales of martyrdom and suffering, the New Cinema of Consensus offers tableaux of mobile young professionals, who play with possibility and flirt with difference, living in the present and worrying about their future, juggling careers, relationships and lifestyles.

Doris Dörrie's *Men* (*Männer*, 1985), more than any German film of the 1980s, articulated a generation's deep disdain for the dreams of 1968 about a better life and an alternative existence. It also took dramatic leave from the New German Cinema. This double reckoning came in the form of a modest television movie made with a budget of 800,000 DM. It quickly was the talk of the nation, a runaway success that combined a snappy dialogue and a nimble dramaturgy in a German comedy of remarriage. Indeed, the film satisfied critics and Zimmermann, winning every imaginable award. It was the most successful German film of the year: 4.2 million tickets were sold within its first six months and five million people saw it during 1986. Dörrie herself maintained that she had inadvertently hit a resonant chord of the *Zeitgeist*. Observers, both domestic and foreign, lauded the film's refreshing departure from the angst-ridden agendas of Fassbinder, Herzog and Wenders.

A manager, Julius, struggles to regain his errant wife who has left him for the somewhat younger Stephan. Julius goes underground and takes a spare room in the artist's commune, redirecting the alternative spirit's energies, and in the end making him over altogether. The film aligns itself with Julius' perspective, presenting his fear of instability and his fantasy of restoration. The narrative might even be interpreted as an extended psychodrama. Early in the film Julius lies in bed with Paula and, to her dismay, snores loudly. Near the film's end the scene is repeated, suggesting that the entire sequence of events between the two moments has been one long dream. In this fantasy scenario, Julius becomes a voyeur, both threatened and fascinated, watching his younger self (in the form of Stephan) carry on with his wife. Fearless and virtually omnipotent, Julius transforms the artist into a mirror reflection, dissolving his competitor's allure for the wife and in that way winning back his old existence. One might call the film *Educating Stephan*: its crucial passages focus on the formation of identity as an exercise in the manipulation of images. Julius remakes Stephan, attiring him in a new wardrobe, redoing his hair, giving him lessons in managerial style, showing him how to gaze, how to negotiate, how to make commercial illustrations more appealing by throwing in a slight touch of the unconventional.

The encounter of dialectical opposites gives rise to a higher synthesis. The bohemian learns from the businessman the art of the deal and the power of the bluff. With only a minimum of resistance, Stephan surrenders to the seductions of consumer society, enacting a scenario that would have us believe that social climbers and social dropouts are at heart kindred spirits – and German *Kleinbürger*.[9] *Men* offers a psychological history of the generation of 1968 from the perspective of the generation that followed it. We hear Eric Burton's 'When I Was Young' throughout the film; it becomes the refrain for the student movement's failed hopes. 'I've been through all the communal forms, I'm dulled by them ... I've lost my utopia', Stephan will admit at a key moment. The aim of the commune was ultimate openness, of all sorts: self-disclosure, self-analysis, self-criticism. So much self-awareness, as we know from Guggenberger, means too much identity. Foregrounding an adaptive and mobile subjectivity, *Men* provided a New Age version of *Mann ist Mann*.[10]

The German Cinema of Consensus has taken Dörrie's impetus and raised it to the higher power. There is in fact a direct line from *Männer* to *Der bewegte Mann*. Wortmann's smash hit of 1995, released in America as *Maybe, Maybe Not*, is a Peter Pan narrative. Axel is a creature of irrepressible desire; he refuses to live up to his partner Doro's expectations that he be a faithful partner and a dutiful future father. Thrown out by Doro, Axel becomes friends with the homosexual Norbert, and even flirts with the prospect of a gay encounter. Here again, though, a character's role-playing involves no risk-taking or threat of radical change. Many recent German films invoke male homosexuality (but curiously rarely lesbianism), but invariably within the context of well-known clichés and the same old jokes.[11] Rarely does one encounter a strong or decisive woman. The essential female centrepiece of German comedies, played by Katja Riemann as a refurbished Doris Day, longs above all for romantic bliss and bourgeois security. Wortmann's work as a whole, and particularly *Der Campus*, is emphatic in its systemic ridicule of feminism and identity politics. In *Der Campus*, 68ers appear as characters without belief, self-promoting careerists who employ political correctness as a vehicle of self-interest, who assume the moral highground to protect their turf and expand their sphere of influence. They are, to a person, figures without depth of being or strength of conviction.

The recent hit, Helmut Dietl's *Rossini*, shows us an array of luminaries, extensions of Julius and Stephan, gathering in a fashionable Munich restaurant. Dietl's new men are film-makers; the world of their projects, like the nouvelle German world of *Rossini*, is one of sex, money and ambition. In a procession of movies about people who are typically graphic artists in the advertising branch or individuals employed as disc jockeys, film-makers, actors, musicians and models, the Cinema of Consensus has replicated – and demonstrated – the workings of a German culture industry that probes every way possible to gain an edge and an advantage. Unlike the generation that produced the New German Cinema, it has published no programmatic statements or collective declarations. That is not to say, however, that it lacks a programme or a larger purpose.

The difficulty of saying we

The disparity between New German Cinema and the Cinema of Consensus bears out competing desires to create images for a nation and to speak as a prominent and privileged voice of that nation. In Edgar Reitz's film essay, *The Night of the Directors* (*Die Nacht der Regisseure*, 1995), New German directors have become elder statesmen. The film imagines a grand museum of German film history in which Leni Riefenstahl sits comfortably between Werner Herzog and Volker Schlöndorff, in which fantasies of the German forest are entertained as if the Nazis had never worshipped blood and soil, where Schlöndorff can speak of Fritz Lang as a great German director, 'even though he was Viennese and part Jewish'. A central emphasis in this film-historical excursion are evocations of a former popular cinema, of alluring stars like Zarah Leander, Kristina Söderbaum and Marika Rökk. Even film-makers whose look back in anger spawned a New German Cinema appear now as a part of a larger legacy that includes Riefenstahl and the Ufa productions of the 1930s and 1940s.[12] Despite the presence of former DEFA film-makers (Frank Beyer and Wolfgang Kohlhaase) and younger directors like Detlev Buck and Peter Sehr, there is no conflict, controversy, or disagreement. Reitz staged this fictional meeting to create a sense of common interests in a national cinema's imagined historical community (Reitz 1995). In this regard at least, New German Cinema now speaks as part of a greater Germany and a German legacy that it once assailed.

The issue of national cultural identity, as Paul Willemen points out, arises only in response to a challenge posed by the other, so that any discourse of national-cultural identity is from the outset oppositional – although not necessarily progressive (1994: 206–19). The other that has helped solidify the self-understanding of today's German film culture is surely not Hollywood, but rather a cinema of unruly authors, oppositional politics and alternative images. Popular cinema – and in this regard Hollywood, Ufa, and German films of the

1950s – has in fact returned as a good object, as a film culture's points of orientation and role models. The dream of many aspiring German film-makers today is to become a Wolfgang Petersen or a Roland Emmerich. If anything, the current mainstream cinema longs for a German film industry as powerful and resonant as a former age's Ufa studio. The Cinema of Consensus consciously seeks ways of saying 'we' in its address to German audiences. Its fantasies of a German Film Empire and a national German tradition are, without question, both problematic and difficult, problematic given post-wall Germany's increasingly heterogeneous and multicultural realities, difficult given German cinema's diverse constituencies and audiences.

The Cinema of Consensus provides an interesting, if ephemeral, chapter in German film history. It does not sell abroad because it is perceived as both too German and yet not German enough. It has stars familiar only to German audiences and generic designs that are not readily exportable because they are done better and more effectively elsewhere. Although it is resolutely stylish, the cinema lacks a distinctive style: however professionally crafted, it is unabashedly conventional in its appearance and structure. The Cinema of Consensus, of course, is a construction, a critical term that I have used to describe a gathering of films and film-makers which have dominated media accounts and industry campaigns devoted to German film's public profile. There are many other forces at work in this nation's film culture, indeed offbeat voices and less reconciled visions, less visible films with a historical ground, a post-national sensibility, and a critical edge. There are numerous noteworthy exceptions to the rule, ragamuffins like Christoph Schlingensief, Heinz Emigholz and Monika Treut, uncompromised auteurs like Ulrike Ottinger, Rosa von Praunheim and Harun Farocki, explorers of darker provinces such as Michael Klier, Jan Schütte, Wolfgang Becker, Heike Misselwitz and Fred Kelemen, the recalcitrant remnants of DEFA with their reflections on a lost world and an uncommodious new situation, pliers of a liminal cinema like Thomas Arslan, Kutlug Ataman, Lars Becker and Eoin Moore who survey the multicultural realities of a post-wall community, ambitious new arrivals like Tom Tykwer (*Winter Sleepers* [*Winterschläfer*]), Hans-Christian Schmid (*23*) and Fatih Akin (*Short Sharp Shock* [*Kurz und schmerzlos*]) with a desire to fathom the psychic and social makeup of today's young Germans – among others. Some contemporary German films have not lost the incendiary potential of New German Cinema, the ability to illuminate a darker world and to bring to light less obvious and for that reason more provocative perspectives. For reasons that I have tried to make apparent, this cinema remains for the most a minority opinion and a marginal perspective, existing in the shadows of the more prominent Cinema of Consensus.

Notes

1   For all of 1997, despite the legendary first quarter, the domestic market share of German films was 17 per cent. The most successful German film of 1997 was

Knockin' on Heaven's Door (3.5 million tickets). In 1998 the market share fell to 9 per cent. *Titanic* alone constituted 15 per cent of all admissions; it sold 18 million tickets. The leading German films of 1998 were *Comedian Harmonists* (2.3 million) and *Run, Lola, Run* (2.0 million).

2 New talent agencies like 'Players' (Cologne), 'm4 management' (Berlin) and 'm4 models' (Hamburg) negotiate aggressively for the stars of the German entertainment industry, see anon. 1996 and H.R. Blum and K. Blum 1997.

3 See Menz 1997: 117–23 and Chervel 1999. For two particularly devastating French assessments of Tykwer's film, see O. St. 1999 and J-M.F. 1999.

4 Since Fassbinder's death, Edgar Reitz's *Heimat* (1984), Dorris Dörrie's *Men* (*Männer*, 1985), Wim Wenders' *Wings of Desire* (*Der Himmel über Berlin*, 1987), Michael Verhoeven's *The Nasty Girl* (*Das schreckliche Mädchen*, 1990), Agnieszka Holland's *Europa, Europa* (*Hitlerjunge Salomon*, 1990) and Sönke Wortmann's *Maybe, Maybe Not* (*Der bewegte Mann*, 1994) are likely to be the only German titles that most American cineastes might call to mind. And even if we may know and perhaps appreciate this handful of German films, we no longer have a sense of this national cinema's larger picture.

5 See, for instance, Buchka 1996.

6 Even if the luminaries of this cinema graced the covers of *Time*, *L'Express* and *Der Spiegel*, New German Cinema never was a popular or a financially viable one. In 1977, for instance, the year of Werner Herzog's *Stroszek*, Rainer Werner Fassbinder's *Despair*, Wim Wenders' *The American Friend* (*Der amerikanische Freund*) and Margarethe von Trotta's *The Second Awakening of Christa Klages* (*Das zweite Erwachen der Christa Klages*), West German films commanded only 4 per cent of the domestic market share.

7 Zimmermann (1985) would justify his film policy in the article, 'Das Publikum muß immer mitbestimmen': 'German films must align themselves more with the expectations of the average viewer. We must support such endeavours to the full extent of our possibilities. This does not mean, however, a populistic levelling or a "flirting with mass taste"'.

8 West German television stations aired 1,294 feature films in 1980; a decade later the annual figure would exceed 7,000 titles. Taking into account all video releases, television broadcasts, and cinema screenings, consumers in the Federal Republic now have potential access each year to well over 12,000 features.

9 Admiring himself while trying on one of Julius' suits, Stephan breaks into song, 'Ich brech' die Herzen der stolzesten Frauen', a famous hit by German cinema's most famous adaptable character and authoritarian personality, Heinz Rühmann. The change of attire and persona also intimates a recourse to an earlier comic role and a previous era of German cinema.

10 In the film's press book, Dörrie maintained that she had worked like an anthropologist, doing field work to comprehend the customs and habits of an unknown tribe.

11 See Martenstein 1996.

12 In Reitz's *Night of the Directors* (*Die Nacht der Regisseure*), Wenders offers a brief dissenting opinion about Nazi cinema. It's hard to imagine, he says, that these films were received in an uncritical way, a perspective distinctly at odds with the emphases of Reitz's other presenters.

Bibliography

Amend, H. and Bütow, M. (eds) (1997) *Der bewegte Film: Aufbruch zu neuen deutschen Erfolgen*, Berlin: Vistas.

Anon. (1996) 'Sterne zu Talern', *Die Woche* 5 January.

Berg, J. (1993) *Am Ende der Rolle. Diskussion über den Autorenfilm*, Marburg: Schüren.

Blum, H.R. and Blum, K. (1997) *Gesichter des neuen deutschen Films*, Berlin: Parthas.

Buchka, P. (1996) 'Nur keine Konflikte', *Süddeutsche Zeitung* 18 April.

Bühler, W.-E. (1980) 'Michelangelo und Sisyphos: Zur Retrospektive des Österreichischen Filmmuseums', *Filmkritik* 24, 10.

Chervel, T. (1999) 'Lola rennt nicht in Paris', *Süddeutsche Zeitung* 22 April.

Crofts, S. (1998) 'Concepts of National Cinema', in J. Hill and P. Church-Gibson (eds).

Etten, M. (1992) 'Der lange Abschied: Fassbinder und die Mythen des neuen deutschen Films', *film-dienst* May, 45, 11: 5.

F., J.-M. (1999) '*Cours, Lola, Cours*', *Le Monde* 7 April.

Folckers, N. and Solms, W. (eds) (1996) *Risiken und Nebenwirkungen*, Berlin: Bittermann.

Franfurter, B. (ed.) (1995) *Offene Bilder*, Vienna: Promedia.

Guggenberger, B. (1987) *Sein oder Design: Zur Dialektik der Abklärung*, Berlin: Rotbuch.

Habermas, J. (1985) *Die Neue Unübersichtlichkeit*, Frankfurt am Main: Suhrkamp.

—— (1997) *A Berlin Republic: Writings on Germany*, trans. S. Randall, Lincoln: University of Nebraska Press.

Hill, J. and Church-Gibson, P. (eds) (1998) *The Oxford Guide to Film Studies*, Oxford: Oxford University Press.

Jansen, P.W. and Schütte, W. (eds) (1992) *Rainer Werner Fassbinder*, Frankfurt am Main: Fischer.

Kluge, A. (ed.) (1983) *Bestandsaufnahme. Utopie Film*, Frankfurt am Main: 2001.

Kreimeier, K. (1992) 'Narrenschiff im Bildersturm', *Arnoldsheimer Protokolle* 1.

Liebman, S. (1988) 'On New German Cinema, Art, Enlightenment, and the Public Sphere: An Interview with Alexander Kluge', *October* 46.

Martenstein, H. (1996) 'Falsche Kerle', *Der Tagesspiegel* 10 October.

Menz, D. (1997) 'Von *Sissi* bis zum *Bewegten Mann*: Vertrieb deutscher Filme im Ausland', in H. Amend and M. Bütow (eds).

Nolden, R. (1989) 'Doris Dörrie: Jeder darf einmal der Narr sein', *Die Welt* 8 May.

Prümm, K. (1996) 'Unbändiges Gelächter. Was ist an der deutschen Filmkomödie komisch?', in N. Folckers and W. Solms (eds).

Reitz, E. (1995) 'Verlust des Wir-Gefühls: Eine Momentaufnahme zur Situation des deutschen Films', *Frankfurther Rundschau* 15 July.

Rhode, C. (1990) 'Kommerzielles Kino auf elegante Weise: Gespräch mit dem Regisseur Dominik Graf über seine neue Arbeit', *Der Tagesspiegel* 4 November.

Roth, W. (1989) 'Die Zukunft des Kinos (4): Gespräch mit Günter Rohrbach', *epd Film* December 6, 12.

Schmidt, G. (1984) 'Neue deutsche Filmemacher: Die vierte Generation', *tip* 15 June.

Schödel, H. (1989) 'Das Kino lebt hier nicht mehr', *Die Zeit* 24 November

Schütte, W. (1992) 'Sein Name: eine Ära. Rückblicke auf den späten Fassbinder (1974/82)', in P.W. Jansen and W. Schütte (eds).

Schwanitz, D. (1995) *Der Campus*, Frankfurt am Main: Eichborn.

Seeßlen, G. (1995) 'Zur Lage des deutschen Films', in B. Franfurter (ed.).

St., O. (1999) 'Lola peut toujours courir', *Libération*, 7 April.

Vahabzadeh, S. (1998) 'Wir können alles machen – wir müssen es nur tun', *Süddeutsche Zeitung*, 5 February.

Weingarten, S. (1990) 'Der Markt ruft', *Tagesspiegel* 8 December.

Wenders, W. (1991) 'Der Akt des Sehens', *Die Zeit* 6 September.

—— (1993) 'Podiumsdiskussion', in J. Berg (ed.).

Willemen, P. (1994) 'The National', in P. Willemen, *Looks and Frictions: Essays in Cultural Studies and Film Theory*, Bloomington, IN: Indiana University Press.

Zimmermann, F. (1985) 'Das Publikum muß immer mitbestimmen', *Die Welt* 12 January.

17

CONTEMPORARY CINEMA

Between cultural globalisation and national
interpretation

Ulf Hedetoft

Introduction

Contemporary cinema, like other types of visual mass communication, is
increasingly embedded in discourses of globalisation. However, as is the case
with globalisation generally, its discrete manifestations are full of paradox and
tension. They are complex, heterogeneous phenomena, caught between their
national or local origin, the homogenising tendencies represented by the global
village and its inroads on the particularities of the national, and the tendency for
those at the receiving end of transnational cultural processes to reinterpret and
reinvent extraneous cultural influences within their own field of mental vision,
their own interpretive and behavioural currency. As Ella Shohat and Robert
Stam have put it, 'Perception itself is embedded in history. The same filmic
images or sounds provoke distinct reverberations for different communities'
(Shohat and Stam 1996: 163).

Earlier in the same article, the two authors theorise that 'media spectatorship
forms a triated plurilogue between texts, readers, and communities existing in
clear discursive and social relation to one another' and that 'the culturally varie-
gated nature of spectatorship derives from the diverse locations in which films
are received, from the temporal gaps of seeing films in different historical
moments to the conflictual subject-positionings and community affiliations of
the spectators themselves' (ibid.: 156–7). In the context of this article it is
important to stress that these 'locations', in time as well as space, to a significant
degree are mediated and defined by the national: national history, national territory, bounded national imaginings, national 'meanings' and so on, and not
infrequently are mediated to as well as by spectators – as part of the 'plurilogue'
– in such a way as to neutralise potential 'gaps' in order perceptually to forge
continuities of understanding and emotion.

Apart from wanting to discuss the push-and-pull dialectic between national
identities and cultural globalisation in a general theoretical idiom, this contribution specifically aims to locate contemporary cinema within such forms of tension
between its transnational forms of production, dissemination and (sometimes)

contents, and its routinely national modes of reception, decoding and interpretation, based on national identities, cultural history and aesthetic traditions, as well as on particular readings of the world informed by a given national *habitus* and certain foreign stereotypes. In particular, it wants to revisit the perennial problem of Hollywood (blockbusters)/globalisation vs national cinema (Crofts 1993; Elsaesser 1987; Higson 1989, 1995). The initial focus will be on Hollywood as the producer of a specific variant of national (i.e. American) cinema. I shall subsequently consider Hollywood as producing a form of global cinematic culture received, interpreted and 'nationalised', less by the ordinary spectator than by a specific category of national mediatic gatekeepers – i.e. reviewers, sneak previewers and 'framers' – the last category referring to authors of articles and interviews in dailies and periodicals intended to place films in historical context, to ferret out directors' underlying motives, to introduce the cast, to discuss sociological or philosophical implications of films and so on.

Empirically the analytical focus – as a case in point – will be reviews and background articles published in three countries (the USA, France and Denmark) dealing with a recent and much-acclaimed Hollywood blockbuster with worldwide dissemination, Spielberg's *Saving Private Ryan*. The aim is to assess the role of 'the national optic' in culturally transcribing, translating and mediating this global/American text to national audiences, and in decoding it so as to 'make sense' of it within the interpretive palimpsest of specific national knowledges, cultural identities and aesthetic and philosophical traditions.

In this way the case study will also provide an indication of the extent to which – and how – 'globalisation' in the cultural cinematic arena factually spells 'homogeneity' at the receiving end, i.e. what kinds of tension, continuity and hybridity exist between national cinema as a cultural and identity-related phenomenon and the global reach of the medium from the point of view of technology, distribution and consumption. As Andrew Higson has put it well, 'the paradox is that for a cinema to be nationally popular it must also be international in scope. That is to say, it must achieve the international (Hollywood) standard' (Higson 1989: 40). This implies, of course, that Hollywood – though often derided and dismissed – in a very significant way represents the model for any (other) national cinema, whose 'film culture is implicitly "Hollywood"' (ibid.: 39, drawing on Elsaesser 1987).

This is undoubtedly a valid point, but still leaves unanswered the questions posed above: will critical reception (here among reviewers etc.) *of* Hollywood also *be* Hollywood, or in a different idiom, will American, French and Danish reviewers highlight the same points, identify the same qualities and evaluate on the basis of more or less the same criteria? Or will these reviewers differ, perhaps significantly, along national lines, about a movie that is produced by an American Jew, deals with a war in which all three countries were (very differently) involved, and very conspicuously wraps itself in the American flag (see further below)? Or differently still, and in universalised terms, is the Hollywood of American production and (often banal) contents identical to the Hollywood global viewers and critics perceive and construct?

National culture in globalisation: frames of reference, public spaces and symbolic analysts

In general terms, relations between nationality and globality are characterised by formal symmetry, but real asymmetry. This means that in spite of the fact that the global system consists of formally equal (nation-)states as the most central units – and that therefore there is no contradiction, but rather complementarity between nationalism and globalisation (Hedetoft 1999) – the real state of affairs is much less idyllic. In the real world of politics and influence, certain nationalisms, cultures, ideas and interpretations are more transnationally powerful, assertive and successful than others. Where the less influential ones are not necessarily less self-congratulatory, they are certainly more inward-looking and always carry the label of national specificity. The more powerful ones (actually or in the making), on the other hand, tend towards a universality of meanings, impact and acceptance, as their national-cultural currency becomes transnationally adopted, mixes and mingles with more long-standing cultural legacies, syncretises with them, is explicitly welcomed as a positive admixture to the culture and identity of other nations, or is treated as an admirable (role) model for emulation. In all cases, such cultures and communicative processes tend to lose their national exceptionalism, and to be seen as more or less naturalised frames of reference at several removes (in time and space) from their national origin. They become semiotically de-nationalised, not because they do not have a national origin, but precisely because they have proved so successful as vehicles of national interests, cultures and identities. As is the case with the English language in the world today, such assertive and hegemonising cultural processes at their most successful turn into a global cultural lingua franca, a transborder space of shared assumptions, material landmarks and discursive references. In this way, 'globalisation' is a very non-symmetrical process and constitutes anything but a level playing-field.

On the other hand, nor is globalisation limited to the cultural effects of American power and the processes often referred to as 'McDonaldisation' (Ritzer 1993), even though American cultural hegemony is undoubtedly a telling case in point. World history contains numerous examples of similar processes (though rarely with the same global reach as today), and in the modern era of national states cases of cultural imperialism and/or dominance come to mind (British, French, Chinese, Russian, Habsburg, Spanish and so on) that in different ways fit the bill described above. Even today, 'Americanisation' is neither a linear, one-way process nor the only dominant player in the contested domain of cultural 'soft power'. Concepts like 'cultural hybridity', 'creolisation', 'clashes of cultures' and 'ethnic diversity'; actors like a host of different national institutes set up to promote the global spread of national cultures (the British

Council, Alliance Française, the Goethe Institutes, even the Danish Cultural Institutes and so on); and political processes like the ongoing struggle between the EU and the US to curb American influence on the European audio-visual market for mass communication – all indicate that cultural globalisation processes at the intersection between national exceptionalism and universal influence cannot be reduced to a series of simplistic relations between one assertive 'sender' and a (number of) passive 'receivers'. National cultures do assimilate outside influences, but for one thing the primary sender (the US) itself constitutes a diverse, assimilationist cultural rag-bag, and second, receivers both react, interact and proact *vis-à-vis* American influences, in the process reforging and reinterpreting them in the context of national history, culture and perceptual optics.

This is by no means to deny the overwhelming impact of American culture on current globalising processes, but rather to place it in the appropriate perspective. If we try to apply this perspective to the film arena, it throws a new slant on the concept of national cinema and the relations between Hollywood blockbusters and 'foreign film' (or 'art film', as it is sometimes labelled, to suggest that other national cinemas can offset the quantitative impact of Hollywood through high quality film-making).

First of all, this perspective reminds us that also 'Hollywood', as a rule, produces national cinema, if by this concept we understand film whose thematic 'aboutness' (Hjort 2000), interpretive framing and sets of ideas and values are rooted in American perceptions of man, nature, society and the world – movies in other words whose taken-for-granted assumptions and common-sense understandings (and occasionally explicit ideological or philosophical loyalties) are of a US origin, no matter how strongly they might parade as global plots, themes or ideas, or how effectively 'American' problems are frequently given an all-human, universalistic spin (by producers or consumers of Hollywood movies).

Second, however, this perspective also calls for a rethinking of the perimeters of 'national cinema'. In most cases, this concept has been linked to notions like 'locus and ownership of production', 'the national character of distributive networks' or films' 'themes and contents'. Others, having recognised the importance of reception and consumption, do stress that, for example, 'imported mass culture can also be indigenized, put to local use, given a local accent' (Shohat and Stam 1996: 149), while pointing out that 'specific communities both incorporate and transform foreign influence' (ibid.). However, such insights are rarely taken to their logical conclusion, which is that such indigenisation processes tend to remould one form of national cinema into another. 'Foreign audiences', that is, other national optics through which American-global cinema is reinterpreted, on the one hand stamp their own national/local vision, common-sense assumptions and locally inspired worldviews on the cinematic products they actively engage with; on the other, the raw material they mentally rework (more or less dramatically, depending on their cultural background and transnational orientation) is still forged in the cauldron of

Hollywood themes and values and both frames and constrains the 'new nationality' of the movies in question. In short, two national contexts meet within the public communicative space of the movie theatre, producing a new national text framed by a more universalised 'transnational imaginary' of American origin. 'National cinema' in the context of globalisation thus reappears as a changeable and non-permanent notion, as a transboundary process rather than a set of fixed attributes. 'Hollywood' (as well as all other national cinemas of international reach) is constantly undergoing a (re)nationalisation process, temporally and spatially, a process which does not stamp out the US flavour of these cinematic products, but which negotiates their transition into and assimilation by 'foreign' mental visions and normative understandings.

This should not, *per se*, be understood as the production of so-called 'third cultures', defined by Mike Featherstone as 'sets of practices, bodies of knowledge, conventions, and lifestyles which have developed in ways which have become increasingly independent of nation-states' (1996: 60). The results might well be 'a third' as compared both with the 'sending' Americanness of the texts and the 'receiving' indigenous frame of national reference, but this third is not – or only rarely – a transnational, cosmopolitan intermediary, floating freely in a contracted global time-space. It is more appropriately captured in terms of a 'third' national/local dimension, a new cultural hybrid integrating, at the level of national specificity, two national cultures (one of global proportions, the other more local) through a process of mental bricolage. This process, it should be noted, is not 'unconscious', but reflexive. Cinema-goers – and reviewers and critics too, of course – are well aware that they are watching a Hollywood blockbuster, and most have a clear hunch that Hollywood products are chock-full of Americanisms. This means that they engage with these movies *as American*, and will tend to bring their pre-understanding of the US (admiring, exotic, sceptical, dismissive, hostile and so on) to bear, more or less directly, on their interpretation of what they are watching. At the same time, at the level where a cognitive and emotional engagement with a film's unfolding plot, represented characters, and constitutive themes takes place, national audiences will apply the optic of their history, identity and values in a process involving a decoding and reframing of the film's content and 'message'.

This reframing process – a constant interaction between acknowledging the 'foreignness' (here: the American nature) of the film and relating to it through reinterpretation – can entail more or less radical reactions to and departures from the 'original' set of meanings and messages embedded in the text. In other words, the hybrid third can be more or less alienated from the original product. The degree of alienation will depend partly on the aesthetic design of the movie, its cognitive message, and the extent to which the receiving culture has generally been inundated by US culture and has assimilated the values, contents and assumptions underlying specific movies, and, finally, will depend on the ways in which the critical film establishment (reviewers, critics and 'framers') wishes to mediate movies to the general public, that is, fulfils its advisory and interpretive gatekeeper functions: national symbolic analysts negotiating between the product and the consumers, between the national origin of the former and the national *habitus* of the latter (more about this below). On the other hand, it is difficult to identify pre-given, universal patterns related to the proximity or distance of parent national cultures and identities. A brief digression – unrelated to the American impact on global cinema – will exemplify this point.

In the article '"I Have a Plan!" The Olsen Gang Captures Denmark and Norway: Negotiating the Culture Gap', Bjørn Sørensen (1994) demonstrates the vast differences of popular as well as critical reception in Denmark and Norway of a series of Danish movies commonly known as the 'Olsen Gang Movies', thirteen films in all produced between 1968 and 1981 (recently, in 1998, a final 14th was added to the series). The tribulations of the movies are interesting in light of the great degree of similarity between the cultures, languages and social structures of these two neighbouring Scandinavian countries. Throughout, the series has enjoyed popular as well as critical acclaim in Denmark. However, the original Danish version fell on deaf ears in Norway. It was subsequently reworked and reproduced ('versionised'), with Norwegian actors, certain changes of plot, locale and titles, a different type of humour, and, not insignificantly, Norwegian rather than Danish national markers – for example, using the Norwegian flag rather than the Danish flag in a number of central episodes. In this new form, the series turned into a major box-office success in Norway, whereas 'the reception by the critical establishment was completely different for each of the two countries' (ibid.: 77). Loved by Danish reviewers, most contemporary Norwegian critics – particularly the Oslo establishment – saw the movies 'as a yearly affront to Norwegian film production' (ibid.), pandering to a common stereotype of rural, unsophisticated and jollicose Norwegianness which Oslo elites were eager to distance themselves from – partly because it is a commonly accepted notion of Norway in Denmark. And interestingly, as Sørensen points out, critical reception was more favourable in the provinces of Norway, 'something that allows a discussion of these films in a broader context of Scandinavian national stereotypes' (ibid.).[1]

The point of this digression is not to enter into a discussion of the details of the discrepancies between the contexts of original national production/reception and the subsequent Norwegian national scenario, but, first, to illustrate the significance of national perception and reception for reframing and, in this case, reproducing a series of movies for a new, culturally similar, national audience, and, second, to exemplify the different (nationally conditioned) roles that film critics and film reviewers can have when trying to mediate between product and audience. The striking thing in this instance is the different types of nationally based responses in Norway. Where mass audiences reacted negatively to the original Danish version, they embraced the indigenised version spontaneously because the series had now been laced with a number of markers of 'Norwegianness' (or put differently, a number of 'Danish' markers had been removed from the movies), which had the effect of Norwegianising the film's context, actors, symbolism and themes. Critics, on the other hand, reacted against the movies on account of these changes, interpreting the indigenisation process as too crude, shallow and stereotypical, and the films as still too much of an import from the former core of the Danish-Norwegian Union. At the back of most critics' minds, then – and reflexively rooted in these symbolic analysts' historical knowledge and cognitive interpretations – lurked an image of more subtle, more authentic and more 'sovereign' Norwegian film – i.e. an alternative, nationally informed scenario, with movies clearly belonging to the category of 'art films' or 'high culture', carrying a national quality stamp that might help Norwegian film production enter the international stage and thus work as leverage toward international acclaim.

Only in this sense did the critics turn out to be less 'national' and more 'global' in their response to the series than the popular masses. Without trying to extrapolate unduly, I would like on the basis of this contrast to provide a few general remarks about the role of critics and the usefulness of studying reviews and framing commentaries, before proceeding to look at our specific case study. The most important variables to keep in mind are the following.

First, reviewers are symbolic analysts (Reich 1992) and as such part of an apparent transnational ecumene within what Castells (1997: 354) terms 'global networks of wealth, power and information'. Their commonality relates to a variety of factors: their international mindset, their knowledge of film and film history, their international travel and encounters at various film festivals, and often their educational backgrounds. More specifically, their common orientation toward the standards and values set by 'Hollywood' constitutes a significant parameter of common identification and professional self-image. To the extent that Hollywood standards are adopted and treated as such a trans-boundary reference point (enthusiastically or perhaps more critically), they significantly contribute toward a font of shared assumptions and historical landmarks that critics draw on and which justifies thinking of these individuals as one group sharing a common professional identity. Hollywood becomes, if not an organic part of their selves, at the very least a very significant other. In this way it does make sense to talk of film critics as part of the same transnational community of identity, passing critical judgement on the basis of universal (i.e. non-national) values, knowledges and assumptions. This cosmopolitan dimension would seem to be strengthened by the fact that critics frequently view films together during festivals and that even on their own national home ground they are presented with movies in previewing sessions, i.e. in spaces separated from the viewing situations of the general public. As Louis Menand has succinctly put this point:

> Reviewers see most movies in screening rooms. It's like seeing them in church. Everyone is quiet and attentive; no one is getting up for

popcorn or rummaging around for a Life Saver. People in screening rooms do not talk back to the movie.

(Menand 1998: 7)

Whereas 'people in movie theaters do. I saw *Saving Private Ryan* in a large theater in midtown Manhattan on a Saturday night. ... It was not an audience in idle search of cheap thrills. They had read the reviews; they were prepared to be affected' (ibid.). Louis Menand then proceeds to give examples of the way in which members of the audience interacted with the movie's characters and commented on the unfolding plot. When, for instance, one of the American soldiers in the movie is confronted with the chance to do away with a German, a 'woman down front' cries out 'Shoot him!'. 'She was clearly', so comments Menand, 'expressing the sentiment of the house'.

Second, however, this way of conceptualising the critical community (and its differences as compared with the more spontaneous, often national(ist) reaction of the ordinary cinema-going public) simultaneously entails the danger of seeing its 'internationality' as running counter to, by-passing (Castells' word again) its basis of national belonging and identification and of overlooking the half-grudging nature of many critics' acceptance of global (= Hollywood) standards. The point is that while their cultural-educational baggage and mental horizons might well be transnational to a significant (though nationally different) degree, 'transnational' need not mean non-national, and culture cannot readily be translated into terms of identification, let alone identity. Two points should be highlighted here: the question of communicative spaces within which reviewers operate, and the determining constituents/frames of their identity. Although both are ambiguous, they do bring the national question back into the picture.

Film critics operate within communicative spaces that are primarily nationally bounded: the papers/journals that they write for (or television stations their commentaries are broadcast on) more often than not define themselves as national, the primary audience targeted is the national citizenry of their respective nation-states, the premiering of movies that their reviews or framing commentaries relate to is usually organised so as to occur simultaneously within specific national circumferences, their reviews are phrased in the national language, and so on. In other words, the entire space-time loop in these instances is subjected to the primacy of the national, and critics/reviewers/framers both explicitly and more covertly need to take account of the cultural, historical, communicative, aesthetic and political assumptions, knowledges and expectations prevalent among members of their target audience. The ambiguity indicated stems from the fact that they also need to convey the 'other-nationality' or the 'globality' of the specific film under review, and that in most cases this matches their self-understanding as belonging to a cosmopolitan ecumene. This makes for a variety of different communicative, 'hybrid' strategies and meaning contents, and also for a lot of similarities in the mediation (particularly the background framing) of movies, but does not eliminate the fundamentally national framework of the critics' gatekeeper function.

Nor, of course, does it eliminate their national allegiances and *habitus*, their belonging to a national community and their application of the 'national optic' to the movie being reviewed. Having a global outlook is no impediment to the maintenance of a national core of allegiance and identification – as previously argued, in the contemporary world global and national attitudes seem to complement each other. The case of the Olsen Gang demonstrated one of the modes in which this complementarity can play itself out: as the rejection of a particular kind of crude (and Danish-inspired) nationalism in favour of more sophisticated and more internationally acceptable/understandable forms of Norwegian cinema, which would base themselves firmly in high rather than popular culture and from which the Norwegian film establishment might hope to attract international kudos. One form of 'inward-looking' Norwegianness is here pitted against a more cosmopolitan, culturally open version. Both, however, are national and cast in the mould of fulfilling certain national-cultural needs.

Naturally the interaction between globality/otherness and nationality on the production-mediation-consumption continuum which movies negotiate in the process of crossing borders can play itself out in a host of other ways. The national rootedness of reviewers can be more or less in evidence, and the syncretic 'third' can therefore manifest itself in a variety of ways. Hollywood blockbusters here present us with a particularly challenging case, because on the one hand they have, as set out above, somehow lost their 'nationality' in the course of the global expansion of American cinema (in the minds of viewers, including many professional film critics), and on the other they also tend to provoke very anti-American, nationally or regionally steeped responses that are informed by the fear of being inundated by American popular culture and losing one's national culture in the process. In this light, let us now look more closely at the critical reception of *Saving Private Ryan* in two EU countries, Denmark and France, and, by contrast, also in its national country of origin, the US.

National thirds, or 'I wonder how the reaction in Europe will be to this film'

This heading is a quote from an amateur review posted on 26 July 1998, by a certain Peter Tong, on the *Washington Post* website, having invited reactions to the movie. The question of course is both interesting and relevant, addressing as it does the core issue of this chapter and showing sensitivity to the problem of European reactions to an American movie thematising an important historical moment of transatlantic interaction. However, seen in context the question is less objective/exploratory and more (nationally) normative than might appear at first blush, for the review goes on to state that 'every drop of American blood shed there was priceless and irreplaceable'. What this spectator (in a manner quite unrepresentative of the general critical reception in the US –

see below) is therefore asking is whether Europeans, in the way they react to the movie, will acknowledge the American sacrifice during the Second World War towards the liberation of Europe from Nazi aggression.

The responses to the question by reviewers and 'framers' in Denmark and France, in spite of similarities, evince a number of interesting differences. Before addressing these 'European' reactions to an unmistakably 'American' movie (no matter how 'Hollywood' and therefore global it may be), a few words on the film itself and the reasons for selecting it as this chapter's 'case' are in place.

The major part of the film is in the nature of a flashback to the invasion of Normandy (described in gruelling and realistic detail during an early, twenty-two-minute long scene) and the story unfolding therefrom, in which a small detail of soldiers are given the special task of locating and rescuing Private Ryan, the only surviving brother of four (the other three having been killed in combat), in order to return him to his family home in Idaho. When they eventually find him, Private Ryan refuses to be saved and instead insists on fighting on and trying to hold a strategically important bridge. Nevertheless, unlike the entire rescue unit, he finally comes out of the showdown with the German forces alive. The opening and closing scenes are set in 'the present', in the cemetery off Omaha Beach to which James Ryan returns fifty years later. Framed by the American flag, which in full-screen format is the first and last image confronting the audience, we see him abjectly kneeling before the grave of Captain John Miller, the head of the rescue unit. In the closing scene he asks his wife, who has accompanied him to the cemetery along with his children and grand-children, whether he has been a 'good man', in this way seeking confirmation of having lived up to Captain Miller's final words to him before dying: 'Earn it!' – an injunction to become worthy of the sacrifices the unit paid to save his life.

Thus, on different levels of thematisation and explicitness, this is both a film about fighting for liberty and against tyranny in Europe, about fighting for the disengagement of one man from this war in the name of moral decency, and about American values and the greatness of patriotic sacrifice. In other words, it is a special cocktail of *American national pride*, the uncomfortable but necessary burden of international engagement and sacrifice that the US has to face and indeed faced in the Second World War (*international idealism*), and (at least on the surface) questions of *universal morality*, the good life that the former two components are meant to secure, the human qualities underlying it and so on.

The film stands out as relatively uncharacteristic for the run-of-the-mill Hollywood movie by the explicitness of its national origin and its patriotic 'message' – a fact not lost on critics in any of the three countries, but nevertheless providing the background for different interpretations, meanings and normative values. For that reason, the point made above about critics and audiences generally engaging with Hollywood movies in a reflexive mode, conscious of their American origin and bringing their knowledge, stereotypes and sentiments regarding the US to bear on the interpretive process, is obviously true in this case, since the movie is not just based on American values and identity, but makes a point of highlighting these in thematic terms. On the other hand, it also tries to construct a narrative of universal human morality, decency and courage, and it is this constellation between processes of marking and unmarking the movie's nationalism in the thematic context of a major war fought on European soil that makes it such an appropriate testing ground for European reviewers' handling of their gatekeeper function between nationality and globality.

Both in Denmark and France press coverage of the movie was extensive, prior to as well as following the release of the movie in late September (Denmark) and early October (France), 1998, approximately two months after its US release.[2] In both countries this coverage consisted of background articles dealing with Spielberg, his life, family and movies, with the history of American Second World War movies and *Saving Private Ryan*'s relationship with them, and with the movie's unashamedly patriotic tone and message. Reviews also focused on the movie itself and on different types of comment to which its Americanisms, morality, realism, romanticism, topicality and cinematic qualities (technique, casting, artistry, direction, etc.) give rise. Naturally, as far as mundane levels of description, paraphrase and historical cinematic parallels are concerned, similarities between the national coverages abound. These national responses are also similar in that they accord to this movie (simply by virtue of being yet another Spielberg film) ample textual space and a significant amount of attention. Finally, certain judgements are shared, particularly that the movie is not quite so special and unique as it would appear on a first viewing and certainly is not Spielberg's best film. However, though quite some common ground exists and the movie in many ways is recognisably the same whether viewed through a Danish or a French set of lenses, nevertheless emphases vary and normative judgements differ markedly on a national basis (rarely fore-grounded in its own right) as regards the triangular configuration around which the movie pivots: nationalism/international idealism/universal morality and the three different kinds of 'us' (national, transatlantic or global) that each of these is linked with and transmits within the communicative context of the movie.

Let me start by reverting to the question: Do these two national critical communities react to the movie by suitably acknowledging the legitimacy of US patriotism and the extent of American sacrifices for Europe during the Second World War, particularly during D-Day? Phrased in slightly more critical terms, do they buy into the didactic part of Spielberg's self-avowed and widely publicised intent and message in this film: to erect a monument to veterans of D-Day and commemorate their sacrifices? While we need to note that there are certain differences within the national communities on this count, still the overall pattern indicates the existence of two nationally different approaches to this crucial question, as regards explicit mention, tone and mediatory strategy.

In this respect, coverage in *France* hovers between extensive mention of the movie's patriotic thrust and a certain US-sceptical dismissiveness of both its crude 'flaggism' and its attempts to situate itself on the moral high ground. The formal means of mediating between the former – which implicitly recognises the legitimacy and interest of Spielberg's patriotic assertiveness for a French public traditionally riven by forces of attraction as well as repulsion in relation to American values – and the latter which tends towards deflating this legitimacy, is extended use of *interviews* with Steven Spielberg himself (e.g. in *Le Figaro*, 26–27 September, and *Le Monde*, 1 October 1998), juxtaposed with critical commentaries in review articles or debate articles. The interviews allow Spielberg ample scope for voicing his own views on the film and its patriotic qualities in an apparently neutral form. Thus, for example, he emphasises that his acceptance of its release in China was conditioned on refusing the Chinese the right to cut out the initial and the final shots of the American flag. At the same time, however, he claimed that although he wanted to use the movie to pay homage to the American war veterans, to reinstate patriotic values and oppose the national 'cynicism' that he sees spreading – still, 'it is not a patriotic film' (*Le Figaro*, 27 September 1998). In the context of the caustically critical comments surrounding the interviews (particularly in *Le Monde*, 1 October 1998), such interviews acquire the function of allowing Spielberg to *expose* a somewhat misplaced and certainly exaggerated nationalism, which is in turn *analysed* in the accompanying pieces. Thus the form and the sheer length of the interviews would seem to recognise his national message and its global importance, but in fact conceal a mostly disapproving subtext. This subtext comprises both outspoken evaluations of the patriotic tenor of the film (such as 'la crétinerie de l'épilogue et du prologue du film', the assessment of Samuel Blumenfeld in his review in *Le Monde* – the very same critic who conducts the interview with Spielberg located next to the review article!), but also other types of evaluations scornfully dismissive of the alleged global megalomania of Spielberg's project and its cultural superficiality (e.g. in the form of comparing it to a Disneyesque theme park – 'The memory of the century as theme park'):[3]

> Spielberg is the greatest Hollywood producer in an era where Hollywood is no longer the geographical epicenter of American cinema, but an industrial international image factory wanting to perfect globalisation in the domains of collective representations. ... [Spielberg] can do nothing but recycle traditional mythologies while covering up the vanity of the operation.
>
> (Jean-Michel Froudon , *Le Monde*, 1 October 1998)[4]

Similar views are expressed in *Cahiers du cinéma* (no. 528, 1998) and *Libération* (30 September 1999). What these reviewers focus on is not just the patriotic message of the movie, but its failure to combine moral didacticism with aesthetic detail and enjoyment, and crude realism with romantic heroism in a way that in any substantial way makes the movie stand out from the conventional war movies. Spielberg is represented as a director who in fact produces little more than a second-order simulacrum 'à la manière de' although he both lectures his audience and exploits their sentiments in an attempt to design the ultimate war movie that will capture war as it really is, the universal truth about war and man. The movie wants to be unique, definitive and eye-opening, but lapses into sentimentality, patriotic affirmation and the utilisation of character portrayals and enemy images that are the stock-in-trade of traditional war movies. This discrepancy between the stated aims of the film – to reinvent patriotic American values, to recognise those who sacrificed their lives for 'our' liberty, and to address a fundamental moral dilemma – and its factual character as yet another tale of heroism, bravery and moral virtue that piggy-backs on a long history of American war films, makes the majority of the French reviewers dismiss Spielberg as a professional manipulator of images and emotions, as a megalomaniac when it comes to visualising and giving cinematic credence to ideas, thoughts and sentiments. In this area he comes across as naive, simplistic and almost childlike, in spite – or maybe because – of his ambitions to create the definitive war narrative, 'to be *all of* film, to capture the totality of History in the global reach of one work' (*Cahiers du cinéma*, no. 528).[5] This review ends on a representative note by pointing out that the film 'is a movie that wants to live on in the injured memory of humanity but which is killed by its details'.

The basic tenor of the critical coverage in France is, therefore, that the patriotism of the film is slightly ludicrous, the universal moralism misguided, trivial or poorly represented, and its international idealism superficial and/or pompous and at bottom mostly identifiable as global, image-making ambitions of Disneyesque proportions. For these reasons – and although more measured and cautious reviews are also in evidence – there is little recognition of the movie's national, or moral message. The movie *grosso modo* comes across to the readership as a partially failed, though in many ways well-intentioned and technically admirable project of a Hollywood producer entrapped by self-aggrandisement and peddling his own homegrown morality in the shape of a rather traditional war film. Without French culture, history, morality or identity being once mentioned in these reviews, the mediated product nevertheless bears the unmistakable imprint both of 'art cinema' as applied yardstick and of negative French US images among the cultural intelligentsia; and in spite of the contribution of US forces during the Second World War towards the liberation of France, the reader is hard put to it to find any utterances of gratitude or acknowledgement for this achievement in the way French reviewers and framers have chosen to handle this Spielberg movie.

For that reason, the French variant of national thirdness in this instance is a peculiar mix on the one hand, of grudging recognition and admiration – primarily manifested in the sheer extent of media coverage of the film and in letting Spielberg have so much of an independent say, but also in the occasional acknowledgement of the legitimacy of patriotism *eo ipso* – and on the other hand a sneering and distanced tone of dismissiveness and occasionally outright sarcasm at the pretentiousness of a movie seemingly trapped between its *American* patriotic ardour and its global ambitions in the vein of a (Disneyised) *universal* morality.

The general tenor of critical reception in *Denmark* on most of these counts is quite different. Not that the American pride and patriotism of the movie is overshadowed by its moral philosophy, but it is accorded quite a different value and recognition. In a commentary in the conservative daily *Berlingske Tidende* (24 October 1998), for example, headlined 'Spielberg viser flaget' ('Spielberg waves the flag'), the paper's editor-in-chief Peter Wivel seemingly sarcastically remarks that the movie 'has the nerve to wrap itself in the American flag'. A read of the article shows, however, that the sarcasm is directed at the imaginary reader who might object to the patriotism of the film. In fact, the article argues in enthusiastic and pro-American terms for the legitimacy of this type of national ardour and emphasises the gratitude European peoples should harbour *vis-à-vis* American sacrifices during the Second World War, for 'we became free human beings thanks to American help'. Hence, Spielberg's project is a laudable work of commemoration for the war veterans and instructive for the younger generations who have no memory of the war. On this analysis, Spielberg wants to generate a mood of acknowledgement in his audience 'for having saved Western civilisation'. Rather than the movie's cinematic qualities, it is here its instructional message and emotional lessons that are at the centre of attention.

Such undiluted gratitude and enthusiasm, verging on apologetics, are not totally representative of the comments and reviews in the Danish media as a whole, but nevertheless do reflect a spirit of acceptance and recognition of the moral legitimacy of this particular manifestation of patriotism, because it is prompted by an international selflessness and has positive consequences for Denmark/Europe/the free world. For some, this legitimacy is underpinned by the anti-heroic 'realism' of the movie, its truthfulness, and its intention 'not to please' or 'entertain'. With the starkness of the war's realities in mind, 'it is hardly shameful to admire [the soldiers] for it [i.e. their sacrifices for Europe's freedom]' (*Kristeligt Dagblad*, 23 October 1998). Other reviewers do emphasise the 'sentimentality' and 'pathos' framing the beginning and end of the film, and quite a few criticise it for its celebration of heroism and for lapsing into the mould of traditional Second World War movies, with nuanced portrayals of Allied soldiers and stereotypical depictions of Germans (*Jyllands-Posten and Information*, both 23 October 1998). However, even these reviews (and framing articles in the same papers) applaud the film for its moral purpose and superior craftsmanship. *Weekendavisen* (23–29 October 1998) thinks Spielberg has performed a major feat by successfully celebrating old-fashioned virtues though this really should not be possible any longer, and finds the strength of the film to lie in its balance between 'realism' and 'heroism'. The reviewer, Bo Green Jensen, claims that American reviewers rejected the film due to its pandering to emotions rather than reason, but he nonetheless 'recommends the movie without serious reservations'.

In most papers, these types of (more or less subdued) accolades are framed by articles about the history of the Second World War movies, Spielberg's career and personality, and background stories on the history of the film. This is consistently done in the third-person format, that is, in a narrative that represents Spielberg's views, rather than allowing them to be presented directly in the context of an interview, as was the case in France. This approach is more in accordance with a basically more positive and admiring position *vis-à-vis* Spielberg, the film and Hollywood generally (information and assessment merge), whereas the French form allows for a disjunction of presentation and evaluation.

The other main feature of the Danish press' reception of the movie that is worth mentioning is that it is consistently compared – and not always as favourably as one might have imagined – with other Hollywood productions featuring the Second World War. Quite a few of the comments tend to downplay the film in that respect, assessing it to be a more ordinary, run-of-the-mill war movie than it would like to be (*Information*, 23 October 1998), or to be inferior to other movies of the same kind (*Jyllands-Posten*, 23 October 1998). However, unlike France, there is no tendency to see it as a Disneyised, copycat war film, nor to criticise it for its ambition of being the war movie that ends all war movies; rather, the reactions in Denmark are common-sensical, cautious of too much enthusiasm, and call for moderation along the lines of 'this is a great movie, but not *that* great'. Basically the movie's premises and self-understanding are accepted, and comments are embedded in a context bounded by the critics' belonging to a transnational universe of knowledge and values, politically, culturally and cinematically. The existence of a transatlantic, Hollywood-dominated ecumene is clearly in evidence, propped up by numerous references to the reception of the movie in the US context. For this reason, US-denigrating or US-sceptical stereotypes are hardly brought into play, in either of the two categories of critical commentary.

Thus, the 'third' produced in the Danish context is rooted in an affirmative appraisal of the movie's moral dogmatism and (putative) celebration of the values of freedom and sacrifice; in other words, its transatlantic internationalism is both accepted and applauded, occasionally by explicitly referring to the historical benefits of American sacrifices for the Danish community. On the other hand, there is also widespread acceptance of Spielberg's American patriotism as legitimate and understandable. Finally, the universalising 'human' dimension and dilemma of the film are admiringly assessed as striking a sensible balance between heroism and anti-heroism. Altogether, the Danish reception is 'globalising', in the sense that it accepts Spielberg as a dignified representative of Hollywood film-making, and US values and contributions to Western civilisation as laudable; the 'us' of the commentaries is one therefore which comprises both producer and receiver/consumer. The American other is one which is (almost) part of ourselves in this case, unlike France, where French cultural nationalism draws a clear-cut boundary between the sophistication of 'us' and the crudeness and pretentiousness of 'them'. Before going on to draw a few conclusions and to fit these analytical remarks into the larger framework of the theoretical reflections set out above, a brief side-glance – as counterpoint – at the critical reception of the movie (two months earlier) on its own home ground, the US, is appropriate. Apart from the fact that commentaries in the US press, true to a general trend in US entertainment culture, are more concerned with actor personalities (like Tom Hanks and Matt Damon), with questions of stardom and possible Oscar nominations following the release of the film than is the case in Europe, three points are worth foregrounding that distinguish the US reception from the two European ones already discussed.

First, the US media are clearly more focused on the stark realism, historical honesty and alleged anti-war message of the movie than either the French or Danish commentators, and they devote quite a lot of space and emotive verbiage to describing the historical realities of D-Day (see e.g. *People*, 3 August 1998). Second, although the patriotic component of the film is mentioned, particularly in connection with Spielberg wanting to erect a monument to the war veterans, much more attention is given to the potentially counter-patriotic, nationally divisive effects of depicting the Second World War in such brutally honest terms; as one headline goes, 'Can America handle "Private Ryan"?' (MSNBC, *Hollywood Voyeur*, 30 June 1998); or as Spielberg remarked to Associated Press on 19 July 1998: 'I don't want to turn Americans away from the patriotism many of us feel, but in the process of the chaos of combat, these were some of the things men were driven to do' (cited from *Yahoo News*). And third, in logical extension of this optic, the major part of both the critical and affirmative commentary concentrates on the movie's universal, moral questions: Why risk eight men's lives to save one? What kind of humanitarian ethic is at work here? What's the place and the worth of dignity, decency and human affections in the midst of the slaughterhouse of war? How do soldiers preserve their humanity, and how do those who are fortunate enough to come out of the war alive make themselves worthy of it?

Interestingly, thus, whereas the two European critical communities both, in various ways, tend to focus their spotlight on the explicit US patriotism of the movie and, as regards Denmark, on the international, transatlantic historical mission of the US, domestic US attention is concerned with the film's potential for negatively impacting patriotic sentiments and stirring up uncomfortable memories among the public at large as well as among war veterans, and further-more with eagerly debating its universal, timeless and globally valid moral questions and the cinematic effects usurped by Spielberg to bring home his message, particularly his appeal to emotional reactions rather than the rational mind. Positive as well as negative reactions in the US media centrally hinge on assessing Spielberg's degree of success in aestheticising this universalist kind of *problématique* while on the one hand condemning the realities of war and on the other celebrating the quiet heroics and solid humanity of people like Captain Miller, 'a decent man of the sort that America was theoretically meant to produce, and perhaps did during the generation in question' (*Variety*, 26 July 1998). This does not, as the quote demonstrates, imply that the patriotism of the movie is absent from reviews. Rather than being explicitly thematised as an important element of the movie's storyline and message, the patriotism is taken for granted as the cultural-historical frame within which Spielberg produced the movie and within which it needs to be received. Thus, Spielberg's own preference for seeing this as 'not a patriotic film' (see previously cited statement to *Le Figaro*) is by and large taken at face value by the American critical community (unlike France, and, differently, Denmark). For the same reason, the international idealism (politically or morally understood, according value to the Western, transatlantic brotherhood) so pronounced in Denmark is subdued, almost non-existent in the US reception. After all, the beneficiary of the anti-heroic heroism of the platoon is Private Ryan (American and everyman in one), not 'Europe' or 'democratic liberties'.

Conclusion

Saving Private Ryan provides a perfect example of a movie which, as I argued above, is rooted in American perceptions of man, nature, society and the world – movies in other words whose taken-for-granted assumptions and common sense understandings are of a US origin, no matter how effectively or frequently 'American' problems are given an all-human, universalistic spin. The interesting point is that it is the American critical reception of the movie which most comprehensively accepts the transformation from 'American' to 'global-universal'. In the other two cases, the US-national(ist) qualities and import of the movie are foregrounded, though they are very differently evaluated. However, both in France and Denmark, critics explicitly engage with the movie as American, as I argued above on a more theoretical note, bringing their pre-understanding of the USA to bear. And in spite of the fact that the Danish reception is by and large considerably more positive and 'globally minded' than the French, it is no closer to either the movie itself or the national receptive pattern in the US than is the French. The nationality of these commentaries is in no way short-circuited by the transnational professional attachments of the critical community, but in both countries interesting national thirds emerge, and in all three countries, critical reception obliquely reflects privileged elite images of self and other as well as period-specific concerns about war and peace, national identity and security, Western values, humanitarian ethics and transatlantic co-operation.

The French 'national third' is a faithful reflection of a national mood *vis-à-vis* the USA which on the one hand is still steeped in a kind of French cultural self-congratulation deeply suspicious of US hegemonic aspirations, dismissive of US cultural superficiality, and mindful of the need to keep French national identity and sovereignty intact in spite of the inroads of US theme-park culture. On the other hand, the admiration for Spielberg's technical craftsmanship and the sheer extent of the commentary accorded to a film somehow thematising transatlantic war collaboration (including extensive interviews) manifest the political and military *rapprochement* between France and the USA in recent years, reflected in French abandonment of the WEU as an independent European security organisation and in the important step to rejoin NATO's military command.

The Danish national optic, in a similar manner, reflects a steadily more pro-American mood and a markedly more affirmative political as well as cultural position as regards the US over the past 6–7 years – including a much more proactive transatlantic and NATO-oriented security policy. Elite (as well as popular) awareness in Denmark regarding the positive effects of US involvement in Europe for the security of a small nation like Denmark has steadily increased and has made Denmark one of the most enthusiastic NATO members overall. Thus, the implicitly assumed transatlantic 'we' found in the reviews and framing commentaries mirrors a broad consensus among Danes, who for that reason do not see their national culture and identity as threatened by Disneyisation and McDonaldisation (much more so by Europeanisation in fact). In this context, the 'flaggism' of the movie is seen as a positive extension of the widespread use of the Danish flag to symbolise national pride, and not as a sign that interests are at work which might constitute a cultural or political threat to Denmark.

Finally, the US reception is indicative of a mood *vis-à-vis* war, international engagements and the sacrifice of American lives which on the one hand recognises the need for international commitment and takes American-cum-human values almost for granted, and on the other tends to shy away from the sacrifice of American blood for purposes that are not clearly in the US interest. On the background of high-tech warfare like the Gulf War (and later the Serbian War) and US public sensitivity to the capture or death of even a single US soldier, the battle scenes in *Saving Private Ryan* manifest a meaningless waste of human (i.e. US) lives, and the plot of the movie – extricating James Ryan from the European battlefields in order to repatriate him to the good life of Middle America – a message that makes a whole lot of patriotic sense (though this potential isolationism is counteracted by the resolve of Ryan not to be 'saved', but to see the battle through and thus save the meaning of the war and the death of his brothers for himself). On that background, the moral focus of the US critical reception reflects a new type of US patriotism, committed to sacrifices and global concerns, but within limits set by the possibility of making 'human' and 'moral' sense of interventions in the light of American interests.

This particular analysis cannot, of course, make any claims to representativeness. Nevertheless, it demonstrates the importance of paying close attention to the minutiae of the national mediation by commentators of even large-scale Hollywood blockbusters. The profile of the movie that media consumers had outlined to them in the three countries contains very important differences of emphasis, evaluation and omission. In important respects, the expectation horizon is thus shaped by critics in three nationally distinct ways: audiences are equipped with three different kinds of pre-understanding with which to unravel and interpret the actual movie they watch unfolding – filters which in turn are locked into elite and public images of transatlanticism and national culture. The theoretical and analytical implications of this production of national 'thirds' must be pursued in another context. What can be concluded here is that if this pattern holds true for this particular Hollywood blockbuster, it will probably be found in other cases too.

Notes

1 It should be added that the series was even more radically changed in Sweden, whereas in the GDR it proved to be a resounding success in its original version.
2 The text corpus on which the analysis is based consists of pre-release commentaries, reviews and 'framing articles' in leading newspapers and periodicals in all three countries, representing different political and intellectual positions. In Denmark: *Aalborg Stiftstidende*, *Aktuelt*, *Berlingske Tidende*, *Information*, *Jyllands-Posten*, *Kristeligt Dagblad*, *Politiken* and *Weekendavisen*. In France: *Cahiers du cinéma*, *Le Figaro*, *Libération*, *Le Monde*, *Le Progrès*. In the USA: *Associated Press* (website), *The Christian Science Monitor*, *CNN Interactive*, *Entertainment Weekly*, *MSNBC* (website), *Newsweek*, *New York Review of Books*, *People*, *Variety*, *Washington Post*.
3 'La mémoire du siècle comme parc d'attractions'.
4 'Spielberg est le plus grand réalisateur hollywoodien d'une époque où Hollywood n'est plus l'épicentre géographique du cinéma des Etats-Unis, mais une imagerie industrielle internationale destinée à accomplir la mondialisation dans les domaines des représentations collectives. ... [Spielberg] peut seulement recycler les anciennes mythologies en masquant la vanité de l'opération'.
5 '[D]'être *tout* le cinéma, de concurrencer la totalité de l'Histoire par la globalité d'une oeuvre'.

Bibliography

Castells, M. (1997) *The Power of Identity*, Malden: Blackwell.
Crofts, S. (1993) 'Reconceptualising National Cinema/s', *Quarterly Review of Film and Video* 14, 3: 49–67.
Elsaesser, T. (1987) 'Chronicle of a Death Retold', *Monthly Film Bulletin* 54, 641: 164–7.
Featherstone, M. (1996) 'Localism, Globalism, and Cultural Identity', in R. Wilson and W. Dissanayake (eds).
Hedetoft, U. (1999) 'The Nation-State Meets the World. National Identities in the Context of Transnationality and Cultural Globalization', *European Journal of Social Theory* 2: 171–94.
Higson, A. (1989) 'The Concept of National Cinema', *Screen* 30, 4: 36–46.
—— (1995) *Waving the Flag*, Oxford: Oxford University Press.
Hjort, M. (2000) 'Themes of Nation', in this volume.
Menand, L. (1998) 'Jerry Don't Surf', *The New York Review of Books*, 24 September.
Reich, R. (1992) *The Work of Nations*, New York: Alfred A. Knopf.
Ritzer, G. (1993) *The McDonaldization of Society*, Thousand Oaks, CA: Pine Forge Press.

Shohat, E. and Stam, R. (1996) 'From the Imperial Family to the Transnational Imaginary: Media Spectatorship in the Age of Globalization', in R. Wilson and W. Dissanayake (eds).

Sørensen, B. (1994) ' "I Have a Plan!" The Olsen Gang Captures Denmark and Norway: Negotiating the Culture Gap', *Velvet Light Trap* 34: 71–83.

Wilson, R. and Dissanayake, W. (eds) (1996) *Global/Local: Cultural Production and the Transnational Imaginary*, Durham, NC: Duke University Press.

18

BIRTHING NATIONS

Jane M. Gaines

Eric Hobsbawm's monumental *Nations and Nationalism Since 1780* (1990) stands firm on its premise that nationalism precedes the nation. This, it seems, is justification for the study of nationalisms without nationhood, semi-fanatical nationalisms that ignite like a bonfire and then die down, or those whose heat increases slowly until everything is in smoke and it is difficult to control the conflagration. In particular, this is a discussion of some of the *uses* to which melodrama has been historically put in the service of nation-building. Here I look at two silent film melodramas, the first based on a case of dramatically failed effort and the second on a case of a somewhat misled attempt at nation-building: D.W. Griffith's *The Birth of a Nation* (US, 1915), and its South African equivalent, *De Voortrekkers* (South Africa, 1916). My interest is in the melodramatic mode in the service of the transmission of knowledge about sexual reproduction. In short, what I call sex education as nationalism and nationalism as sex education.

The question of the *national melos* of *The Birth of a Nation* has an obvious logic for readers familiar with the history of the political as well as the emotional turmoil surrounding the film, particularly in the years of its original release and its re-release in the 1920s in the US. For it is well known that the film which was intended to produce resonant feelings of sympathy for the creator's cause instead prompted audiences to respond with outrage and expressions of hostility. Imagining, or perhaps fantasising a community, director Griffith and producer Thomas W. Dixon created a recruitment film for a cause whose time had clearly passed. Of the two, Dixon, author of two novels upon which *The Birth of a Nation* was based, *The Leopard's Spots* and *The Clansman*, was perhaps the more rabid son of the old South, but it is fair to say of both that they were guilty of the charge of wanting to fight the Civil War over again. The futility of their vision of the South as a separate world, a land, a people, a nation, is only emphasised by the fact that what was known as the 'Lost Cause' or the 'Southern Legend' had clearly run its course by 1914 (Merritt 1982). *The Birth of a Nation* would be released at the *end* of the heyday of Southern radicalism, not the beginning, and was more precisely the swan-song of that political movement rather than the herald of a new dawn for Southern sympathisers (Taylor 1998; Williamson 1984, 1986).

By the time of its release, fifty years after the end of the Civil War, the South as a separate nation was no longer conceivable, and yet, it is *not* the union of North and South that the film seems to imagine (despite its protests and insistent references to the connection of the Aryan peoples in the North and the South). Instead, the film advocates *a nation that never was*. Contrary to most interpretations of the film that stress the constitution of the American union, the nation that is 'birthed' in the film is really the impossible, 'invisible' nation that only exists in the minds of stalwart Southerners. Perhaps it is time to assert that the film's union of former enemies and the evaporation of hostilities between them is not now and never was really believable. For purposes of this paper, then, the 'nation' in that famous title, refers not to the unified North and South but to the Confederate South. National melos, as exemplified by *The Birth of a Nation*, must thus be a narrative lament, a sad song of loss, and yet, simultaneously and contradictorily, it is a hate narrative. As has been noted by countless commentators since its release, the film is a venal expression of disdain for and distrust of black Americans, particularly in the role they played in reconstruction. And this is why Griffith's sad film struck sympathetic chords with such a select few at the time of its release.

Earlier, I have discussed the role of the Joseph Carl Breil score and its contribution to the construction not only of the melos but of the musical characterisation of the 'barbarism' ascribed to characters of African descent in the film (Gaines and Lerner, forthcoming). The analysis of the composite musical score and its motifs, however, is only one approach to defining the melodramatic formal system in Griffith's flawed work. It has seemed to me that after all that has been written about this film, we are only now beginning to grasp its function as a melodrama, as we move beyond its dualisms and feuding parts, to consider the particularity of its hyperbole. *The Birth of a Nation*, it could be argued, is not only overblown as all melodrama will be, overstating its dramatic case in the most exaggerated and elongated of terms. Griffith's feature is excessively obsessive and frenetic. A dramatic overreaction, its responses are out of proportion to the threat posed, and its celebrated rhythms create nothing more nor less than the representation of panic. By the end, the film has worked itself up to a fevered pitch. Something is seriously wrong. But an overreaction to what?

The Birth of a Nation has long been notorious for its portrayal of black characters and has been accused of racism by community groups, beginning with the NAACP (National Association for the Advancement of Colored People) protests in the year of its release and continuing into the present. We suspect that the aestheticisation of frenzy in Griffith's film has something to do with racism, and I want to return to the question of the feverishness of much of the film but first let me attend to the question of the *where* and the *when* of racism. Earlier I have discussed the difficulty of attributing racism to a work of photographic representation (Gaines 1992). And recently, Anthony Appiah, thinking of the eighty-year struggle of the NAACP against *The Birth of a Nation*, has cautioned us to consider the way in which we speak about racism in film and television in the wider culture, arguing that a film 'is not racist in the same way that a person is' (Appiah 1993: 82–3). Calling our attention to the systematic and structural function of racism, Étienne Balibar echoes the same theme when he says that 'Racism is a social relation, not the mere ravings of racist subjects' (Balibar 1991: 40). We are thus disinclined to make any assumptions about the location of racism in the text. Accordingly, I will be careful here to refer to the racism *attributed to* the cinematic text. But does this question of the *where* of racism lead to the assertion that the society's racism is the same as or different from the racism that has historically been attributed to films such as *The Birth of a Nation*? The question becomes more interesting when we introduce the example of the production and the reception of *De Voortrekkers*, or, rather, the *uses* to which the film was put by the Afrikaner Nationalist Movement.

The possibility that we can think of the racism attributed to a motion picture as in one place and the racism of the society as in another is enabled by the contemporary consensus among critical race theorists that we need to consider racism in the plural, that is, to think multiple and undulating racisms, differing relations of race not only across cultures but within a single culture. But before we think the correspondence or the non-correspondence between so-called racist cultural texts and the racist societies that spawned them, we need to wonder as well about the possible correlation between racism and nationalism. After all, the connection made by anthropologist Ruth Benedict suggested that there might be a scientific coincidence here (Benedict 1942). But Étienne Balibar has pointed out that Benedict's example is narrow since Nazi anti-Semitism is not exactly the same as colonial racism and that as 'we do not all live in equally racist societies', it follows that racism may have significantly different ingredients from nation to nation. The mix that produced South African apartheid, he goes on to argue, would be one part Nazism, another part colonisation, and another part slavery (Balibar and Wallerstein 1991: 35, 40). It would be tidy to contend that the cult of origins and the 'chosen people' consciousness that often characterises nationalism simultaneously produces the hate reaction that is racism, especially since the two films we are considering could be taken as exemplifying such an equation. Balibar, however, introduces a corrective. 'Racism', he wants to argue is 'not necessarily an inevitable consequence of nationalism' (ibid.: 35). Actually, he says, racism should be considered as over and above nationalism, a 'supplement' to it, in 'excess' of it (ibid.: 54). This is not to say that there is not a strong historical correlation here, for Balibar's thinking owes everything to the assumption that nationalism and racism are governed by a certain historical reciprocity (ibid.: 53). My motive in theorising the relation as somewhat more of a disjuncture than an equation is intended to allow for the historical opportunism of racism. Like the question of the frenzy of the text, this is a point to which I will return.

Afrikaner nationalism and *De Voortrekkers*

If racism and nationalism are never necessarily in the same place, the ostensible racism of the hypernationalistic text and the racism of the society in question need not correspond either, raising the question of the *when* of racism. Here, *De Voortrekkers* is illustrative. Cited as the South African equivalent of *The Birth of a Nation*, presumably because it has an association with a defeated group whose history is glorified in the film, *De Voortrekkers* has historically been associated with the rise of Afrikaner nationalism (Strebel 1979: 25). Clearly on this count, the historical resemblance is striking if one compares the Southern losses in the Civil War with the Afrikaner defeat at the hands of the British in the Boer War of 1899–1902. Where *The Birth of a Nation* is nostalgic for the Southern plantation life long gone (the 'Plantation Illusion' as it has been called), the South African film is enamoured with the story of the Great Trek, a moment in Afrikaner history that was retrospectively discovered as the expression of pioneer courage that justified the Boers' entitlement to land and consequently their imagination of nation.

But if the single temporal disjunction between the 1915 release of *The Birth of a Nation* and the heyday of the Confederate South is striking, *De Voortrekkers* is best understood in relation to a set of historical disconnections that are unparalleled in their complexity. The narrative of the 1916 film follows the Great Trek, really a mass exodus that began in 1836, a migration northward from the British Cape Colony of people of Dutch descent who had become dissatisfied with British policies, particulary those the Boers perceived as unfairly favouring native Africans. Their goal, in the words of the inter-titles is 'to establish a Model Republic for our paternity', a 'Free Dutch Republic' that they say they intend to found by the purchase of land from the reigning Zulu monarch, Dingaan. The trekkers, under the command of Piet Retief, however, are betrayed by Portuguese traders who are instrumental in turning Dingaan against them, and after the signing of the treaty deeding Natal to the Boers, the Zulus slaughter Retief and his people *en masse*. General Pretorius, however, is notified immediately of the massacre and rushes to the rescue. In what would become known as the glorious Battle of Blood River, 16 September 1838, he defeats the Zulus, largely, according to the inter-titles, because the backward people encounter fire-arms in battle for the first time.

'Getting its history wrong is part of being a nation', as Ernest Renan observed in his famous lecture 'What is a Nation?' (Renan [1882] 1990). South African observers have uniformly noted that *De Voortrekkers* makes a blatant and obvious error, casting the Portuguese and the Zulus as the enemy in this story and not the British who had so recently been the villains in the Boer War devastation from which the wounds would have been still fresh in 1916. This misconstrual of events, this substitution of the Zulus for the British, is one of the film's historical lapses that leads Keyan Tomaselli to conclude that it is not finally about Afrikaner nationalism at all. *De Voortrekkers*, he wants to argue, is

301

about imperialist expansion, an ideology that borrowed the narrative of the Great Trek, the martyrdom of Piet Retief, and the vanquishment of Dingaan's army at the hands of General Pretorius (1986: 38). And clearly the production history of the film would support this argument. Produced by African Film Productions Ltd., a British corporation, and directed by an American, Harold Shaw, the film was produced for a British market (ibid.: 39). Ironically, the British overseas market explains the existence of such films because the domestic South African audience was not large enough in 1916–20, the span of the life of the company, to allow the company to more than break even (Gutsche 1972). British distribution secured the profits.

So *De Voortrekkers* produced the illusion of unity between former enemies, the two white factions merged in the figures of the white conquerors of the dark continent, no doubt emphasised by the film's subtitle, 'Winning a Continent'. But in emphasising the political economy questions, Tomaselli must necessarily de-emphasise the question of reception. For it is the Afrikaner *claim* on the film that produces it as a text of Afrikaner Nationalism, beginning with its premiere at the Krugersdorp Town Hall on Covenant Day (later Dingaan's Day), the day commemorating the Boer victory over the Zulus at Blood River. The beginning of a long association with Afrikaner tradition and ritual, the film screening was also wrapped up in the inauguration of the Paardekraal Monument which to the devout stood for the victory over the British as well as the black Africans (Strebel 1979; Tomaselli 1985: 36). Other parallel developments place *De Voortrekkers* within the forcefield of a seething dissatisfaction with the British and a throbbing nationalist sentiment. For the would-be conquerors had themselves been conquered, after all. Afrikaans was made an official language in 1918 and by 1925 it had replaced Dutch as the language spoken in parliament. The double inter-titles in English and Afrikaans mark the first use of the new African language in this manner (Strebel 1979: 26). Finally, the association between *De Voortrekkers* scenarist Gustav Preller and the Afrikaner movement is intimate, the author of the biography of Piet Retief as well as Andries Pretorius having figured significantly in the discovery of the Great Trek as the key chapter in the history of the brand new nation (Thompson 1985: 36). It is Preller who is credited with the documentary accuracy of *De Voortrekkers*, with adding the detail to the portrayal of the lives of the Trek Boers from whom he descended. All of which is to say that ironically the British had produced the very vehicle that would be used in the engineering of a new nation within the nation of South Africa, a group that aspired to define the rest of the nation for white others as well as for black African others. By 1948, Afrikaner nationalism would seem to be secure as that year nationalists were able to win a majority in elections and gain control of the government (ibid.: 26). Quite the opposite of *The Birth of a Nation* whose appearance produced some isolated outbreaks of enthusiasm for the lost cause in the form of Ku Klux Klan-sponsored screenings, *De Voortrekkers* contributed to a gradual build of nationalist sentiment, mostly as part of ritual celebration.

1838, 1916, 1938: 'mimetic imitations' of the past

What is remarkable about *De Voortrekkers* and puts it in a category with no other silent film, is its continual use in classrooms after its initial release in 1916 but also its function as a technologised national narrative on a mass scale before the advent of television. The critical reception highlight occurred in 1938, the year of the centenary celebration of the Great Trek, and again as at the premiere of the film, twenty-two years before, the exhibition of *De Voortrekkers* would be linked with the phenomenon of trekkers travelling in ox-wagons, with a mass reenactment of the struggles of the Boer ancestors (Tomaselli 1986: 36). The numerical size of the audience for *De Voortrekkers* cannot compare with the original audiences for Griffith's *The Birth of a Nation*, which, despite protest and censorship, was a US box office record-breaker in 1915 and again at its re-release in 1921. However, *De Voortrekkers'* association with the mass waves of the Afrikaner movement and the public exhibition of fervour without opposition place it in a special category of mass consciousness builder. At the 1938 celebration, eight ox-wagons driven by trekkers in vintage costume made long trips from key points in Southern Africa to the Pretoria hill where the Voortrekker Monument was to be erected. The commemoration drew one tenth of the population, around 100,000, and at the climactic arrival of torches relayed to the site, the women were said to have touched the corners of their handkerchiefs to the flames, producing scorched mementoes (Thompson 1985: 39). Such a ritual claim on such a mass scale settles the question of the film's relation to the Afrikaner cause. The film was opportunistically mobilised to meet a nationalist need at a crucial moment, a moment twenty-two years after the original release date, hence the strange historical disjuncture. Also, *De Voortrekkers* was surprisingly prescient. By 1938, the real foe of the Afrikaner cause was no longer the British but had become the Africans who had stood in for the British in the 1916 film as scapegoats for Boer failures.

The Afrikaner centenary celebrations, for which women wore long skirts and men grew beards in imitation of their ancestors, stand as the motion picture itself in mimetic relation to the historic past. Much was made of the extras who were said to have been descendants of the 1938 trek Boers, a kind of guarantee of the directness of the blood lines, an unsurpassable example of genetic realism (Strebel 1979: 26). In its marvellous mimesis, *De Voortrekkers* shares some things with *The Birth of a Nation*, that prototype of the epic as genre in the silent era. The stuffed frames and grandiose aspirations to stage the impossible – from Zulu-Boer battle scenes to the foraging of the Orange River in ox-carts – suggest that the film admires the crowded opulence and near fanatical empiricism of *Intolerance* (1916), a film which received wide distribution in South Africa (Tomaselli 1986: 36). Vivian Sobchack has written about the epic as genre, stressing its representation of historicity in the empirical 'verifiability' of its excess of detail (Sobchack 1995: 288). Further, she has observed that the epic is characterised by a mimetic relation between the scale and the difficulty of the film's production and the magnitude of the historical adversity dramatised on screen. It is as though the genre 'celebrates and represents the historic struggles under which it produced itself as *mimetic imitation* of the events it is dramatising' (ibid.: 293). Such celebration is generally found in the promotional materials, and here *De Voortrekkers* exemplifies the strategy. In an article in the South African *Stage and Cinema*, director Harold Shaw talks about the production in terms of feats successfully performed – the ten million gallon artificial river constructed, the dynamiting of a kopje (hill), and, most compelling, the direction of 6,000 African miners who were employed in the Blood River Battle reinactment. Yet here, to my mind, is also one of the most unsettling aspects of this elaborate mimesis – the story of the recreation of the Battle of Blood River that turned into a race riot (Shaw 1916: 2). As Elizabeth Strebel describes the incident, an actor playing a voortrekker accidentally shot off his gun, provoking a genuine fighting reaction from the Zulus who swarmed down on the pretend wagon laager (circular grouping) and attacked the whites, as one might say colloquially, 'for real'. For a moment until police authorities arrived, Africans and white settlers acted out present hostilities under the guise of past hostilities, and the proper distance between act and reenactment was fatally broached (Strebel 1979: 27). Perhaps the shooting of *De Voortrekkers* represents the most deadly case on record of a mimesis of a mimesis. The incident urges us to consider some of the same questions raised by the myth of the pornographic 'snuff' film – the cheapness of lives and the dispensability of colonial others in the service of the exotic picture.

Genre: nation

'With regard to location, it is instructive to note just how closely the notion of genre parallels that of nation', says Rick Altman in his discussion of the incoherence of genre. While we might want the concept of genre (as nation) to cohere, to prove itself as compact as the term (genre), that concept is as large and unwieldy as the examples that constitute it (Altman 1999: 86). Altman wants to analogise genre and nation, those concepts filled out and constrained by their examples, but we need to take him further – to suggest that nations and nationalism can find formulaic expression in genre. Going beyond the literary notion of national narrative, we would want to consider the question of what Jennifer Peterson has called 'scenic nationalism', the defining features of landscape as it becomes *mise-en-scène*, a phenomenon she identifies in early travel films. Here is the point at which the land becomes emblematic through its representation on the wide screen, and the male imperialist figure is understood as able to stake a claim as far as his eye can see (Pratt 1992: 60). Until recently, the only film genre studied in such explicitly nationalist terms has been the American Western, although Richard Dyer has made a productive comparison between the West of the Western and narratives set in the South, particularly as they subscribe to their own myths of origins, suggesting the existence of what might be called the 'Southern'. Dyer finds two genres of national origins: one a 'success' genre, the other a 'failure' genre (1996: 35–6), and, thinking of *The Birth of a Nation*, he describes a genre whose concerns, like the obsessions of the Confederate South, are the breeding 'of slaves and white dynasties' (ibid.: 36). And yet, the South encounters trouble in its attempt to breed perfectly white people. Since things are never light enough, says Dyer (1996) in a breath-taking argument, 'lightness' must paradoxically be brought down from the North, imported into the film as Northern imagery. If the South is distracted and worried about the whiteness of whiteness, the Western, says Dyer, assumes purity, largely by maintaining a world without women (ibid.: 36). In American history, this comparison certainly says, red men have never constituted the threat to the bloodlines that black men have.

While *De Voortrekkers* can sustain the comparison with *The Birth of a Nation* as a national narrative preoccupied with historical ancestry and retrospective glory, it has an odd relation to the purity melodrama enacted in *The Birth of a Nation*. Here I am thinking of the encounters between the white virginal characters (Flora Cameron and Lucie Stoneman) and the sexually dangerous blacks (Sylas Lynch and the hapless Gus). Like the Western, *De Voortrekkers*, with its emphasis on the trek over dangerous terrain and the battles with savages, is a narrative of 'mastery', in Dyer's terms (ibid.: 36). Also like the Western, the narrative of Afrikaans origins assumes rather than asserts racial purity. However, this is not to say that Afrikaner nationalism will not be concerned as well with purity, only that this concern will surface some years later, as we will see. One could say that the apparent disinterest in the question of sexual purity in the *De Voortrekkers* allows us no basis whatsoever for comparisons with a film like *The Birth of a Nation* whose obsession with the protection of Flora and Lucie over-whelms the narrative. But I have a way of getting around this apparent stalemate. In order to force these two films into sharp relief on the question of the female body as it relates to cults of origin, I want to attempt to complicate the question of purity, suggesting how both of these films are implicated in notions about the menarche, or first menstruation. As I will show, versions of the cultural significance of this event have remained relatively unchanged across the centuries, or at least core assumptions have remained resistant to change.

The authors of *The Curse: A Cultural History of Menstruation* thus open their first chapter: 'Greater than his fear of death, dishonor, or dismemberment has been primitive man's respect for menstrual blood' (Delaney *et al.* 1988: 7). A premise seldom tested in either empirical or interpretive studies of culture until recent years, this powerful feminist assertion has the potential to transform entrenched readings of canonical texts. Such an entrenched reading, I would argue, is the analysis of Flora Cameron's tragedy in *The Birth of a Nation* as her 'rape' at the hands of the newly freed Negro Gus. Earlier, I have discussed the overwhelming tendency on the part of scholars to want to read Gus' pursuit of the girl and Flora's leap from the cliff as the enactment of 'rape', the act of black man against white woman that in the historical moment of the film would surely incur the wrath of the lynch mob. While I realise the importance of fore-grounding these issues in one of the major cinematic texts of the century, I have remained unconvinced by readings of the scene as a 'rape' (Gaines forth-coming). More compelling is Joel Williamson's discussion of Thomas Dixon's obsession with his mother's biological history, beginning with his written recol-lection that she was forced to marry his father at thirteen before the appearance of her 'mensus', an unusual spelling of *menses*, suggesting a pseudo-scientific knowledge of female development (Williamson 1986: 107; see also 1984: 172). According to Williamson, Dixon was fixated on this fact of the marriage at thir-teen, pencilling over the '3' several times, and linking her difficulties with childbearing and later painful menopause to the premature marriage (1986: 107–8). While Williamson would like to use Dixon's focus on his mother's reproductive troubles as an explanation for his fanaticism, I want to temper this somewhat by suggesting his typicality, to suggest that Dixon leads us to see Flora as enacting more than the fear of defilement by the black beast. Flora enacts the menarche as defloration, illustrating what the authors of *The Curse* tell us is a failure to make a distinction between menstrual blood and the blood of the hymen that has historically appeared at first intercourse.

Although this confusion characterised the 'primitive mind', the authors argue, the association between these two occasions of bleeding has continued to produce in the male mind a strong association between menstruation and inter-course, even the belief that the latter causes the former (1986: 30–4). Thus the child who is married at thirteen could be understood as experiencing inter-course and menstruation simultaneously, the one bloody act bringing on the other, providing self-evident proof (to the primitive male mind) that early menarche was the sign of precocious depravity.

This is the cumulation of meanings surrounding Flora who must be seen as bearing more than the burden of victimhood at the hands of a black rapist. Long before the contemporary concerns that articulate terror of sexual abuse and assault, child-women would have been initiated into a different culture of trepidation, one surrounding the menarche. I read the displacements of concern in the iconography of the napkin, the bleeding orifice, the brother's horror, and the ritual use of magical blood. In fact, it is the iconography of *The Birth of a Nation* that persuades me that we need to see more possibilities in the flitting about of little Flora who is so strongly associated with images of absorbent cloth. For all of those viewers who have been struck by the strangeness of the raw cotton Flora pats on to her collar and the title 'Southern ermine' as well as the secretiveness of the work of ripping up old sheets, the representation of menstruation appears as a viable explanation for the emphases of *The Birth of a Nation*. Surely, then, the momentousness of Ben Cameron's gesture of wiping the blood from his sister's mouth is explained (see Figure 18.1). That he uses the corner of the red and blue Confederate flag that she has wrapped around her waist only reinforces this reading of the flag as a menstrual rag. This is the stained cloth that he will later dip in a crucible of water and hold on high in the

Figure 18.1 Ben Cameron wipes the blood from his sister's mouth: *The Birth of a Nation* (1915)

Ku Klux Klan ceremony that sends the night riders into action after the lynching of Gus. The inter-title, Cameron's invocation, emphasises the symbolic value: 'Brethren, this flag bears the red stain of the life of a Southern woman, a priceless sacrifice on the altar of an outraged civilisation'. Michael Rogin has read this scene as the 'sacramentalisation' of Flora's death, a ceremonial use not only of her own 'communion blood' but of Gus' castration, a double ritual that comes dangerously close to 'mixing their blood together' (Rogin 1985: 178). But the problem with this reading is that it emphasises Gus' castration without understanding Flora's, for primitive myth as well as more modern psychoanalysis have seen menstruation as a bleeding wound and therefore a kind of symbolic castration (Delaney *et al.* 1988: 75).

My earlier analysis has emphasised the incident as a paternal warning to white daughters, an attempt to ensure their fear of black men, a project consumed with its own terror of the interracial sexuality that did not actually exist in any significant proportion after the American Civil War (Gaines 2001). On second consideration, however, it seems to me that the ostensible rape alone is not enough to produce the terror I read in the eyes of Ben Cameron who both shuns and clasps the body of his little sister. The warning to white daughters comes on top of or in addition to the much more deeply implanted fear of their own biological processes, fear of strange forces within them that produce the mysterious bleeding that comes without warning, bleeding that could be caused by intercourse. All of the worst things that could happen to a woman come at once for Flora and it does not matter symbolically whether she has had intercourse by

307

rape or not since menarche, as I have noted, was so consistently confused with the first sex act.[1] Finally and most significantly, this new interpretation is intended to downplay the significance of race which seems to me is not absolutely essential to the representation of Flora as victim. She is traumatised by her own vaginal bleeding. Here, the bloody body of the female child is read as violated whether the source of the bleeding is internal or external. To return to Thomas Dixon's memoir, we learn here that it hardly mattered who had violated his mother at thirteen (since he apparently never held this against his father) but the fact that his mother had *suffered* a trauma to her reproductive organs at such a helpless stage produced the necessity of a defence, became a convenient rationale for a grand cause and a racial vendetta. That the Gus character is a convenient scapegoat but hardly a sufficient explanation for what happens to Flora emphasises the trumped up nature of the black male crime but also something more, something perhaps suggested by Balibar's assertion that racism is in excess of nationalism, a 'supplement' in his words, you will recall (Balibar and Wallerstein 1991: 54). Gus is supplementary here to the project of the essentialisation of the national, in itself a deep force and a mythos founded on the mysterious phenomenon of female bleeding. This is not to say that Gus' threat does not represent racism as nationalism, it is to suggest that it also represents the excessiveness of the racism in the rape charge. That is, the excessiveness that works to produce the much too much sensibility of melodrama also foments nationalist fervour in other forms and on other occasions: rallies, church services and ritual pageantry. It is no coincidence, considering the preferred terrain of the woman's body as national battlefield, that the location of the struggle at the edge of the cliff in *The Birth of a Nation* is also the location of the biological justification for national belonging. Thus it should become more clear that what I mean by national melos is the combination of a blood mythology, a suffering victim, stirring music, symbolic ritual and reenactment in the name of an historical story of origins. The heart-wrenching narratives of dramatic fiction have their equivalent in the pulse-quickening moments of mass worship and especially ritual song. We have yet to see exactly how racism adds to, perhaps enhances, nationalistic fervour. It should be clear that I want to align racism with that cinematic excess, that aesthetic supplement as evidenced in the swelling music in addition to the frenzied cutting and the breathlessness produced by the telescoped representation of temporality. The question of racism in relation to both *De Voortrekkers* and *The Birth of a Nation* is in that which is always over and above and thus in its hyperbole might be seen as an invitation to extremism and zealotry.

National melos and sex education

We have discussed how the ingredients of the national melos can include the cult of origins, a narrative of origination, really, and how the melodramatic aesthetic provides the opportunity for racism in appeals to the senses. But racism offers much more to the nationalist project. It offers nothing less than a philosophical system.

> Theoretically speaking, racism is a philosophy of history ... a historiography which makes history the consequence of a hidden secret revealed to men about their own nature and their own birth ... [it] makes visible the invisible cause of the fate of societies and peoples ... '
> (Balibar and Wallerstein 1991: 54)

Racism, says Balibar, provides an *explanation*. If the destiny of a people is obscured to them, racism promises to make that destiny visible; if the cause of the success or failure of its campaigns is unclear, racism makes it clear. Racism offers an explanation of the success or the failure of the nation, to use Dyer's terms again, and it is knowingly a philosophy of history that begins with the secret processes of the body. Interesting, isn't it, that the question of the nation should be located in that most mysterious of places, that the nation's history should be seen as emanating from its secrets? For genetic makeup is at once the most secret and the most telling of structures.

The telling or keeping of secrets about birth, about the birth of the nation, would seem to be at the heart of many narratives of national origination, and as a segue back into the South African situation, I want momentarily to consider the story of the birth of Shaka, the legendary founder of the great Zulu nation, who, since his life (1787–1828) paralleled that of the European emperor, is often compared with Napoleon. As a tale illustrating the customs of the Zulu peoples, the story of the illicit coupling of Shaka's parents became a feature of at least two of the popular histories of the Zulu peoples (Ritter 1955; Morris 1965). As both of these versions explain the aberration from custom that produced Shaka, the parents, Senzangakona, a young and attractive Zulu chieftain, and Nandi, equally royal, but too closely related to Senzangakona for the two to be considered ideally marriageable, met in the woods. There, although they might have engaged in the sanctioned practice of *uku-hlobonga*, sex play that did not involve intercourse, they got carried away, as the myth goes, and abandoned the rules. Nandi found herself pregnant, and the response of the tribal elders to the news was that there was a mistake – the cessation of her menses must be explained as the work of the I-Shaka, the intestinal beetle who was traditionally blamed for any menstrual irregularities. As the story goes, Nandi's people threw the elders' diagnosis back in the face of the Zulus, and requested that Senzangakona's people come to claim Nandi and her 'I-Shaka'. Thereafter, or at least given the emphasis in the white South African versions of the Zulu tale, the great ruler's very name would carry the connection with the 'suppression of menses' (Morris 1965: 44; Ritter 1955: 26). Again, what we have here is evidence of the attribution of special powers to menstrual blood and the almost deliberate confusion of processes of intercourse and childbirth, although with the difference in the ingenuity of the transformation of the mysterious blood into the beetle and the beetle into the baby. I will ask the same question of Nandi's story as I did of Flora's: Why tell the narrative of national origins as a lesson in sex education?

Questions remain about the sources of the Shaka Zulu stories, and whether one looks to the infamous diaries of the British doctor Henry Francis Fynn or even Zulu oral tradition, one is suspicious, knowing how early the ideological layering must have begun. In more recent years, the question of whose history through whose eyes emerged with a vengeance in the controversy over the South African Broadcasting Corporation's 1986 *Shaka Zulu* mini-series, some of which was based on E.A. Ritter's sensationalistic history (Hamilton 1989: 17). The relationship between the Shaka mythology and the rise of Afrikaner nationalism, our subject here, is yet an open but fascinating topic and here I hope to be suggestive since there will always be the difficulty of separating out the British and the Boer contributions to the enlargement of the Zulu legacy, a problem that, we will recall, Keyan Tomaselli has already signalled in his argument that *De Voortrekkers* was originally a British project. That the history of the Zulus had early been annexed to that of the Boers is clearly evidenced in *Day-Dawn in South Africa*, the version of Afrikaner entitlement written by *De Voortrekker* scenarist Gustav Preller in 1938, the occasion of the centennial celebrations that would mark the turn in the fortunes of the nationalist effort.

Preller would select some of the most sensational of the stories about Shaka to include in his history, although avoiding the sexual detail that would surface in the later popularised history. We thus find references to the failed *ukuhlobonga*, to the size of Shaka's genitals and his own sexual abstinence, and to what at least one author referred to as his 'latent homosexuality' (Morris 1966: 46). Important to Preller, it would appear, is the legend of the mass executions of the cowardly, and the capricious murder of four hundred women, 'assegaied' to death (that is, speared by the Zulu 'assegai'). But perhaps Shaka's most incomprehensible action (and therefore the strongest evidence of his barbarism) was his extreme reaction to the death of his mother, Nandi, described as a mass genocide in which ten girls were buried alive with her, and for the following year, the command given that no woman could give birth to a child and all milk had to be spilled on the ground. Preller's account mentions the eye-witness who counted seven thousand Zulus dead as a result of Nandi's death, and adds this toll to the evidence that supports the idea of Shaka as an absolute despot (Preller 1938: 175). *De Voortrekkers* gives us a clue as to the efficient utilisation of the myth of Zulu cruelty. In one scene, the Zulu ruler Dingaan, Shaka's half-brother who succeeded him after participating in his assassination, orders the murder of his own child. Title: 'No child of mine is to live. Take it away. The birds want food'. The image of the chief, holding the baby upside down by one leg, provides the rationale for the conversion of Sobuza, the Zulu warrior who is so repulsed by the offence to the inherent Christianity of his sensibility (an internalisation of 'Thou shalt not kill'), that he becomes a Christian.[2]

Figure 18.2 Sobuza, the Zulu warrior who converts to Christianity: *De voortrekkers*
(1916)

The Afrikaners' incorporation of Zulu history into their own would be a double move, a glorification that turns immediately into denigration. First, there is probably a self-congratulatory gesture in the portrait of the fierce people and the leader whose military discipline produced a strong state and an immense territory. These, after all, were the people who had been conquered by the Boer forces of far smaller numbers. Further, the construction of the black African nation may be a parallel to the construction of a white South African nation, although the concept of nationhood would be imposed from without on the structure of the Zulu 'kingdom'. It is curious to think of black Africa as providing a model for a new nation which, as Grant Farred has urged, wanted to be a 'distinctly (white) "African nation"' a nation 'belonging' to Africa (Farred 1992: 17). This apparent contradiction, 'white African', has ideological difficulties from the start, and would require nothing less than the invention of an entirely new language that would grow out of the land, but the greatest difficulty would be in supplanting the Africans who so greatly outnumbered the Boer farmers, indigenous Africans who we now know could not finally be contained on a fraction of the land that had belonged to their ancestors. But if there was a necessary enlargement of the Zulu myth, there was also the requisite distancing from the black African which betrayed a concern that the Boer should stand above and apart from these people. There would be the legacy of white Boer indolence that would need to be lived down. As J.M. Coetzee summarised the European attitude toward him, 'The Dutch Boer in Africa was

311

Figure 18.3 Zulu assegais and swords fill the frame: *De voortrekkers* (1916)

subjected to close and censorious scrutiny ... because his sloth, his complacent ignorance, his heartlessness towards the natives, his general slide into barbarism seemed to betray the whole imperial side' (Coetzee 1988: 3). By 1938, it would be important for the Boers to distance themselves from both the British (constructed as responsible for racial intermingling) and the black Africans, understood as a 'totally distinct subspecies' (Thompson 1985: 29). Thus, Gustav Preller's statement of the Boer credo, like the integration of Zulu legend, becomes part of Afrikaner history in *Day-Dawn in South Africa*:

> Of all European nationalities who up to the present time have come into contact with the African native, the Boers have been entirely unique in successfully avoiding bastardisation. Despite the infamous things that irresponsible individuals have written, it remains the proud boast of the Voortrek that the Boers managed to keep their blood pure.
>
> (Preller 1938: 151)

I offer the above historical backdrop as a way into the obsessions of *De Voortrekkers*, a myth-in-the-making that shares this problem of the paradox of racial distinction with *The Birth of a Nation*. Two white groups at ideological odds with each other must both claim commonality with one another in order to distinguish themselves from people of African descent. However, in order to distinguish themselves from *each other* they claim that the other white group has not distinguished itself sufficiently from the black group. White Southerners, 'calling the kettle black', accuse white Northerners, as represented by August Stoneman and his mulatto mistress Lydia, of 'intermarriage', while white South Africans of Dutch descent, as in Preller's version of history, accuse British South Africans of 'bastardisation'. While this version of South African race relations might have taken a full century to develop, beginning with the 1838 Trek Boers' flight from the Cape Colony and the objectionable British leniency towards natives, *De Voortrekkers* marks the three-quarters point with the visualisation of black Africans as an exotic sub-species. The problem of the representation of the numerical advantage as well as the sexual threat of the Zulus is resolved in the film by their anthropologisation. The directors of the film opt for a mix of documentary-style footage with dramatic enactment that primarily produces the Zulu people as a horde and fills the frame with assegais and shields, prominent signs of authenticity (see Figure 18.3 opposite). But the crowdedness of the frames in *De Voortrekkers*, while achieving an anthropological look at these people, contradicts any vision of the emptiness of the landscape, the visual standpoint that characterises the Western. *De Voortrekkers*, whether intentionally or inadvertently, represents South Africa as already full, as peopled. The challenge for the Trek Boers and their ancestors will be to corral the mass of black figures that cover every corner of the frame. In representing the magnitude as well as the invincibility of their foes, white South Africans unwittingly figure their own inevitable future.

Conclusion

'Racism', to paraphrase Balibar, 'makes history the effect of a secret revealed only to a few about their inner nature and the circumstances of their birth'. Things seemingly inexplicable are made clear and the fates of entire societies are laid out comprehensively. The scale differential here is remarkable – that something so small as a birth secret should have its effect on whole civilisations and continents – that the rituals of the menarche, so shrouded in secrecy, should be so determining in the fates of nations. To dramatise this principle, I have juxtaposed two historically discrepant tales of first menstruation and sexual intercourse – the stories of Flora and Nandi. The one bleeds profusely, the other doesn't bleed at all but produces a son whose name carries the memory of his peculiar birth. 'Shaka', the mythical menstrual beetle, is a concept that both explains the Zulu leader's greatness and contains the seeds of his destructive obsession. Flora, like Nandi, becomes the sacrificial token whose death drives the zealot into a killing rampage. While the ride of the Ku Klux Klan and Shaka's campaign to avenge Nandi's death would seem to have little in common politically, they share a vision of nation-building as monomania. Further, these drives of death have their root in the principle of sex education as nation formation.

Thanks to Keyan Tomaselli and Ingrid Byerly for help with sources for this article.

Notes

1 I have also argued (Gaines 2001), that in hurling herself off the cliff Flora performs a primitive abortion, and could thus be seen as miscarrying the black foetus. My interest in conflating all of these reproductive processes in my interpretation is to stress the historical confusion that surrounds these processes as well as the symbolic interchangeability of the stages of female reproduction.
2 Later in the film, Sobuza will kill Dingaan, ridding the Boers of the threat to their settlement. While in the film, the character is a Zulu, Preller's own history spells the name 'Sopuza' and identifies the historical figure as a Swazi chief who was, however, close to General Pretorius in his campaign against the Zulus, and who was said to have killed Dingaan around 1840 (Preller 1938: 183–4).

Bibliography

Altman, R. (1999) *Film/Genre*, London: British Film Institute.
Anderson, B. (1991) *Imagined Communities*, New York: Verso.
—— (1992) 'The New World Disorder', *The New Left Review* 193: 3–13.
Appiah, A. (1993) ' "No Bad Nigger": Blacks as the Ethical Principle in the Movies', in J. Matlock, M. Garber and R.L. Walkowitz (eds).
Balibar, É. (1994) *Masses, Classes, Ideas: Studies on Politics and Philosophy Before and After Marx*, trans. James Swenson, London: Routledge.
Balibar, É and Wallerstein, I. (eds) (1991) 'Racism and Nationalism', *Race, Nation, Class: Ambiguous Identities*, New York: Verso.
Benedict, R. (1942) *Race and Racism*, London: Routledge.
Coetzee, J.M. (1988) *White Writing: On the Culture of Letters in South Africa*, New Haven, CT: Yale University Press.
Cripps, T. (1977) *Slow Fade to Black: The Negro in American Film 1900–1942*, Oxford: Oxford University Press.
Delaney, J., Lupton, M.J. and Toth, E. (1988) *The Curse: A Cultural History of Menstruation*, Urbana, IL: University of Illinois.
Dixon, T. (1902) *The Leopard's Spots: A Romance of the White Man's Burden, 1865–1900*, New York: Doubleday.
—— (1905) *The Clansman: An Historical Romance of the Ku Klux Klan*, New York: Grosset and Dunlap.
Dyer, R. (1996) 'Into the Light: The Whiteness of the South in *The Birth of a Nation*', in R.H. King and H. Taylor (eds), *Dixie Debates: Perspectives on Southern Culture*, London: Pluto Press.
—— (1997) *White*, London: Routledge.
Fanon, F. (1963) *The Wretched of the Earth*, trans. Constance Farrington, New York: Grove Weidenfeld.
Farred, G. (1992) 'What Formation? The New South African Nation?', *Alphabet City* 2: 14–18.
Fleener-Marzec, N. (1980) *D.W. Griffith's The Birth of a Nation: Controversy, Suppression, and the First Amendment As It Applies to Filmic Expression, 1915–1973*, New York: Arno Press.
Fynn, H.F. (1986) *The Diary of Henry Francis Fynn*, J. Stuart and D. McK. Malcom (eds), Pietermaritzburg: Shuter and Shooter.
Gaines, J. (1992) 'Who is Reading Robert Mapplethorpe's Black Book?', *New Formations* 16 (Summer): 24–39.
—— (2001) *Fire and Desire: Mixed Race Movies in the Silent Era*, Chicago, IL: University of Chicago Press.

Gaines, J. and Lerner, N. (forthcoming) 'The Orchestration of Affect: The Motif of Barbarism in Breil's *The Birth of a Nation* Score', in R. Abel and R. Altman (eds), *The Sounds of Early Cinema*, Bloomington, IN: Indiana University Press.

Gutsche, T. (1972) *The History and Significance of Motion Pictures in South Africa 1895–1940*, Cape Town: Howard Timmins.

Hamilton, C.A. (1989) 'A Positional Gambit: *Shaka Zulu* and the Conflict in South Africa', *Radical History Review* 44: 5–31.

Hobsbawm, E.J. (1990) *Nations and Nationalism Since 1780: Programme, Myth, Reality*, Cambridge: Cambridge University Press.

—— (1992) 'The Opiate Ethnicity', *Alphabet City* 2: 8–11.

Kristeva, J. (1993) *Nations Without Nationalism*, New York: Columbia University Press.

Matlock, J., Garber, M. and Walkowitz, R.L. (eds) (1993) *Media Spectacles*, London: Routledge.

Merritt, R. (1982) 'Dixon, Griffith, and the Southern Legend: A Cultural Analysis of *The Birth of a Nation*', in R. Dyer MacCann and J. Ellis (eds), *Cinema Examined*, New York: E.P. Dutton.

Morris. D. (1966) *The Washing of the Spears*, London: Abacus.

Peterson, J. (1999) 'World Pictures: Travelogue Films and the Lure of the Exotic, 1890–1920', upublished Ph.D. dissertation, University of Chicago.

Pratt, M.L. (1992) *Imperial Eyes: Travel Writing and Transculturation*, London: Routledge.

Preller, G. (1938) *Day-Dawn in South Africa*, Pretoria: Wallachs' P & P Co. Ltd.

Renan, E. (1882) 'What is a Nation?', in H. Bhaba (ed.), *Nation and Narration*, London: Routledge, 1990.

Ritter, E.A. (1955) *Shaka Zulu*, London: Penguin.

Robinson, C. (1997) 'In the Year 1915: D.W. Griffith and the Whitening of America', *Social Identities* 3, 2: 161–92.

Rogin, M. (1985) ' "The Sword Became a Flashing Vision": D.W. Griffith's *The Birth of a Nation*', *Representations* 9: 150–95.

Shaw, H. (1916) 'Filming the *Voortrekkers*', *Stage and Cinema* 30 December: 2.

Sobchack, V. (1995) ' "Surge and Splendor": A Phenomenology of the Hollywood Historical Epic', in B. Grant (ed.), *Film Genre Reader II*, Austin, TX: University of Texas Press.

Sorlin, P. (1980) *The Film in History: Restaging the Past*, Totowa, NJ: Barnes and Noble Books.

Staiger, J. (1994) '*The Birth of a Nation*: Reconsidering its Reception', in Lang (ed.), *The Birth of a Nation*, New Brunswick: Rutgers University Press.

Strebel. E. (1979) '*The Voortrekkers*: A Cinematographic Reflection of Rising Afrikaner Nationalism', *Film and History* 9, 2: 25–32.

Taylor, C. (1998) *The Mask of Art: Breaking the Aesthetic Contract – Film and Literature*, Bloomington, IN: Indiana University Press.

Thompson, L. (1985) *The Political Mythology of Apartheid*, New Haven, CT: Yale University Press.

Tomaselli, K. (1985) 'Popular Memory and the Voortrekker Films', *Critical Arts* 3, 3: 15–24.

—— (1986) 'Capitalism and Culture in South African Cinema: Jingoism, Nationalism and The Historical Epic', *Wide Angle* 8, 2: 33–44.

White, H. (1990) *The Content of the Form: Narrative Discourse and Historical Representation*, Baltimore, MD: Johns Hopkins University Press.

Williamson, J. (1980) *New People: Miscegenation and Mulattoes in the US*, New York: Free Press.

—— (1984) *The Crucible of Race: Black/White Relations in the American South Since Emancipation*, New York: Oxford University Press.

—— (1986) *A Rage for Order: Black/White Relations in the American South Since Emancipation*, New York: Oxford University Press.

Zyl, H. van (1980) '*De Voortrekkers*: Some Stereotypes and Narrative Conventions', *Critical Arts* 1, 1: 24–31.

NAME INDEX

SUBJECT INDEX

CPSIA information can be obtained at www.ICGtesting.com
Printed in the USA
LVOW101151210911

247244LV00002B/65/P